Senecan Tragedy and the Reception of Augustan Poetry

CHRISTOPHER V. TRINACTY

OXFORD
UNIVERSITY PRESS

Oxford University Press is a department of the
University of Oxford. It furthers the University's objective
of excellence in research, scholarship, and education
by publishing worldwide.

Oxford   New York
Auckland   Cape Town   Dar es Salaam   Hong Kong   Karachi
Kuala Lumpur   Madrid   Melbourne   Mexico City   Nairobi
New Delhi   Shanghai   Taipei   Toronto

With offices in
Argentina   Austria   Brazil   Chile   Czech Republic   France   Greece
Guatemala   Hungary   Italy   Japan   Poland   Portugal   Singapore
South Korea   Switzerland   Thailand   Turkey   Ukraine   Vietnam

Oxford is a registered trade mark of Oxford University Press
in the UK and in certain other countries

Published in the United States of America by
Oxford University Press
198 Madison Avenue, New York, NY 10016, United States of America

© Oxford University Press 2014

All rights reserved. No part of this publication may be reproduced,
stored in a retrieval system, or transmitted, in any form or by any means,
without the prior permission in writing of Oxford University Press,
or as expressly permitted by law, by license, or under terms agreed with
the appropriate reproduction rights organization. Inquiries concerning
reproduction outside the scope of the above should be sent to the
Rights Department, Oxford University Press, at the address above.

You must not circulate this work in any other form
and you must impose this same condition on any acquirer.

Library of Congress Cataloging-in-Publication Data
Trinacty, Christopher V., author.
Senecan tragedy and the reception of Augustan poetry / Christopher V. Trinacty.
pages   cm
Includes bibliographical references and index.
ISBN 978-0-19-935656-0
1. Seneca, Lucius Annaeus, approximately 4 B.C.–65 A.D.—Criticism and interpretation.
2. Intertextuality.   3. Latin poetry—History and criticism.   I. Title.
PA6685.T75   2015
872'.01—dc23   2013043445

1 3 5 7 9 8 6 4 2
Printed in the United States of America
on acid-free paper

CONTENTS

Acknowledgments v

Introduction 1
1. Seneca the Reader 26
2. Intertextuality and Character 62
3. Intertextuality and Plot 127
4. Intertextuality, Writers, and Readers 186
Epilogue 233

Bibliography 237
Index of Passages 249
Subject Index 261

ACKNOWLEDGMENTS

I have been blessed with strong support while I have worked on this book. David Christenson first pushed me to explore intertextuality in Latin poetry and has been my friend and mentor throughout my career. At Brown University, Jeri DeBrohun listened to my ideas about Senecan tragedy and encouraged me to formulate them into my dissertation. She has always been willing to discuss my thoughts about Seneca and provide astute guidance. Michael Putnam directed my special author exam on Senecan tragedy and recommended that I simply reread the texts whenever I suffered from writer's block, advice that has served me well throughout my career. Conversations with my fellow graduate students at Brown influenced my thoughts on Seneca, especially conversations with Michael Fontaine, Max Goldman, Zoe Kontes, Peter Lech, Ben Low, Sarah Nix, and Heather Vincent. Positions at the University of Arizona, Amherst College, and the University of Missouri allowed me to work on this book, and I thank my various colleagues, students, and friends for all their help and advice: Justin Arft, Norman Austin, Michael Barnes, Sara Brenneis, Alex Dressler, Richard Foley, Justina Gregory, Frederick Griffiths, Luca Grillo, Dan Hooley, Jun Ishii, Max Kaisler, David Konstan, Eph Lytle, Raymond Marks, Anatole Mori, Melissa Mueller, Arum Park, Andreola Rossi, Maureen Ryan, C. Michael Sampson, David Schenker, Rebecca Sinos, Marilyn Skinner, David Soren, Dennis Trout, Timothy Van Compernolle, Christopher van den Berg, Gonda Van Steen, Rex Wallace, Katherine Wasdin, Cynthia White, and Amanda Wilcox. At Oberlin College, I have been inspired by the support of my colleagues Benjamin T. Lee, Kirk Ormand, Thomas Van Nortwick, and Drew Wilburn. All have assisted in innumerable ways. The readers and editors of Oxford University Press helped to strengthen this book greatly, and I offer my sincere gratitude to them. The Thomas Cooper Fund for Faculty Research provided funding for production costs. Portions of this book have appeared in *Classical Journal*, *Phoenix*, and *Classical and Modern Literature*. Individual chapters also benefited greatly from the questions of audiences at Brown University, Cornell University, Kenyon College, Smith College, the University of Arizona, the University of Manitoba, the University of Western Ontario, and Wake Forest University.

My family has always encouraged me throughout my career, and this project could not have been completed without them. I dedicate this book to my wife, Emily Troiano, who is simply the best.

Introduction

> All words are pockets into which
> now this, now that is put,
> and sometimes many things at once.
> —Nietzsche, *The Wanderer and His Shadow*

How does Seneca approach the composition of his tragedies? Why does he choose to write about such mythological subject matter, and how does the tragic genre grant the fullest expression of his literary aims? Senecan tragedy has received increased attention in recent decades, which has resulted in multiple readings of the tragedies ranging from Lacanian analyses of language (Segal) to expositions of the metatheatrical and literary elements in the plays (Boyle, Erasmo, Littlewood) and a Freudian exploration of the dark themes and troubling conclusions of the *Thyestes* (Schiesaro).[1] While many scholars now shy away from reading the tragedies as didactic Stoic lessons, recent work has reinvigorated philosophical readings of the plays through careful application of certain tenets to the works.[2] Historicist critics, who once saw the grim visage of Nero or the crazed smile of Caligula behind Atreus or Agamemnon, now are more likely to discuss the propensity for dissimulation under tyrants and to examine the broader political issues behind the tragedies.[3]

---

[1] See Segal (1986), Boyle (1997) 112–37, Erasmo (2004) 122–39, Littlewood (2004), Schiesaro (2003). Other recent work on Seneca includes Inwood (2005), Ker (2009), Bartsch and Wray (2009), Staley (2010), and Star (2012). Even Pseudo-Seneca has been well served by Ferri's (2003) and Boyle's (2008) commentaries on the *Octavia*.

[2] Marti's (1945) belief that the works showed the progression of the Stoic *sapiens* has been largely refuted. In its place, sophisticated studies by Fitch and McElduff (2002), Bartsch (2006), and Star (2006, 2012) find the tragedies both elucidate and question Stoic ideas of character, decision making, and psychology (respectively).

[3] For Henry and Walker (1985) the characters embody specific individuals. More general applications of dissimulation and politics can be found in Rudich (1993), Bartsch (1994), and Beacham (1998) 197–254.

This study places Senecan tragedy in its Roman literary context and explores Seneca's relationship with his literary predecessors, in particular, the strong influence of the Augustan poets (Vergil, Horace, and Ovid).[4] Seneca develops his plots, characters, and tragic ideology, in part, through a reading of his Augustan predecessors, and their works inspire Seneca's dramatic poetry.[5] Intertextuality can help us understand the innovative manner in which Seneca stitches together this literary material as well as his reception of Augustan poetry. Kallendorf describes how intertextuality can be seen as a locus of reception:

> The alluding author begins the process by reading an earlier text, then working out an interpretation of that text. As he or she begins writing, the new text unfolds in dialogue with the old one, in such a way that the potential meaning of one or more words resonates against their original usage in another text, where they meant something that is seen as relevant again.[6]

The critic, in seeing various intertextual connections, must try to understand how they are being used and find a rationale for such echoes in Seneca's work. Seneca's tragedies are notable because of the stress he places on his language—teasing out and examining the rhetorical as well as poetic ramifications for his tragic language at every turn.[7] This brief introduction discusses Seneca's tragic style in relation to his contemporary era, before turning to Seneca's interest in poetic composition and indicating how his use of intertextuality can help the reader to understand issues such as character, plot, poetics, and genre in his tragedies.

---

[4] See Jakobi (1988) for examples of the linguistic influence of Ovid on Seneca's tragedies. Ter Haar Romeny (1887) and Spika (1890) provide Vergilian and Horatian parallels (respectively). From an interpretative standpoint, the works of Tarrant (1978), Putnam (1995) 246–85, Hinds (1998), Schiesaro (2003) 26–31, 221–8, and Littlewood (2004) 259–301 have influenced my intertextual readings of Seneca most significantly. One can find traces of additional Augustan poets (Propertius, Tibullus, Varro of Atax, etc.), but Vergil, Horace, and Ovid are the three authors who influence Seneca most thoroughly in his tragedies.

[5] Schiesaro (2003) 223 claims that this creates the characteristic "belatedness" in Seneca's plays since "they represent an anachronistic return to the past, a frustrated desire for lost forms mediated by an overwhelming and oppressive intertextual memory. Senecan tragedy validates its existence (and its novelty) by displaying total awareness of its epigonic nature and by laying bare its internal mechanisms."

[6] Kallendorf (2006) 68.

[7] Eliot (1950) 54 famously claimed, "In the plays of Seneca, the drama is all in the word, and the word has no further reality behind it."

Roman Tragedy and Senecan Tragedy

Seneca's tragedies concern myths and characters that are, in many ways, overdetermined. Many previous poets had elaborated the well-known stories of Medea, Phaedra, and Oedipus, in genres as diverse as epic, tragedy, lyric, and love elegy. The complex relationships and visceral motivations of these mythical characters were considered the primary material for tragedies at least from the time of Aristotle.[8] Burian comments on the interplay between these traditional narratives and their expression in the tragic genre:

> Tragic praxis can be seen as a complex manipulation of legendary matter and generic convention, constituting elaborate networks of similarities and differences at every level of organization. Such a praxis supplies the poet with constructive elements predisposed to favour certain actions, character types, issues, and outcomes, and provides the audience with a significant frame or control for the interpretation of what they are witnessing. The particular shape and emphases of a tragic plot, as the product of variation in the shape and emphases both of known legendary material and of familiar formal constituents, can forcefully direct or dislocate spectators' attention, confirm, modify, or even overturn their expectations.[9]

A similar "tragic praxis" motivates Seneca's plays, which respond broadly to the Greek mythic background while emphasizing their particular place in the Roman literary tradition by intertextually referencing that tradition. Burian notes that the spectators bring expectations to these characters and that the Greek tragedians play off these expectations. Seneca's tragic material was likewise familiar to his Roman audience, and he challenges their assumptions about character, plot, and action. Tarrant's seminal article, "Senecan Drama and Its Antecedents," draws attention to the influence of Augustan writers on Seneca for his "conception of tragic form and style, as well as much of the content of his plays."[10] As works of literature, Seneca's tragedies rely on the reader's knowledge of both the Greek dramatic foundation and the Augustan literature from which he repeated and markedly draws.

Seneca inherits a theatrical tradition that was still alive and well at Rome even if the vicissitudes of transmission have obscured our evidence of dramatic

---

[8] Cf. *Poet.* 1453a18–21.
[9] Burian (1997) 179.
[10] Tarrant (1978) 214.

productions, of the quality of the plays, and of the playwrights themselves.[11] Latin drama began with Livius Andronicus and the performance of one of his plays at Rome in 240 BCE. The *cothurnatae* of Livius, Naevius, Ennius, Pacuvius, and Accius survive only in fragments but, nonetheless, exhibit powerful alliteration, a Roman sensibility, and a fascination with locating themselves in the Greek tradition.[12] Although tragedies continued to be written after the death of Accius (86 BCE), it appears that fewer new tragedies were staged, and much of our evidence from this period concerns the restaging of classic Republican tragedies.[13] Horace complains that the tragedies of his day were overblown spectacles more suited to the eyes than to the ears, and Cicero's description of the dedication of Pompey's theater in 55 BCE testifies to the visual pretentiousness of Republican tragedy.[14] Unfortunately, only a manuscript notice of Varius' *Thyestes* and a few lines of Ovid's *Medea* survive—two Roman tragedies that Quintilian finds comparable to the finest of Greek tragedy.[15] Seneca's tragedies often treat similar subjects as those of his Roman predecessors, but, at the same time, his works diverge from the earlier tradition and reflect his unique style and preferences.

Seneca renovates the tragic genre primarily through his strong response to Augustan literature and his use of the rhetoric of his day; in essence he is creating dramatic *poetry*, and his plays should be read as poems.[16] Seneca's works are rhetorically accomplished, and their rhetorical power extends beyond mere verbal brilliance to the skillful exploitation of intertextuality (an aspect of oratorical

---

[11] Jory (1986) 144 believes "the heyday of the Roman theatre was not in the Republic but in the Empire."

[12] Beare (1951) 25 writes how Roman dramatists "tried, in a general way, to render their originals faithfully; but their native genius and their instinctive knowledge of popular taste compelled them to infuse a Roman flavour into everything they wrote." Boyle (2006) gives the most comprehensive overview of tragedy in Rome, and Manuwald (2011) of Republican theater. Jocelyn (1969) 12–23 discusses Hellenization.

[13] Part-time tragedians include famous authors and statesmen such as Julius Caesar, Augustus, C. Julius Strabo, and C. Asinius Pollio. Few tragic fragments survive from these authors. Note the way older plays are reinterpreted in their new historical context at Cic. *Pro. Sest.* 118–25, and *Ep. Ad Att.* 2.19.3.

[14] Hor. *Ep.* 2.1.187–8. Cic. *Fam.* 7.1 describes Pompey's dedication. Horace did consider Varius one of the best Roman poets (cf. *Carm.* 1.6) but his view of contemporary tragedy as a whole seems bleak, in spite of the fact that he devotes much of his *Ars* to dramatic matters.

[15] Quint. *Inst.* 10.1.98. Quintilian finds only Pomponius Secundus (60 CE) worthy of mention after Ovid. Codex Montecassinus 1086, fol. 64 contains the notice of Varius' *Thyestes*.

[16] This is not to say that early Republican tragedy or Greek tragedy did not have a strong rhetorical background, but simply that Seneca's rhetorical style is indicative of his time. *Ep.* 114.13: *oratio certam regulam non habet; consuetudo illam civitatis, quae numquam in eodem diu stetit, versat* ("Oratory does not have concrete rules; the custom of society, which never remains constant for long, changes it."). Mastronarde (1970) focuses on Seneca's *Oedipus* as a poem.

training that is often overlooked).[17] Seneca's dramaturgy both revolves around and questions the meaning of the spoken word. Goldberg commends this focus on language:

> Rather than simply observing, and then dismissing, rhetoric as the source of mannerisms and verbal pyrotechnics (though it was certainly that), we might productively argue that rhetoric—in particular declamation—was a positive influence on Roman tragedy because it asserted the primacy of language over spectacle. The declamatory model that shaped Seneca's idea of tragedy thereby brought the genre out of the intellectual doldrums that had so exasperated Cicero and Horace.[18]

Seneca invites his audience to enjoy his linguistic complexity, and this shift from visual bombast to verbal bombast is one of the defining features of his work.[19] This is a changed tragedy, one that owes less to Athenian drama or the tragedies of Cicero's time and more to the literary, rhetorical, and philosophical climate of Seneca's day.[20] One can imagine that the audience was primed to applaud the witty and urbane words of Seneca's characters in much the same way the audience for declamations appreciated arresting and audacious verbal ingenuity in the work of Seneca the Elder.[21] The writers of the Neronian Renaissance are known for their fondness for paradox, striking *sententiae*, oscillating between elaboration and concision, and their literary and mythological erudition.[22] Neronian

---

[17] The Elder Seneca comments on the use of *imitatio* and allusion at *Contr.* 7.1.27 and *Suas.* 3.4–7. If rhetoric can be seen broadly as "the ability to motivate the linguistic sign" (Conte (1986) 23), then intertextuality can be seen as fundamental to that motivation. Canter (1925) focuses on the rhetorical aspects of Senecan tragedy. Leo (1878) 158 famously judged Seneca's tragedies to be "declamations patterned after tragedy and divided into acts."

[18] Goldberg (1996) 276.

[19] Cf. Goldberg (1997) 197, where he extols Seneca's rhetorical tragedies: "Senecan tragedy demands careful listening. Daring to make language the prime vehicle of meaning was a decision with important consequences. It reversed the tendency toward action and spectacle we saw developing in Cicero's day." M. Wilson (2007) provides a valuable overview of Seneca's rhetorical techniques.

[20] Valuable studies of this time period include Gordon Williams (1978), Mayer (1982 and 2005), Hutchinson (1993), Rudich (1993), Conte (1994b), and Fantham (1996). Casamento (2002) discusses the influence of declamation on Senecan tragedy. I prefer the term "Renaissance" to "Silver Latin," because of the value judgment inherent in "Silver" vis-à-vis the "Golden Latin" of the Augustans.

[21] This can be seen time and again in the *Controversiae* and *Suasoriae*. Seneca often notes how speakers will confront one another with charges of plagiarism, an issue examined in McGill (2013) 146–77. In this monograph, I do not investigate the question of the performance of Seneca's tragedies, although I endorse the possibility of performance. Cf. G. W. M. Harrison (2000) and Kohn (2013).

[22] Boyle (1994) 13 provides an overview.

authors such as Lucan and Petronius likewise share Seneca's interest in learned allusions and the rhetorical trends of the day, but do so within the generic confines of epic and the novel. Seneca's tragic plots, speeches, and characters exhibit a strong relationship with their literary predecessors, and recall other poetic genres, including elegy, epic, lyric, and pastoral.[23] Tarrant comments on this predilection, "One might fairly say that Seneca applies to tragedy the blending of genres so widely practiced by the major Augustan poets, and does so using predominantly Augustan material."[24] Senecan tragedy allows these different voices to coexist, and their combination—as suits the tragic genre—adds to the literary richness of the work by supplying innovative perspectives on the material.[25]

Why Tragedy?

Seneca's literary output is wide-ranging, and he has quite rightly been called a "man of many genres."[26] From philosophical dialogues on issues such as anger, divine providence, and gift-giving to a long treatise on Stoic physics (*Naturales Quaestiones*), Seneca's prose displays the philosophical and rhetorical inclinations for which he was famous. His letters to Lucilius provide a more "day-by-day" glance at the philosophical interests of Seneca in his final years and stress the importance of self-reflection, study, ethics, and friendship.[27] In his Menippean satire, *Apocolocyntosis*, Seneca unleashes his acerbic wit against Claudius and the inadequacies of his rule, and blends both prose and verse to critique Claudius.[28] The *Apocolocyntosis* also allows us to see Seneca writing in a mock-tragic vein when he

---

[23] Littlewood (2004) 283–5 finds pastoral elements in the opening song of the *Phaedra* that act as instances of "deviant intertextuality." Tragedy always consisted of a multiplicity of genres and types of speech, which could highlight "such encounters of differing voices as a means of producing opacity and ambiguity in the language of the plays" (J. Barrett (2002) xvi).

[24] Tarrant (1995) 225.

[25] Cf. Farrell (1992) 261 on his reading of Ovid's *Metamorphoses*: "There can be no question of individual elements borrowed from different genres, each retaining its pastoral, epic, or elegiac character. Instead, each of these elements takes on a new character, provisional and unique to this telling of this story."

[26] Ker (2006).

[27] Henderson (2004) and Wilcox (2012) offer close readings of the *Epistulae*. M. Wilson (2001) and Inwood (2007) discuss the importance of their epistolarity.

[28] Relihan (1993) is a good overview on the genre, and Leach (1989) and Damon (2010) offer perceptive readings of the *Apocolocyntosis* that take into consideration its genre and political ramifications. Damon's claim that "perhaps the most striking evidence of the work's generic travails is the way its poetry and prose compete to say the same thing" (60) can be applied to certain moments of Seneca's tragedies in which the chorus and characters offer varied interpretations of the same event and probe its possible meanings.

introduces the character of Hercules to be the gatekeeper of Olympus, who "acts tragically in order to be more terrifying" (*et quo terribilior esset, tragicus fit*, 7.1)[29] and delivers a speech in iambic senarii (the typical meter of tragic dialogue). The similarities between this speech and passages from Seneca's *Hercules Furens* helped Fitch to determine a relative dating system for Seneca's tragedies, spanning, at least, the Claudian and Neronian periods.[30] We should not think of Seneca only writing tragedies at one point in his life (e.g., in response to Nero's love of the stage), but rather as part of a lifelong project of composition. The manuscript tradition preserves nine tragedies (the *Phoenissae* is incomplete) and one *praetexta* under Seneca's name, but scholars agree the *Octavia* is not by Seneca and the *Hercules Oetaeus* probably is not his.[31] Senecan tragedy touches upon issues found in his prose works: the power of anger, a tyrant's lust for power, Stoic *sympatheia*, contemplation of death, the laws of fate, the allure of vice, and the difficulty of action for those with only partial knowledge of a predicament.[32] Role-playing is a common theme in Stoic philosophy and the world of declamation, and one can tease out how these philosophical and rhetorical foundations influence Seneca's tragedies as well as reflecting the historical period in which he lived.[33] The role-playing in which Seneca's characters engage also evokes Stoic ideas of the self, and here again intertextuality, through its presentation of alternative roles, raises evocative questions about how these characters both view themselves and are viewed (by other characters, the author, and the audience).[34] My primary interest in Stoicism rests in Seneca's conception of character and his manner of describing the roles that his characters play. Littlewood comments on the parallelism between the theatricality of these characters and a Stoic view:

---

[29] All translations are mine unless otherwise indicated.

[30] Fitch (1981) suggests the tragedies should be grouped into early plays (*Oedipus, Agamemnon*, and *Phaedra*), middle plays (*Troades, Hercules Furens*, and *Medea*), and late plays (*Thyestes, Phoenissae*). There is no way of knowing if the "early plays" could possibly have been written under Caligula or even Tiberius.

[31] Cf. Boyle (2006) 221–9 for a brief overview on the question of authorship and the primary aims of both the *Octavia* and the *Hercules Oetaeus*.

[32] Rosenmeyer (1989) finds the underpinnings of Stoic cosmology ever-present in Senecan tragedy. Littlewood (2004) 15–36 passim indicates how Stoic morality can help us identify "the broken world" of Seneca's tragedies. Star (2012) points out the importance of Stoic self-command in the tragedies.

[33] Bartsch (1994) and Rudich (1993, 1997) detail the issue of dissimulation and role-playing under Nero; Boyle (2006) 182 notes, "As works such as Petronius' *Satyricon* exhibit, the cultural and educative system had generated a world of actors."

[34] C. Edwards (1997) and Inwood (2005) 322–52 discuss the concept of "self" in Seneca's philosophical works. This concern with the self has been seen as a distinguishing trait of Stoicism in the Empire that is embodied in the writings of Seneca, Epictetus, and Marcus Aurelius; cf. Foucault (1986, 2005).

The representation of life as a role, as something fabricated, draws attention to the possibility of it being fabricated otherwise. Existence is no longer a given, a common necessity, but something to be asserted and fashioned. Not only the individual but his/her reality is a matter of perspective. This autonomy of the metadramatic character plays interestingly with the autonomy, the private perspective, of the Stoic.[35]

Thus, for the characters always to want someone present to observe their actions is not merely a ramification of metatheater but also a Stoic position.[36] As Edwards states, "In Stoicism, the actions of an individual acquire meaning insofar as they are witnessed."[37] While Seneca stresses in his *Epistulae Morales* the need for consistency in playing one's role, his tragedies challenge that assertion by presenting mutable characters that consistently follow a path divergent from that of the Stoic *sapiens*.[38]

Because of his philosophical works, it has been tempting to view Seneca as a writer of "philosophical" tragedies and to find ways in which the tragedies illustrate his Stoic beliefs.[39] My study, however, focuses primarily on Seneca as a reader of the Augustan literary tradition. Philosophical language and ideas are present in Seneca's plays, but Seneca calls attention again and again to the *literary* makeup of his tragic world and "in doing so...reminds the reader that the world it represents, its events and its laws, are constructions."[40] Seneca writes tragedies in particular because it is in the DNA of tragedy to be a mélange of different genres; the tragic genre allows him to shape the poetic material according to the tragic concerns of the play, and he aims to use tragedy as a lens through which to view the Latin literary tradition. In addition, the tragic genre does not provide one overriding point of view or narrator, but consists of various characters struggling to make sense of (or control) the tragic situation. This dramatic dialectic inspires the characters to debate their motivations and desires, and helps to create the tragic conflict at the heart of these works.[41] Seneca's characters wrestle with the ramifications of their thoughts and actions for one another and for themselves, and the tension and clash of viewpoints allows Seneca to explore the various thematic nuances of the plays.

---

[35] Littlewood (2004) 57.

[36] Cf. Boyle (1997) and Erasmo (2004) for more on metatheater in Seneca.

[37] C. Edwards (2002) 383.

[38] Most emphatically in Medea and Atreus. For more on Medea's relationship to Stoicism, cf. Bartsch (2006) 244–81.

[39] Staley (2010) 24–41 summarizes the various positions of Stoic interpreters of Senecan tragedy.

[40] Littlewood (2004) 17.

[41] Cf. Rosenmeyer (1989) 77: "Again and again in Senecan drama, through the dovetailing of irreconcilables, judgments and feelings are made to clash, and are compacted into a poetry of oppression. For in drama the discordant strains are not serialized and disengaged...but are forged into an overwhelming tissue of syntheses."

Of course Seneca's tragic themes run the gamut of human experience, illuminating, among other ideas, "power, impotence, delusion, self-deception; the futility of compassion; the freedom, desirability, and value-paradox of death; man, god, nature, guilt."[42] Seneca is also drawn to tragedy's emphasis on pathos and the expression of events of suitable *atrocitas, maiestas,* and *gravitas.*[43] Tragedy allows Seneca the fullest expression of his poetics. The literary features of his plays should be viewed with the same eye for detail as a Horatian ode or a book of the *Aeneid,* and Seneca's skill as a poet shines through in each line. His intertextuality is one aspect of his poetics, and it is the primary topic of this study.

The *Epistulae Morales* as Literary Criticism

Although Seneca never presents a unified theory of literary interpretation and never cites his tragedies directly in his other writings, he does concern himself with literary matters from time to time.[44] In his prose works, Seneca generally quotes poets (Vergil most often, then Ovid) in order to illuminate moral subject matter, and occasionally he appraises poetry from philosophical and literary points of view.[45] For example, he critiques Vergil's *Georgics* and Ovid's *Metamorphoses* and, in so doing, reveals his concern with poetic genres and literary objectives. He claims that the true purpose of the *Georgics* was not didactic but rather the reader's pleasure, as Vergil "did not wish to teach farmers, but to please his readers" (*nec agricolas docere voluit, sed legentes delectare, Ep.* 86.15), and illustrates Vergil's ignorance of certain agricultural matters by quoting lines from the *Georgics.*[46] In his *Naturales Quaestiones,* Seneca argues that the fanciful detail of wolves swimming with sheep (**nat** *lupus inter oves, Met.* 1.304) found in Ovid's description of the flood

---

[42] Boyle (2006) 197. This is just a sampling of the themes and ideas that Boyle mentions.

[43] Regenbogen (1927-8) famously stresses these aspects of Senecan tragedy.

[44] Some have viewed the "tragic" Hercules of the *Apocolocyntosis* 7.1 as a parody of Seneca's own *Hercules Furens.* Cf. Eden (1984) ad loc. and Fitch (1987a) 50–3. A fine overview of his style can be found in G. Kennedy (1972) 469–81. Staley (2010) draws upon Seneca's prose works in order to hypothesize a Stoic tragic model behind his dramas.

[45] Fantham (1982) 19–34 gives examples of Seneca's attitude towards poetry and rhetoric. Merchant (1905) gives an overview of Seneca's theory of style and concludes, "He fell short, to some extent, of his ideal. But a failure to realize fully in practice what he aimed at proves no insincerity in the aim" (59). Mazzoli (1970), Setaioli (1985), and Batinski (1993) offer important interpretations of Seneca's view of literature.

[46] At *Ep.* 86.16 he critiques an additional passage about the harvesting of beans and millet, although Spurr (1986) believes Seneca is too quick to judge Vergil's knowledge and points out how Vergil may give correct agricultural information. Henderson (2004) 129–38 discusses how the refutation of Vergil here is emblematic of the ethical strategy embodied in the *Epistulae Morales.*

(*Met.* 1. 253–312) is inappropriate for such a serious topic, while other Ovidian lines are more suitable to the magnitude of his theme (*pro magnitudine rei*).⁴⁷ This criticism comes at the conclusion of Seneca's own prose account of a cataclysmic flood, and Seneca ends by offering his own spin on Ovid's weakest point, "You will know what befits [this flood] if you conceive that the whole world is swimming" (*Scies quid deceat, si cogitaveris orbem terrarum* **natare**, *Nat.* 3.27.15). These comments show what we might have expected, that Seneca was concerned with matters of poetic propriety and was willing to venture his own opinions on the successes and failures of his predecessors. In the final example, we can also see how Seneca highlights his criticism of Ovid's childishness (*pueriles ineptias*) by encouraging Lucilius (in language that reverberates with Ovid's own) to envision a flood which features not just animals swimming but the entire world.⁴⁸ In two of his letters to Lucilius (*Ep.* 79 and 84), Seneca examines the writing process in more extensive detail, and in each epistle one can find continuity between the substance of the letter and the literary sensibility of Seneca's tragedies. Although these letters were in all probability written after the majority of his tragedies, they show the creative manner in which Seneca responds to the Augustan poets in contexts dealing with poetics.

Writers and orators of Seneca's time did not consider familiar myths and topics passé or uninspiring. These topoi (precisely because they were already so well-known) allowed the writers to exercise their creativity and intellect in a way that showcased their writing and speaking ability. The *Controversiae* and *Suasoriae* of the Elder Seneca offer similar opportunities for the orators to dazzle their audiences with their verbal dexterity, wit, and sententiae.⁴⁹ In order to show the sophistication and intricacy of Seneca's intertextual technique and its importance for his poetics, an investigation of Epistle 79 is imperative. In this letter, Seneca instructs Lucilius about the poetic opportunities that a description of Aetna can provide (*Ep.* 79.5–7). He encourages Lucilius to write about Aetna although Vergil, Ovid, and Cornelius Severus have already tackled the subject (*Ep.* 79.5):

---

⁴⁷ *Nat.* 3.27.14: *non est res satis sobria lascivire devorato orbe terrarum* ("It is not a sufficiently sober attitude to play when the whole world has been destroyed"). Seneca's response to Ovid's *Metamorphoses* in Book 3 of the *Nat.* shows the importance of Ovid as a source, especially for flood narratives. This passage has engendered much comment, see Degl'Innocenti Pierini (1990) 177–210, Setaioli (2000) 177–9, Hine (2009) 318–20, and Gareth Williams (2012) 129–32. Seneca the Elder similarly finds Ovid too clever for his own good at *Contr.* 2.2.12 and *Contr.* 9.5.17.

⁴⁸ Cf. Hutchinson (1993) 128–31 and Morgon (2003) for more on Seneca's criticism of Ovid.

⁴⁹ Although the *Controversiae* are notably unusual and spectacular, various orators recite on the same topic. Cf. Bonner (1949) and Winterbottom (1974) xi–xviii.

Omnibus praeterea feliciter hic locus se dedit, et qui praecesserant, non praeripuisse mihi videntur quae dici poterant, sed aperuisse.

Moreover, this subject has given itself to all with happy results, and previous authors seem to me not to have preemptively seized all that could be said, but only to have opened the way.

According to Seneca, it is beneficial to be the latest in a long line of writers (*Ep.* 79.6):

Multum interest utrum ad consumptam **materiam** an ad subactam accedas: crescit in dies, et inventuris inventa non obstant. Praeterea condicio optima est ultimi; parata verba invenit, quae aliter instructa **novam faciem** habent. Nec illis manus inicit tamquam alienis; sunt enim **publica**.

It makes a great difference whether you approach a subject already worn out or one where there is still work to be done; in the latter case, the topic grows daily, and what has been discovered does not stand in the way of new discoveries. Besides, the best position is to be the latest writer; he finds at hand words which, when deployed differently, show a new face. And he is not stealing them, as if they belonged to someone else, for they are public property.

A similar aesthetic motivates his tragedies, because they concern mythological figures whose stories were related countless times. While it may seem unduly challenging or simply impossible to successfully follow Vergil or Ovid, Seneca does not feel that way, and he relishes the poetic possibilities, especially because he can incorporate their own language to "show a new face." In fact, this passage does just that. The use of *novam faciem*, "new face," recalls a line from Vergil's *Aeneid*—when Aeneas addresses the Sibyl's report of his future sufferings, saying, "For me not any strange or unexpected form of labor arises, O maiden, for before now I have foreseen all these things" (*non ulla laborum, / O virgo,* **nova** *mi* **facies** *inopinave surgit; / omnia praecepi...Aen.* 6.103–5). Seneca discussed this line at the conclusion of Epistle 76, a mere three letters earlier, in a philosophical context as an apt summation of the idea of Stoic *praemeditatio futurorum malorum* (*Ep.* 76.33).[50] Surely Seneca still could have this phrase in his mind as he penned Epistle 79. He is now giving this phrase a "new face" in this epistle and displaying how the *Aeneid* can be utilized to endorse this idea of intertextual poetics.

---

[50] For more on the philosophical ramifications of *praemeditatio*, cf. Armisen-Marchetti (2008).

In addition, a variation of this phrase is also found near the close of Ovid's *Tristia* 2, when Ovid protests that he has written serious works (including his own tragedy) and offers a description of his *Metamorphoses*: "I have also reported about bodies changed into new forms, although the final edit was lacking from what I began" (*dictaque sunt nobis, quamvis manus ultima coeptis / defuit, in **facies** corpora versa **novas**, Tr.* 2.555–6). These lines cleverly refer to and rewrite the opening of the *Metamorphoses*.[51] Ovid's use of *facies novas* here is a particularly dexterous move as *facies* is never paired with the adjective *novus* in the *Metamorphoses*. Thus, this line embodies the sort of change Ovid may have wished to make, if he had the time for a final revision of his epic. Seneca's use of *novam faciem* recalls both Vergil and Ovid in order to include both of these poets intertextually, and to give their words a novel function in his epistle.

Seneca considers such poetic material "public property" (*publica*), a term previously used by Horace in his *Ars Poetica* to indicate his own attitude towards dramatic subject matter (***publica materies**, Ars* 131).[52] In this passage, Horace encourages writers to not be mere translators or imitators of the Greek material (*Ars* 133–4). That context may still be on Seneca's mind as he reveals that he is not being a mindless follower, but appropriating language from Horace, Ovid, and Vergil to express his own poetic principles. The letter continues to rebrand the language found here when later discussing virtue, the primary topic of the second half of the epistle. Seneca writes, "The day will come which will reveal virtue even if it is hidden and obscured by the spite of contemporaries" (*veniet qui conditam et saeculi sui malignitate conpressam dies **publicet**, Ep.* 79.17). That sort of repetition is key to understanding how Seneca will subtly shift meanings from metaphoric to literal, or from literary critical to philosophical, in the course of his prose works (and a similar method can be seen in his tragedies). Often the language Seneca picks up from the intertextual source is manipulated throughout his own work as a way to indicate his own reading of that material. This methodology will be stressed throughout this study and is one of the primary ways of revealing Seneca's reception of the Augustan material. To further underline this tendency, one need only look at the conclusion of this letter, where Seneca muses on the flimsiness of lies and pretense compared to the certainty of virtue: "Posturing does no good. An external appearance

---

[51] *In nova fert animus mutatas **dicere** formas / **corpora**; di, **coeptis**...Met.* 1.1–2.

[52] Cf. Fantham (1982) 24, Setaioli (1985) 846–7, and Martina (1992) for more on the Horatian term here. Cf. Peirano (2013) 90–1 for the legal tone of Horace's *publica materies*. Seneca finds philosophical material from a variety of sources to likewise be *publicae* at *Ep.* 33.1. Seneca's figuration of the poetic material as a field may derive from his reading of Horace (cf. Brink (1963) 182–3), or from his father's work on declamation (*Contr.* 1 *praef.* 10; McGill (2005) 345–6). Seneca later applies the verb *publico -are* when discussing virtue, which indicates an additional supplement to the earlier formulation (*Ep.* 79.17). For more on Seneca as a reader of Horace's *Ars*, cf. Chap. 4.

lightly put on deceives few; truth is consistent in every part" (*Nihil simulatio proficit; paucis inponit leviter extrinsecus inducta **facies**: veritas in omnen partem sui eadem est. Ep.* 79.18). The intertextual material now comes to emphasize philosophical truth, yet another new "face" to enhance the argument of Seneca's letter.

In addition, as any reader of Horace's *Ars* knows, Aetna itself appears in that poem as the final resting place of the *Siculi poetae* (*Ars* 463), Empedocles. Thus the very subject matter that Seneca encourages Lucilius to sink his teeth into responds to the finale of Horace's *Ars*. Seneca gives Horace's injunction his own spin as he manipulates the very language of his literary predecessors in offering his own syncopated *ars poetica*. He reveals how the words of the Augustan poets can be given a fresh significance in his epistolary confines and includes the third of the great Augustan poets in the letter, *intertextually*, after explicitly mentioning Ovid and Vergil. In his tragedies, Seneca finds himself in the enviable position of being the latest poet to tell the stories of figures such as Medea and Hippolytus. Seneca's advice in Epistle 79 parallels the intertextual nature of his tragedies, in which the words of previous authors can be employed in an original manner to elucidate his particular view of the subject matter.[53] In this letter, Seneca practices what he preaches, and his understanding of the Augustan poets is essential for the literary criticism offered therein.

If authors continue to treat mythological topics, how can they produce something novel? In Epistle 84, Seneca writes to Lucilius about the proper manner of reading and writing, and his comments there also provide a glimpse into his theory of literary composition and imitation. He develops the analogy that the good writer is like a bee both because he blends the practice of writing and reading and mingles the material from a variety of sources. In doing so he will imitate the actions of bees in their production of honey (*Ep.* 84.3):

> Apes, ut aiunt, debemus imitari, quae vagantur et flores ad mel faciendum idoneos carpunt, deinde quidquid attulere disponunt ac per favos digerunt et, ut Vergilius noster ait,
>
> liquentia mella
> stipant et dulci distendunt nectare cellas.

---

[53] Cf. Sen. *Suas.* 3.7: *Hoc autem dicebat Gallio Nasoni suo valde placuisse; itaque fecisse illum quod in multis aliis versibus Vergilii fecerat, non subripiendi causa, sed palam mutuandi, hoc animo ut vellet agnosci.* ("Moreover Gallio was saying that his friend Ovid liked this phrase very much and therefore did what he had done with many other verses of Vergil, not as an act of plagiarism, but openly borrowing and wishing that his borrowing be noticed."). Cf. Setaioli (1985) 846–56 for more on Seneca's principles of *aemulatio* in this letter and *Ep.* 84.

We ought to copy bees, as they say, which flit about and light upon those flowers suitable for making honey, and then, whatever they have gathered, they sort and distribute among the honeycombs, as our Vergil says,

> They pack away
> The flowing honey and stuff their combs with sweet nectar.

When thinking of bees, Seneca naturally turns to Vergil, although the quotation he provides comes not from the *Georgics* but from the *Aeneid* (1.432–3). If the previous letter exploited intertextual connections to point out the literary texture, this one focuses on quotation to do something similar.[54] This *Aeneid* passage, however, derives in large part from the *Georgics* (4.162–9), and these words are almost identical to the lines in the *Georgics*. In the *Aeneid*, Vergil applies his own previous description of the bees in an extended "epic" simile (for the Carthaginians building their city), whereas the original account of the bees was followed by a simile comparing the bees to the Cyclopes.[55] It is no coincidence that Seneca thinks of Vergil when mentioning bees—this quotation links both the *Aeneid* and the *Georgics*, and its context in each of the models features extended similes. Seneca recalls this framework, as his letter also features a large number of similes and metaphors to describe the *contaminatio* of influences at play in any work of literature.[56] Vergil is specifically added to the mix of the letter in order to show the principle of literary imitation (*imitari*) at work—note how Seneca signposts that he will be relying on the accounts of earlier authors with *ut aiunt* even before the direct quotation.[57] Seneca repeats this formulation without the Vergilian quote soon after (*Ep.* 84.5):

> **Nos quoque has apes debemus imitari** et quaecumque ex diversa lectione congessimus separare (melius enim distincta servantur), deinde adhibita ingenii nostri cura et facultate in unum saporem varia illa libamenta confundere, ut etiam si apparuerit unde sumptum sit, aliud tamen esse quam unde sumptum est appareat.

---

[54] See Chap. 1 for discussion of quotation vs. intertext in Seneca's oeuvre.

[55] Cf. Austin (1971) *ad* 430 ff., Thomas (1988b) *ad* 162–9, and Briggs (1980) for discussion of this phenomenon.

[56] While *contaminatio* traditionally is associated with Roman comedy and Terence in particular (cf. Beare (1959)), it can be seen as an effective way to understand Senecan tragedy as well as much of Latin literature (cf. Larmour (1990)). Seneca's technique indicates that he believes such a mixture does not "spoil" or "sully" the work as a whole, but rather improves it.

[57] Cf. Ross (1975) 78 and Hinds (1998) 1–3 for more on the use of certain phrases (*ferunt, fama est, dicuntur*) as signposts for "Alexandrian footnotes."

We also ought to copy these bees, and sift whatever we have gathered from our varied reading (for such things are better saved if kept distinct); then, by applying our supervising care and knowledge we should combine those varied flavors into one delicious mixture that, even though it reveals its origins, it nevertheless is clearly something different from the original.

Instead of featuring another quote from Vergil or an intertextual nod, Seneca now stresses his own viewpoint and interpretation of the Vergilian lines from a compositional standpoint. His primary thesis is that one must incorporate a variety of models in one's writing.[58] While one may come to resemble the author whom one particularly admires, Seneca stresses the independence of the imitator: "I want you to be like him in the manner of a son, not an image: for an image is a dead thing" (*similem esse te volo quomodo filium, non quomodo imaginem: imago res mortua est, Ep.* 84.8). Here, the use of *imago* resonates in the Roman mind with the wax death masks (*imagines*) that were prominently displayed in a Roman family's shrine and leads to the idea that slavish or word-for-word imitation is a "dead thing" (*res mortua*).[59] If honey was one metaphor for poetic production, so wax too can be shaped into the form of the literary predecessor whose work one resembles, but Seneca highlights that the filial status (*filium*) allows for individual development (and if Seneca is thinking of his father's words on *imitatio*, one can see a further rationale for this comparison).[60] Seneca continues the parade of metaphors, claiming that when one has thoroughly digested the material of previous poets, one can produce a unified creation that brings to light what has been made from those sources.[61] This work is like a chorus, which, although made up of many singers, results in one voice

---

[58] This idea probably derives, in part, from the rhetorical formulation of *imitatio/aemulatio* espoused by his father, cf. *Contr.* 1. *praef.* 6, Berti (2007) 263–4, and Trinacty (2009) 263–5. One may also think of Hor. *Carm.* 4.2.27–32, where Horace develops the extended metaphor that he writes his poems in the same manner (*more modoque*, 28) as bees make honey.

[59] Cf. Usher (2006) ad loc. Cf. Dressler (2012) for the importance of this letter in understanding Seneca's "performative language of metaphor and *exemplum*" (173).

[60] The wax used in the death masks would have been made from beeswax and wax was employed to coat writing *tabulae*. Seneca posits that the blended raw materials come from his literary predecessors, "as though they provided the wax, and he the die or stamp" (Fantham (1978) 110).

[61] Seneca believes the mind will be able to do this and "hide everything by which it was helped, and show only the thing itself which it produced" (*omnia, quibus est adiutus, abscondat, ipsum tantum ostendat, quod effecit, Ep.* 84.7). Seneca likens the process to the digestion of food at 84.6, which repeats an idea from *Ep.* 2.2. Ker (2006) 34–5 concentrates on how this letter reveals Seneca's notions of "adjusting, and especially of circumscribing, one's area of focus and changing an existing literary model into a new form that is qualitatively different."

(*Ep.* 84.9).[62] This letter stresses again and again that such a method of imitation is a creative transformation of the models, and thus "the emphasis on the unrecognizability of the final product is not... a counsel of dissimulation to hide one's thefts, but rather the simple evidence of mature individuality."[63] Seneca composes his tragedies in keeping with this very manner of literary production. He combines themes, imagery, and language from the previous poetic tradition and creates something new from its diverse parts. His dramatic works thus exhibit elements of the grand tragedies of Euripides and Sophocles, of Vergil's *Aeneid*, and of Horace's *Odes*, as well as moments taken directly from the more ludic poetry of Ovid. In spite of the contributions of these various authors, however, the resulting product is "clearly something different from the original," both reflecting Seneca's dramatic concerns and embodying his view of intertextuality.

Intertextuality and Interpretation

Seneca's tragedies reveal the poet's close reading of his predecessors and his desire to utilize their accounts in order to flesh out his characters, themes, and dramatic plot. If the Augustan poets often looked back to classic Greek models in their practice of *aemulatio* (Horace with the lyric poets, Vergil with Homer, Ovid with Callimachus among others), for later authors the Augustan poets were the classics. Because of their strong influence on setting the "standards" for all subsequent Latin poetry, the Augustan poets are those with whom Seneca continually engages in formulating his dramatic poetry. The impulse to respond to the Augustan poets can be seen in other writers of this period as well (e.g., Lucan writing his *Bellum Civile* as an anti-*Aeneid*), and their classic status ensured that later authors both relied on and critiqued their works.[64] While a

---

[62] From a philosophical point of view, Seneca is willing to take ideas from all sources, cf. *Ep.* 58.26: *Hoc ego, Lucili, facere soleo: ex omni notione, etiam si a philosophia longissime aversa est, eruere aliquid conor et utile efficere* ("I am accustomed to do the following, Lucilius, and try to search out and make useful something from every field of thought, even if it is very far removed from philosophy.").

[63] Greene (1982) 74. Greene stresses the importance of this letter for theories of *imitatio* in the Renaissance. His stance on *imitatio* for the "Renaissance creator" could easily be applied to that of the post-Augustan Latin poet: "*Imitatio* produced a vast effort to deal with the newly perceived problem of anachronism; it determined for two or three centuries the character of most poetic intertextuality; it assigned the Renaissance creator a convenient and flexible stance toward a past that threatened to overwhelm him" (2).

[64] Cf. Fantham (1982) 21: "Virgil was now universally known, guaranteeing to the writer who introduced a Virgilian allusion into his argument the full understanding of quotation and context by his readers." Ker (2006) 28 points out how Seneca's decision to write tragedy may have been influenced in part by his contemporaries' choices of genre: "Since the genres engaged in by such writes as Seneca the Elder (history), Lucan (epic), Persius (verse satire), Cornutus (etymology, theology),

majority of my readings stress the world of the tragedy as its own *mundus significans*, the historical moment in which Seneca is writing offers a possible rationale for certain intertexts to the Augustan poets.[65] Seneca observes the promise of the Augustan period steadily eroding around him, and selected references draw attention to fissures already present in the works of Vergil and Ovid, especially references to issues such as civil war and the drawbacks of rule by one man.[66]

A reading that takes into account such interconnections recognizes the opaque nature of Seneca's tragic language. Words consistently manifest multiple meanings according to their immediate dramatic context and their intertextual dialogue with previous poetry. Intertextuality occurs when the reader finds a connection between two (or more) texts because of linguistic, metrical, or contextual similarities.[67] I stress the reader's role in the creation of intertextual meaning (that is, necessarily, my own readings of these intertexts), although I do believe a majority of the intertextual references detected in this study would also have been perceived by Roman readers and planned by Seneca.[68] Indeed, his frequent inclusion of the intertextual language elsewhere in his tragedies would seem to demand Seneca's intent. Barchiesi remarks on the creative relationship between the intertextual model and its new context:

> The relation that joins a text to a model involves the interpretation not of one text but of two. Both these interpretations are ever on trial, in process, and continually influencing one another. The new text rereads its model, while the model in turn influences the reading of the new text—indeed when recognized, it often has the power to do so.[69]

Columella (agricultural manual), Petronius (prose fiction), Calpurnius Siculus (pastoral), and others, are all ones which Seneca conspicuously avoided."

[65] Cf. Greene (1982) 21:

> To read in terms of a *mundus* is not to close off the polyvalence of the text, but to seek its potency within the richness of the writer's play with his own codes. The codes themselves moreover cannot be isolated from the usages and structures of the language that supplies their counters. The *mundus* can be thought of as foregrounding certain semiotic potentialities against a background of neglected potentialities coextensive with the language. The *mundus* focuses that power in language to shape and respond to our mental activity.

[66] Cf. Chap. 1 pp. 51–9, Chap. 3 pp. 160–4.

[67] Cf. Wills (1996) 18–23 for more linguistic features of reference.

[68] Cf. Farrell (1991) 21–4 and Edmunds (2001) 39–62 for more on the question authorial intent in allusion. Laird (1999) 38 argues for the importance of the reader in intertextuality: "Instances of irony, parody, or stylization in texts or utterances—which are manifestations of intertextuality—are notorious for not being evident to everyone.... They are actualized only by readers or hearers with a certain competence."

[69] Barchiesi (2001) 142. For a dissenting view, cf. Irwin (2004) 236.

The deployment of intertexts is not fixed but changes with the dramatic situation of the characters and the themes that Seneca wishes to stress. One should not think that each reminiscence of Vergil's *Aeneid* (or even the same line of the *Aeneid*) is necessarily static in what it signifies for Seneca. This flexibility allows for the creation of fresh meaning that takes into consideration Seneca's interpretation of his model and its placement in the tragic genre.

Intertextuality can also be seen as a constituent part of the reception of previous literature and, therefore, reveals Seneca's role as a reader of the Augustan tradition. Martindale reflects that "one useful approach to certain great 'imitative' texts is to see them as rereadings of the works imitated."[70] As Seneca looks back to the poetry of Ovid, Vergil, and Horace, he acts as a critical interpreter of their work in the inventive manner in which he reemploys their language, thought, and poetics. Within the tragic framework, the model work is given new life that additionally can hint at Seneca's view of the tragic genre. Putnam's investigation of Senecan allusion to Vergil's *Aeneid* finds Seneca "reiterating in play after play evidence of man's destructiveness as if he felt that his role as interpreter of Vergil's poem lay in insisting upon vital aspects of the epic which eulogists of empire and emperors would shunt aside or, at best, undervalue."[71] Seneca's project in his tragedies includes deconstructing the language of the Augustan poets, and refiguring it through the perspective of his tragic protagonists. In doing so, he positions himself as a critic of the Augustan tradition and reveals a poetic voice that often subverts the classical ethos of that tradition.

Intertextuality and Genre

As intertexts can recall a particular moment in the model text, so they can recall the genre of that model.[72] The different genres of Roman poetry each offer their own perspective on the world, as Conte elaborates: "It is a language, that is, a lexicon and a style, but it is also a system of the imagination and a grammar of things. Genres are the expressive codification of a culture's models; indeed, they are those very models subjected to a process of stylization and formalization which gives them a literary voice."[73] Tragedy as a genre is an amalgam of different genres, from the lyric chorus to the nearly epic narrative of the messenger speeches; and genre is one way in which their language is codified and understood.

---

[70] Martindale (1993) 35.

[71] Putnam (1995) 279.

[72] Cf. Fantham (1982) 19: "The Romans traditionally thought in terms of genre, relating specific genres to certain types of material, but in the post-Augustan generation, genre itself was in the melting pot."

[73] Conte (1994a) 132.

In the absence of a single narrator, the various characters engage in an active contestation of meaning; tragedy itself can be seen as the collision of various points of view. Because Seneca's tragedies incorporate so many different genres of poetry, he is able to create a dialogue between these genres and show how they can influence his characterization of dramatic figures, their actions, and tragedy itself.[74] Therefore, when Seneca's Medea reformulates language from Ovid's *Heroides*, its original elegiac background and Ovidian context influence the ramifications of such material in its new tragic setting.

This propensity for dialogue between genres approaches the tenets of Bakhtinian thought, namely, the concepts of dialogism and heteroglossia.[75] Dialogism can be seen as the way a text incorporates two different discourses and allows their distinct perspectives, languages, and implications to come into contact with and evaluate one another. For Bakhtin, the novel was the representative genre that could encompass a variety of genres and meanings, but this is partly because of his limited view of poetry as essentially monologic and representative of only the poet's voice.[76] Bakhtin states, "The language of the poetic genre is a unitary and singular Ptolemaic world outside of which nothing else exists and nothing else is needed. The concept of many worlds of language, all equal in their ability to conceptualize and to be expressive, is organically denied to poetic style."[77] Bakhtin, however, may downplay the ability of poetry to be dialogic, especially tragic language, which is not only subject to the focalization of various

---

[74] For a similar view of generic dialogue in Plato, cf. Nightingale (1995) 3: "When Plato incorporates the text or discourse of another genre into a philosophical dialogue, he stages a scene in which the genre both speaks and is spoken to."

[75] Dentith (1995) 218–19 offers the following summary definition of the term:

> Heteroglossia, once incorporated into the novel (whatever the forms for its incorporation), is *another's speech in another's language*, serving to express authorial intentions but in a refracted way. Such speech constitutes a special type of *double-voiced discourse*. It serves two speakers at the same time and expresses simultaneously two different intentions: the direct intention of the character who is speaking, and the refracted intention of the author. In such discourse there are two voices, two meanings and two expressions. And all the while these two voices are dialogically interrelated, they—as it were—know about each other (just as two exchanges in a dialogue know of each other and are structured in this mutual knowledge of each other); it is as if they actually hold a conversation with each other.

[76] Cf. Blevins (2008) 16 on dialogism and lyric:

> Bakhtin's notion of dialogism is an important, thoughtful understanding of the dynamic nature of language, both inside and outside of literary discourse, but Bakhtin simply miscalculated the dialogic nature of lyric and thus failed to explore what dialogism truly means for lyric poetry and how the recognition of lyric's multivoiced construction might offer substantive insights into the lyric genre.

[77] Bakhtin (1981) 226.

characters but also often references various other semantic fields (legal, political, philosophical) in its own right.[78] As Vernant and Vidal-Naquet state:

> The tragic message, when understood, is precisely that there are zones of opacity and incommunicability in the words that men exchange. Even as he sees the protagonists clinging exclusively to one meaning and, thus blinded, tearing themselves apart or destroying themselves, the spectator must understand that there are really two or more possible meanings.[79]

Key terms in Senecan tragedy such as *ira, amor, virtus, pietas,* and *furor* are often subjects of conflict for the characters, and throughout his corpus Seneca finds ways to unlock the "many worlds of language" inherent in his poetry. The language of tragedy exists on a multiplicity of levels, and intertextual references provide another layer of signification to the way in which Seneca's language communicates with its reader. Tragedy's inherent mélange of generic registers adds an additional dialogic element as the lyric choral songs redefine the actions and themes of the play, while different characters struggle to understand the tragic world surrounding them. Seneca's tragedies offer a textual space for the inclusion of a vast array of different genres, and the incorporation of epic or elegiac tropes breathes new life into his concept of tragedy.

Through intertextual echoes, a character such as Seneca's Phaedra can be seen to resemble Vergil's Dido, Ovid's Phaedra of *Heroides* 4, and even Ovid's Dido of *Heroides* 7.[80] Seneca's characters often seem aware of their own intertextual life, and this leads to a bifurcation of their roles, in which they appear to remember their past *literary* feelings and actions, and even attempt to model their behavior according to these past accounts. Such moments allow for fruitful insight into intertextuality and character development. As Seneca's Medea attempts to emulate a previous representation of herself in the pages of Ovid, so Seneca himself is emulating the Ovidian material in his characterization of Medea. These characters show themselves to be knowledgeable interpreters of their literary lives, and this self-conscious conceptualization creates opportunities for self-reflection that verges on literary criticism.[81] When Seneca's Medea casts her spell in language that recalls the incantation of Ovid's Medea (*Met.* 7.192–293), one can see that

---

[78] Batstone (2002) and the articles contained in Blevins (2008) reveal how ancient lyric poetry may be dialogic.

[79] Vernant and Vidal-Naquet (1988) 43.

[80] Cf. Fantham (1975) for Vergil's Dido and Phaedra, T. D. Hill (2004) 159–75 for Ovid's Dido and Phaedra.

[81] Goldberg (1996) 275–83 finds that such metapoetic critiques can involve rhetorical concepts as well.

Seneca is attempting to improve upon Ovid's account while also refashioning it in his tragic world. Such metapoetic turns happen often in Senecan tragedy, as characters comment on their position in the play *and* on the drama's position within the larger context of Latin literature.

Intertextual Excursus

In the course of the following chapters, I analyze intertextuality in a number of ways stressing how the recognition of an intertext reinforces major themes of the play, offers metapoetic commentary, and stresses the "readerly" nature of these tragedies. For instance, in Seneca's *Phaedra*, the Nurse lectures the chaste hunter Hippolytus about the importance of sex for preserving life on earth (*Phd.* 466–8):

> Providit ille maximus mundi parens,
> cum tam rapaces cerneret Fati manus,
> ut **damna** semper subole **repararet** nova.

> When the greatest father of the universe saw
> How greedy were the hands of Fate, he decided
> To always repair the losses with new offspring.

This is part of a speech that both draws upon various Epicurean tenets and even Stoic language to encourage Hippolytus to "follow Nature as a guide" (*sequere naturam ducem*, 481) and to enjoy his youth. While this sentiment echoes Stoicism's primary maxim ("to follow Nature," *Ep.* 41.9, 90.4, 90.16), it is difficult to read the Nurse as a voice for Stoic values in the play.[82] The Nurse looks at the natural world that Hippolytus devoutly extols and points to the necessity of procreation for the maintenance of that world. The Nurse believes such an argument may convince Hippolytus to give up his chastity and engage in an affair with Phaedra, but Hippolytus' subsequent misogynistic rant shows that in his mind it may be "natural" to hate all women.[83]

---

[82] Cf. Hine (1994) for the difficulty of such Stoic readings and Armisen-Marchetti (1992) for more on the polyvalence of the Nurse's role in this play. Cf. Rosenmeyer (2000) for more on Seneca and *natura*.

[83] Hippolytus claims, "I detest all women, I bristle, I flee, I curse all / Whether it is reason, or nature, or harsh madness: / It pleases me to hate them" (*Detestor omnes, horreo fugio execror. / sit ratio, sit natura, sit durus furor: / odisse placuit.* 566–8). Note how Hippolytus' own view equates two of Stoicism's primary positive guides (*ratio, natura*) with an antithetical value (*furor*).

While the philosophical and rhetorical pull of this speech may be central to the Nurse's purposes (she is pulling out all the stops in her attempt to persuade Hippolytus), this passage also grimly foreshadows the play's conclusion through an intertext with one of Horace's most famous odes (*Carm.* 4.7). In this poem, Horace observes the natural world and the changes of the seasons, causing him to muse upon the passing of time and the inevitability of death. He writes (*Carm.* 4.7.13–6):

> **damna** tamen celeres **reparant** caelestia lunae:
>   nos ubi decidimus
> quo pater Aeneas, quo Tullus dives et Ancus,
>   pulvis et umbra sumus.

> While the quick waxing of the moon repairs heavenly losses:
>   When we have descended to the place
> Where father Aeneas, where rich Tullus and Ancus are,
>   We are dust and shadow.

The contrast of nature's constant renewal and the everlasting death of men provides the common theme in the speech of the Nurse and Horace's ode, and the use of similar language shows Seneca's debt to Horace here. While the Nurse attempts to use such an argument to encourage Hippolytus to sow his wild oats, for Horace it leads to contemplative meditation on the inescapability and immutability of death. A reader with full knowledge of Horace's poem will also remember the close of that poem, and Horace's use of Hippolytus himself as exemplum of death's permanence (*infernis neque enim tenebris Diana pudicum / liberat Hippolytum*, "For Diana cannot free pure Hippolytus from the infernal shades," *Carm.* 4.7.25–6).[84] Within the Nurse's speech, Seneca has embedded Hippolytus' imminent destruction and, through the Horatian intertext, pointed to the inevitability of the play's concluding death tableaux. This type of intertextual play is common in Senecan tragedy and allows Seneca to undercut a character's speech with subversive meaning or foreshadow future events if the reader comprehends the full context of the model text. The recognition that Horace's "pure Hippolytus" (*pudicum…Hippolytum*) is unable to escape Hades also may key the reader into the importance of forms of the adjective *(im)pudicus* for the latter half of Seneca's play.[85] Phaedra's final confession before her suicide stresses that Hippolytus was "pure and guiltless" (*pudicus, insons*, 1196) and that Theseus, a fellow sufferer in

---

[84] Garrison (1991) ad loc. remarks on the final stanza, "Hippolytus' chastity did not save him from death, nor did the friendship of Theseus save Pirithous. The grim point of the final stanza is that death conquers love."

[85] When Hippolytus recognizes that Phaedra is propositioning him, her body becomes "impure" (704, 707), whereas the Nurse's stratagem is to call Phaedra "pure" (728, 735) compared to the

Horace's poem (*Carm.* 4.7.27–8), is the cause of his own son's death.[86] Like the ominous music that underscores foreboding moments in film, so the reader who hears the words *damna…reparant* and understands their Horatian pedigree will find the Nurse's words worrying. The complete Horatian context colors the Nurse's words and leads the reader to understand the inevitability of Hippolytus' death in this very play.

Overview

What kind of a reader was Seneca? The opening chapter explores moments in which Seneca quotes passages of Ovid and Vergil in his prose works and then recalls the same passages as intertexts in his tragedies. By studying these parallel passages, one can view the differences (and similarities) in his approach and gain insight into Seneca's manner of reading. Seneca finds in the Ovidian and Vergilian lines evocative language as well as fertile ground for reinterpretation. Whether it is a philosophical letter or a speech of a dramatic character, the literary context of Seneca's work provides a critical frame for the interpretation of the Augustan passage. In general, however, the prose works offer a more monologic take on the poetic quote because Seneca strives to fit its meaning into the ethical framework of his essay; his tragic intertextuality operates in a more dialogic way and opens up a conduit between the two texts. Seneca's tragedies are shown to be representative examples of Bakhtinian dialogism in which more than one "consciousness" is able to speak.[87] The words of the model text are often repeated and rebranded in the course of the play, revealing Seneca's interest in not only testing the limitations of the language's meaning but also its application to the tragic tale.

In the second chapter, I examine how intertextuality influences Seneca's development of two characters, Medea and Phaedra. Seneca's Medea is a fusion of the Ovidian Medea(s) of the *Metamorphoses* and *Heroides*, and the drama

---

"rapist" Hippolytus. The *Phaedra* accounts for six of the seven times that forms of this adjective appear in Seneca's tragedies.

[86] Horace is also "correcting" a variant tradition, followed by Vergil and Ovid, that Hippolytus was saved by Diana.

[87] Cf. Holquist (1990) 20–21:

> Dialogism argues that all meaning is relative in the sense that it comes about only as a result of the relation between two bodies occupying *simultaneous but different* space, where bodies may be thought of as ranging from the immediacy of our physical bodies, to political bodies and to bodies of ideas in general (ideologies)…. Conceiving being dialogically means that reality is always experienced, not just perceived, and further that it is experienced from a particular position.

This position can be seen as both Seneca's active experience of writing the tragedies as well as the (modern/ancient) reader's experience constructing meaning through his tragedies.

explores different facets of her character before she attains her superhuman position at the close of the tragedy. Seneca stresses the literary makeup of Medea's character, and she comes to stand-in for an authorial figure as she directs the action of the play.[88] In the *Phaedra*, the characterization of Hippolytus and Phaedra indicates the strong connection between Ovid and Seneca, but these characters (unlike Medea) are unable to come to terms with their own self-presentation. Language from Ovid's elegiac poetry abounds in Seneca's play, but now the tropes and imagery from Ovid's *Amores* and *Ars Amatoria* have a sinister air and point to the failure of Phaedra's desire. Phaedra attempts to define herself as an elegiac lover and strives to maintain the persona that Ovid's Phaedra, from *Heroides* 4, assumed, but comes to realize the tragic implications of the intransigence of Hippolytus' view and her own shifting self-definition.

While several of the characters actively control the plots of their plays, in many of Seneca's tragedies, the characters appear to be swept along by the plot and thus are unable to control their actions. My third chapter examines the formal aspects of Seneca's tragedies (prologue speakers, choruses, messenger speeches) and analyzes how intertextuality supplements the plots of his tragedies and offers commentary on the dramatic action. An investigation of the prologues of *Hercules Furens* and *Oedipus* reveals that intertextual references found in these speeches haunt the resulting action of the play. In a similar manner, Seneca's choruses often recall the poetry of Horace, and an examination of Horatian intertexts brings to light Seneca's interpretation of Horace's lyric poetry. By tracing how various choral songs echo Horace's odes, one can understand Seneca's own interest in manipulating lyric discourse in his tragedies. This chapter concludes with an analysis of messenger speeches from the *Phaedra* and the *Troades*. In these speeches, epic tropes are questioned and reevaluated as the messengers relate their stories about the deaths of heroic figures. The polygeneric nature of tragedy, with its blend of lyric choral passages, epic narrative (in messenger speeches), and iambic dialogue ideally fits Seneca's view of literary creation, and impels him to provide a multifaceted exploration of the tragic action.

The final chapter (Chapter 4) deals broadly with the concepts of poetics and genre and proposes a reading of Seneca's tragedies that stresses his unique conception of the tragic genre. While my readings throughout the book indicate how generic enrichment and intertextuality go hand in hand to provide Seneca's interpretation of the Augustan poets, this chapter focuses on particular moments in which Seneca manipulates the works of his predecessors in a metapoetic manner. His tragedies act as a critical forum for the Augustan poets, in which the meanings of their works are questioned. An examination of Seneca's use of Vergil's *Georgics* reveals how the famous preface to the third *Georgic* informs the poetics

---

[88] Cf. Pavlock (2009) for a similar technique in Ovid's *Metamorphoses*.

of Seneca's tragedies. In addition, Horace's *Ars Poetica* offers important material for Seneca's concept of poetics; significant intertexts to Horace's *Ars* reveal how Seneca aims to produce dramatic poetry that embodies or questions Horace's strictures. By developing or eliding aspects of his predecessors' works, Seneca indicates how the manipulation of the source material matters for the interpretation of his tragedies. As Martindale explains, "The signifier is so charged with an excess of energy that it generates further fictions, fictions which serve to answer unanswered questions, fill 'gaps', explain perceived 'contradictions', provide sequels and allow for appropriations in view of new circumstances."[89] Seneca's use of intertextuality encapsulates his reception of the Latin literary tradition, and I show how he incorporates criticism of that tradition in his tragedies. This is seen both in the use of metapoetic language and imagery as well as in characters who act as creators of poetry and those who try to interpret poetry. Surrogate writers and readers populate Seneca's tragedies, and my examinations of Cassandra in the *Agamemnon* and Oedipus in his eponymous tragedy show how Seneca inscribes his own reading and writing techniques in these two characters. This book offers a series of suggestive analyses, which hint at the complexity of Seneca's reception of the Augustan poets, while validating his position as an erudite reader of the Latin poetic tradition.

[89] Martindale (1993) 37 on the idea of the "supplement" to a word or text.

1

Seneca the Reader

> If you think about it, reading is a necessarily individual act, far more than writing. If we assume that writing manages to go beyond the limitations of the author, it will continue to have a meaning only when it is read by a single person and passes through his mental circuits. Only the ability to be read by a given individual proves that what is written shares in the power of writing, a power based on something that goes beyond the individual.
> —Italo Calvino, *If on a Winter's Night a Traveler*

The language, themes, and imagery of the Augustan poets enrich the textual brilliance of Seneca's prose and poetic works. But is there a difference in the way Seneca utilizes these poems, depending on whether they are found in his prose works or his tragedies? Does the genre (whether of the model text or Seneca's) affect how such material is used? The answer is not a simple yes or no, but his desire to reinterpret the Augustan work in its new (Senecan) context is manifest in both Seneca's prose and poetry. In his prose works, Seneca quotes Augustan authors (among others) to add punch and persuasiveness to his philosophical arguments, or because the quote appears apposite to the subject under discussion, even it is often wrenched out of its original context. In many cases, Seneca incorporates an interpretation of the quoted passage into his larger philosophical discussion. As an avowed Stoic, one may expect him to follow the Stoic hermeneutic position and, therefore, employ allegorical and etymological exposition when interpreting poetry.[1] One finds, however, that Seneca usually dismisses such a methodology, instead concentrating on the ethical message to be found in the poetic lines, no matter their source.[2] Modern accounts that have

---

[1] Lacy (1948) presents the basic tenets of a Stoic view of poetry. Long (1996) 58–84 offers an overview of Stoic readings of Homer (note Seneca's own skepticism of Stoic interpretations of Homer at *Ep.* 88.5). What a Stoic interpretation of his tragedies may imply can be seen in Nussbaum (1993) and Hine (1994).

[2] E.g., *Ep.* 8.8: *Quam multi poetae dicunt, quae philosophis aut dicta sunt aut dicenda!* ("How many poets say things that have been said or ought to have been said by philosophers!"). He derides

tried to discover a single strategy that Seneca adopts in reading poetry often run aground because of Seneca's eclectic appropriation of poetic quotes and his differing interpretations of those quotes.³

When Seneca expressly interprets a quotation, he does so by integrating the language and message of that quotation into the larger body of the letter or prose treatise. A similar strategy is at play when intertexts to the Augustan poets appear in his tragedies, although, obviously, without the explicit analysis found in his prose writings. Both quotations and intertexts can be seen as metaphors inasmuch as they signify something *more* than the simple definitions of the words themselves. Worton and Still comment on the metaphorical qualities of quotation:

> In each encounter with a quotation, the reader perceives that, while there is an obvious conflict between sameness or identity and difference, there is also a covert fusion of differences *within* the single utterance. We would therefore suggest that every quotation is a metaphor which speaks of that which is absent and which engages the reader in a speculative activity.⁴

In this chapter, I show how Seneca engages in such "speculative activity," as he further muses upon and modifies the quoted material.⁵ In order to gain insight into Seneca's way of reading poetry, I believe it is important to look at these selected quotations within their Senecan context, while keeping in mind their original background, and, if possible, to cross-examine these same quotations when they are used as intertexts in his tragedies.⁶ This is possible only in a small number of cases, but it sheds considerable light on Seneca's reading of the Augustan poets.

One caveat that must be addressed is the tendency, in such comparative studies of Seneca's prose and poetic works, to favor the prose (i.e., the philosophical) interpretation. The argument usually follows the line that Seneca's tragedies are merely the honey on the cup of philosophy, and that Seneca's "true" opinion is to

---

philosophical quibbling and syllogisms often in the epistles (e.g., *Ep.* 45.5–13; 49.8–10; 82.9–10; 88.42–5). For an examination of poetic vocabulary in Seneca's prose works, cf. Hine (2005).

³ Auvray (1987) believes that Seneca read the *Aeneid* as a Stoic work. Mazzoli (1970) helpfully gathers all the quotations from Seneca's prose works.

⁴ Worton and Still (1990) 11–12.

⁵ Cf. Ker (2009) 122–3 for an example of a "selective quotation" in which the larger context of the quote provides "obvious incongruities" with the thesis being argued.

⁶ Tarrant (2006) 3 points out that sometimes Seneca quotes an Augustan author and includes "in close proximity…allusive reference to the same texts" with an example from *Nat.* 3.27.13–3.28.2.

be found in his prose treatises and letters.[7] This belief has been formative in the study of Senecan tragedy as scholars, including some of the first commentators, tried to explain the Stoic touches of his poetic works through his prose works (in the words of Del Rio, "Seneca is his own best commentator").[8] My study does not aim to uncover hidden Stoic meaning in the tragedies, but rather to investigate the manner in which the works of previous poets are incorporated autonomously in Seneca's prose and poetic works. Frequently Seneca *philosophus* provides a Stoic interpretation of such lines in his letters and dialogues, but such an interpretation is often far away from the sentiment of Seneca *tragicus*.

It may be impossible (and incorrect) to posit one single "reading strategy" on Seneca's part as he approaches the work of previous poets. For Staley, Seneca is a Stoic reader of Vergil in his prose works, and, therefore, "when Seneca turned to writing his own poetry, he continued in this same spirit...writing 'Vergil' in the same way he read him."[9] Others have stressed that Seneca's alluding to and reading of Vergil's *Aeneid* should be given a political dimension: as Vergil gave voice to the legacy of civil war and suffering under Augustus, so Seneca may hint at similar circumstances under Nero.[10] My contention is that Seneca unearths distinct and disparate applications of Augustan poetry as his context demands and that, in general, he will exploit the polyvalence of tragic intertextuality to explore diverse themes and interests. Busch comments on the range of perspectives found in his tragedies: "What results is a dialogic orchestration of voices addressing subjects that the discursive prose treats in a more monologic fashion. While the tragedies make room for the Stoicizing voices that dominate the prose, in this generic setting they represent one ideological constituency among many."[11] As Seneca will take up different subjects and persuasive strategies in his

---

[7] Marti (1945) and Pratt (1983) attempt to read Seneca's tragedies as an explication of his Stoic thought.

[8] See Mayer (1994) for a survey of the views of early Neostoic commentators, like those of Del Rio. Fitch (2002) advises against reading the plays as Stoic works, as "such attempts have invariably led to distorted readings of the plays, by reason of the very different nature of the two genres: moral philosophy in antiquity is optimistic, which tragedy is not; philosophy of a particular school takes a single systematic view of the world, which poetry does not" (22).

[9] Staley (2000) 349. The author suggests that Seneca's monsters, which often feature aspects of Vergilian intertextuality, "are to be read by us as vivid illustrations of passion, just as Vergil's were so read by Seneca himself" (349). However, Staley (2010) 50–1 recognizes that "Seneca does not advocate a narrowly moralistic or philosophical reading of poetry."

[10] Cf. Schiesaro (1992) 61: "*Thyestes* condenses in the polarized contrast between two brothers the horrors of civil strife, a theme with obvious, obsessive resonances in first-century literature.... By alluding to Vergil, Seneca characterizes his own writing as repetition, as a painful, irresistible return to horrors which had already been sung." Bishop (1985) finds political allegory behind the plots of Seneca's tragedies.

[11] Busch (2007) 265.

letters, so the characters of his tragedies present differing points of view for the literary material being employed. In each case, the voice remains Seneca's but the ramifications for interpretation change.

As these case studies progress, the question arises whether there is any difference between a quotation and an intertext. In each case the language takes on additional significance, as it engages the reader in a complex hermeneutic event. As Worton and Still write, "To quote is not merely to write glosses on previous writers; it is to interrogate the chronicity of literature and philosophy, to challenge history as determining tradition and to question conventional notions of originality and difference."[12] While a quote is granted an additional signpost of its interference in the text (e.g., "As Vergil writes…"), and therefore will enact a response from the reader (as one identifies the author and source of the quote), intertexts can be missed. Seneca, however, expects his readers to engage with his material from an informed perspective and to recognize the wide variety of sources behind a poetic production.[13] When he quotes poetry in his prose works, Seneca provides his own interpretation of the material and often includes language from the quote in the surrounding context to show how he continues to respond to the quote. A similar process can be seen in his intertextual engagement with the same material in his tragedies. The *imitatio* he practices as a writer reflects his own critical reading of the source texts, and, through the collocation of material, one can view the authors most important to Seneca's idea of tragic poetry. As Eliot writes, "If we approach a poet without this prejudice [of originality and difference], we shall find that not only the best, but the most individual parts of [an author's] work may be those in which the dead poets, his ancestors, assert their immortality most vigorously."[14] The tragedies offer their own poetic context for interpretation, and often the repetition of language from the intertextual source will act as a leitmotif for the larger world of the play. In the following studies (as well as the following chapters), the intertextual material may resonate with a variety of dramatic concerns such as characterization and plot twists, or with concerns outside the play itself (poetry, politics, philosophy).

Multiple Perspectives, Multiple Readings

First, I want to offer a quick overview of Seneca's strategies for approaching a text and his rationale for the use of poetic quotation in his prose works. In Epistle 108,

---

[12] Worton and Still (1990) 12.
[13] As seen in the discussions of Epistles 79 and 84 in the introduction.
[14] Eliot (1941) 24, quoted in Worton and Still (1990) 12.

Seneca discusses the ability to explicate a text in various ways (whether one is a *grammaticus, philologus,* or *philosophus*).[15] This letter (appropriately for the *Epistulae Morales*) focuses on the importance of philosophy for living a life of consequence, and mentions how poetry can often get to the heart of the matter more quickly and powerfully than prose.[16] But poetry can be dangerous. Because of its beauty, it may lead one to falsehood or embroil one in a passionate response to a fictional situation. However it can also rouse one to action—Seneca provides examples of theatrical *sententiae* that caused the audience to applaud their everyday wisdom.[17] Seneca quotes a saying of Cleanthes (*Ep.* 108.10):

Quemadmodum spiritus noster clariorem sonum reddit cum illum tuba per longi canalis angustias tractum patentiore novissime exitu effudit, sic sensus nostros clariores carminis arta necessitas efficit.

Just as our breath gives a louder sound, when a trumpet magnifies it and it passes through the long tight pipes and then out from a larger opening, so the concise force of poetry influences our senses more strongly.

Seneca's letters utilize poetry to do just that, and he quotes and interprets the poetry of Vergil, Ovid, and others in order to channel the power of their language to challenge and to clarify the subject matter at hand.[18] These poets offer true insight and do so in a memorable manner. For Seneca, poetry is able to influence even the greatest reprobate (*sordidissimus, Ep.* 108.9), and it is the meter, rhythm, and beauty of poetry that increases its impact.[19] This artistry can effectively enhance the moral message of philosophy.

---

[15] Von Albrecht (2004) 68–98 discusses *Ep.* 108 more generally. A similar divide between the *grammaticus* and the *philosophus* can be seen in *Ep.* 88 (esp. 88.37–46). Seneca knows of Stoic, Epicurean, Peripatetic, and Academic interpretations of Homer (*Ep.* 85.5).

[16] Seneca often encourages Lucilius to read with an eye towards ethics (*quicquid legeris ad mores statim referas*, "Whatever you read, apply it at once to your habits," *Ep.* 89.18).

[17] For an overview of Stoic views of poetry, cf. Nussbaum (1993). *Ep.* 108.8–9, 11–12 discusses how lines from the theater cause the listener "to be led to the acknowledgment of truth" (*ad confessionem vertatis adducimur, Ep.* 108.12). His own tragedies provided "philosophical" *sententiae* for countless writers of the Renaissance and beyond.

[18] See Mazzoli (1970) 157–264 for a chronological list and analysis of poetic quotation in Seneca. Seneca first incorporates a quotation in his second epistle, and they appear frequently thereafter.

[19] Cf. *Ep.* 108.10: "When rhythm is added and fixed meter has encompassed a notable idea, that very sense is hurled, as if with a stronger arm" (*ubi accessere numeri et egregium sensum adstrinxere certi pedes, eadem illa sententia velut lacerto excussiore torquetur*). Note how this use of Seneca's own tragedies predominated in the Renaissance, as Eliot (1950) states, "In the plays, indeed, the Stoicism is

In the context of *Ep.* 108, Seneca provides readings of texts such as Cicero's *De Republica* and Vergil's *Georgics*, illustrating that one can find different meanings in the texts, depending on what one is looking for (*Ep.* 108.29):

> Non est quod mireris ex eadem materia suis quemque studiis apta colligere; in eodem prato bos herbam quaerit, canis leporem, ciconia lacertam.

> Nor should you wonder that it is possible for each [different type of reader] to collect information befitting their own studies from the same source, for in the same field the cow searches for grass, the dog searches for the rabbit, and the stork searches for the lizard.

He goes on to show the different approaches one could employ to interpret Cicero's *De Republica*, giving lengthy "philological" and "scholarly" interpretations of certain phrases, before turning to the philosophical perspective he favors. It is notable that Seneca reveals himself to be a talented and acute reader from each one of the viewpoints he adopts. His *philologus* notes the particulars of early Roman political and social history, tracing governmental institutions back to figures such as Romulus and Numa (*Ep.* 108.30). The *grammaticus* concentrates more on the language itself and finds linguistic parallels for the change in definition or usage of words (*Ep.* 108.32–4). This *grammaticus*, much like a modern commentator, is also interested in chasing down *loci communes*, and he thinks himself blessed (*felicem, Ep.* 108.34) if he discovers that Vergil had appropriated an Ennian line (which is "stolen" (*subripuisse*), in turn, from Homer).[20] While Seneca does not endorse this type of reading here, it shows his knowledge of and skill at scrutinizing instances of *imitatio* and *aemulatio*.[21] The tracing of sources was common to ancient (and modern) critics in an attempt to elucidate the originality of writers and to construe their language. Such investigation will aid in the interpretation of his tragedies, but in this letter Seneca downplays this strategy and stresses the philosophical reading of poetry, claiming, "Listening to philosophy and reading should be applied to the proposition of living the blessed life" (*auditionem philosophorum lectionemque ad propositum beatae vitae trahendam, Ep.* 108.35).[22]

---

present in a form more quickly to catch the fancy of the Renaissance than in the prose epistles and essays. Half of the commonplaces of the Elizabethans—and the more commonplace half—are of Senecan origin" (57).

[20] This language of *imitatio* can also be found in Seneca the Elder's description of Ovid's use of Vergil (*Suas.* 3.7).

[21] Cf. Skutsch (1985) 788–9 for more about Seneca's reading of this passage of Vergil's *Georgics* (3.260–1). See the introduction for Seneca's view of *imitatio* and *aemulatio* in *Ep.* 79 and 84.

[22] Seneca tends to diminish the value of poets as ethical teachers, especially when read in a literal manner (*De Ben.* 1.3.10; *Dial.* 10.16.5; *Ep.* 88.3, 9, 20).

This letter specifies some of the manners of reading that were practiced in Seneca's time, and Seneca proves himself to be an adept reader from each perspective. While the letters generally focus on the philosophical significance that poetic quotations can possess, he grants that different readers will understand lines of Vergil or passages of Cicero according to their own tastes. Both the context (poetic, philosophical, philological) and personal predilections of the reader influence the meaning of these lines. Classic works of literature or political philosophy can encompass these different interpretations, like Calvino says: "A classic is a book that has never finished saying what it has to say."[23] An investigation of the Vergilian quote that Seneca first discusses in this letter will provide a preview of the critical methodology that will be used throughout this chapter.

Disease and Grim Old Age: Tragic Scenes of the Underworld

Seneca does not wish the philosophical impact of moral exhortation and poetry to be diminished by scholarly attention to minute details. In this way, he says, "philosophy has become philology" (*Itaque quae philosophia fuit, facta philologia est, Ep.* 108.3). He contrasts the *philosophus* with the *grammaticus* who searches for parallels to Vergil's idea that "time flees" (*fugit inreparabile tempus, Georg.* 3.284) but disregards the force of such a statement. In this context, the *grammaticus* is excited to find the following parallel from earlier in Vergil's *Georgics* (*Ep.* 108.24 quoting *Georg.* 3.66–8):

> **optima** quaeque **dies** miseris mortalibus aevi
> **prima fugit**; subeunt morbi tristisque senectus
> et **labor**, et durae rapit inclementia mortis.

> The most pleasant day of life for wretched mortals flees first;
> Disease and grim old age and hardship follow close behind,
> And the harshness of cruel death snatches you away.

The *grammaticus*, too focused on philological trivia, does not understand the true pathos of the statement, which Seneca proceeds to elucidate (*Ep.* 108.27):

> Itaque toto hoc agamus animo et omissis ad quae devertimur, in rem unam **laboremus**, ne hanc temporis pernicissimi celeritatem, quam retinere non possumus, relicti demum intellegamus. **Primus** quisque tamquam **optimus dies** placeat et redigatur in nostrum. Quod **fugit**, occupandum est.

---

[23] Calvino (1982) 128.

Let us, therefore, act with great courage and leave behind distractions; let us work for this one thing, lest we are left behind and understand too late the very quickness of swift time, which we are not able to stop. Let each day, as soon as it dawns, be considered most pleasant and let it be rendered ours. We must catch that which flees.

Seneca finds this Vergilian passage to be a helpful encouragement to make the most of one's time, and he also incorporated it earlier in his *De Brevitate Vitae*, interpreting it in much the same manner.[24] One must make the most of each day, and the knowledge of impending sickness, old age, and death should act as a spur to live according to Stoic strictures. His aim, in both passages, is to explicate the Vergilian statement and relate the poetic language and imagery to his philosophical message. Seneca cleverly interprets Vergil's line with language and imagery taken from the *Georgics* context, stressing what it means for the day to be *optimus*, redefining what work (*labor/laboremus*) needs to be accomplished, and adding hunting imagery pertinent to the use of *fugit*.[25] This is a common strategy in his prose works, and one finds a similar desire on Seneca's part to rebrand language from intertexts in his tragedies. For Seneca, each day that one awakens and claims for oneself is "best" (*optimus*), especially those days of one's youth, which are fitting for work and study.[26] If the most pleasant day of life for wretched mortals flees first (*Optima quaeque dies miseris mortalibus aevi / prima **fugit***), then, as Seneca claims, "we must catch that which flees" (*Quod **fugit**, occupandum est*). Seneca's persona as moral teacher informs his analysis, and the body of the letter (or dialogue) points out how such poetry can be claimed by a Stoic in order to exhort proper "care of the self."[27]

Seneca's *grammaticus*, however, unimpressed by the sentiment of the line, focuses on the pairing of "disease and grim old age" (*morbi tristisque senectus*), which he also finds

---

[24] Cf. *Dial.* 10.9.2. Note the similar usage of "seize the day" language (*Nisi occupas, fugit.*), appeals to Vergil's authority being nearly divine (*tamquam missum oraculo, Ep.* 108.26; *velut divino ore instinctus, Dial.* 10.9.2), and Seneca's complementary metaphors denoting a similar sentiment. The Vergilian quote has struck other notable writers and thinkers as well (cf. Mynors (1990) ad loc.). Seneca echoes this line at *Phd.* 450–1 (*optimos vitae dies / effluere prohibe*) as the Nurse urges Hippolytus, "Stop wasting the best days of your life." A similar moment involves *Aen.* 2.354, *una salus victis nullam sperare salutem* ("the only salvation for the defeated is to hope for no salvation"), which is echoed at *Phoen.* 89–90, *Oed.* 108–9, and *Troad.* 453, but quoted at *Nat.* 6.2.2.

[25] Note *Ep.* 108.27 with its repetition of *optima*. *Labor* is one of the major themes of the *Georgics* as a whole, and the toil of farming is here contrasted with the toil involved in living a philosophically self-aware life.

[26] *Ep.* 108.27: "Why 'best day'? Because, when we are young, we are able to learn to turn our nimble and still malleable minds to nobler pursuits; because this age is right for work" (*Quare **optima**? Quia iuvenes possumus discere, possumus facilem animum et adhuc tractabilem ad meliora convertere; quia hoc tempus idoneum est **laboribus***). The hunting imagery found here foreshadows the description of the field with different animals searching for their prey.

[27] Cf. Foucault (1986) 39–68 and the importance of a Stoic regimen passim.

personified in the description of the Underworld in Vergil's *Aeneid* ("Lurid Disease and grim Old Age dwell," *pallentesque habitant Morbi tristisque Senectus, Aen.* 6.275). Once again we can see the variability in readings of Vergil according to one's interests, but this connection allows further insight into Seneca's own reception of Vergil. Seneca's *grammaticus* finds links between Vergil's *Georgics* and *Aeneid* because of the similar language used about disease and old age. The reader of the *Epistulae Morales* who comes upon the line in this letter quickly recognizes that this very line was recently employed in the previous missive. It would appear that Seneca had been thinking of this passage of Vergil's poetry, and the ability of poetry to encourage Stoic activity.[28]

In Epistle 107, Lucilius is troubled because some of his slaves have run away, and Seneca uses this opportunity to lecture him on the importance of negative visualization and, implicitly, the insignificance of such a loss.[29] Responding to the grief that Lucilius is enduring and chiding him for his overreaction (a putative cry of "O for Death!"), Seneca writes (*Ep.* 107.3):

> Mori vult? praeparetur animus contra omnia; sciat se venisse ubi tonat fulmen; sciat se venisse ubi
>
> > Luctus et ultrices posuere cubilia Curae
> > pallentesque habitant Morbi tristisque Senectus.
>
> In hoc contubernio vita degenda est. Effugere ista non potes, contemnere potes; contemnes autem si saepe cogitaveris et futura praesumpseris.

> Does one wish to die? Let the mind be prepared for everything; let it know that it has arrived where the thunderbolt resounds. Let it know it has arrived where
>
> > Grief and the avenging Cares have placed their couches
> > And lurid Disease and grim Old Age dwell.
>
> You must spend your life among such comrades. You are not able to flee them, but you can consider them of little value. Moreover you will consider them of little value, if you often think about and anticipate future events.

---

[28] As *Ep.* 108 includes Cleanthes' injunction on poetry, so *Ep.* 107 features Seneca's translation of a hymn of Cleanthes, elucidating the Stoic conception of fate (and showing Seneca's own ability as a translator).

[29] Cf. *Dial.* 6.9.1–5, *Ep.* 98, Manning (1976), and Irvine (2009) 65–84 for the importance of "negative visualization" for Stoic askesis.

Seneca believes that anticipating potential troubles will lead to tranquility, and his letter stresses the inevitability of troubles and suffering because such events are fated. Seneca instructs Lucilius that life is difficult (*Non est delicata res vivere*, 107.2), and he utilizes Vergil's description of the Underworld in part to make his imagery more concrete.[30] Seneca essentially calls Lucilius' bluff, "If you want to die, here's your *katabasis*!" only to modify Vergil's sentiment. Playing off the idea in the quote that the personified Grief and Cares "have placed their couches" in Hades, Seneca comments that these are one's "comrades," and the Latin *contubernio* indicates that they are to be thought of as sharing one's tent or habitation, like one's fellow soldiers.[31] Lucilius (a quasi-Aeneas?) needs to realize that these evils are present in one's everyday life and that the truly heroic activity (*magnum sumere animum et viro bono dignum*, 107.7) is "to boldly suffer the vicissitudes of chance and to harmonize one's life with Nature" (*fortiter fortuita patiamur et naturae consentiamus*, 107.7). This letter shows the consolatory spirit that Seneca practices often in his prose, but now used to chide Lucilius for his hyperbolic distress.[32] In the course of the letter, Seneca attempts to assuage Lucilius through a variety of consolatory techniques; the quotation of Vergil is one way that he attempts to point Lucilius to the correct attitude towards life's scrapes and dilemmas.[33]

If one believes the loss of his slaves a worthwhile cause for suicide, Seneca finds that Vergil's lines illustrate the Hades on earth that awaits those individuals who believe they can go through life without any pain. In fact, such personified evils as grief, care, disease, and old age will affect all of us, and one does not have to die to experience them. Reading Vergil's line in the different contexts of Epistles 107 and 108, as well as from the different perspective of the *grammaticus* and the *philosophus*, provides insight into not only Seneca's erudite application of the

---

[30] Here we can follow Seneca's thought process as the initial thought of death leads to the literary depiction of the world of the dead found in Vergil's *Aeneid*, and the quote (which seems to be on his mind at the time of writing *Ep.* 107 and 108), which is then provided with a typical Senecan twist.

[31] *OLD* s.v. *contubernium* 1 and 4. As part of the larger metaphor for the difficulty of life's journey, Seneca comments, "At one point you will leave a comrade behind, at another you will bury one" (*alio loco comitem relinques, alio efferes*, 107.2), which also may have prompted the Vergilian quote and subsequent explanation. Cf. Mayer (1991) 142 for more on the importance of *contubernium* for *exempla*.

[32] Cf. M. Wilson (2007) 431 on Seneca's rhetorical strategy "that aims at provocation, shock and surprise rather than predictability and orderliness of exposition. His favored literary modes are the epistolary and consolatory, both of which allowed, in fact demanded, great flexibility in structure depending on the character and situation of the addressee."

[33] The concluding translation of Cleanthes (*Ep.* 107.11) reveals in a nutshell how poetry and philosophy can work together to achieve the philosophical ends Seneca desires in the *Epistulae Morales*. The translation itself manifests many qualities of Senecan tragedy; cf. Dahlmann (1977).

Vergilian line but also his ease in appropriating Augustan material for his own diverse ends.

While the prose works bring to light the philosophical importance of Vergil's lines and show Seneca's familiarity with Vergil's *Georgics* and *Aeneid*, Seneca also includes variants of this line (*Aen.* 6.274–5) in two of his tragic depictions of the Underworld. Is there an innovative interpretation given to the line in its tragic context, as in the philosophical epistles? Or is it merely an apposite application of an intertextual source (i.e., Vergil is writing about the Underworld, and therefore Seneca includes the line in his own depiction of the Underworld)? As Seneca gives distinctive interpretations of the Vergilian quote in his prose work, so the surrounding tragic context influences the interpretation of the Vergilian intertext in Seneca's *Hercules Furens* and *Oedipus*.

The *Hercules Furens* includes a long description of the Underworld, in which Theseus narrates to Amphitryon the horrors of Hades. He catalogues the personified ills of mankind to be found (693–6):

> Metus Pavorque, Funus et frendens Dolor
> aterque **Luctus** sequitur et **Morbus** tremens
> et cincta ferro Bella; in extremo abdita
> iners **Senectus** adiuvat baculo gradum.

> There are Fear and Trembling, Death and rending Pain,
> Dark Suffering follows them and shaking Disease
> and War girded with steel; at the back, hidden,
> slow Old Age aids his steps with a staff.

On the surface level, the repetition of figures such as Luctus, Morbus/i, and Senectus are consistent with representations of the Underworld, and one would expect such denizens there. Seneca, however, reiterates Vergil's figures and provides notable details to stress their importance for this play as a whole. In fetching Cerberus from Hades, Hercules has breached the divide between the living and the dead, and his punishment (and that of his family) incorporates imagery dependent on this description of the Underworld.[34] Hercules' madness is described as a "disease" (*morbi*, 1052), and the grief (*luctus*, 1027, 1200) that both Amphitryon and Hercules suffer springs from his insane killing spree. This grief, however, is redefined in the course of the denouement as Amphitryon and Theseus attempt to talk Hercules out of suicide. Amphitryon tells Hercules that while "the grief is yours, the crime is your stepmother's; this calamity is not your fault" (***luctus*** *est istic tuus, / crimen novercae;*

---

[34] Cf. Fitch (1987a) 276: "Theseus' narrative has important connections with the rest of the play in terms of both theme and characterization."

casus hic culpa caret, 1200–1). Amphitryon begs his son to spare him the misfortune of living in miserable old age without him: "Spare my destitute old age" (***senectae parce desertae***, 1249).[35] Such pleas and Amphitryon's threat to commit suicide if Hercules takes his own life eventually convince Hercules to live, in response to which Amphitryon claims he will clasp his son's hand, and he says, "I shall go, leaning on this hand" (*hac nisus ibo*, 1320).[36] The description old age found in the Underworld has now been given the support of a caring son to guide its steps (and not the mere staff found at 696). Seneca rebrands the personifications found in Vergil's description of Hades in his *Hercules Furens*. The play's context and its plot development cause such terms to be modified and to be given a more positive spin, while pointing back to their possible Underworld origins.[37] In many ways this is like the interpretation found in *Ep.* 107 in which these personified "evils" are the very stuff of life, but now taken to a Herculean extreme.[38] Characters such as Amphitryon and Hercules can persevere through the disease and grief that cause anguish in one's life. Through their reliance on friends and family, they can be given a helpful guide in one's old age or at least help one another endure the crucible of tragic suffering.[39]

In turning to the *Oedipus*, a similar use of the Vergilian material can be observed. As in the *Hercules Furens*, these figures appear in a description of the Underworld; Creon describes to Oedipus the horrors of the necromancy performed by Tiresias (592–4):

Luctus avellens comam
aegreque lassum sustinens **Morbus** caput,
gravis **Senectus** sibimet et pendens Metus.

---

[35] Previously Amphitryon had apostrophized his old age as "too alive old age" (*nimis vivax senectus*, 1025–6), when observing the murder of his grandchildren.

[36] Note that Seneca makes a similar argument for choosing not to commit suicide himself when faced with the old age (*senectus*) of his father in *Ep.* 78 (esp. 78.2).

[37] Fetching Cerberus from Hades was part of Juno's plan (604–6) and indicates the extent of her hatred, not his own ambition (46–7). Cf. Shelton (1978) 50–7 on the way this scene creates "an ambivalent picture of Hercules by including elements which detract from the magnitude of the deed" (56).

[38] Cf. Fitch (1987a) 30: "In brief, then, Hercules' madness has a psychological origin. While sane, he is characterized by habitual aggression, ambition, and megalomania; in other words he is already close to insanity in his daily *modus vitae*. At this moment, when he has reached the highest pitch of megalomania, his mind topples over into madness.... Seneca explores the *continuity* between the sane and insane mind."

[39] Cf. Lawall (1983) 10: "The true dramatic climax of the play is thus not the madness and slaying of children and wife (horrific as those events are) but the final act with the anguished response of Hercules to what he has been made to do, the help that he receives from Amphitryon and Theseus, and his own final labor of self-conquest."

> Grief is there, tearing her hair,
> and Disease barely keeping up his tottering head,
> Old Age grievous to itself and Fear hanging overhead.

Once again the repetition of Luctus, Morbus, and Senectus recalls Vergil's lines in a parallel setting, and once again Seneca adds details that are important for his rendition of the Oedipus story. First, this lengthy ecphrasis acts as a central metaliterary reflection for the play as a whole, as Schiesaro explains, "The *vates*, who through his song, that is through carefully chosen words endowed with active power, *rata verba*, can bring to life the Underworld's demonic creatures, is analogous to the poet, whose inspiration vivifies the characters of tragedy."[40] That Vergilian intertextuality contributes to the poetic fabric of this scene befits this moment of Seneca's tragedy. As a father figure (Laius) is summoned to prophesize the troubles that plague Thebes, so Seneca turns to one of his poetic "fathers," Vergil, for fitting details of the Underworld. In addition, these terms are significant for the diseased world of the *Oedipus*. Forms and compounds of *luctus* indicate the effects of the plague on the people of Thebes from the very beginning of the play, as the cycle of grief seems self-perpetuating (62–3):

> quin **luctu** in ipso **luctus** exoritur novus,
> suaeque circa funus exequiae cadunt.
>
> Even in the midst of grief, new grief arises,
> The attendants fall dead during the funeral.

The grief caused by the plague is to be seen as a consequence of Oedipus' patricide and incestuous relationship with his mother, and Luctus is found in Hades in a standard pose of lamentation, ripping out its own hair. Seneca repeats Vergil's Senectus, in part, to uncover Oedipus' murder of his father. When recalling this killing, he pointedly remembers Laius as an old man, "when first a haughty old man pushed me out of the way with his chariot" (*cum prior iuvenem **senex** / curru superbus␣pelleret*, 770–1). In Hades, these personified evils hint at the troubles that Oedipus has caused as well as their source, namely, the killing of Laius. At the close of the play, Oedipus acts as a scapegoat for the misery of the Thebans, and wishes to lead away with him the personified attributes of the plague

---

[40] Schiesaro (2003) 9. Schiesaro (2006) focuses on such *loca horrida* as representative of a Senecan response to pastoral poetry: "The intertextual dialogue with Vergil and Ovid which is a core component of his *loca horrida* shows that Seneca already found anxiety and horror in his predecessors' landscapes" (449). See my discussion of this passage in Chap. 4.

including "the shuddering tremor of Disease" (*horridus **Morbi** tremor*, 1059).[41] It is questionable whether the troubles will end with the departure of Oedipus—Seneca's *Phoenissae* certainly indicates continuing trouble in the House of Laius. But Seneca shows Oedipus' attempt to harness and to dispel the powers of the Underworld in his final speech by repeating the language of the necromancy scene.

Vergil's personifications of Underworld evils clearly had an impact on Seneca's prose and poetry. Seneca's tragic descriptions of Hades can be seen as rival elaborations of the *katabasis* of the sixth book of the *Aeneid*, but they also exhibit rhetorical and thematic expansion germane to the tragedies at hand. Whereas his prose works often will provide a nuanced ethical interpretation of Vergilian quotes, his tragedies provide a larger verbal and thematic frame for the intertext that suggests distinctive meanings for the reader. In the plague-infested world of the *Oedipus*, figures such as Morbus and Luctus haunt the play from the opening lines (note how the fire of the sun is called "grief-causing" (*luctifica*, 3), and the necromancy reveals Oedipus as the true cause of such malevolence.[42] While Oedipus may hope to purge such evils from Thebes, these terms (and others that are etymologically related) arise again and again to stress Oedipus' hand in the sufferings he caused.[43] The *Hercules Furens* indicates how characters can temper the negative connotations of such terms as they attempt to endure the consequences of tragic madness. Even in such an integrative allusion as the repetition of these personifications, one can see the way that Seneca's tragic setting acts to question the terms under consideration as they apply to the protagonists of the tragedies.[44]

Self-Fashioning and Literary Mimicry

In order to further define the differences between Seneca's philosophical and tragic projects vis-à-vis the use of intertextuality and quotation, I wish to turn to a section of Seneca's fragmentary work *De Amicitia* ("On Friendship"), and the language of self-fashioning found in his *Epistulae Morales* and *Phaedra*. The fragment of *De Amicitia* includes a Vergilian quotation that is also referenced in Seneca's *Troades*, while the Vergilian tag "to fashion yourself worthy of a god"

---

[41] Oedipus calls the plague a *morbus* elsewhere (70, 1052). Seneca only uses this word one other time (*Ag.* 97) in the corpus of his tragedies.

[42] Laius' ghost claims that the cause is not "the grief-causing wind" (*luctificus Auster*, 632) but the current polluted king, Oedipus.

[43] Note that forms of *senex* appear over fifteen times in the play.

[44] Cf. Conte (1986) 66–7 for the term "integrative allusion" (one in which the source- and target text complement one another).

(*te...dignum finge deo, Aen.* 8.364–5) becomes problematic in the turbulent world of Seneca's *Phaedra*.

While most of Seneca's *De Amicitia* is lost, the surviving fragments show a concern with rectifying disagreements among friends, keeping friends in mind in spite of absence, and the rarity of true friendship.[45] In one of the three surviving fragments, Seneca quotes Vergil's *Aeneid*, in his reflection on remembrance (*F* 59.5–6):

> Quod ne possit accidere, omni ope resistamus, et fugientem memoriam reducamus; utamur, ut in prima parte dicebam, animi velocitate, neminem a nobis amicum abesse patiamur, in animum subinde nostrum revertantur; futura nobis promittamus, praeterita repetamus:
>
> > sic ille manus, sic ora ferebat.
>
> **Imago effingatur** animo notabilis et e vivo petita, non evanida et muta.
>
> > sic ille manus, sic ora ferebat:
>
> adiciamus illi quae magis ad rem pertinent: sic loquebatur, sic hortabatur, sic deterrebat, sic erat in dando consilio expeditus, in accipiendo facilis, in mutando non pertinax.

> So that we do not [forget] them, let us resist with all our power and let us recall the fleeing memory; let us use the quickness of the mind (as I was saying at the beginning), let no friend be absent from us, let them return to our mind repeatedly; let us engage ourselves in the future, let us call back the past:
>
> > "So were his hands, so was his face."
>
> Let his recognizable image be fashioned in your soul and one sought from life, not faded and silent.
>
> > "So were his hands, so was his face."
>
> Let us add something more particular to this: so he was accustomed to speak, to encourage, to deter, to give advice when sought, to accept the advice of others easily, to change his own advice freely.

---

[45] Cf. Vottero (1998) for a critical edition of the fragments with Italian translation and commentary.

The Vergilian quote comes from the third book of the *Aeneid*, in which Andromache sees Aeneas' son Ascanius and, clearly being reminded of her own dead son, Astyanax, calls attention to the similarity of their features.⁴⁶ It is a poignant moment in the epic as Aeneas prepares to leave the Trojan colony at Buthrotum, and, in the context of the *De Amicitia*, it adds pathos to Seneca's description of an absent friend. In this fragment, Seneca is able to bridge the distance between friends by adding details "from life" (*e vivo*). These details are prompted by similar verbal repetition (note the anaphora of *sic*), and provide representative moments of shared friendship (conversation and the giving and receiving of advice) that cannot be experienced by Vergil's Andromache.⁴⁷ The memory of a friend is to be triggered (or paralleled) in part by the memory of a *literary* text, but such a recollection can be further embellished with one's own experiences.⁴⁸ Seneca as the reader here directs our interpretation of the Vergilian quote through his expansion of the material in the active construction (*effingatur*) of the *imago*, a process that individual readers may choose to formulate differently. As Ker states, "The construction of an *imago* and the structures of memory, both in Seneca and in epic narrative, are not about total mimesis: they are about selective memory, misremembering, outright forgetting, and invention."⁴⁹ One can question and elaborate on the individual memory according to one's own preferences, exposing the process of reception, and making an image in some sense come alive. Such a process can be seen as analogous to Seneca's use of Augustan poetry within his tragedies, as can be illustrated further by looking at this Vergilian line in another manifestation, Seneca's *Troades*.

The *Troades* markedly responds to both Vergil's *Aeneid* and Ovid's *Metamorphoses*, as the protagonists react to the fall of Troy and await their imminent enslavement.⁵⁰ If Aeneas' tale to Dido (encompassing the second and third books of the *Aeneid*) provides his own "take" on events after the Trojan War, Seneca's *Troades* follows the immediate aftermath of Troy's fall among those not able to escape. Seneca exposes the cycle of suffering endemic to the figures of the Trojan War by providing the perspectives of the surviving Trojan women and their children. In the third act, Andromache is startled by a dream of her dead husband,

---

⁴⁶ *Aen.* 3.490.

⁴⁷ Cf. Ker (2009) 281–3 for a sophisticated reading of this passage.

⁴⁸ Cf. Gowing (2005) 71–2 for similar moment of Seneca utilizing Vergilian poetry to preserve memory.

⁴⁹ Ker (2009) 283. Cf. Lethem (2011) 111–2: "By necessity, by proclivity, and by delight, we all quote. Neurological study has lately shown that memory, imagination, and consciousness itself are stitched, quilted, pastiched. If we cut-and-paste our selves, might we not forgive it of our artworks?"

⁵⁰ See further Chap. 3 on intertextuality and plot.

Hector, who tells her she must hide their son Astyanax, whom the Greeks wish to kill.[51] He is to be murdered, in part, because he resembles his father too closely, and therefore may grow up to avenge the Greek destruction of Troy. Andromache addresses Astyanax (*Tr.* 464–8):

> hos vultus meus
> habebat Hector, talis incessu fuit
> habituque talis, **sic tulit** fortes **manus**,
> **sic** celsus umeris, fronte **sic** torva minax
> cervice fusam dissipans iacta comam.

> My Hector was
> Accustomed to have this expression, such
> Was his gait, such was his disposition,
> Thus he bore his strong hands, thus he was tall in his shoulders,
> Thus he threatened with grim visage, scattering his long hair
> With neck thrown back.

This expansion of the Vergilian material (*sic ille manus, sic ora ferebat*) is notable for its close repetition of Vergilian language (*sic, manus*, forms of *fero*), as well as for its evocative details that stress Astyanax's position as a Hector *recidivus*. In this recollection of Vergil, Seneca also foreshadows Astyanax's death, because Andromache's words from the *Aeneid* occur long after Astyanax's death (both Seneca's Astyanax and Andromache become "Vergilian," in a sense, through this intertext). In their commentaries, Boyle and Fantham note the intertext and Seneca's dramatization of the material (Boyle notes that the use of *sic* here could be a stage direction), and the strong focus on Astyanax's body is later emphasized in his death scene.[52] In the fifth act, the messenger tells of Astyanax's courageous death, but in his suicidal fall from the tower, his face and body are reduced to a bloody pulp. Andromache's bitter reaction to this is "In this way he is also similar to his father" (*Sic quoque est similis patri, Tr.* 1117). As a response to the previous description and intertext, Seneca's Andromache calls attention to the similarity (*sic,*

---

[51] Seneca uses a dream of Hector to forewarn of the destruction of Astyanax in the same way that Vergil has a dream of Hector warn Aeneas of Troy's fall (*Aen.* 2.270–97). For Andromache, Astyanax is emblematic of Troy itself: "Not yet has the fate of falling Troy come to an end" (*nondum ruentis Ilii fatum stetit, Tr.* 428), and, as Hecuba bitterly states, the end of the war is the moment of Astyanax's and Polyxena's deaths: "A boy and girl have fallen: the war is over" (*concidit virgo ac puer: / bellum peractum est, Tr.* 1167–8).

[52] Boyle (1994) ad loc.; Fantham (1982) ad loc.

similis) of Astyanax to Hector, and the reader recognizes Seneca's grim application of Vergilian material. If Astyanax was "too similar to his father" (*nimiumque patri similis*, 464) earlier in the tragedy, so here he has come to embody the *Vergilian* Andromache's lost son. The intertext both influences the initial description of Astyanax and is picked up on later in the play when the physical attributes that spurred her memories of Hector are destroyed. When describing his corpse, Seneca stresses the obliteration of his "fine features, face, and the traces of his father" (*signa clari corporis / et **ora** et illas nobiles patris notas, Tr.* 1112–3) in language that picks up on Vergil's description. Through the intertext, Seneca comments that only the (Vergilian) memory continues to exist, but the body of Seneca's tragic Astyanax is now unrecognizable (*deforme corpus*, 1117). Although Seneca finds the Vergilian quote a useful "tag" in his prose work to spur remembrance and make the *imago* seem alive, the tragic Seneca shows a sinister side to such resemblance—the Greeks destroy Astyanax because of his Hector-like qualities, and the Vergilian intertext works to foreshadow the annihilation of Astyanax and the Trojan royal line.[53]

In the prose passage, Seneca shows how a "recognizable image [can] be fashioned in your soul" (*Imago effingatur animo notabilis*), and embellished with details from life. This fashioning (*effingatur*) of images as well as individuals is a major feature of Seneca's prose and poetic works. Authors such as Edwards and Bartsch have stressed the project of self-fashioning that pervades Seneca's prose works, and Littlewood has seen the importance of self-representation as a theme in the tragedies.[54] Seneca's letters encourage Lucilius to begin to fashion himself according to Stoic strictures, and aspects of this transformation can be seen from a Vergilian quote employed in two differing manners. In *Ep*. 18, Seneca informs Lucilius of his attempts to show contempt for wealth and to "practice" poverty—on certain days Seneca would only eat "scanty and very cheap food" (*minimo ac vilissimo cibo, Ep*. 18.5) and dress in the Roman equivalent to a hair shirt (*dura atque horrida veste, Ep*. 18.5). In doing so, Seneca taught himself that poverty was not to be feared; he employs a Vergilian quote to indicate the results of such training (*Ep*. 18.2–13):

> aude, hospes, contemnere opes et te quoque dignum
> finge deo.

Nemo alius est deo dignus quam qui opes contempsit.

---

[53] His death looks back to the death of Priam described earlier in the play (*Tr*. 140).
[54] C. Edwards (1997); Bartsch (2006) 183–229; Littlewood (2004) passim.

> Dare, my friend, to scorn wealth and, in addition, fashion yourself
> Worthy of god.

No one else is worthy of god except the man who has scorned wealth.

One can approach a state of near divinity through such an askesis, as a man who prepares for poverty and toil will be able to endure it, should it become necessary.[55]

In order to indicate Lucilius' moral progress, Seneca exploits part of the same quote thirteen letters later, in Epistle 31. This letter, the second of his fourth book, has been seen as an important milestone for Seneca's epistolary "relationship" with Lucilius. The opening, "I recognize my Lucilius" (*Agnosco Lucilium meum*, *Ep.* 31.1), and argument stress that Lucilius has begun to make real progress in his ethical development.[56] Neither wealth, nor beauty, nor power can help in one's moral progress, but a virtuous soul combined with an active pursuit of knowledge is the key. At this point Seneca makes use of the Vergilian line (*Ep.* 31.11):

> et te quoque dignum
> finge deo.

Finges autem non auro vel argento; non potest ex hac materia imago deo exprimi similis; cogita illos, cum propitii essent, fictiles fuisse.

> And, in addition, fashion yourself
> Worthy of god.

Moreover you will fashion it not of gold or silver; from this material it is not possible to cast a statue similar to god; remember those were made of clay, when they used to be propitious to men.

Seneca abridges the line (eliding the first half of it) but expects his audience (especially Lucilius) to remember what was missing ("Dare to scorn wealth").[57] Stat-

---

[55] *Ep.* 18.8: *Et ne inparatos fortuna deprehendat, fiat nobis paupertas familiaris* ("And, lest Fortune take us unprepared, let poverty become known to us").

[56] *Ep.* 31.8: *Hoc est summum bonum. Quod si occupas, incipis deorum socius esse, non supplex* ("This is the highest good. If you acquire it, you begin to be a friend of the gods, not a suppliant"). For more on the structure of Seneca's books cf. Maurach (1970) and Hachmann (1996). Book 4 appears to be a turning point (Wilcox (2012) 132–40), as Seneca ceases to give the closing quotes, and encourages Lucilius to understand the complete philosophical context of works and not merely choice maxims and epitomes (*Ep.* 33.1–4).

[57] How much does the recognition of Lucilius at the beginning of the epistle hinge on Lucilius' own ability to recognize a previously discussed quotation? Seneca implies that the correspondence is

ues of the gods (note the use of *imago*) made of precious metals are unlikely to advance one's philosophical progress, and, in fact, such material wealth hinders one's moral advancement. As in the eighteenth epistle, poverty will bring one closer to god, and in both letters the original context of the line (Evander's invitation to Aeneas, *Aen.* 8.364–5) emphasizes such an interpretation. If one practices poverty, one will be living according to the Roman values of the heroic age, and one must not believe that indifferent goods such as wealth or beauty will aid in one's ethical progress. The literary exemplum of Aeneas can be as convincing as the historical exempla (figures like Cato, Regulus, even Seneca himself) that Seneca encourages Lucilius to emulate elsewhere in the *Epistulae*.[58] In these two letters Seneca provides a slightly different spin on the quote, but in each letter we can see how his epistolary persona finds Vergil's poetry useful raw material for further amplification in the quest to create oneself.

The verb "to fashion" (*fingere*) continues to be important for Seneca's letters (it appears over fifteen times), but figures less often in his tragic works.[59] Of the ten appearances of the verb, however, seven occur in Seneca's *Phaedra*, and its very first appearance in this play seems to recall Vergil's line.[60] The *Phaedra* revolves around the fragmented and turbulent personae of Phaedra and Hippolytus and the catastrophic results of their ignorance and errors in judgment. Additionally, this verb can mean "to play the part of, pose as" (*OLD* s.v. *fingere* 7c), and the metatheatrical sense of this term lurks behind its appearances in this play. No longer is the concern with positive self-fashioning (as in the letters), but the tragedy probes the motivation behind the creation of the characters' personae and details, in particular, the breakdown of Phaedra's various personae. Intertextually, the words of Vergil reappear when the Nurse attempts to combat Phaedra's desire for Hippolytus, claiming, "Foul lust, favoring its own vice, fashioned the story that lust was a god" (***Deum*** *esse amorem turpis et vitio favens /* ***finxit*** *libido, Phd.* 195–6).[61] The repetition of a form of *fingo* with *deum* suggests that Seneca may have been thinking of the Vergilian line, although the meaning

---

ongoing, and the structure of the books of letters seems to imply some organizational method (although what that method *is* remains debatable; cf. Cancik (1967)).

[58] Cf. Mayer (1991). Quintilian argues, "However much the Greeks take the prize for precepts [*praecepta*], Romans take the prize for moral examples [*exempla*], which is more important" (*I.O.* 2.2.30). The importance of literary figures for self-creation has been downplayed in Seneca's philosophical works, but is incredibly important for the creation of characters in his tragedies (see Chap. 2). In a sense, the poetic quotations found in Seneca's prose works act as special *praecepta* because of the literary context in which they were once embedded.

[59] See C. Edwards (1997) 29–30 for more about *fingere* in the letters.

[60] It appears once in the *Thyestes*, *Troades*, and *Oedipus*, but in none of these does it seem to echo Vergil.

[61] Cf. *Dial.* 7.26.6 and *Dial.* 10.16.5 for similar formulations about the gods (especially as related to poetry).

has been drastically changed. Phaedra's Nurse is not commenting on the way one can become like a god, but rather on the sham belief that lust *is* a god. As the play continues, Seneca stresses the *mis*representation that this verb can denote as the characters misconstrue the language and actions of one another.[62] The Nurse continues her description of the attributes of Venus and Cupid's bow (again with *finxit*, 203), and further uses this verb to describe Phaedra's madness as she oscillates between wearing her hair free or styled (*solvi comas / rursusue fingi*, 371–2). Hippolytus employs this verb when speaking about the lies that people tell now (*verba fingit*, 496) as opposed to in the virtuous Golden Age, which serves as his moral litmus test. Theseus, misreading Phaedra's *fictions* about Hippolytus, claims that his severity and purity was a mere put-on: "Where is that face and that feigned majesty?" (*ubi vultus ille et ficta maiestas viri*, 915). Theseus' gullibility and quick anger lead to Hippolytus' death, underlining the ramifications for such turbulent self-fashioning and the associated belief that things are not what they seem. When Phaedra admits her guilt, she reveals that she had made up the plot (*mentita finxi*, 1194) before killing herself. The bloody pieces of Hippolytus are brought back to Theseus, and now he has to refashion what remains of his son's body (*corpusque fingit*, 1265).[63] In the *Phaedra*, one cannot fashion oneself into someone worthy of divinity, and the characters (and their views of the gods) are shown to be fallible projections of their own desires and fears. If the Nurse's first lines (195–6) cause the reader to recall Vergil's words, we can see how Seneca develops the literary significance of this idea through the repetition of the verb in the course of the play, while subverting the positive message the line possessed in the *Aeneid* as well as in Seneca's own philosophical writings.

Rainbows and Knowledge: Interpreting Ovid's Tapestries

As an understanding of the source (the *Aeneid*) created additional significance for Seneca's employment of the quote/intertext in the previous example, so a

---

[62] For more on this see Chap. 2.

[63] Coffey and Mayer (1990) comment on the witty synonym for traditional burial language (*corpus componere*), but neither they nor Boyle (1987) note the ironic parallel with *Aeneid* 8.634 (where the she-wolf of Rome licks the bodies into shape = *illam* [*lupam*] ***corpora fingere*** *lingua*) and *Fast.* 2.418 (also about the she-wolf who "fashions their two bodies with her tongue," ***fingit*** *lingua* ***corpora*** *bina sua*). While the she-wolf will succeed in fashioning the bodies of Romulus and Remus, Theseus will fail, and the gaps in Hippolytus' body are indicative of the futile actions of the characters. Theseus' attempt is summed up by T. F. Curley (1986) 75: "Theseus' futile attempt to put his son back together best captures the central thrust of the play. It is a systematic deconstruction of the various methods by which men flatter themselves that they can master their fortunes."

similar methodology aids in the interpretation of a passage from Ovid's *Metamorphoses*, which is found in Seneca's *Naturales Quaestiones* and *Oedipus*. In his account of the weaving contest between Arachne and Minerva, Ovid lavishes attention on the density of colors found in the competitors' works (*Met.* 6.61–8):

> illic et Tyrium quae purpura sensit aënum
> texitur et tenues parvi discriminis umbrae,
> qualis ab imbre solet percussis solibus arcus
> inficere ingenti longum curvamine caelum,
> in quo diversi niteant cum mille colores,
> transitus ipse tamen spectantia lumina fallit:
> usque adeo quod tangit idem est; tamen ultima distant.
> illic et lentum filis inmittitur aurum,
> et vetus in tela deducitur argumentum.

> On it, the purple which felt the Tyrian cauldron
> Is woven, and the shades of color are of such subtle variation,
> Just as a rainbow, when the rays of the sun are struck from a storm,
> Is accustomed to dye the sky broadly with his huge arc,
> In which, although so many thousands of diverse colors shine,
> The boundaries between the colors deceive one's attentive eyes:
> The bordering colors are so similar; yet the extremities are so different.
> On it pliant gold is intertwined with the threads,
> And an ancient tale is spun down from the warp.

Ovid's rainbow simile points to the finely woven and Callimachean nature of their projects (*tenues*, 62; *deducitur*, 69) and their creation of patterned scenes (*argumentum*, 69), which are then described by narrator.[64] As a metaphor for the creation of narrative, weaving has a long pedigree, and it is clear that Ovid exploits the connections in his report of the two tapestries.[65] Rosati comments on the pervasive metapoetics of this tale: "The Ovidian story of Arachne is thus the most complete narrative illustration of the metaphor of *textus*, indeed the *aition* of the metaphor itself."[66] Ovid's discussion of the colors of the rainbow

---

[64] For more on Arachne as a poetic surrogate for Ovid himself, cf. Pavlock (2009) 3–6. *Argumentum* can also mean "the plot of a play" (*OLD* s.v. *argumentum* 5a).

[65] Cf. Feeney (1991) 190–4 and Feldherr (2010) 42–3, 60–1.

[66] Rosati (1999) 250.

influences two of Seneca's works, and in each case the metaliterary importance of the Ovidian context influences its interpretation.[67]

In his *Naturales Quaestiones*, Seneca discusses rainbows among the various phenomena of the sky that are difficult to explain. In his investigations, he cites the opinions of numerous authorities about the formation of rainbows. Seneca references an excerpt of Ovid's description as evidence for the variety of colors found in a rainbow, but one can see that Seneca had the larger Ovidian passage in mind (*Nat.* 1.3.4):

Poterat enim verum videri, si arcus duos tantum haberet colores, si ex lumine umbraque constaret. Nunc,

diversi niteant cum mille colores,
transitus ipse tamen spectantia lumina fallit:
usque adeo quod tangit idem est, tamen ultima distant.

Videmus in eo aliquid flammei, aliquid lutei, aliquid caerulei et alia **in picturae modum** subtilibus lineis **ducta**. Ut ait poeta, an dissimiles colores sint, scire non possis, nisi cum primis extrema contuleris. Nam commissura decipit, usque eo mira arte naturae: quod a **simillimo** coepit, in **dissimillimo** desinit. Quid ergo istic duo colores faciunt lucis atque umbrae, cum innumerabilium ratio reddenda sit?

For it would be able to seem true (that rainbows are caused by shadow and light), if a rainbow only had two colors; if it was made up of light and shadow. Now,

Although so many thousands of diverse colors shine,
The boundaries between the colors deceive one's attentive eyes:
The bordering colors are so similar; yet the extremities are so different.

We see in a rainbow some red, some yellow, some blue and other colors, as in a painting, drawn in thin lines. As the poet says, you are unable to know whether the colors are different, unless you compare the last with the first. For the joints are deceptive, so wonderful is Nature's art that what began from similarity ends with dissimilarity. Therefore, what do the two colors of light and shadow do in this case, when an explanation for innumerable of colors must be given?

---

[67] See Busch (2007) 232–5 for a divergent reading of these Ovidian quotations/intertexts.

Seneca chooses to quote a portion of Ovid's simile, but his explanation picks up on the language used elsewhere in Ovid's description. Trying to debunk the idea that rainbows can be formed by merely shadow and light, Seneca omits those portions of Ovid's description that may be used to support such a thesis (*tenues parvi discriminis umbrae*, *Met.* 6.62). Although the stories are spun down (*deducitur*, *Met.* 6.69) in Ovid's version, for Seneca the comparison is to a painting (*in picturae modum*) on which the colors are drawn (*ducta*) in thin lines (Seneca may be thinking of Horace's famous dictum *ut pictura poesis*, *Ars* 361).[68] Seneca is trying to outshine Ovid's description (much like the competitive contest between Minerva and Arachne), and to do so by mimicking Ovid's language in the creation of an image that improves upon the *Metamorphoses*. Seneca, in his own way, is trying to reproduce the art of Nature (*arte naturae*), a task necessarily more difficult and challenging than Ovid's scene.[69] For Ovid, thousands (*mille*) of colors can be seen in the rainbow, which for Seneca are now characterized as innumerable (*innumerabilium*). He cleverly mimics the sound pattern of *mille* in his claim "What began from similarity ends with dissimilarity" (*quod a simillimo coepit, in dissimillimo desinit*), thus showing how dissimilar colors contain the seeds of similarity, but terminate in distinctive shades.[70] This response can be read as a snapshot of Seneca's poetics and the way in which analogous material can be transformed through *aemulatio*, even when included as a quotation.

A comparable motivation is involved in Seneca's intertextual nod to this passage in his *Oedipus*.[71] In a novel scene not found in previous treatments of the Oedipus story, Tiresias and Manto are set to engage in an *extispicium* in order to discover the cause of the Theban plague.[72] In the preliminary activity for sacrifice, Tiresias asks his daughter Manto to describe the flame emitted by incense on the altar (314–20):

> Non una facies mobilis flammae fuit:
> imbrifera qualis implicat varios sibi
> Iris colores, parte quae magna poli
> curvata picto nuntiat nimbos sinu

---

[68] Likewise *commisura* is a technical term for mixing pigments; cf. Parroni (2002) 489.

[69] A germane comparison may be with Seneca's description of a spider web in *Ep.* 121.22–3: "Do you not see how the intricacy of a spider's web is unable to be imitated by man ... that art is born, not taught" (*non vides, quam nulli mortalium imitabilis illa aranei textura ... nascitur ars ista, non discitur*).

[70] Williams (2012) 66 sees this as indicative of the work as a whole: "But in their seemingly incidental way, the invisible transitions between the rainbow's colors also reproduce and exemplify the seamlessness that Seneca associates with the cosmic whole."

[71] The formal connections are well covered by Jakobi (1988) 101 and Töchterle (1994) ad loc.

[72] Cf. Ahl (2008) 121–3 for more on this scene and the way "the timeless Teiresias has adapted his methods to the writer's contemporary Roman world" (122).

(quis desit illi quive sit **dubites** color),
caerulea fulvis **mixta** oberravit **notis**,
sanguinea rursus; ultima in **tenebras** abit.

The shifting flame did not have one appearance;
As rain-bringing Iris weaves herself with various colors,
When she arches across the broad expanse of the sky
And announces storms with her painted bow
(you would hesitate to say whether a color was absent or present),
Blue, mixed with yellow sparks, wanders about,
Then blood-red flashes; at the end it disappears into darkness.

The connections with the Ovidian passage (both in language and the hesitancy to identify the different colors) prove that Seneca's text is responding to Ovid's. Manto attempts to give an accurate description of the variegated flame, but finds it difficult to vocalize: "You would hesitate [*dubites*] to say whether a color was absent or present."[73] This sort of hesitancy is later connected with both Oedipus' cross-examination of Phorbas ("Do you hesitate to speak? Why do you cheeks change color?" *dubitas? cur genas mutat color?*, 849)[74] and Jocasta's address to Oedipus.[75] As Iris (315) acts as a messenger of the gods, so this rainbow gives information even if it is not understood at the present dramatic time. The scene as a whole is premised on the idea that the natural world will provide providential information, if only it can be interpreted correctly.[76] Therefore, when language that is reminiscent of the flame and rainbow imagery appears later in the play, one may attempt to connect it with this original formulation.[77] Such language foreshadows Oedipus' later deliberations—"A way is sought by which you may wander, isolated from the dead and distant from the living" (*quaeratur via / qua nec sepultis **mixtus** et vivis tamen / exemptus*

---

[73] Cf. Boyle (2011) ad loc. for more on the *dubius* motif throughout the play.

[74] If one thinks back to Manto's description (esp. 316, 318), it may be notable that color figures in Phorbas' guilt. A reader tuned to the rhetoric of the day may find the stress on *colores* evocative of the technical term for "the apt and inventive twists given to familiar topics" (Goldberg (1996) 277). Also cf. Chap. 4 on the use of *color* in *Medea*, pp. 194–6.

[75] Cf. 1010: *dubitas? natus es: natum pudet* ("Do you waver? You are my son: it shames you to be my son."), and the chorus's description of Jocasta's hesitation (*dubitat afflictum alloqui*, 1007). T. F. Curley (1986) 91–100 sees the "*dubius* motif" as important for our understanding of the *Oedipus* as a whole.

[76] Cf. Busch (2007) for an attempt to link the *extispicium* with Oedipus' blinding, and the ambiguity of the language: "If the scene's language is confusing, that is not because it has ceased to function rationally in accord with nature's laws, but because it describes natural phenomena which are anomalous, though still capable of being assimilated into nature's rational signifying structure" (253).

[77] Cf. Bettini (1983) for a thorough examination of many of these terms in the *Oedipus*.

erres, 949–51)—and punishment, as the blind Oedipus states: "This darkness pleases me" (*iuvant **tenebrae***, 999). The description of the flame acts as a sign (*notis*, 319), which should be interpretable by Tiresias but perplexes the famous seer. This parallels Oedipus' own unreliable interpretation of signs in the play, despite his claim that "it is given to Oedipus alone to know riddles" (*ambigua soli **noscere** Oedipodae datur*, 216).[78] As the language hints at Oedipus' future blindness, so here Tiresias' own inability to understand the signs show the difficulty in piecing together the truth of the situation.[79] While the competitive framework of Arachne and Minerva may not appear to relate to the basic myth of Oedipus, through this intertext, we can see how Seneca may figure Oedipus as a victim of the gods similar to Arachne. The metaliterary dimension can likewise be stressed as Seneca once again attempts to improve upon this "Ovidian" lychnomancy (divination through fire) with his exhaustive account of the *extispicium*, replete with more signs (*certas notas*, 352) specifically connected with Oedipus and his family.[80] Seneca has found in Ovid's description language that can be pertinent to his dramatic situation, and as the colors of the rainbow change from blood red to darkness, so Oedipus' brutal self-blinding will transform this hero from an answerer of riddles to a riddle himself.

Otium and the *Eclogues*

I turn now to Seneca's interpretation of Vergil's first *Eclogue* in his epistles, his *De Beneficiis*, and his *Thyestes* in order to analyze the differences in interpretation as well as the possible political implications for Seneca's handling of the *Eclogues* in the *Thyestes*.

Epistle 73 is concerned with the relationship between philosophers and kings. In the course of the epistle, one that has excited interest because of the possible biographical information it contains (it discusses why philosophers should be able to retire from political life, as Seneca had done), Seneca refers to Vergil's first *Eclogue* to express the gratitude the philosopher feels in times of peace (*Ep.* 73.10–11):

---

[78] Cf. Oedipus' ironic claim that he knows himself better than the gods do (765–7) and the repetition of forms of *notus* throughout the play (235, 331, 352, 509, etc.), which are cognate to *noscere* here.

[79] As he had previously admitted that "a great part of truth is hidden to the blind" (*visu carenti magna pars veri latet*, 295).

[80] Cf. Boyle (2011) ad 324–7.

> Confitebitur ergo multum se debere ei, cuius administratione ac providentia contingit illi pingue otium et arbitrium sui temporis et inperturbata publicis occupationibus quies.
>
>> O Meliboee, deus nobis haec otia fecit:
>> namque erit ille mihi semper deus.
>
> Si illa quoque otia multum auctori suo debent quorum munus hoc maximum est,
>
>> ille meas errare boves, ut cernis, et ipsum
>> ludere quae vellem calamo permisit agresti,
>
> quanti aestimamus hoc otium, quod inter deos agitur, quod deos facit?

> Therefore the philosopher will admit that he owes a great debt to the ruler who, by his directions and foresight, makes it possible for him to experience rich leisure, control of his own time, and serenity unbroken by public business.
>
>> O Meliboeus, a god has made this peace for me:
>> For that man will always be a god to me.
>
> And even if such leisure owes a great debt to its creator, this is its greatest reward:
>
>> As you can see, that man has allowed my oxen to wander,
>> And has allowed me to play whatever I want on my rustic pipe.
>
> How greatly should we value this leisure [of the philosopher], which is spent among the gods, which makes [us] gods?

Here Seneca draws a contrast between the vigorous *otium* of a philosopher and the *otium* of the bucolic shepherd-poet whose herds can graze without threat, and who can while away the day in song.[81] In the first *Eclogue*, Tityrus sings of the pastoral bliss he has been able to obtain due to the intervention of someone in Rome

---

[81] Seneca claims, "Leisure without study is death" (*otium sine litteris mors est*, 82.3), to describe the *otium* of philosophers. Cf. M. Wilson (1988) 110–9 for a reading of that epistle. Reydams-Schils (2005) 99–113 discusses *otium* in Seneca and other Roman Stoics. *Otium* is important in many of Seneca's works, especially (naturally) *De Otio*.

(probably Octavian).[82] The leisure that philosophers enjoy will allow them to commune with the gods and even create gods (in a wonderful inversion of the Vergilian *deus nobis haec otia fecit*, Seneca writes *otium...quod deos facit*). Seneca goes on to describe how a Stoic *sapiens* can be considered the equal of Jupiter (*Ep.* 73.14–5), and how one must cultivate the seed of the divine in his soul to be truly good (*Ep.* 73.16).[83] Seneca employs the Vergilian quote both to differentiate the *otium* of the philosopher from that of the poet and also to indicate the implicit difference between the *otium* that he has eked out for himself under Nero and Vergil's under Octavian. While Tityrus' panegyric indicates his conception of Octavian's divinity, for Seneca, the emperor will not be praised in poetry because the Stoic will spend that time improving his soul, "by observing thrift, self-restraint, and courage" (*hac secundum frugalitatem, hac secundum temperantiam, hac secundum fortitudinem, Ep.* 73.15). However, Nero (if Nero read the *Epistulae Morales*, that is) should not lose heart, as the letter itself expresses gratitude to the ruler, "because they provide to nobody more than philosophers the ability to enjoy peaceful leisure" (*Nullis enim plus praestant quam quibus frui tranquillo otio licet, Ep.* 73.1). While calling attention to the separate genres of pastoral poem and philosophical epistle, Seneca's reading of Vergil concentrates on the differing outcomes of *otium* on the shepherd-poet and on the philosopher.

This Vergilian passage also inspired Seneca to muse upon the thanks owed to god in *De Beneficiis*. This treatise was written sometime in the late 50s or early 60s CE, and Griffin believes it could have been finished as late as June 64.[84] For most of this time Seneca was firmly attached to Nero as advisor to the princeps, and the concerns of Epistle 73 may underlie this passage as well. Once again the underlying theme of gratitude leads Seneca to cite Vergil's lines as he responds to his interlocutor's statement: "God gives no benefits" (*Non dat deus beneficia*, 4.5.1). Seneca details features of the natural world (trees, rivers, fields) and claims that one should praise god for the blessings of nature and show gratitude (4.6.4–5):

> Nonne, si gratus es, dices:
> Deus nobis haec otia fecit.

---

[82] Cf. Clausen (1994) 31: "Virgil deliberately confuses the private with the public sense of *libertas*, and by so doing solves his literary problem, that of expressing gratitude to Octavian in the pastoral mode."

[83] This broader cosmic view is paralleled in his *De Otio*; cf. Williams (2003) 10–2, who stresses this "view from above." It is possible that Seneca recognized that Octavian is often paired with Jupiter in Vergil's writings and therefore gives his own take on the philosopher "becoming" Jupiter-like. Thomas (2001) 42 examines the passages of Vergil's poetry that mention Octavian and finds that "there is a single and dominant function to all of these passages: each one creates a close identity between Octavian and Jupiter."

[84] Griffin (2013) 12–4 for dating *De Beneficiis*.

>   namque erit ille mihi semper deus, illius aram
>   saepe tener nostris ab ovilibus inbuet agnus.
>   ille meas errare boves, ut cernis, et ipsum
>   ludere, quae vellem, calamo permisit agresti.

Ille deus est, non qui paucas boves sed qui per totum orbem armenta dimisit, qui gregibus ubique passim vagantibus pabulum praestat, qui pascua hibernis aestiva substituit, qui non calamo tantum cantare et agreste atque inconditum carmen ad aliquam tamen observationem modulari docuit, sed tot artes, tot vocum varietates, tot sonos alios spiritu nostro, alios externo cantus edituros commentus est.

Will you not, if you are grateful, say:
>   A god has made this leisure for me,
>   For that man will always be a god to me, whose altar
>   Often a tender lamb from my folds will stain,
>   As you can see, that man has allowed my oxen to wander,
>   And has allowed me to play whatever I want on my
>   rustic pipe.

But he is a god who has liberated not just a couple oxen but herds throughout the whole world, who supplies fodder to the wide-ranging flocks, who offers pastures in summer and then in winter, who has not only taught how to play the pipe and to create a song that, although pastoral and common, yet shows some attention to form, but has invented numberless arts, the thousands of variations of the voice, the thousands of tones that will produce songs, some by the breath of our body, others given by the breath of an instrument.

Seneca's conception of the divine expands and caps the words of Vergil's Tityrus while mimicking some of the language found in the first *Eclogue*. This god is responsible for all the herds on earth, and is the source for all the arts and music that man can develop. He picks up on Vergil's language, but now it is not simply Tityrus' *boves* but *armenta*, and not a *calamo* but all arts and voices (*tot artes, tot vocum varietates*). In like manner, the *inconditum carmen* that Seneca identifies with the pastoral poet probably derives from *Eclogue* 2 and the description of Corydon's song there as *incondita* (*Ecl.* 2.4). The *deus* of Vergil's pastoral poem takes on characteristics of the universal god that can be identified as the creator and custodian of the natural world. In the context of the treatise, it is important for Seneca's god to bestow a great many benefits without expecting anything in return, "since he does not need to have anything given, nor are we able to give anything to him; therefore, a benefit is something that is desirable in itself."⁸⁵ This treatise thus displays a view of divinity at odds with the deification of powerful men (and future emperors) implicit in the first *Eclogue*.⁸⁶ Having lived under Nero and having observed his megalomania, Seneca draws the conception of a universal god who transcends the earthly reality of the pastoral shepherd and is identified with Nature itself, "for what is Nature other than god and the divine reason which unites the whole world and all its parts" (*quid enim aliud est natura quam deus et divina ratio toti mundo partibusque eius inserta?* 4.7.1). It is a wholly Stoic view, paralleling the universalizing concerns of the treatise at this point in which "the imitation of the gods is most pervasive, as a model both for giving benefits and for showing gratitude."⁸⁷

Both of these prose works highlight a Stoic interpretation of Vergil's poem, a position stressed in the work of Setaioli, Staley, and Maguinness. In his investigation of Vergilian quotation in Seneca's works, Maguinness finds that "a philosophical, symbolical, or allegorical twist is given to a quotation that in its context does not admit, or at least does not require, the interpretation given by the philosopher."⁸⁸ This particular passage of Vergil seems to have struck a chord in Seneca when discussing issues of gratitude, godhead, politics, and the philosophical use of *otium*. Seneca gives the Vergilian quote an interpretation that helps prove his philosophical point and, as these examples reveal, often can exhibit subtle variation according to its context. These two works show how the same passage can be used to stress the uses of *otium* for philosophical progress, as well as the power and influence of gods and rulers in the world.

Seneca's *Thyestes*, a horrific tragedy detailing the revenge of Atreus on his brother Thyestes, echoes the same passage of Vergil's *Eclogues*, but develops an interpretation of the passage in a manner that befits the tragic framework. The chorus's celebratory song (546–622) reveals that they have not been privy to Atreus' deceitful machinations, and a sense of foreboding (enhanced by intertextual nods to the *Eclogues*) undercuts the song's optimism.⁸⁹ The chorus responds to the feigned truce that has arisen between Atreus and Thyestes and claims it is an instance of fraternal *pietas* which can "lead even the unwilling to peace" (*ducit ad pacem Pietas negantes*, 559).⁹⁰ The chorus wonders (*Thy.* 560–6):

---

⁸⁵ *De Ben.* 4.9.1: *quoniam nec ille conlato eget nec nos ei quidquam conferre possumus; ergo beneficium per se expetenda res est.*

⁸⁶ One can see his scathing view of the apotheosis of an unworthy emperor in the *Apocolocyntosis*.

⁸⁷ Griffin (2013) 119.

⁸⁸ Maguinness (1956) 93.

⁸⁹ An echo of Horace *Carm.* 2.1.17–8 at *Thy.* 573–6 also suggests the hopeful reversal of the recent civil war. In that section of Horace's poem, he focuses on the imaginative power of Pollio's civil war narrative.

⁹⁰ Atreus, however, has expressly dismissed *pietas* in preference for the Furies (*Excede, Pietas, si modo in nostra domo / umquam fuisti*, 249–50).

Otium tanto subitum e tumultu
quis **deus fecit**? modo per Mycenas
arma civilis crepuere belli:
pallidae natos tenuere matres;
uxor armato timuit marito,
cum manum invitus sequeretur ensis,
sordidus pacis vitio quietae;

What god has made sudden peace from such tumult?
Recently the weapons of civil war sounded throughout Mycenae,
Pale mothers held their children, the wife feared for her husband in arms,
Since the sword (rusted through the harmful effects of peace)
Reluctantly followed his hand.

As in *Ep.* 73, and *De Beneficiis*, this line owes much to Vergil's first *Eclogue*, in which the shepherd Tityrus claims that his peaceful state was created by a god (*Ecl.* 1.6–8):

O Meliboee, **deus** nobis haec **otia fecit**.
namque erit ille mihi semper deus, illius aram
saepe tener nostris ab ovilibus imbuet agnus.

O Meliboeus, a god has made this leisure for me,
For that man will always be a god to me, whose altar
Often a tender lamb from my folds will stain.

For Tityrus, young Octavian has granted him freedom and the land to tend his herd, and he expresses his gratitude by worshipping him as a god. Tityrus makes this assertion under the backdrop of the land confiscations that followed the battle of Philippi in 42 BCE, and the troubling implications of civil strife should be read into the intertext. In particular, the larger context of *Eclogue* 1 and the sufferings of Meliboeus indicate the stark reality for many during this period.[91] In the *Thyestes*, the chorus claims that civil war recently shook Mycenae (*modo per Mycenas / arma civilis crepuere belli*, 561–2), and their hope is that a god has reconciled Atreus and Thyestes, leading to peace. Seneca interprets Vergil's line within its original historical context, as Tarrant postulates: "By opposing *otium* to the *arma civilis… belli*, Seneca makes explicit a connection that remains below

---

[91] Clausen (1994) 32: "Virgil's sympathies are usually engaged on the side of defeat and loss; and here, in a poem praising Octavian, it is rather the dispossessed Meliboeus than the complacent Tityrus who more nearly represents Virgil."

the surface of Vergil's poem. Vergil's confident assertion has become a question, another instance of uncertainty about the gods' activities or even existence."[92] Such an interpretation is further supported by the only previous mention of *otium* in the play. In the preceding choral passage, the chorus hopes to enjoy "gentle quiet" (*leni…otio*, 395) and a life "unknown to any Roman" (*nullis nota Quiritibus*, 396). While Seneca can place anachronistic Roman touches in his tragedies, this is the only time "Quirites" is used and speaks to the Roman sentiment and the hope for peace and calm. Here, the chorus's ignorance and their hopeful belief that a god has intervened point to their fallible understanding of the dramatic situation. The intertext emphasizes the gulf between the chorus's conception of events and the truth of the situation: Atreus and Thyestes are still very much at war (especially in the mind of Atreus), and *otium* will not be found in Seneca's tragic world. If the gods do exist, their role is taken over by Atreus, who becomes godlike (*dimitto superos*, 888), even sacrificing children, not Vergilian lambs, on altars (*ornatur arae*, 684; *stat ipse ad aras*, 693), while the "peace" that occurs is an interlude in a much longer war.[93]

Seneca's cynical reading of the *Eclogues* as a whole can be seen later in the *Thyestes* as well.[94] In the fourth choral song, the chorus reacts to the disappearance of the sun (which has fled in response to Thyestes' cannibalistic consumption of his own children). They claim (*Thy.* 877–80):

> in nos **aetas ultima venit**?
> O nos dura sorte creatos,
> seu perdidmus solem miseri,
> > sive expulimus!

> Has the final age come to us?
> O we were born to a harsh lot,
> We, wretches that we are, either have lost the sun,
> > Or we have driven it away!

The world as they know it is coming to an end, and, in this cosmic reversal, the chorus surprisingly echoes the optimistic prophesy of Vergil's fourth *Eclogue* (*Ecl.* 4.4–5):

---

[92] Tarrant (1985) ad loc. Previous questioning of the gods appears at *Thy.* 122–35 and 407.

[93] The "sacrifices" that Atreus performs at the altars involve Thyestes' children, whose blood stains the altar (*aras sanguine extinguens suo*, 742) much like the lamb of *Ecl.* 1.

[94] Tarrant notes only the first instance (*Ecl.* 1.6) in his index of moments when Vergil is "echoed or imitated by Seneca."

Ultima Cumaei **venit** iam carminis **aetas**;
magnus ab integro saeclorum nascitur ordo.

The final age of the Cumaean Sibyl's song now has come;
The great order of the centuries is born anew.

The repetition of the words *ultima*, *venit*, and *aetas* signals the appropriation, but how is this intertext operating in its new poetic context?[95] Seneca's choral ode details the destruction of the ordered constellations and underscores the sinful world of the tragedy that the characters inhabit. The natural order has been destroyed by the actions of Atreus, and the Golden Age that Vergil expectantly hopes for is seen to be a cataclysm of hatred and despair. The optimism of the eclogue has been completely shattered by the incorporation of this line in the *Thyestes*—the life (*aetas*, 397) of quiet introspection that the chorus had earlier hoped for is seen to be illusory, and the only *ordo* of the *Thyestes* is the correct ordering of the children's sacrifice (*servatur omnis ordo*, 689). In this tragic world, children are born to be objects of or instruments for revenge, and will not presage a new era of peace and prosperity.

Seneca responds to Vergil's *Eclogues* in a variety of ways, according to genre and context, and in this example historical and political considerations should be kept in mind. If Seneca tended to view the first *Eclogue* within the framework of rulers and those ruled (whether that power dynamic was kings and court philosophers or gods and individuals), might the use of the same line in the *Thyestes* also carry a hidden criticism of Nero? In such a tragic environment, even a work as hopeful as the fourth *Eclogue* can be inverted into a bleak comment on power and the chasm between hopeful expectations and harsh reality. The *Thyestes* is usually given a Neronian date,[96] and the sinister ramifications given to these passages of the *Eclogues* emphasizes the distance between Nero's first five "good" years and the tyranny he was exercising at the end of his reign. It acts as a stark reminder of the volubility of rule, and the further politicization of pastoral poetry (as seen in Seneca's possible contemporary Calpurnius Siculus).[97] At the beginning of Nero's reign, Seneca could celebrate the young emperor as ushering in a new Golden Age (*aurea...saecula*, *Apo*.4.9; cf. *Ecl*. 4.9: *gens aurea*) and destined to be worshipped like the sun, but near the end of his life Seneca sees

---

[95] Additionally, Seneca's *digni* (876) echoes the previous line of the *Eclogues*: *si canimus silvas, silvae sint consule **dignae*** (*Ecl*. 4.3).

[96] Cf. Fitch (1981), Nisbet (1990).

[97] Cf. Braund (2009) 11–6 for an overview and bibliography of the poetic panegyrics surrounding Nero's accession. Cf. Mayer (2011) 454–6 for more on the question of his date, but his political overtones and penchant for panegyric are unquestionable.

how far such hopes have fallen.⁹⁸ As the pastoral theme of *otium* has been perverted in the course of the *Thyestes*, so the Vergilian language surrounding the Golden Age that accompanies a new ruler has been transformed from its laudatory purpose in the *Apocolocyntosis* and given tragic ramifications in the *Thyestes*.

One reader who made this connection between the destruction of the Golden Age and Nero's descent into tyranny is the author of the *Octavia*. Because the *Octavia* appropriates language found in Seneca's tragedies and includes Seneca as a character, it may be seen as a useful guide to the author's view of Seneca.⁹⁹ Before Nero's entrance onstage, the character of Seneca mentions that the vices collected over so many lifetimes (***aetates***) have overwhelmed Rome and that "we are oppressed by a grim age" (***saeculo** premimur gravi*, 430).¹⁰⁰ We can see the use of language common to the fourth *Eclogue* and Seneca's own *Thyestes* now foreshadowing the arrival of Nero himself. When the character of Nero appears, he displays the negative results of passion, luxury, and vice (his first words demand the deaths of Plautus and Sulla). As Ferri explains, "*Octavia* may be the earliest witness in the history of political and libertarian interpretations of Senecan tragedy. When Nero repeats the thundering *sententiae* of Seneca's mythological tyrants, the point is probably made that all those fictional characters were aliases of Nero."¹⁰¹ While these recollections to the fourth *Eclogue* may be more subtle, they may be just as important as a way to understand how a later reader identified a subversive intertext already present in Seneca's *Thyestes*.

Conclusions: Quotation and Intertext

These examples have stressed the independence of Seneca's analyses and the way heterogeneous meanings can be formulated from the same lines of Vergil or Ovid. The context of the source material and its reconfigured position in Seneca's prose or poetic works grant the line particular significance from a philosophical or poetic point of view. In both cases, Seneca has a penchant for including the terms from the quotation or the intertext in the surrounding material and,

---

⁹⁸ Cf. *Apo*. 4.25–32 for Nero as Sol. This identification pleased Nero, and his iconography often included identification with Sol. Seneca's Atreus also takes on such a role, leading Volk (2006) 199 to conclude "that the *Thyestes* is indeed an anti-Neronian play and that Atreus' reaction to the eclipse—his reference to his own transformation into the sun god—serves additionally to drive home the similarities between the ruler of Argos and that of Rome."

⁹⁹ The recent commentaries of Ferri (2003) and Boyle (2008) detail the pervasive connections between the *Octavia* poet and the Senecan corpus.

¹⁰⁰ Seneca's speech provides a description of the ages of man and the decline from the Golden Age. Cf. Ferri (2003) ad loc. for more details.

¹⁰¹ Ferri (2003) 70.

therefore, offering further commentary on his interpretation of the line. Conte has written about the difference between quotation and allusion as follows:

> [Quotations] openly acknowledge the work of another, so that no tension is established between the two texts. No "expropriation" of an older text occurs, because the new verbal segment does not rework the old one dialectically; it simply inserts the only text statically within itself. Thus no interpenetration occurs between the two texts—no violence is done to the "propriety" of the old text, and the new text sets up no new meaning to add to its own evident sense (so that there is no complication of sense or of the artistic process).[102]

In his prose works one can see how Seneca weakens Conte's position by his questioning and rewriting of the quoted material. In the cases considered above, Seneca very rarely allows a quote to stand unchallenged or uninterrupted by his philosophical musings. Often one observes an "interpenetration" between the texts as Seneca strives to develop the quotes within his ethical framework and finds ways to show his personal understanding of the quoted material. That being said, it is his *own* interpretation (or the persona of "Seneca" the writer) that is being pushed in his philosophical works, whereas in his poetic works he allows for the full dynamic of intertextual dialogue to be determined in the mind of his reader. As the intertext is further complicated by the perspective of the characters or the dislocation of the material in Seneca's tragic world, the reader must come to terms with the extensive layering of meaning that certain lines or even single words may contain. In a later work Conte explains:

> In fact, a work's meaning and structure can only be grasped in relation to models, while the models themselves are derived from a long series of texts of which they are the invariants. Looked at in this way, every literary work becomes distorted, even opaque; it turns into a highway system with signs indicating towns, roads, places that recede into infinity.[103]

In this chapter I have tried to show how Seneca provides certain signposts in his prose and poetic works through the frequent repetition of marked terms from his models, and by pinpointing the original context from which he derived his borrowing. In this way, he casts light upon the density of his poetic language and reveals the dialectical method that he wishes his reader to pursue when confronted with an intertext or quotation.

---

[102] Conte (1986) 60.
[103] Conte (1994a) 137.

Seneca's reading of these poets stresses the polyvalence of their poetry, especially in his own tragic interpretations, where the adoption of Vergilian and Ovidian language can lead to many different consequences. At times such intertexts can add authorization to descriptions, such as his accounts of the Underworld in the *Oedipus* and *Hercules Furens*, but that language is then further incorporated into the tragic world of the play. By doing so, Seneca indicates that the intertextual potential persists in those terms and shades their later use. At other times, Seneca can be seen to actively undermine the tradition (as with his use of the *Eclogues*), but he is always questioning the texts and allowing the full spectrum of their meaning to come to light. In the merger of the source material with Seneca's tragic perspective, new meanings can be coaxed from the text in the same way a particularly striking metaphor provides a fresh viewpoint on a common object or theme. What is most important for the reading of Seneca's tragedies is to treat them as poetry, which Mastronarde stresses:

> Indeed, one might argue that a fuller understanding of Seneca's peculiar qualities as a Latin poet is to be attained by ignoring the usual questions... and instead treating his works merely as poems—not portrayals of action, but verbal paintings of almost static situations well known to the reader, but depicted in ever fuller detail as the work progresses.[104]

In his tragedies, Seneca's close attention to language, rhetoric, and imagery foregrounds the potency of the word. His propensity to quote and interpret the Augustan poets in his prose works indicates his knowledge of their poetry and how these poets may be of use for ethical and moral improvement. Seneca's pervasive reformulation of the Augustan poets in his tragedies indicates his desire to transcend their works, while noting his indebtedness to them. As Seneca celebrates Lucilius' ability "to signify more than you say" (*plus significas quam loqueris, Ep.* 59.5), so Seneca embodies such a poetics in his tragedies, which exploit literary tropes and language for the fullest expression of his distinctive tragic vision. Intertextuality grants his language additional resonance that colors not only Seneca's plays but also the Augustan originals as he interprets their works in a tragic context.

---

[104] Mastronarde (1970) 291.

2

Intertextuality and Character

> You should know that it is a great thing to play a single man. Apart from the wise man, however, no one plays *one*: the rest of us take on many forms. At one moment we will seem to you to be frugal and serious, the next moment wasteful and frivolous. We change our mask in turn, putting on the opposite of the one that we removed. So demand of yourself that, whatever kind of man you began by showing yourself to be, you keep yourself as that kind of man until the end. Try to make it so that you can be praised, but if not, that you can be recognized.
> —Seneca, *Ep.* 120.22

In the quotation above, Seneca comments on the tendency for individuals to exhibit different sides of themselves (*multiformes sumus*), while encouraging Lucilius to present an unified "self" that can be recognized. While *multiformis* can indicate the multiplicity of roles or moods one displays, it is also indicative of the ability of a writer such as Ennius, whose versatile nature, apparently, led to the various genres of his writings.[1] As we saw in the previous chapter, Seneca himself is a "man of many genres," and his varied literary and philosophical projects not only take on diverse forms but also comment on the same quotes/intertexts in heterogeneous ways. In the context of this chapter on intertextuality and character, it is apparent that Seneca recognizes the problematic nature of selfhood and the various pressures on an individual to develop a stable character.[2] In the prose writings exempla of great men (Cato, Scipio) are often related for Seneca's addressee (e.g., Lucilius, Nero) to emulate. The poetic works, however, rely on intertexts to literary figures for his characters to emulate, and these previous

---

Epigraph: Cf. Ker (2009) 116 for this translation and discussion of the passage.

[1] Fro. *Aur.* 2: *In poetis autem quis ignorat ut gracilis sit Lucilius, Albucius aridus, sublimis Lucretius, mediocris Pacuvius, inaequalis Accius, Ennius multiformis?* ("Among poets, who does not know how Lucilius is refined, Albucius dry, Lucretius sublime, Pacuvius mediocre, Accius uneven, and Ennius multifaceted?")

[2] Cf. Bartsch and Wray (2009) for more on Seneca and the concept of the self, and Star (2012) 62–83 for self-command in Senecan tragedy.

poetic figures can be seen behind the characterization of Seneca's tragic protagonists.[3] However, one can also see behind the word *multiformis* the multiplicity of different poetic sources that comprise each of Seneca's literary characters. In characters such as Medea and Phaedra (the subjects of this chapter), the literary/mythological source materials offer a variety of roles for these protagonists, and their ability (or inability) to come to terms with the various facets of themselves creates much of the dramatic tension and dramatic irony in these tragedies.

Nevertheless, Seneca's characters have often been faulted for being static and more fit for the declaimer's platform than the tragic stage. Seneca strives to impart a tragic grandiosity to his characters in part through their bombastic and multilayered language. This excess should not be looked at as an obstacle to the appreciation of Seneca's characters, but rather as a supplement to our understanding of their passions and motivations. While many characters have a penchant for long-winded monologues and self-examination, this is because Seneca is interested in the psychological lives of his characters. Hadas comments on this feature of Seneca's dramaturgy:

> The heart of a drama is character; plot, dialogue, setting are all really means for expressing character.... In Seneca's country it may be the custom to wear one's heart outside instead of inside one's clothes and to shriek for attention to it by all contrivances of color and sound and gesture; but that does not mean that the hearts are identical. The contrary would seem to be indicated: the heart is so important a human document that any peculiarity must be remarked.[4]

Seneca's characters can be rewardingly studied as exempla of passions at their breaking point (Medea), of wrathful avengers realizing their goal (Atreus), or of the extremes of suffering (Hecuba), and the rich details of the language provide a multidimensional view of these tragic figures.

Seneca delves into the literary tradition surrounding his characters, manipulating the material in order to grant his creations depth and distinction. Figures such as Hercules or Ulysses have a long and complex literary history; Seneca highlights details in their mythological traditions in his tragedies in order to bring to the fore the tragic themes of his plays. Goldhill explains how intertextuality emphasizes the textual nature of the characters of Greek tragedy:

---

[3] Cf. Fantham (1975) for the influence of Vergil's Dido on Seneca's heroines, especially Phaedra.
[4] Hadas (1939) 227.

As literary inventions, then, the characters of Greek drama draw on, define themselves through, and develop in relation to other texts. These characters may not have psychological pasts or futures beyond the texts but they carry around the echoes of their verbal pasts, earlier readings, earlier writings. The boundaries of personality and the boundaries between personalities are continually being transgressed by such defining intertextual differences.[5]

Seneca draws his characters with a similar regard for the literary tradition and genre behind them, and this tradition acts as a kind of personal history of the characters. Sometimes, as in the case of Ulysses and Atreus, the characters appear to knowingly base their actions on previous literary representations.[6] Thus, Ulysses can urge himself to "call forth all of Ulysses" (*advoca...totum Ulixem*, *Tr.* 614–5), as if he is playing the trickster role known through his characterization in the Homeric epics and the dramatic tradition. Other characters, however, may be seen to be at the mercy of the literary tradition, and figures such as the Trojan women of the *Troades* derive much of their pathos from the reader's knowledge of their past, present, and future sufferings.[7] This gap in knowledge between the reader and the characters can lead to dramatic irony, surprise, and mockery, as well as metaliterary reflection. For a writer as concerned with the literary tradition as Seneca, each moment of intertextuality must be analyzed for possible additional significance, and in the creation of characters, that significance may touch upon the themes of the tragedy, the characters' intertextual "life," and Seneca's view of the self.

Seneca's characters continually probe the concept of self, and are prone to quick alterations, self-doubt, and changes in behavior. Seneca investigates the psychological makeup of his characters as they question their emotions and actions. The Latin term *persona* has a variety of meanings and can indicate a fictional character, the dramatic mask, or the true personality of an individual.[8] The "inner nature" of these characters is problematized in these tragedies as they act in multifarious manners and shift in temperament in the course of what can be

---

[5] Goldhill (1986) 188. Greek tragedians always have Homer in mind, while Seneca keeps Ovid, Vergil, and Horace close at hand.

[6] Schiesaro (2003) 70–138 points out the strong influence of the Procne/Philomela/Tereus story on Atreus' character.

[7] As Littlewood (2004) 300 writes of Phaedra, "What for characters is a biological repetition is a textual phenomenon for the reader."

[8] Much good work has been done on the slippage between these terms in Seneca's works. Cf. Edmunds (2001) and T. D. Hill (2004) 159–75. Garton (1972) 3–40 studies differences between person, persona, and personality.

viewed as a search for their character. For a Stoic, "the challenge...was first to establish his own character and then to actualize it, even to the bitter end."[9] The characters' attempts to find a role and "actualize it" actively create the tragedy in the *Phaedra* and can be seen throughout the *Medea* when Medea questions what behavior best fits her role(s). The intertextual relationship between Seneca's characters and the works of Ovid can help to pinpoint the role the characters try to personify or to cast doubt upon the efficacy or motivation behind a role. It raises the question whether there is a true "Medea" or simply a conglomeration of textual roles that Seneca's Medea can take on, as if merely selecting from a roomful of masks.

Seneca and Ovid

This chapter focuses, in particular, on Seneca's use of Ovidian material in his creation of Medea and Phaedra.[10] While other authors and commentators have noted many of the intertextual echoes that I will be analyzing, most have not read them as an example of Seneca's reception of Ovid's work nor linked the intertexts with the larger themes and issues of the tragedies. Why focus on Ovid in particular? The rhetorical impulses that Ovid developed and flaunted in his poetry are even further refined in Seneca's writing and are among of the most recognizable aspects of his writing.[11] Ovid also experimented extensively with genre in his works, which makes him a model for Seneca's inclusion of various genres in his tragedies.[12] Often Ovid relates tales found in tragedy in works as diverse as the *Ars Amatoria* and the *Tristia*, peppering his *Heroides* and *Metamorphoses* with mythological figures from tragedy, and he wrote a (lost) *Medea*.[13] Tragedy was clearly important to Ovid;[14] Seneca recognizes this and writes his tragedies as a response to Ovid's tragic interests, teasing out his own

---

[9] C. Edwards (2002) 387. Long (1996) 264–85 also stresses consistency in the representation of the self.

[10] This is not to deny the importance of additional intertextual source material, but a full analysis of every possible intertext is (probably) impossible. Jakobi (1988) collects linguistic parallels, and my study is indebted to his work throughout. Schiesaro (2003), Littlewood (2004), Hinds (2011) and the commentaries to individual plays also provide copious examples of Ovid's impact on Seneca.

[11] Seneca the Elder writes of Ovid's striking sentiments that could be taken too far (*nescit quod bene cessit relinquere, Contr.* 9.5.17) and his knowing use of radical poetic neologisms (*Contr.* 2.2.12). Quintilian devotes an entire section in his work to censuring Seneca's style, in part because of its popularity among young orators (10.1.125–31).

[12] Cf. Tarrant (2002) 20–32 with suggested bibliography.

[13] Heinze (1997) 223–52 provides an edition with commentary of Ovid's *Medea*. Cf. Hinds (2011) 22–8 for the importance of Ovidian "Medeas" to Seneca's plays.

[14] D. Curley (2013) appeared too late for me to take into consideration.

tragedies from the multigeneric Ovidian material. Seneca employs Ovidian language and imagery in order to elaborate the various facets of his characters and also to highlight the different genres that comprise the tragic genre. For instance, elegy's distinctive reduction of perspective—namely, the way the poet/*ego*'s perspective of the external world is defined solely through his relationship to his beloved—is shown to be vulnerable on the dialogic tragic stage.[15] In addition, Seneca stresses transformation through the pervasive echoes of the *Metamorphoses*, but these characters illuminate the limits of *human* reversals and changes.[16] As the characters, buffeted by the emotional frenzy of love and anger, attempt to understand themselves and their own behavior, Seneca draws upon the Ovidian tradition to give nuance to his portrayals, to get at the inner workings of their minds, and to comment on his tragic project as a whole.

In each case Seneca exploits particular aspects of the Ovidian source material—whether it be generic, situational, linguistic, or thematic. Seneca's Medea and Phaedra both look back to their characterizations found in Ovid's *Heroides*. The fact that the *Heroides* consists of letters written by the heroines allows him to question the efficacy of letters within a myth that hinges upon a letter (*Phaedra*), and to manifest the power of action as opposed to mere elegiac complaints (*Medea*). The literary background of these characters can be reified through attempts by the characters themselves to understand their motivations and behavior. At these times Seneca has them look back to previous moments in their own (literary) lives for commentary on their actions.[17] Seneca often will incorporate language of the intertext in the larger verbal and thematic patterns of his tragedy to momentous effect, indicating his interest in exploring the implications of the intertextual material. As characters repeat the terms the reader can see how such references continue to influence the action or are found to be wanting or insufficient. In essence, this approach provides a glimpse of Seneca's reception of Ovid's works. By reinscribing Medea and Phaedra into the tragic genre, Seneca is reclaiming them from Ovid, and his elaboration on Ovidian themes and language points to his attempt to make something innovative (and greater) from the Ovidian material.

---

[15] Cf. Barchiesi (2001) 32: "What distinguishes [elegy] is its peremptory reduction of every external matter to its central focus, the persona of the poet-lover and his all-consuming purpose: the conquest and defence of love. The identifying feature of elegy is precisely this monologic reduction; as a rule, elegy has room for one voice only."

[16] E.g., in Seneca's *Troades* the stress is on Hecuba's fall from queen to slave, not from human to dog (*Met.* 13.565–75). Also, it is notable that aside from Juno in the *Hercules Furens*, the gods do not appear as characters in Seneca's plays.

[17] Cf. Ker (2009) 115–25; Bartsch (2006) 216–29.

Phaedra

Both Hippolytus and Phaedra struggle with their self-identities in the course of Seneca's play, and Seneca shows how the instability of Phaedra's personae leads to Hippolytus' death and her eventual suicide. Phaedra takes on different roles in an attempt to win Hippolytus or to explain her behavior to the Nurse, Theseus, and, ultimately, herself. Fitch and McElduff, in their investigation of the concept of the self in Senecan tragedy, find that Phaedra's mutable self-representation "can misidentify and fragment the authentic self, leading to alienation from that self and ultimately to its destruction, as well as the destruction of others."[18] The various intertextual sources help to define the fragmentation of Phaedra's character as she oscillates between preserving her honor and following her passion.[19] Ovid gives two lengthy accounts of the story of Hippolytus and Phaedra (*Met.* 15.497–546, *Her.* 4), and mentions it in other works.[20] Seneca draws upon these accounts as well as additional Ovidian material that features the themes of illicit or incestuous love. In the course of his tragedy, the intertextual matrix points to similarities between Seneca's Phaedra and characters such as Myrrha Byblis, and Medea from the *Metamorphoses*, as well as the elegiac Phaedra of *Heroides* 4.

I begin this analysis with the argument between Seneca's Phaedra and her nurse, which introduces us to Phaedra's character and the Nurse's role as advisor. Such scenes often appear in Senecan tragedy to display the emotional state of the protagonist and the ineffectual advice of a subordinate.[21] In the *Phaedra*, this scene also recalls Ovid's *Amores* and *Remedia Amoris*, and displays the manner in which Seneca responds to Ovid's erotic poetry by "updating" it for the dramatic situation at hand. Phaedra espouses the view that love is unable to be controlled, and, therefore, she must give in to her passion (or commit suicide). I follow with a discussion of the choral ode on love (274–357) in order to explain the impetus for the changes of personae that Phaedra undergoes, and to show how Seneca foreshadows the destructive nature of her passion with intertexts from Ovid's *Amores*. Next I examine those characters from the *Metamorphoses* that also share in unnatural desire (Myrrha, Byblis), as well as Medea (both as a paradigmatic *noverca* and as a co-sufferer of passion). Ovid draws upon elegiac imagery and topoi in his development of these heroines and their struggles to come to terms with their desires, and

---

[18] Fitch and McElduff (2002) 36.
[19] The fragmentation of Hippolytus' character will be physically manifested at the conclusion of the play in the form of his mangled body.
[20] Cf. *Fast.* 6.737–62; *Rem.* 64, 743–4; *A.A.* 1.511, 744. In this chapter I deal only with those moments when Seneca exploits Ovid to characterize his Phaedra.
[21] Cf. Tarrant (1978) 192–3.

Seneca utilizes this imagery as well in his *Phaedra*.[22] Seneca's Phaedra believes her passion cannot be controlled (like Medea) and relies on the tenets of elegiac poetry (like Byblis) to formulate her desire. The final intertext I will examine is *Heroides* 4, Phaedra's letter to Hippolytus, in order to show how Seneca modifies Ovid's representation of Phaedra and to reveal the ramifications of placing an elegiac Phaedra in the tragic genre. Seneca stages the moment in which Phaedra reveals her desire for Hippolytus (which is the purpose of Phaedra's epistle), and Seneca redeploys language from the letter in a new, dramatic context. It may not be surprising that the confrontation scene contains many recollections of this poem, but what may be surprising is how Seneca critiques Ovid's elegiac Phaedra and shows the macabre results of elegiac role-playing in his tragic world.

Phaedra's *Remedia Amoris*?

Phaedra's opening speech positions her as a woman unhappy in her marriage and stricken with passion for an unnamed individual (although the references to her desire for hunting directly after Hippolytus' hunting song leave little doubt). Phaedra's desire is countered by the Nurse, who does not sympathize with Phaedra's love, but chooses to reinforce the traditional roles women should play as wives, mothers, and daughters. In effect, Seneca's Nurse responds both to Phaedra's speech and to Ovid's elegiac poetry as she attempts to demolish the elegiac tropes and motifs that foul desire has created (*turpis et vitio favens / finxit libido*, 195–6), those same tropes that Phaedra follows and applies to her love.[23] The elegiac behavior that Seneca's Phaedra appears to have learned from Ovid's erotic poetry is now opposed by a novel application of Ovid's own *Remedia Amoris*.

Phaedra's initial speech emphasizes her change in behavior, her Pasiphae-like desire, and her belief that Venus has cursed her family. She identifies her passion with her mother's (112–4):

> Quo tendis, anime? quid furens saltus amas?
> fatale miserae matris agnosco malum:
> peccare noster novit in silvis amor.

> Where do you move, soul? Why, maddened, do you love groves?
> I recognize the fateful evil of my pitiable mother:
> Our love knows how to sin in the woods.

---

[22] Seneca recognized that some aspects of Byblis' story recall *Heroides* 4, and these will be especially helpful in the examination of Phaedra's character.

[23] *Fingo* is an important word in the *Phaedra* as each of the primary characters uses it to define themselves and their behavior (cf. 496, 1194, 1265). See Chap. 1 for more on this term.

Phaedra believes that the wild Hippolytus can be conquered in the woods and that she has learned such behavior from her mother (*amore didicimus vinci feros*, 240). The recognition (*agnosco*) motif and the concept of learning (*novit/didicimus*) promote the idea that Seneca's Phaedra is dependent on previous literary representations of Pasiphae.[24] The verb *agnosco* acts as a signpost of intertextual borrowing as well as Phaedra's self-conscious awareness "of her family history to push her into action even as she is repelled by the vision before her."[25] In this particular example, the idea of the woods as a locus for illicit passion recalls the representation of Pasiphae in Ovid's *Ars Amatoria*, where she is said to have wandered the groves and woods in her love for the bull (*in nemus et **saltus** thalamo regina relicto / fertur*, 1.311–2). Phaedra creates a persona for herself that follows the exemplum of her mother and concludes her initial formulation of her passion by concluding, "No Minoan girl has ever gotten off with an easy love, it is always yoked to crime" (*nulla Minois levi / defuncta amore est, iungitur semper nefas*, 127–8).[26] From a metaliterary perspective, an "easy love" is more suitable for the lesser genre of elegy as opposed to tragedy's more serious nature, and the yoking imagery that pervades the play becomes more and more menacing as it progresses.[27]

The Nurse questions Phaedra's conception of passion and attempts to dissuade her from following in the footsteps of her mother. Coffey and Mayer comment on the Nurse's speech: "The present speech of dissuasion gives a glimpse of S[eneca]'s imitative technique. Ovid composed a work to help us avoid love, *Remedia amoris*; S[eneca] borrows from it some arguments for the Nurse to use with Phaedra."[28] The Nurse tries to allay Phaedra's fiery passion by dousing it with the cold water of Ovid's *Remedia*. Phaedra's Nurse recommends (132–5):

> quisquis in primo **obstitit**
> pepulitque amorem, tutus ac victor fuit;
> qui blandiendo dulce nutriuit **malum**,
> **sero** recusat ferre quod subiit **iugum**.

---

[24] Cf. Coffey and Mayer (1990) ad 113 for the additional intertexts to Vergil's *Ecl*. 6.56 and *Aen*. 4.23. Phaedra knows her mother was successful in her pursuit of a wild bull, and mentions it at Ov. *Her*. 4.165–6.

[25] Armstrong (2006) 288.

[26] Cf. Ov. *Am*. 3.1.35–6 for more on the interplay between elegy and tragedy. *Tr*. 2.381–3 notes that tragedy defeats every genre in its "weightiness" (*gravitate*); the "lightness" of elegy is a commonplace (cf. *Am*. 1.1.19 and McKeown (1989) ad loc.).

[27] Paschalis (1994) examines the bull and horse imagery of the *Phaedra*.

[28] Coffey and Mayer (1990) ad loc.

Whoever rejects and repels
Love at the beginning, he is safe and successful;
He who nurtures the sweet evil with caresses,
Too late he complains of the yoke to which he has succumbed.

Seneca's Nurse repeats the advice of Ovid's *magister amoris* of the *Remedia*, who directs his reader to act quickly to withstand any passion (89–92):

quale sit id quod amas, celeri circumspice mente,
    et tua laesuro subtrahe colla **iugo**.
principiis **obsta**: **sero** medicina paratur,
    cum **mala** per longas convaluere moras.

Regard with a quick mind what sort of thing it is you love,
    And draw your neck from the troubling yoke.
Resist at the start: medicine is prepared too late,
    After evils have strengthened through long delays."[29]

Seneca infuses his account with language from the *Remedia* that encourages Phaedra to fight her passion at the start and also happens to resonate with the larger dramatic context. Seneca finds a moment from the *Remedia* that speaks to the particular situation at hand and cleverly situates the language within the larger mythological context.[30] Phaedra herself has deemed her desire a "fateful evil" (*fatale...malum*, 113), and the use of *malum* for love is consistent throughout the *Phaedra*.[31] While the reference to the yoke is rather common in elegiac poetry, it is particularly appropriate to the love of a Cretan woman (***iungitur semper nefas***), especially as the parallels with Pasiphae have already been stressed.[32] Such language also will appear later in the play as Seneca connects the imagery surrounding yoking with Phaedra's final death wish as she claims, "It was not permitted to join souls, but surely it is permitted to join fates" (*non licuit*

---

[29] Cf. Jakobi (1988) ad loc. Hine (1994) also finds Lucretian parallels (4.1068–72, 1149–54) for the Nurse's advice.

[30] One may recall that Ovid boasts his *Remedia* would be able to cure the passions of both Pasiphae and Phaedra: "Give Pasiphae to me, and she will put aside her love for the bull; give Phaedra to me, and the foul love of Phaedra will disappear." (*da mihi Pasiphaen, iam tauri ponet amorem; / da Phaedran, Phaedrae turpis abibit amor.* 63–4). Segal (1987) traces the yoking imagery in the play.

[31] Cf. *Phd.* 101, 113, 115, passim. Note that the phrase *fatale...malum* looks back to *Tr.* 5.1.59: *est aliquid, **fatale malum** per verba levare* ("It is something to lighten a fated evil with words"). This passage relies on the identification of elegy as an appropriate meter for lament, whereas Seneca formulate the *malum* strictly as an erotic "evil."

[32] Cf. McKeown (1989) ad 1.213–6 for more on "the taming of oxen and horses as an erotic image."

*animos **iungere**, at certe licet / **iunxisse** fata*, 1183–4). Seneca pairs Phaedra and the Nurse, here embodying the tenets of elegiac poetry and the *Remedia*, respectively, to contend with one another, while the language itself foreshadows later disaster for both Phaedra and Hippolytus.

Phaedra persists in claiming that she has been overcome by love (*amoris in me maximum regnum fero*, 218) and that she will follow Hippolytus anywhere he may flee. She formulates herself as a huntress as well as a Hippolytus-like figure, and her language mimics both Hippolytus' earlier song as well as the elegiac topos of erotic hunting (233–5):

> Hunc in ***nivosi*** *collis* haerentem iugis
> et aspera agili saxa calcantem pede
> **sequi** per *alta nemora*, per **montes** placet.

> Although that man lingers on the peaks of a snowy mountain
> And treads harsh rocks with his agile feet,
> It pleases me to follow him in the deep groves, through the mountains.

Seneca repeats language found earlier in Hippolytus' lyric hunting song in order to point out that Phaedra is trying to model herself, in part, on Hippolytus himself.[33] There, Hippolytus urges his fellow hunters to go where "the grove is shaded with high alder" (***nemus alta****/ texitur alno*, 9–10) and to climb "hills eternally white with Riphaean snow" (***colles*** *semper canos /* ***nive*** *Riphaea*, 7–8). In elegiac poetry, the lover must follow the beloved, no matter where she may flee.[34] Commenting on a passage of Ovid's *Amores* (2.19.36), Conte claims that such pursuit is "the motto that can emblematically represent the torment of the elegiac form of love: *quod sequitur, fugio; quod fugit, ipse sequor.*"[35] Ovid famously conceives of the lover as a soldier in *Amores* 1.9, and his lover undergoes labors similar to those Phaedra imagines for herself (9–12):

> mitte puellam,
> strenuus exempto fine **sequetur** amans;

---

[33] Cf. Littlewood (2004) 268: "Erotic hunting is so familiar that there can be little material which admits desire more easily." De Meo (1978) 51 and Littlewood (2004) 289–90 discuss how this passage recalls Hippolytus' song.

[34] Cf. Prop. 2.26.29ff., Tib. 1.4.41ff. After Hippolytus rejects her advances, Phaedra realizes this is her fate: "I recognize the destiny of our house: we seek what should be fled" (*et ipsa nostrae fata cognosco domus: / fugienda petimus*, 698–9). See discussion below.

[35] Conte (1994a) 63. Phaedra responds to the Nurse's claim that Hippolytus will flee by saying, "If he should flee through the very sea, I would follow" (*per ipsa maria si fugiat, sequar*, 241).

> ibit in adversos **montes** duplicataque nimbo
> flumina, congestas exteret ille **nives**.

> Send the girl away,
> The vigorous lover will follow to the ends of the earth;
> He will cross hostile mountains, rivers swollen by rain,
> That man will crush snowdrifts.

Phaedra seems to have learned her behavior both from her mother as well as from the traditional elegiac portrayals of a lover's actions. In the *Phaedra*, Seneca grants this language additional relevance because of the centrality of hunting and the woods to Hippolytus' characterization.[36] Forms of the verb *sequor*, found in the intertext and important to the theme of hunting, appear twenty times in the play and act to bind the actions of the main characters.[37] Phaedra stresses how she will follow Hippolytus, no matter where he may go (*per ignes, per mare insanum sequar / rupesque et amnes*, 700–1), culminating in her suicide to "follow" him into the Underworld (1180). For Hippolytus the woods are a safe environment precisely because they are devoid of women and their deceitful machinations.[38] Phaedra's erotic hunting counters Hippolytus' chaste identification with Diana and hunting, and this creates one of the conflicts between the two protagonists as each misunderstands the language of the other.[39] In a sense, their misunderstanding revolves around the very fact that each character is thinking in a different genre: for Phaedra, the woods have elegiac connotations, but for Hippolytus his conception centers on a Golden Age reverie, more attuned to pastoral or didactic principles.[40]

This opening act between the Nurse and Phaedra involves an active questioning of the Ovidian tradition and the presence of elegy in the tragic genre. Seneca's Phaedra exhibits the typical *furor* (102, 178, 184) and *dolor* (99) associated

---

[36] Cf. *Phd.* 483–539.

[37] Cf. *Phd.* 60, 178, 235, 239, 241, 254, 396, 481, 491, 596, 618, 700, 849, 987, 1034, 1051, 1077, 1180, 1210, 1240. Diana "harries" (*sequitur*, 60) deer, Theseus "investigates" (*exsequor*, 1210) a false charge, Hippolytus is said to "take vengeance upon" (*persequitur*, 239) all women, and the monster from the sea continuously "follows" (*sequitur*, 1077) Hippolytus' chariot.

[38] Cf. *Phd.* 559–64. In addition the city is host to people who "hunt after" (*sequitur*, 491) vain honors.

[39] It is notable that the chorus believes the woods to be an unchaste locale. Cf. Segal (1986) 64: "Phaedra evokes a fantasy-picture of Hippolytus: not a virginal recluse, but a desirable and available sex-object, like the Endymion and Hylas of whom the chorus sings just after her sexual fantasies reach a catastrophic end."

[40] Cf. *Phd.* 483–564 and the treatments of Segal (1986) 77–105, which clarifies the savage primitivism underlying Hippolytus' belief, and Littlewood (2004) 285–93.

with the elegiac lover,[41] but the Nurse (and Phaedra) are quick to point out that such passion leads, in this case, to a crime (*nefas*; 128, 143, 153), incest. Seneca draws upon Ovid's *Metamorphoses* extensively in this scene (to be discussed below), but also subtly applies moments from the *Ars Amatoria*, *Remedia Amoris*, and *Amores* that are particularly apt for the dramatic situation. Seneca shows himself to be interested in questioning the various tropes of elegiac desire and the problems that an elegiac sensibility may cause in his tragic environment. Phaedra's opening salvo with the Nurse indicates her conception of love as a force more powerful than any other and her belief that the only alternative to pursuing her passion is suicide, another elegiac trope (250–66). The Nurse quickly recants and decides to help Phaedra in her attempt on Hippolytus, figuring him as a particularly savage opponent (*intractabilem*, 271; *ferum*, 272; *immitis*, 273). The language of elegiac love will continue to appear in the play, but often with more sinister connotations.[42] Phaedra's view about the power of love, however, is supported by the subsequent choral ode, which directly follows upon the debate between the Nurse and Phaedra, as the chorus points out the transformative potential of desire.

Change of Heart (*Phd.* 274–357)

Seneca's *Phaedra* problematizes how characters attempt to present themselves to the world, and the mutable nature of such self-representation.[43] As Seneca's Phaedra succumbs to her desire, she becomes increasingly unstable in her conduct, and her erratic behavior impels much of the tragic action.[44] The second choral ode (274–357) ponders the power of "uncontrollable" (*impotens*, 276) and "brash" (*lascivus*, 277) love, and catalogues the ways in which love causes transformation in all creatures, great and small.[45] This choral song stresses that love is universal among beasts (335–51), mankind (290–5), gods (296–316), and

---

[41] Within the first poem of Propertius' *Monobiblos* one finds both *furor* (1.1.7) and *dolor* (1.1.38) as characteristic features of elegiac love. Conte (1994a) 54 finds "the ideology of elegy, in fact, associated love and *furor* in a strict rhetorical bond and, by entrusting erotic passion to the logic of impetuous impulses, denied it the positivity of a stable satisfaction."

[42] Note how quickly her longing to follow Hippolytus (*sequar*, 241) can be changed to following her husband, Theseus, who is in the Underworld (*virum sequamur*, 254).

[43] Cf. Star (2006) for an attempt to show that Seneca's characters desire *constantia* in a way not incompatible with his Stoicism.

[44] The Nurse claims that Phaedra's passion (*furor*) is uncontrollable (363), and that she continually changes (*semper impatiens sui / mutatur habitus*, 372–3). When Phaedra appears onstage (387ff.), she wishes to discard her regal attire and become Amazon-like (to please Hippolytus or hunt him?).

[45] Coffey and Mayer (1990) ad loc. notes, "The reference to gods transformed for love is bound to recall Ovid's *Metamorphoses*," and goes on to list the parallels with Ovid's work.

heroes (317–29). Once again intertexts to Ovid's works are manipulated to endorse the chorus's vision—in this case the mixture of lines from the *Metamorphoses* and the *Amores* demonstrates that love is one of the primary reasons for transformation and that it will redefine the personal relationships of the protagonists throughout the play.

While emphasizing its geographical reach, Seneca also recalls two programmatic passages from Ovid's *Amores* in order to comment on the power of love in this tragedy. The first is rather minute, but also features a telling *contaminatio* with Ovid's *Metamorphoses*. It comes from the opening of *Amores* 2.1, in which Ovid restricts his audience (*theatra*, 2.1.4) to "the maiden who is not frigid at the sight of her beloved, / and the boy touched by love for the first time" (*in sponsi facie non frigida* **virgo**, */ et rudis* **ignoto** *tactus* **amore** *puer*, 2.1.5–6). In response to this circumscribed audience, Seneca's chorus speaks of the fire that Cupid wields and its impact on all the peoples of the world, of all ages (290–5):

> iuvenum feroces
> concitat flammas senibusque fessis
> rursus extinctos revocat calores,
> **virginum ignoto** ferit **igne** pectus—
> et iubet **caelo** superos **relicto**
> vultibus falsis habitare terras.

> Love stirs up the fierce flames
> Of youth and recalls the snuffed-out heat
> Of tired old men. He strikes the hearts of maidens
> With unknown fire—
> And orders the gods to leave the heavens
> And inhabit the earth with false appearances.

Seneca picks up on Ovid's language, but expands the scope of Cupid's power. In addition, the move from *amore* to *igne*, while a common enough identification in erotic poetry, is stressed throughout this play and in this very chorus (*impotens flammis* 276, *arsit* 309, *sacer…ignis* 330, *flammam* 337, *ignibus* 355).[46] Although Ovid wishes to limit his audience to those who are first experiencing passion, Seneca's chorus finds Love's influence to be universal and inescapable. This passage also shows Seneca's clever ability to unite passages from across Ovid's corpus of poetry—the phrase *caelo…relicto* derives from Ovid's *Metamorphoses* and, contrary to the sentiment of Seneca's line, from a story that does not involve trickery on the part of the gods. In this case, it stems from the story of Mercury, who is enflamed with love

---

[46] Cf. Segal (1986) 46–50 for more on fire imagery in the *Phaedra*.

at first sight for Herse (*exarsit*, 727). Unlike a majority of stories involving the love of gods for mortals, he eschews any masquerade (*Met.* 2.730–1):

> vertit iter **caelo**que petit terrena **relicto**
> nec se dissimulat: tanta est fiducia formae.
>
> He turns his path and, leaving the heavens, seeks the earth
> Without a disguise: such is his confidence in his beauty.

Love will cause Mercury (costumed or not) to come to earth—Seneca echoes *terrena* with *terras*.[47] Seneca includes intertexts to both the *Metamorphoses* and the *Amores* in order to display the power of love and to transcend moments in Ovid's texts in which the discussion of erotic passion is restricted due to age (*Amores*) or a god simply combs his hair and arranges his robe in an attempt to woo the object of his affection (*Metamorphoses*). In the latter case, it is noteworthy that Mercury ultimately does not achieve his goal (a rarity in the *Metamorphoses*)—perhaps he should have changed his form as per Seneca's chorus. By employing two intertexts that go against the grain of the chorus's argument, Seneca corrects the Ovidian accounts and suggests the opposite—namely, that love is all-powerful and will alter one's behavior.

Further indicating Seneca's engagement with Ovid's poetry, the first poem of the *Amores* acts as the intertextual model for another section of this choral ode. Seneca's chorus comments on Cupid's sphere of influence (330–4):

> Sacer est ignis (credite laesis)
>   **nimiumque potens**.
> qua terra salo cingitur alto
> quaque per ipsum candida mundum
>   sidera currunt,
> hac **regna** tenet **puer** immitis...
>
> The fire is heaven-sent and too powerful
> (Trust those who have been wounded).
> Where the land is ringed by deep ocean,
> Where shining stars run through their orbit,
> In that place the fierce boy holds power.

---

[47] The confidence in his *forma* that Mercury manifests is questioned repeatedly in the *Phaedra* (cf. *anceps forma bonum mortalibus*, 761; *res est forma fugax*, 773, passim). See below for Hippolytus' problematic *forma*. Anderson (1996) 321 notes how in the *Metamorphoses* "among human beings, *forma* causes nothing but frustration and trouble." Mercury was struck initially by Herse's beauty (*obstipuit forma, Met.* 2.726).

Seneca's Cupid resembles Ovid's description of Cupid in the opening poem of his *Amores*, and Seneca calls attention to his poetic assimilation of Ovid's character intertextually (*Am.* 1.1.13–4):

> sunt tibi magna, **puer, nimiumque potentia regna**;
> cur opus adfectas, ambitiose, novum?
>
> Your reign is great, boy, and all too powerful;
> Why do you ambitiously strive after a new work?

In this choral song, Seneca further delineates the expanse of Cupid's power, and brings the powerful figure of the *Amores* into his tragedy.[48] In *Amores* 1.1, the narrator complains that he does not wish to write love poetry until he is stricken by Cupid's arrow, and Seneca's chorus likewise shows the difficulty of escaping Love's influence.[49] In addition, the claim that Cupid's fire is "too powerful" (*nimium...potens*) recurs twice later in the play, exposing the importance of this sentiment for Phaedra and Theseus. When Phaedra attempts to convince Hippolytus to have an affair, she corrects his use of the name "mother" for her: "The name of mother is overbearing and too powerful" (*matris superbum est nomen et **nimium potens**,* 609). The intratextual echo shows that Phaedra is still under the influence of Cupid's power, and this opens a speech in which she endorses the concept of *servitium amoris* (see below). After hearing of Hippolytus' horrific death, Theseus exclaims, "O too powerful nature, how strongly do blood ties hold parents!" (O ***nimium potens*** / *quanto parentes sanguinis vinclo tenes* / *natura!,* 1114–6). This expression, Theseus' first words after the messenger speech, directs the reader once again back to this choral song, indicating not only that Cupid was behind Hippolytus' death but also the conflation of *amor* and *natura* at work in sections of the play.[50] Seneca calls attention to the elegiac imagery and concerns that motivate the action of his play through intratextually returning to this phrase and placing it on the lips of different characters. By echoing language from the programmatic poems of the first two books of *Amores* (1.1 and 2.1), Seneca signposts the elegiac influence of Ovid's poetry on his own tragic song, although the metrical variation of this chorus (Sapphic hendecasyllables and anapests) reveals part of the way in which he transforms his model.

---

[48] The phrase *sacer...ignis* (330) additionally recalls the destructive power of the plague in both Lucretius (6.660, 1167) and Vergil (*Georg.* 3.566) and thus highlights the damage passion can cause.

[49] The chorus may also be hinting that Cupid (i.e. elegiac poetry) can be found in tragedy.

[50] Cf. Boyle (1987) 18–24 for *natura* in the *Phaedra* and the role of this chorus: "The divinities of sexual love and the goddess of the moon, wilderness and the hunt seem to represent in fact complementary aspects of nature's power, savagery and violence; for it is with *natura* that the ode seems concerned."

Seneca's *Phaedra* highlights the damage (*credite laesis*) and changes that can be caused by passion, and intertextual connections to the *Amores* indicate the elegiac topoi that will influence the imagery surrounding Phaedra and the representation of erotic desire in the play.

The chorus accentuates the complete reversals in behavior that Love compels: the elderly gain vigor (291–2), timid stags look to fight (341–2), and Hercules assumes female attire and spins thread (317–24).[51] The gods are not immune and the chorus stresses how Love manipulates not only their behavior, but even the forms they assume. Jove himself has often feigned lesser forms (*induit formas quotiens minores*, 299), becoming both a swan (301–2) and a bull (303–8) in order to satisfy his passion, stories found in Ovid's *Metamorphoses*.[52] The chorus concludes (352–7):

> vindicat omnes
> natura sibi, nihil immune est,
> odiumque perit, cum **iussit amor**;
> veteres cedunt ignibus irae.
> quid plura canam? vincit saevas
> cura novercas.

> Nature claims all for herself,
> Nothing is immune, and hate dies
> When love orders; old angers yield to desire.
> What more shall I sing?
> Care defeats savage stepmothers.[53]

The chorus here appeals to *natura* in its guise of sexual desire and places Phaedra within the larger context of the influence and transformative power of passion.[54] The phrase *iussit amor* can be found in elegiac contexts,[55] and two from Ovid are particularly pertinent here. In *Amores* 2.1.3, Ovid programmatically claims that

---

[51] The representation of Hercules is influenced by *Her.* 9 (Deianira's letter to Hercules), cf. Coffey and Mayer (1990) ad loc.

[52] Cf. Ovid *Met.* 2.846–75, esp. 850, **induitur** *faciem tauri*; *Met.* 6.103–9.

[53] Boyle (1987) ad loc. comments, "*Cura* is almost a technical term in Roman elegy for passionate, anxiety ridden love: see Propertius 1.3.1, 1.15.31." Seneca uses elegiac language to stress the elegiac love that Phaedra hopes to attain with Hippolytus and her position as an elegiac lover. This overcomes the traditional hatred of stepmothers (*novercae*).

[54] Cf. Boyle (1987) ad loc. for more on *natura* in this chorus. Vergil's description of love at *Georg.* 3.219ff influences the conclusion of the choral song and shows how Seneca adapts material from other genres in his tragedy. At *Georg.* 3.282 *malae novercae* use hippomanes to kill their stepsons; although Seneca alludes to this passage, he gives it a different significance—love will change stepmothers.

[55] Cf. Prop. 2.16.39–40, Tib. 1.6.30, Ov. *Her.* 20.230.

he will detail his love affairs in this book because "Love ordered this" (*hoc quoque iussit Amor*).⁵⁶ The opening poems of the first and second books of Ovid's *Amores* lurk behind the chorus's sentiments in part because of their marked position as programmatic *elegiac* poems (and we will see that *Amores* 3.1 is especially important for Seneca's *Medea*). Similarly, the importance of *Heroides* 4 on Phaedra's characterization will become apparent as the play progresses; this phrase is found emphatically near the opening of that poem when Phaedra writes, "What modesty forbids me to say, love has ordered me to write. Whatever love orders, it is not safe to disregard" (*dicere quae puduit, scribere **iussit** amor. / quidquid **Amor iussit**, non est contemnere tutum*, 4.9–10). Seneca positions the reader to recognize the influence of *Heroides* 4 on his *Phaedra* by including this phrase in the choral ode and indicating the source of Phaedra's fiery passion for Hippolytus. The chorus, always an individual voice in Senecan tragedy, seems to support Phaedra's claims from the first act that Love cannot be avoided and even should be conjoined with the larger idea of nature itself. Now "nature claims all for herself" whereas earlier Phaedra understood her passion as a vendetta of Venus against her family (*Venus… **vindicat***, 124–5).⁵⁷ Boyle comments on the merger of nature and love:

> In Phaedra's initial, perceptive analysis, in the Nurse's subsequent rejoinder, the Cretan princess' love for Hippolytus was presented as monstrous passion, a perversion of nature (esp. 173–77); from the perspective of the first choral ode it is *natura* itself, which claims its victims like the goddess of the hunt.⁵⁸

In some sense, Seneca is one-upping the literary tradition of transformations caused by desire that are found in works such as the *Amores* and *Metamorphoses*, while pointing to the underlying motivation for such drastic alterations in behavior (and form). The changes that Phaedra undergoes in the course of the play reflect the turbulence of those struck by love and even concludes the argument of the chorus. While the metamorphoses of gods and heroes and behavioral upheavals of animals may be astounding, what really proves the power of Love (*quid plura canam?*) is the passion that a stepmother, Phaedra, expresses for Hippolytus.

---

⁵⁶ Cf. McKeown (1998) ad loc. for the recollection of *Am.* 1.1.24 and the idea that Ovid's poetry is written "at divine behest."

⁵⁷ Note Phaedra's bitterly sarcastic use of this verb later in the play: "This one crime was lacking, for you to enjoy Theseus' bed as if it was avenged and you still pure" (*hoc derat nefas, / ut **vindicato** sancta frueris toro.* 1186–7). These are the only three uses of this verb in the play.

⁵⁸ Boyle (1987) 20–21.

Multiple Phaedras

To stress the possibility of transformation and the presence of the themes of incest and forbidden passion in Phaedra, Seneca utilizes the Ovidian characters of Byblis and Myrrha to examine the consequences of Phaedra's incestuous desire. These characters struggle to fight their illicit passions, attempt to explain their actions through comparison with previous elegiac lovers, and endure metamorphosis because of their love. Ovid's Medea (from the *Metamorphoses*) also informs Seneca's depiction of Phaedra, both when Phaedra attempts to negotiate the severity of her passion and as a precedent for the actions of a stepmother.[59] These Ovidian characters provide explanations and suggest possible outcomes for Phaedra's passion. Intertextual echoes help to provide a new treatment of the theme of destructive passion as the language and imagery of Ovid's heroines shape Phaedra's depiction. By combining some of the paradigmatic stories from the *Metamorphoses* that center on incestuous desire, Seneca creates a Phaedra who becomes the culmination of these incestuous characters. If passionate love can cause transformation, as the first choral ode seems to imply, how will Phaedra transform in the course of the play? In a manner like Myrrha or Byblis or in another way altogether? Seneca's play shows the all-too-human (and tragic) results of the diverse personae Phaedra assumes in her pursuit of Hippolytus and its resultant catastrophe.[60]

Medea, Myrrha, Byblis, and Phaedra

Seneca's Phaedra attempts to renegotiate her familial position with respect to Hippolytus by denying her tie to him as his stepmother (*noverca*). Stepmothers were notorious for evil in Latin declamation and poetry, and Medea was one exemplum of the evil intentions of stepmothers through her attempted poisoning of Theseus.[61] However, Ovid's depiction of Medea's youthful love for Jason in his *Metamorphoses* also displays the power of passion. Intertextual links between Seneca's Phaedra and Ovid's Medea unite the desires of these characters, while the focus on Phaedra's role as stepmother also indicates the danger of acting in a Medea-like manner in the genre of tragedy.

In the *Metamorphoses*, Ovid's Medea struggles with her passion for Jason, and this struggle is formulated as a battle between desire and reason: "She was not

---

[59] Cf. McAuley (2012) for more on Medea in the *Phaedra*.

[60] It can be argued that the monster from the sea is a physical embodiment of her monstrous passion (see Chap. 3 for more on the representation of the monster).

[61] Cf. *Met.* 7.405–24. Boyle (1987) ad 356 discusses the conventional savagery of stepmothers in Latin poetry.

able to defeat her passion with reason" (***ratione furorem*** / *vincere non poterat*, Met. 7.10–1). Medea goes on to question her desire, wondering if some god obstructs her (*nescio quis **deus** obstat*, 7.12), before describing her helplessness (7.17–21):

> excute virgineo conceptas pectore flammas,
> si potes, infelix. si possem, sanior essem.
> sed trahit invitam nova vis, aliudque cupido,
> mens aliud suadet; video meliora proboque,
> deteriora **sequor**.

> Cast off the fires which possess your maiden heart,
> If you are able, unhappy one! If I could be, I would be healthier!
> But a strange power draws me unwilling. Desire persuades me one way,
> And my mind persuades differently: I see the better and I approve it,
> But I follow the worse.

Medea's love for Jason overcomes her ties to her family and her fatherland, and, despite a clear knowledge that her actions are wrong (*video meliora proboque*), she chooses to help Jason in his heroic endeavors. These lines strongly influence Seneca's representation of Phaedra's passion. After the Nurse has expressed her abhorrence of incest and compared Phaedra's actions to Pasiphae's, Phaedra responds (177–9, 184–5):

> Quae memoras scio
> vera esse, nutrix; sed **furor** cogit **sequi**
> peiora....
> quid **ratio** possit? vicit ac regnat **furor**,
> potensque tota mente dominatur **deus**.

> I know what you say
> Is true, Nurse, but passion compels me to follow the worse....
> What can reason do? Passion conquers and rules,
> A powerful god has dominion over my whole mind.

Like Medea, Phaedra also feels that she is incapable of fighting her desire, and, despite her recognition of the veracity of the Nurse's advice, she finds it impossible to govern her passion.[62] Whereas Ovid's Medea wondered what god hindered her, Seneca's Phaedra knows all of Cupid's attributes, including his

---

[62] This allusion to Ovid's *Metamorphoses* also includes a second reference, to Phaedra herself in Euripides' *Hippolytus*. Cf. *Hipp.* 380–3 and Jakobi (1988) ad loc. The use of *furor* for desire appears often in the play (96, 268, 279, 363, passim); cf. Merzlak (1983) for discussion.

power over the gods and, presumably, an afflicted mortal woman like herself (186–94).⁶³ The concept that Phaedra must "follow the worse" becomes a leitmotif throughout the play: Hippolytus claims her crime is worse (*peior*, 689) than her mother's, the chorus claims that Fortune (especially in tragedy?) always favors the worse (*peiora*, 980), and Phaedra claims that Theseus has acted worse than a stepmother in his vengeance (*peior*, 1192).⁶⁴ This term becomes indicative of Seneca's quest to explore the depths of tragic suffering for all the characters of the play and may hint at one of the roots of the suffering: after all, *peior* is the comparative form of the adjective *malus*, and Phaedra often describes her love as a *malum*.⁶⁵

While the reference to the young Medea stresses Phaedra's passion at the start of the play, she will later be identified as a *noverca* in the tradition of the older Medea. Remember that the chorus, in singing of the power of love, saves the example of *novercae* for the conclusion of their ode, "What more can I say? Love defeats savage stepmothers" (*quid plura canam? / vincit saevas cura novercas*, 356–7). Throughout the play, Hippolytus considers stepmothers the most savage of beasts (*taceo novercas: mitius nil est feris*, 558),⁶⁶ and he uses Medea as his primary example: "Alone, the wife of Aegeus, Medea, will prove women to be a fearsome race" (*sola coniunx Aegei, / Medea, reddet feminas dirum genus*, 563–4).⁶⁷ When Phaedra admits her love to Hippolytus, he claims that her actions surpass Medea's: "This evil is greater, greater than the Colchian stepmother" (*Colchide noverca maius hoc, maius malum est*, 697).⁶⁸ After Hippolytus' death, Phaedra compares her actions as *noverca* to those of Theseus: "Listen, Athenians, and you, a father worse than a murderous stepmother" (*Audite, Athenae, tuque, funesta pater / peior noverca*, 1191–2). Although Phaedra hopes to

---

⁶³ As discussed above, Seneca provides the answer to Ovid's Medea, providing a possible rebuttal of Cupid's power (195–217).

⁶⁴ Additionally, the Nurse claims that fame is "kinder to those deserving worse, and worse for the good" (*peius merenti melior et peior bono*, 270).

⁶⁵ The use of a comparative in this fashion is reminiscent of Schiesaro's (2003) discussion (31–36, 130–31) of the *maius* motif in the *Thyestes*. If the Fury wishes to amplify the *nefas* (*maiore numero*, Thy. 57), then "any repetition of *nefas* is necessarily worse than its model—more obsessive, more painful, more 'guilty'. At the level of poetics, the repetition will encourage the exploration of a more intense and emotionally loaded language of recursive patterns and of elaborate internal echoes" (31–2). Also see Seidensticker (1985) for the *maius* motif in Senecan tragedy as a whole.

⁶⁶ Cf. Fitch (2004b) 118 for the various possible manuscript readings of this line.

⁶⁷ Cf. McAuley (2012) 56 on how Medea "functions rhetorically in *Phaedra* as a silent yet immanent presence, defining the play's moral limits, haunting its protagonists like a half-forgotten nightmare, infusing with savage irony its narrative of familial prejudice, self-delusion, and manipulation."

⁶⁸ Note his different use of the word *malum*. Hippolytus and Phaedra misunderstand each other's language throughout the play. Inspired by Hinds (2011) 23, McAuley (2012) 50 comments on this line, "This hyperbolic language is distinctively Seneca, but the alliterative associations of *maius*, maleficence, monstrosity, and motherhood also make it unmistakably *Medean*."

transcend the implications of being a stepmother, she comes to embody this dangerous stereotype as the play progresses. After she kills herself, Theseus believes he must learn from her actions: "Learn from a stepmother: bury yourself in the regions of Acheron" (*disce a noverca: condere Acherontis plagis*, 1200). In the *Metamorphoses*, Theseus escapes the plots of Medea against his life because of his father's recognition of his sword, but his son is not so lucky against a surrogate Medea. Hippolytus' sword, left behind when he fled from Phaedra, convicts him of his "guilt." Seneca describes the sword in language that mimics Ovid's account, which leads the reader to believe it is the *same* sword.[69] Therefore, Phaedra becomes a second Medea against Theseus' family, and Seneca traces her development through allusions to Ovid's *Metamorphoses*. Both the irrational passion of Medea and her role as a stepmother inform Seneca's portrait of Phaedra, and Seneca hopes to bring the mythological tradition of Medea into play in order to foreshadow the actions of his Phaedra.

If Medea acts as a model for a stepmother's behavior as well as the tendency for passion to overcome reason, Myrrha's incestuous desire for her father (*Met.* 10.298–502) provides a paradigm for Phaedra's incestuous passion and the disastrous outcome of such desire. Both Phaedra and Myrrha struggle with their passions until they are led to the brink of suicide, but, in both cases, their nurses intervene and ultimately help to broker the affair.[70] When describing the possible affair between Phaedra and Hippolytus, the Nurse asks (171–2):

> miscere **thalamos patris** et gnati apparas
> **utero**que prolem capere confusam **impio**?

> Are you preparing to mix the marriage chambers of father and son
> And to accept a confused brood in your impious womb?

While the Nurse is still speaking hypothetically, her language echoes the precise moment from Myrrha's tale when she has first left her father's bedroom (10.469–70):

---

[69] Cf. *Phd.* 899–900: *regale patriis asperum* **signis ebur** / **capulo** *refulgent, gentis Actaeae decus*, and *Met.* 7.422–3: *cum pater in* **capulo** *gladii cognovit* **eburno** / **signa** *sui generis facinusque excussit ab ore*. Segal (1986) 150–79 illustrates Seneca's dramatic use of the sword to "create a dialectic not only between acting out and repression, but also between muffled verbal effects and grandiose, shocking gestures." Hinds (2011) 6–8 takes this as the representative example of "a potent Ovidian presence within the imaginative space of Senecan drama. Tragic and intertextual repetition, mythic and poetological paternity, the problematic transfer of meaning from generation to generation."

[70] Anderson (1978) 501 points out how details from Myrrha's story are dependent on Euripides' *Hippolytus*. Seneca's transferal of the material back to tragedy can also be seen in his use of the *Heroides* of tragic figures in his plays.

plena **patris thalamis** excedit et **impia** diro
semina fert **utero** conceptaque crimina portat.

She leaves the bedroom of her father pregnant and impiously
Bears his seed in her dreadful womb, carrying away the conceived crime.

Seneca calls attention to the similarities between these tales only to outdo Ovid by stressing the confusion of the marriage chambers of father and son (*patris et gnati*).[71] In fact, later in the play, as Phaedra contemplates suicide after Hippolytus' death, she recalls this line as she asks, "Shall I seek the bedroom of my husband, made impious by such a deed?" (*coniugis **thalamos** petam / tanto **impiatos** facinore?*, 1185–6).[72] Although Myrrha's offspring will be the beautiful Adonis, the symbolic offspring of Phaedra's passion is the monster from the sea that destroys Hippolytus.[73]

Augmenting his reception of the Myrrha's story, Seneca echoes Ovid's tale of Byblis' incestuous love for her brother, Caunus (*Met*. 9.454–665). Byblis' behavior evokes that of a *scripta puella* who has misread the elegiac genre; Seneca likewise depicts Phaedra as the embodiment of certain elegiac commonplaces.[74] Byblis constructs her persona through elegiac poetry (especially through Ovid's own *Heroides*), and her "elegiac failure" results, in part, from her gender, because in elegy it is the male lover who must pursue the female beloved.[75] Ovid and Seneca both look back to *Heroides* 4 in the construction of their characters, and this connection, in addition to verbal similarities, functions to tie the two stories together. If Ovid's Byblis shows the inability of elegiac love to exist unaltered in the epic world, so Seneca's Phaedra will show a similar inability for love to exist unharmed in the tragic world.[76]

---

[71] Cf. Coffey and Mayer (1990) ad loc.: "A child of Phaedra and Hippolytus would be both stepson and grandson to Theseus (hence *confusam*)."

[72] Theseus' curse on Hippolytus also features the emphatic contrast of forms of *pater, gnatus*, and *parens* (947–8).

[73] Note that the monster's hybridity also recalls the Minotaur, the result of Pasiphae's passion. Cf. Davis (1983) 119: "In both cases indulgence in unnatural love causes the creation of a monster. Seneca uses heredity to account for one aspect of Phaedra's psychology, her predisposition to perverse lust, and to suggest that hers is a crime against nature." Note the birthing imagery surrounding the monster (*Phd*. 1019–20).

[74] Cf. Janan (1991) and Raval (2001) for more on the literary background of Ovid's Byblis. Ahl (1985) 211 remarks on the Greek pun of Byblis' name (βύβλος)for the writer and the written.

[75] Raval (2001) 306. Phaedra also attempts to take the active role of the lover in her pursuit of Hippolytus, as Littlewood (2004) 280 explains: "Her male voice, apparently awkward, reinforces her assumption of Hippolytus' role and the reversal by which she becomes the hunter and he the prey."

[76] Jenkins (2000) also makes the point that Byblis' crisis occurs when she sends the letter and it has an unsympathetic reader. It is notable that Ovid has introduced the letter to the Byblis myth, whereas other renditions have Byblis verbally confessing her desire. Similarly, Phaedra's attempts to

Byblis was possessed by a love for her brother (*Byblis Apollinei correpta cupidine fratris*, *Met.* 9.455), and is presented as a lesson that girls should only love lawfully.[77] At the inception of her passion, Byblis appears unaware of her feelings, but the customary forms of address for her brother no longer seem suitable (9. 466–7):

> iam dominum appellat, iam **nomina** sanguinis odit,
> Byblida iam mavult quam se **vocet** ille **sororem**.

> Now she calls him master, now she hates the name of brother,
> Now she prefers that he call her Byblis, and not sister.

Seneca's Phaedra also understands the power inherent in names and variant forms of address as she attempts to convince Hippolytus not to address her as his mother or stepmother. Much like Byblis, Phaedra attempts to reformulate her relationship with Hippolytus in accordance with elegiac standards through a change of title (609–12):

> matris superbum est **nomen** et nimium potens:
> nostros humilius nomen affectus decet;
> me vel **sororem**, Hippolyte, vel famulam **voca**,
> famulamque potius: omne servitium feram.

> The name of mother is haughty and too powerful;
> A more humble title befits my feelings:
> Call me sister, Hippolytus, or slave;
> Slave is better: I will bear every form of servitude.

Phaedra attempts to obfuscate her relationship with Hippolytus with a "more humble title" in order to convince him that she is a suitable erotic partner for him.[78] Seneca cleverly alludes to the Byblis story by having his Phaedra include the term "sister" (*sororem*) before changing the term of address to "slave" (*famulam*).[79] Seneca's Phaedra then positions herself as a slave to love (*omne*

---

portray herself to Hippolytus as a fitting lover will fall on unsympathetic ears—no physical letter will appear in Seneca's rendition.

[77] *Met.* 9.454: *Byblis in exemplo est, ut ament concessa puellae*. Iphis will later be described as *correpta cupidine* (9.734), which reveals the similarities of these two stories.

[78] Cf. Jakobi (1988) ad loc. for *famula* and *soror* as "female companion" or "mistress." As pointed out earlier, the use of *nimium potens* would remind the reader of the first choral song's depiction of love.

[79] The concept of *servitium amoris* is common in elegiac poetry, cf. Copley (1947) and Murgatroyd (1981). For both Byblis and Phaedra, the gender roles are reversed as they act like elegiac lovers who must "undergo punishments and…undertake duties which in real life were felt to be

servitium feram, 612), taking up the suggestion from Byblis that Caunus be her "master" (*dominus*), as well as the elegiac commonplace of *servitium amoris*. Phaedra and Byblis both anticipate that a change in name will indicate that an erotic relationship is permissible. Byblis believes it will allow them to be united (*si liceat mutato nomine iungi*, 9.487). Raval explains how Byblis hopes a change in title will assist her desire:

> The phrase *mutato nomine* explicitly articulates the connection that Byblis draws throughout the episode between the linguistic and the erotic levels. She endows language with the ability to alter her situation, believing that a change in name will remove the obstacles that prevent her from having a romantic relationship with her brother.[80]

Seneca's Phaedra hopes for a similar result. Both Ovid's Byblis and Seneca's Phaedra rely on elegiac poetry for the foundation of their self-conception. As Fitch and McElduff claim, "The persona of slave has a particularly useful ambiguity, since through it she can and does evoke established connotations of the *servitium amoris*."[81] It is her position as a slave to love or even as a lover (634, 671) that gives Phaedra the false confidence that her plan may succeed and that reveals Seneca's interrogation of elegiac topoi in his play.

Heroides 4 connects Seneca's Phaedra and Ovid's Byblis because it provides the common intertextual background to both characters as they attempt to define themselves in their longed-for relationships. Both Byblis and Phaedra feel the flames of love, both ask their beloveds to pity their love, and both follow their passions obsessively to their demise.[82] Byblis decides to write a letter explaining her desire for Caunus, like Phaedra in *Heroides* 4, whereas Seneca's Phaedra, despite her dramatic history as a letter writer (Eur. *Hipp*. 856-9), prefers to approach Hippolytus directly. The first line of Byblis' letter, "The good health which, unless you grant it, she will not have" (**quam, nisi tu dederis,** non est habi-

---

peculiar to the slave alone" (Copley (1947), 285). Note that the chorus tells of Apollo's servitude to Admetus because of love (296-8), which was the locus classicus for the idea of *servitium amoris* in Tibullus (2.3.11-30).

[80] Raval (2001) 294. Also cf. Segal (1986) 158: "Phaedra must break down the name of 'mother' and replace it with the language of erotic passion. The first step in her seduction, then, is a linguistic transformation. This in turn displays her passion in contrasting registers of language. She speaks with the authority of the Roman *matrona* in her *domus*, but she also uses the words that one would expect to find in the demi-monde of Roman elegy."

[81] Fitch and McElduff (2002) 32.

[82] The fiery nature of passion is an erotic commonplace (*Phd*. 103-4, 188-94, 641-4; *Met*. 9. 464-5, 541); Seneca especially stresses the pity that may help aid the love affair (*Phd*. 623, 636, 671: *miserere amantis*), but Ovid's Byblis also hopes it will be effective (*Met*. 9.561: *miserere fatentis amorem*). Byblis follows (*sequitur*, 9.640) Caunus until she is transformed into a fountain.

tura **salutem**, 9.530), strongly mimics the opening of Phaedra's *Heroides*, "The good health which, unless you grant it, she will lack" (***quam nisi tu dederis**, caritura **est** ipsa, **salutem**,* 4.1). Ovid's elegiac representation of Phaedra in *Heroides* 4 presents a paradigm for the incestuous desires of Ovid's Byblis and Seneca's Phaedra, but the epistle proves ineffective for Byblis. Although Ovid skips over the details of the face-to-face confrontation between Byblis and Caunus (9.631–4), Seneca dramatizes the confrontation in a form replete with echoes of the *Metamorphoses* and *Heroides* 4 (see below).

The intertextual ties between Ovid and Seneca continue to stress the link between language and lawful relationship. Byblis believes that her familial relationship with her brother will disguise any erotic relationship—"We will conceal our hidden joys by the name of brother" (*dulcia fraterno sub **nomine** furta **tegemus**,* 9.558)—an idea that she discovered in *Heroides* 4: "Blame can be concealed by our familial name" (*cognato poterit **nomine** culpa **tegi**,* 138). Seneca's Nurse likewise believes Phaedra may hide her crime by means of a cunning trick: "Let us suppose we conceal the crime through trickery" (*credamus tamen / astu doloque **tegere** nos tantum nefas,* 152–3)—but the play reveals the futility of such attempts.[83] Both Byblis' and Phaedra's epistles are unable to convince their beloveds, and Seneca's tragedy points out the impossibility of hiding such a *nefas*, no matter how clever your language may be. When Byblis' letter fails, Byblis believes it is because of the medium, not the message. She figures that she should have spoken to Caunus (9.586–9):

> quid, quae celanda fuerunt,
> tam cito commisi properatis **verba** tabellis?
> ante erat **ambiguis** animi sententia dictis
> praetemptanda mihi.
>
> Why did I so quickly write down on hurried tablets
> Words that should have been hidden?
> First I should have tested his opinion about me
> With ambiguous statements.

What Byblis imagines to have been the problem becomes the reality in Seneca's *Phaedra*. When Phaedra accosts Hippolytus, he complains about her vague language (full of elegiac commonplaces and double entendres): "You utter ambiguous words with a muddled voice; speak openly" (***ambigua** voce **verba** perplexa*

---

[83] The concealment of desire or crime is found throughout *Phaedra* ("Although it may be concealed, her madness is betrayed by her face," *quamvis **tegatur**, proditur vultu furor,* 363; "Your twisted words conceal some great matter," *perplexa magnum verba nescioquid **tegunt**,* 858).

iacis: / effare aperte, 639–40). After Phaedra finally reveals her love for him, Hippolytus claims that her crime is even worse than Pasiphae's, figuring the Minotaur in language now conspicuous for its intertextual and intratextual ties as a "ambiguous offspring" (***ambiguus** infans*, 693).[84] Seneca stages the violent results of Byblis' hoped-for meeting to show that obscure language will not help Phaedra's attempted seduction, but will instead cause more trouble.

Seneca follows Ovid's tales of Byblis and Phaedra in order to further define his Phaedra as an elegiac lover and to show the self-deception implicit in elegiac language. Like Byblis, Phaedra's love will fail and her pursuit will be in vain, but, in addition, Phaedra's desire causes the deaths of both Hippolytus and herself. The grave consequences of her obsessive passion and her instable self-fashioning reveal Seneca's larger dramatic interests. He chooses moments from his intertextual models that he can dramatize or embellish (often through repeating the language in the larger context of his *Phaedra*). In addition, the metaphors and imagery of elegiac poetry are realized in Seneca's *Phaedra* in a concrete manner that exposes the distance between elegy and tragedy. For example, Phaedra's fiery passion leads directly to the fires of the Underworld, as Phaedra states, "I will follow you madly through rivers of fire" (*per amnes igneos amens sequar*, 1180). Seneca's Phaedra hopes to be considered Hippolytus' slave and to be protected in his arms (***sinu** receptam supplicem ac servam tege*, 621), but her desire will help to produce the monster from the deep (*nescioquid onerato **sinu** / gravis unda portat*, 1019–20), and she will only be accepted into the arms of death at the close of the play (*confugimus ad te: pande placatos **sinus***, 1190). Vernant and Vidal-Naquet comment that this ambiguity of language defines tragic discourse: "The irony of the tragedy may consist in showing how, in the course of the action, the hero finds himself literally 'taken at his word,' a word that recoils against him, bringing him bitter experience of the meaning he was determined not to recognize."[85] Seneca consistently probes the alternative meanings of Phaedra's erotic language that stress the concrete pain and suffering that will impact every member of the royal household resulting from her desire. No longer are the elegiac tropes merely figurative; Seneca reveals the harrowing reality of such language in this play.

Hero(id)es and Villains

When Phaedra finally confronts Hippolytus, Seneca stresses the similarities to *Heroides* 4 only to surpass the scope of that letter and enact the conflict that results from Phaedra's admission of love. The correspondences between Ovid's

---

[84] Forms of *ambiguus* appear also at *Phd.* 840 and 1141.
[85] Vernant and Vidal-Naquet (1988) 114.

work and Seneca's have been noted and are so numerous that the Cambridge commentary on Seneca's *Phaedra* includes the text of *Heroides* 4 as an appendix.[86] While Ovid plays with the generic ramifications of taking a tragic heroine and placing her in an elegiac and epistolary world, now Seneca brings this elegiac Phaedra back into the tragic realm. Phaedra's epistolary proposal to Hippolytus focuses attention on her self-representation as an available and willing erotic partner who attempts to persuade him to begin an affair.[87] Ovid's Phaedra sheds the customary roles for women in society (mother, wife, daughter) and tries to take on the active role of a lover seeking a new liaison.[88] Many of the characteristics of Seneca's Phaedra are prefigured in Ovid's poem, including her struggle between *pudor* and *furor*, her desire to mimic Hippolytus' hunting behavior, her belief that her family was cursed by Venus, and her hope that Hippolytus will be sympathetic to her appeal.[89] Ovid influences Seneca's work by giving an elegiac vocabulary to Phaedra's passion and suggesting imagery that Seneca develops in the course of his tragedy. For Seneca, *Heroides* 4 provides a snapshot of Phaedra's present mental state, but he wishes to stage her proposal and the consequent suffering in his tragedy.[90] While any reader of Seneca's play would expect a letter to play some part in the action, Seneca surprises the audience by showing Phaedra's direct proposal to Hippolytus and her subsequent ambiguous "confession" to Theseus.[91] Seneca, in a sense, provides the letter that the reader expects through his intertextual references to *Heroides* 4. His intertexts with this poem at the pivotal moment of the tragedy endorse Ovid's elegiac representation of Phaedra while indicating the generic limits of that representation.[92]

---

[86] Coffey and Mayer (1990), Grimal (1963), Jakobi (1988), DeVito (1994), and Littlewood (2004) 269–301 passim call attention to the allusive relationship between the two texts.

[87] In utilizing a letter to propose a relationship, Ovid's Phaedra follows the precepts of Ovid's *A.A.* 1.437–40. Cf. Knox (1995) 25 for more on the similarities.

[88] Seneca's Phaedra likewise gives up her traditional familial and societal roles (*Phd.* 103–9).

[89] For *pudor* and *furor* cf. *Her.* 4.9, 51, 155 and Henry and Walker (1966) 223–8 for the importance of these concepts in Seneca's *Phaedra*; for hunting mimicry cf. *Her.* 4.37–8, 43–6, 78–83 and *Phd.* 110–2, 394–404, 699–702; for Venus' curse on the family cf. *Her.* 4.54–66 and *Phd.* 124–8; for compassion cf. *Her.* 4.165–76 and *Phd.* 623, 636, 671. Cf. Armstrong (2006) for more on the parallels.

[90] In staging the proposal of the affair, Seneca may be following Euripides' first Hippolytus play, cf. W. S. Barrett (1964) 11–2.

[91] Cf. *Her.* 4.3–6 and Fulkerson (2005) 140: "As the external reader knows, Phaedra habitually writes letters." While the Euripidean Phaedra's letter falsely accuses Hippolytus of rape, Seneca's Phaedra utters indefinite statements because "it seems most likely that she is ashamed to utter outright falsehoods. At least she can salvage for herself the appearance of honour, even if she cannot possess its substance" (Davis (1983) 123).

[92] Cf. DeVito (1994) 329: "If Seneca did pattern Phaedra's confession of love on Ovid alone, it would be almost impossible to believe that he considered *Heroides* 4 to be anything other than a poem showing just what he wished to show in his play, the tragedy of a woman's subjugation to love's power."

Intertextuality and Character 89

In the third act, Phaedra and Hippolytus finally meet, and intertextual references to *Heroides* 4 expose how Seneca wishes to elaborate Ovid's portrayal of the relationship. Hippolytus has just denounced all women and shown the intransigence of his misogyny.[93] Phaedra, having fainted, revives in Hippolytus' arms and steels herself to the task of seducing him.[94] Coffey and Mayer comment on the creative manner in which Seneca uses Ovidian material as his Phaedra describes her desire in language reminiscent of *Heroides* 4:

> S[eneca] has composed an adroit speech for his heroine in which the dangerous issue of sexual desire is neatly hinted at behind a veil of comparisons and allusions. He has moreover successfully indulged his taste for literary rivalry (*aemulatio*) in going a step further than Ovid, whose Phaedra could not address Hippolytus directly but had to write a letter instead (*Her.* 4.7–10).[95]

The interaction between Phaedra and Hippolytus displays the extent of Phaedra's passion (*malum*, 637), and the false hope (*spes*, 634) that love can produce.[96] Phaedra claims that Hippolytus' physical beauty overwhelms her, and reminds her of Theseus' former good looks: "One house has seized two sisters" (***domus** sorores **una** corripuit **duas***, 665). This line restates an identical claim in the *Heroides*, "One home pleased the two of us, your beauty captured me, my sister was taken with your father" (*placuit **domus una duabus**; / me tua forma capit, capta parente soror*, 4.63–4). Phaedra ties her desire once again into her family line (this time Ariadne acts as the exemplum), while also portraying Hippolytus as a second (new and improved) Theseus.[97] This furthers her belief, remarked upon previously, that her passion is somehow destined because Seneca now points to similarities between the sisters Ariadne and Phaedra. The beauty (*forma*) of Hippolytus is stressed throughout the play as being particular to Hippolytus (743), but an untrustworthy boon (761–3). It ultimately becomes a concrete reminder of his destruction when Theseus looks to replace a part of

---

[93] *Phd.* 578–9: *solamen unum matris amissae fero, / odisse quod iam feminas omnes licet* ("I have one consolation for the death of my mother: / now it is possible for me to hate all women.").

[94] *Phd.* 592–9.

[95] Coffey and Mayer (1990) ad loc.

[96] Which reminds the reader of the previous use of the term *malum* above pp. 69–70.

[97] Cf. Fulkerson (2005) 122–42. She traces the influence of Ovid's Ariadne (*Her.* 10) on Phaedra (*Her.* 4) in order to defend Phaedra's belief that she has been abandoned and to show Ariadne as "the spokeswoman for deserted women." Davis (1983) 199 remarks on the Hippolytus/Theseus comparison, "In falling in love with her stepson Phaedra is falling in love with a more perfect version of her husband."

Hippolytus' dismembered corpse and pauses on a piece "foul and lacking in beauty" (*forma carens / et turpe*, 1265–6). While the *forma* of Hippolytus is static in the epistolary context, Seneca's drama can modify how exactly Hippolytus' *forma* disintegrates in the course of the play.

Seneca's Phaedra elaborates upon Hippolytus' beauty by comparing him to his father: "How that man gleamed! The fillets pressed his hair and a golden modesty tinged his tender cheeks" (*quis tum ille fulsit! presserant vittae comam / et **ora flavus** tenera **tinguebat** pudor*, 651–2). This resembles the Ovidian Phaedra's comments about Hippolytus: "Your garments were white, your hair encircled with flowers, a shy ruddiness tinged your golden face" (*candida vestis erat, praecincti flore capilli, / flava verecundus **tinxerat ora** rubor*, 4.71–2).[98] Seneca's Phaedra illustrates Hippolytus' beauty through mention of his father, and this description shows how an intertextual reference can entwine the familial connections even more tightly. Seneca's Hippolytus resembles a young Theseus, but that Theseus resembles the Hippolytus of *Heroides* 4! Armstrong notes how this identification "is thus given astonishing intensity. Phaedra's self-examination, her recognition of patterns, has resulted in an extreme form of self-delusion which collapses in on itself in a tangle of paradox: the virginal non-virgin makes a speech of undisguised erotic passion destined never to be consummated."[99] The attraction felt can quickly move from father to son as similar language equates their comeliness and leads to this one house ruining the two sisters of the House of Minos. Predictably for Seneca's intratextual tragedies, it is Hippolytus' beautiful face (intertextually marked) that bears the brunt of his punishment, as he falls "headlong on his face" (*praeceps in **ora** fusus*, 1085).

These descriptions are clearly marked as intertextual through the repetition of language and the similar subject matter. At this point in Seneca's play, one may expect to find a large number of references to Ovid's *Heroides* 4, because this is the moment in which Phaedra attempts to seduce Hippolytus. In fact, nearly every line recycles language from *Heroides* 4, which points to the almost inevitable nature of Phaedra's passion and the sense that Seneca wants to explore the generic implications of placing Ovid's Phaedra into this tragic world.[100] Seneca continues to problematize Ovid's version when Seneca's Phaedra ends her first proposition by falling dramatically to her knees (665–8):

En **supplex** iacet
adlapsa **genibus** regiae proles domus.

---

[98] It is notable that the beauty of Hippolytus and a young Theseus is now absent in the love-struck Phaedra, who has "no purple blush tingeing her shining face" (*non **ora tinguens** nitida purpureus **rubor***, Phd. 376).

[99] Armstrong (2006) 291.

[100] Jakobi (1988) and Coffey and Mayer (1990) list the copious parallels.

respersa nulla **labe** et intacta, innocens
tibi **mutor** uni. certa descendi ad **preces**.

        Lo, she lies as your suppliant,
Fallen on her knees, the offspring of a royal house.
Stained by no blemish and pure, innocent
I am changed by you alone. Resolute I have lowered myself to prayer.

At this moment, Seneca's Phaedra enacts the imagined scene that Ovid's Phaedra wrote in her epistle: "I am not ashamed to get on my knees and pray.... Defeated, I pray and stretch my royal arms around your knees" (*non ego dedignor **supplex** humilisque **precari**.... victa **precor genibus**que tuis regalia tendo / bracchia*, Her. 4.149, 153–4). Seneca puts into action the claims issued in Ovid's letter in order to show how the "real" situation would play out with Hippolytus present. Phaedra acts as a suppliant to Hippolytus, although the sympathy she hopes for in *Heroides* 4 is turned upside down when Hippolytus draws his sword to sacrifice Phaedra to the goddess Diana.[101] In addition, this passage reveals that Seneca's Phaedra is concerned with her quasi-virginal reputation, which Ovid's Phaedra also stresses ("If my purity has to be marked by unknown blot..." *candor ab insolita **labe** notandus erat*, Her. 4.32). Seneca's Phaedra strongly claims that she changes for Hippolytus alone (*tibi mutor uni*), and Ovid's Phaedra had previously marked her desire to pursue hunting in similar terms ("I am changing to unknown pursuits," *ignotas **mutor** in artes*, Her. 4.37).[102] At this dramatic highpoint, Seneca has incorporated *Heroides* 4 in order to show the transformation that Phaedra has undergone in the course of the play. She has imperiled her regal position, become similar to an elegiac hunter, and compromised her reputation.[103] Seneca's *Phaedra* both endorses the elegiac portrait of Phaedra found in *Heroides* 4 and vividly depicts the destruction that it can cause by staging what happens next (an action that cannot be depicted in the *Heroides*) and recasting key terms in a negative manner throughout the play.

When Hippolytus rejects Phaedra's overture, Phaedra finds herself in a position common to those in her family. Her continual identification with the elegiac portraits of her mother and sister leads to her personal definition. The pride that she felt at the start of the play has been tempered by the recognition of the sins of the house. After Hippolytus denounces her as an evil worse than Medea (*Colchide noverca maius hoc, maius malum est*, 697), Phaedra responds (698–9, 703):

---

[101] Phd. 704–9.

[102] This is the only time this form of *muto -are* is used in all of Senecan tragedy and all of Ovid's *Heroides*.

[103] Cf. Littlewood (2004) 263: "Phaedra and the nurse have both articulated the plot against him through the inversion and erotic contamination of the rhetoric of the hunt: Phaedra plays a huntress and an Amazon in whose erotic pursuit the virgin hunter becomes prey."

> et ipsa nostrae fata cognosco domus:
> fugienda petimus; sed mei non sum potens....
> iterum, superbe, **genibus** advolvor **tuis**.

> And I recognize the fate of our house:
> We seek what ought to be avoided; but I am not in control of myself....
> Again, arrogant one, I fall prostrate before your knees.

As her mother desired the bull, as Ariadne followed Theseus, so Phaedra commits herself to an unattainable passion. She assumes the position that Ovid's Phaedra pictures in her letter, stretching out her arms around the knees of Hippolytus for a second time (***genibus**que **tuis**, Her.* 4.153). The words that could only be written and the actions that must be imagined in Ovid's letter are revealed not only to displease Hippolytus but also to lead to the deaths of both characters. These intertextual examples show the clear reliance of Seneca on Ovid's *Heroides* 4, but what exactly was he aiming to do in his appropriation of Ovid's Phaedra? Seneca places an elegiac representation of the protagonist into his tragedy in order to point out how tragedy can both incorporate and question the version presented in Ovid's work. The polyvalent viewpoints of tragedy expose the problems inherent in the monologic and self-absorbed perspective of elegy. If love orders, it would appear that one must follow and change accordingly (*Phd.* 354 ~ *Her.* 4.9–10), but such transformations not only affect the individual, they affect the world as well. So Phaedra may follow Hippolytus in an elegiac hunt, but he is truly hunted by the monster of the sea (*sequitur adsiduus comes*, 1077)—just one of many examples of the way Seneca makes concrete the tropes of elegiac poetry. Seneca's dense intratextual repetitions underline how the language from these intertexts continues to influence the action of the play. Seneca shows the far-reaching results of Phaedra's desire as it touches each of the characters of the play.[104]

While love often motivates the transformation of gods and heroes in Ovid's *Metamorphoses*, Seneca offers a more human depiction of Phaedra's shifts in persona, even as monsters of Ovidian pedigree loom on the horizon.[105] Despite her attempts to create a respectable self-image, her identification with honorable

---

[104] Cf. Mastronarde (2010) 26 on tragedy's ability to evaluate from various perspectives: "Drama is inherently a multivocal representation, and none of the voices in it have absolute authority, transparency, or reliability for an audience in its efforts to interpret what it sees and hears. Tragedies may present important areas of ambivalence, impasse, or open-endedness in their scrutiny of psychological, ethical, and social issues."

[105] This is also the subject of the choral ode discussed above. Note the *minores...formas* that the gods assume (*Phd.* 299). For more on the monster from the sea as an example of generic and intertextual *contaminatio*, cf. Chap. 3.

familial figures is unable to stand up against her passion.[106] The intertexts suggest the difficulties in Phaedra's situation because the elegiac and epic exempla stress the motivation for violence, upheaval, and, ultimately, her suicide. All of these characters (and genres) help to show the difficulty of maintaining a single self-representation under emotional duress. The generic differences between epic and tragedy or elegy and tragedy are put on display when Seneca exploits the language of elegiac lovers or Ovidian characters from the *Metamorphoses* and employs them in his development of Phaedra's character. If Ovid's epic world is one defined by "forms changed into new bodies" (*in nova... mutatas dicere formas / corpora*, *Met.* 1.1–2), Seneca displays his interest in the problems that arise from the multiple forms that each of us assumes (*multiformes sumus*, *Ep.* 120.22). His Phaedra becomes the culmination of various traditions of incestuous love (Myrrha, Byblis), uncontrollable passion (Medea, echoes of *Amores*), and hereditary misfortunes (Pasiphae, Ariadne). These intertexts increase our sympathy for Phaedra because they emphasize that passion is uncontrollable and has laid low many a heroine preceding Phaedra. By combining their stories in his characterization of Phaedra, Seneca works to underscore her passion as something both *greater* and *worse* than these Ovidian antecedents and to assert that tragedy is the appropriate genre for considering the results of Phaedra's love.

Seneca's *Medea*

Seneca developed the character of Medea, in part, through her previous manifestations in the works of Euripides, Apollonius, and Ovid. Seneca does not merely parrot previous accounts but presents a complex figure that vacillates between the emotional fragility of a young girl in love, the superhuman power of a witch (granddaughter of the sun), and the anxious concerns of a mother.[107] His play, in some sense, is about Medea's self-discovery, and how Medea comes to terms with the various facets of her character. Medea rehearses various roles in the course of the drama, and her journey through different roles mimics the position of Seneca rewriting prior accounts.[108] The Ovidian material is the most influential intertextual model on which Seneca draws, and one can map certain roles (wife, mother, witch) onto moments of the *Heroides* and *Metamorphoses* in

---

[106] Of course her family provides both positive and negative examples of behavior.

[107] These roles were highlighted in the preceding works (e.g., Apollonius' Medea as, primarily, the young girl in love).

[108] This is not to say that earlier accounts were static in their treatment of Medea. Graf (1997) 25 comments on Apollonius' Medea: "Apollonius had to take pains to ease the tensions between the maidenly—and impossibly infatuated—Medea that he wanted to present and another Medea, already familiar to his readers, who was skilled in magic and a priestess of Hecate."

order to show how Seneca has interpreted this material and made use of it in his tragedy.[109]

Ovid's only tragedy, *Medea*, has been lost, but his other accounts of Medea (*Heroides* 6 and 12, *Metamorphoses* 7.1–424) provide distinctive views of her.[110] In the *Heroides*, Medea is both the powerful "other woman" about whom Hypsipyle complains and the caring mother who muses upon her past love for Jason while the wedding procession of Creusa passes.[111] In the *Metamorphoses*, Ovid gives us a varied portrait of Medea, but he focuses primarily on her magical skills and ability to change the world. Seneca's play reacts to these Ovidian accounts—his Medea accepts or rejects certain roles (and genres) in the play before she fully develops into the complex semidivine heroine at the tragedy's conclusion. The other characters attempt to control and define Medea, whether by hoping she will just disappear (the first chorus) or trying to bribe her (Jason), but Medea dominates the action and controls the plot. Seneca's Medea worries about her self-representation, and her violent moods lead her to question her relationship with Jason and the actions performed on his behalf. At certain moments she hopes to rekindle her love for Jason and wishes to strengthen their marriage tie. No longer a princess, no longer a wife, now a mother with no access to her children, a foreigner denied refuge: How will Medea handle this new situation? Of course, the reader knows the tragedy that springs from Medea's stay in Corinth, but Seneca's version of events reflects his own vision of Medea's character. At the conclusion of the play, Medea's guilt for her brother's murder and her betrayal of her father contribute to her bloody exit, but it is primarily her love for Jason, now curdled into black hate, that leads to her tragic departure.

Critics have often commented on the intertextual background of Medea in Seneca's play, and Wilamowitz famously claimed, "This Medea has read Euripides."[112] Seneca's Medea betrays knowledge of the actions she has performed in the pages of Ovid and Euripides and even aims to improve upon her past crimes. The "role" she is playing is defined by previous literary accounts, but as the play unfolds Seneca makes Medea into a quasi-author of the plot and active compiler of the texts she wishes to enact. Metapoetic language reveals her transcendence into a semidivine dramaturge, possibly standing in for Seneca himself.

---

[109] Cf. Guastella (2001) for a similar interpretation of the *Medea* without as much attention paid to the intricacies of these intertexts, but with an eye to the model of revenge found in *De Ira*. Trinacty (2007) focuses exclusively on the role of the *Heroides*.

[110] Seneca alludes to each of the two surviving lines of Ovid's *Medea*, which makes one wonder how many more undetectable allusions there must be.

[111] These two dissimilar roles in the *Heroides* are predicated on the different writers of the letters (Medea herself and Hypsipyle). In *Her*. 6, Hypsipyle views Medea as a threat to her relationship with Jason, while Medea portrays herself as a good mother and wife who has been wronged in *Her*. 12.

[112] Wilamowitz-Moellendorff (1919) 3:162.

Before discussing the play as a whole, I will briefly examine Medea's character in Ovid's *Heroides* and *Metamorphoses* and show how Ovid creates different roles for Medea in these works. I will then turn to Seneca's *Medea* and examine three roles that Medea assumes in Seneca's play—mother, wife, and witch—before discussing their resolution in the final act.[113] Each of these roles recalls passages from the *Heroides* and *Metamorphoses*, and Seneca's interplay with Ovid helps to further characterize Medea as a tragic amalgam of these Ovidian works. Each role also involves a critique of Ovid's poetry; Seneca's language and imagery point out the differences between the tragic genre and Ovid's genres, and this metaliterary dimension shows how Seneca constructs his characters and the plot with a view to supplementing these Ovidian Medeas.

Ovid's Medea: The *Metamorphoses* and *Heroides*

When Ovid treats the myth of Medea in the *Metamorphoses* (7.1–424), he coolly passes over the tragic events in Corinth in a mere four lines (394–7), focusing instead on Medea's initial passion for Jason, the power of her magic to effect good (Aeson) and evil (Pelias), and her travels around Greece. Ovid's account vies with Apollonius' description of Medea as a young girl in love (1–158) before turning to her magical exploits (159–349).[114] In the latter section, Ovid focuses on Medea as witch, and he delights in describing the preparations for, and results of, her sorcery. When Seneca alludes to the Medea of the *Metamorphoses*, his references evoke particular moments of Medea's life from Ovid's epic (e.g., young girl in love, full-grown witch). Because Ovid's *Metamorphoses* recounts multiple stories narrated in multiple manners and generic registers, one cannot impose a single "epic" way of regarding Seneca's adoption of Ovidian material.[115] Seneca uses Ovid's *Metamorphoses* for depictions of Medea that he can broadly confirm or reject in his tragedy. In the fourth act (670–848), Seneca composes an incantation scene inspired by Ovid's *Metamorphoses* (7.159–349) in order to show continuity with Ovid's depiction of Medea as witch. This scene is absent from Euripides' *Medea*, who stresses Medea's humanity throughout his play, and it allows Seneca to develop the superhuman powers of Medea. Seneca exaggerates Medea's characterization as a witch

---

[113] Under the role of "wife," I place Medea's memories of her youthful love for Jason, which is the foundation of their marriage, and the wedding imagery found in Seneca's play.

[114] Cf. Ap. Rhod. *Argon.* 3 passim.

[115] Cf. Hinds (1992) 82 on the *Metamorphoses*: "Broadly speaking, two things characterize the Augustan poet's approach to genre: an abiding concern for the traditional, stereotyped boundaries of a genre; and, in tension with this, a strong interest in testing and going beyond those boundaries—which are, however, retained as the theoretical norm against which any experimentation is measured."

in order to show her active control of the dramatic situation. Her magical ability allows her to become a stand-in for the playwright himself as she creates or destroys the world of the play. The metapoetic implications of Medea's magical ability were also hinted at in the *Metamorphoses*, as Liveley comments: "Close reading suggests that Medea undergoes a secondary and more complex metamorphosis in identity, transformed from witch to poet.... Medea's words and spells (*verbis et carmine*—7.203) here reflect Ovid's own transformative poetics."[116] Whereas transformation is stressed in the *Metamorphoses*, in Seneca's play the magic is used purely for destruction, hinting at one of the major generic differences between the two versions of Medea.

We see a much different characterization of Medea in Ovid's *Heroides* from that in the *Metamorphoses*. Here, Ovid is interested in exploring scenarios and actions that are not part of the traditional literary accounts of Medea (and Hypsipyle), which gain rhetorical point and literary poignancy through their relationships with previous literature. While Hypsipyle (in *Heroides* 6) describes Medea as a barbarian witch who has enchanted her rightful husband, the Medea of *Heroides* 12 sounds much like Hypsipyle herself, a woman lamenting the loss of her husband. Both women try to convince Jason to return to them, and both offer similar arguments based on children, loyalty, and love in their self-presentation as wronged wives and abandoned lovers. Medea and Hypsipyle bemoan their positions, and their complaints focus on the Jason they once knew and with whom they fell in love.[117] Both *Heroides* reveal the powerful deeds that Medea has performed in the past and retell these events through an elegiac perspective. In *Heroides* 12, Medea laments that she has betrayed her family and country for a man who leaves her despite the acts done on her behalf. For Hypsipyle, her rival must possess supernatural powers to keep Jason away.[118] Both Verducci and Lindheim stress that Hypsipyle becomes more Medea-like over the course of her epistle.[119] Seneca notices this progression as well, and his Medea assumes and manipulates the language of both Ovid's Hypsipyle and Medea. These *Heroides* are two of the building blocks of Seneca's *Medea* and allow Seneca to give nuanced information about the love that his Medea felt for Jason almost in shorthand. As language from these elegiac epistles reappears in Seneca's tragedy,

---

[116] Liveley (2011) 78.

[117] Cf. Hinds (1993) 28 for his discussion of similar language in the two *Heroides* and its indication that "it is always the same story with Jason and his women." The *Heroides* as a whole highlight that elegy is the fitting poetry of lament; cf. Knox (1995) 281.

[118] Despite Hypsipyle's assurance, Prince (2003) points out the inefficacy of love magic in elegy.

[119] Verducci (1985) 65–6 reads this as Hypsipyle dissolving her bourgeois and conservative self-representation into her inner Medea, while Lindheim (2003) 123–35 finds that Hypsipyle mimics Medea to supplant her as Jason's "eternal object of desire." Cf. the use of *credula / credulitatis* at *Her.* 6.21 and *Her.* 12.119–20.

the reader recalls the full context of the source text. As in the *Phaedra*, the effect of reintroducing this tragic heroine into the genre in which she had originally been inscribed is striking.[120] There are subtle changes in characterization due to the Ovidian contexts (and genres), and these changes ultimately allow Seneca to comment on the generic differences between the worlds of the *Heroides* and his tragedy.

Seneca's Medea: Mother and Wife
(Love and Marriage)

Let us now return to Seneca's *Medea*. Seneca stresses the different roles Medea assumes in the play and how these personae influence Medea's actions.[121] Medea questions her place in society and her relationship with Jason throughout much of the play until, taking advantage of her supernatural powers, she finally destroys her rival, murders her children, and escapes Corinth. Medea's different personae correspond generally to her love and anger, emotions whose power and violence are stressed throughout the play and can be broadly mapped onto the *Heroides* and *Metamorphoses*.[122] The intertextual relationship between Seneca and Ovid adds depth and motivation to these roles of Medea, and Seneca defines his tragic Medea as the culmination of Ovid's elegiac and epic Medeas.

In the first act, Medea stresses her position as spurned wife and mother, indicating the two roles that derive from her relationship with Jason. In her self-definition as Jason's wife, Medea cannot believe he has essentially divorced her with his recent marriage to Creusa. Seneca relies on the reader's recollection of Ovid's *Heroides* to understand Medea's former love for Jason, and the elegiac genre highlights the passion she once felt for Jason. In addition, the *Heroides* offer a view of the relationship from the heroine's own perspective; after all, it is Medea and Hypsipyle who compose their letters. Seneca's Medea, however, fulfills the threats of Ovid's heroine and, in doing so, points out how quickly and completely love can turn to hate and thus how her story can be transformed from an elegy to a tragedy.

When Medea emerges on stage, she is already plotting revenge, even if she is unsure what it will entail. Medea presents herself as a wronged mother in addition to a betrayed wife. Seneca applies maternal language and imagery to Medea

---

[120] Hinds (1993) 39 points out the opposite correlative: "Medea, the tragic heroine par excellence, enters a collection of elegiac epistles, but she does not come quietly: her tragic identity is not suppressed, but rather is set in productive tension with her new epistolary environment."

[121] Cf. Bartsch (2006) 255–81 for more on Medea's personae from a Stoic point of view.

[122] Cf. *Med*. 867–70: *frenare nescit* **iras** */ Medea, non* **amores**; */ nunc* **ira amor**que *causam / iunxere: quid sequetur?* ("Medea does not know how to control her anger, nor her love; / now anger and love have joined causes: What will follow?").

in order to adumbrate the eventual murder of her children as well as to indicate her need to transcend previous roles. Medea wants to harm her enemies, and her language foreshadows even more destructive behavior (23–6):

> me coniugem optet, quoque non aliud queam
> peius precari, liberos similes patri
> similesque **matri** – **parta** iam, **parta** ultio est:
> **peperi**. Querelas verbaque in cassum sero?

> May he long for me as his wife, and (I can think
> Of no worse curse) children resembling their father and mother.
> My revenge is born, it is already born: I have given birth.
> Do I compose complaints and speeches in vain?

This passage contains many verbal clues to a vengeance that will involve Medea's children.[123] By claiming "My revenge is born," Medea seems to point to the infanticide that concludes the play. This play on language also appears in *Heroides* 12 and establishes a connection between Seneca's Medea and Ovid's. At the conclusion of that poem, Ovid's Medea knows that Jason has agreed to marry Creusa and therefore has lost everything. She contemplates revenge and claims, "My anger labors over great threats" (*ingentis* **parturit** *ira minas*, 208).[124] In Seneca's play, Medea's speech indicates a connection between motherhood and revenge, and words such as *pario* (25, 26, 50, 55) and *gravior* (49) emphasize this parallel.[125] Medea's logic requires that she perform greater crimes as she grows older (48–50):

> levia memoravi nimis:
> **haec virgo feci**; gravior exurgat dolor:
> maiora iam me scelera post **partus** decent.

> I have recalled things too light:
> I did these things as a girl; a heavier bitterness arises:
> Now greater crimes are fitting after I have given birth.

---

[123] Both Ovid's Medea and his Hypsipyle comment on the resemblance of their children to Jason in their respective *Heroides* (*Her.* 6.124–5; *Her.* 12.189–90).

[124] Cf. *Her.* 12.188 where Medea worries that "a savage stepmother will rage against my children" (*saeviet in partus dira noverca meos*); note the use of *partus*. Hinds (1993) 41 points out that the *ingentis…minas* implies "by an etymologizing suggestion found several times elsewhere in Latin poetry, threats abiding in Medea's own 'generative' powers, threats within and against her own '*gens*.'" I would add that Seneca connects this further to Medea's inborn quality when Medea claims, "Now I am Medea; my genius has grown through my evils" (*Medea nunc sum; crevit* **ingen**ium *malis*, 910).

[125] The metapoetics of birthing language can also be seen in the possible echo of Horace's *Ars* 139: ***parturient*** *montes, nascetur ridiculus mus* ("The mountains will labor, and a laughable mouse will be born").

The deeds she accomplished as a girl will not suffice. Her language points to her new roles as Jason's wife and mother of his children, but now she wishes to redefine these roles. Seneca's Medea highlights the correspondence between her position in Jason's home and her upcoming departure: "The house was gained by crime, it must be left by crime" (*quae scelere **parta** est, scelere linquenda est domus*, 55). Thus Medea tinges her language with a darker meaning as motherhood and birth are linked with future crime.

This language also helps the reader understand the position of Seneca's tragedy and its relationship with elegy. Medea's need to improve upon deeds that she once accomplished, and her contemplation of greater actions than she has attempted before prefigures the tragic events that will ensue. At the conclusion of *Heroides* 12, Ovid's Medea writes, "My mind surely plots something greater" (*nescio quid certe mens mea **maius** agit*, 12.214), and this claim foreshadows the tragedy that will result from her feelings of desertion and anger. Barchiesi comments on this passage, "Medea is suggesting that a new poetic kind is called for: she could not write a letter about her 'greater' actions, and this material, unspeakable for elegiacs, is reserved to the heights of a *cothurnata*."[126] Here, one is reminded of *Amores* 3.1, in which a personified Elegy and Tragedy quarrel over Ovid's services as poet, and of Tragedy's urge to Ovid (23–4),

> tempus erat, thyrso pulsum **graviore** moveri;
> cessatum satis est—incipe **maius** opus!

> It is time that you were moved by the stroke of a greater thyrsus;
> You have wasted enough time—begin a greater work.[127]

Seneca picks up on this language of "generic ascent" in his tragedy, and Medea strives throughout the work to perform "greater" crimes and transcend her previous Ovidian representations.[128]

---

[126] Barchiesi (1993) 345. Earlier in *Heroides* 12, Medea claims that when she entreats Jason she uses words "too humble for her spirited soul" (*nunc animis audi verba **minora** meis*, 12.184). In Seneca's play, her language and actions will soon become greater (*maior*) and fit her soul and character.

[127] Cf. Similar uses of *maius* to indicate poetic escalation at Virg. *Ecl.* 4.1, Prop. 2.34.65–6, Sen. *Thy.* 267.

[128] Cf. S. J. Harrison (2002) for the term "generic ascent," which signifies the way poets such as Ovid represent their transitions from "lower" genres such as elegy or pastoral to "higher" ones like tragedy or epic. Hinds (2011) 27: "It is arguable that the cumulative effect of Ovid's interventions in the already-crowded Medea tradition is to program all subsequent Medeas in Latin, and perhaps the majority of subsequent tragic (and quasi-tragic) protagonists in Latin, as meta-Medeas, post- and proper-Ovidian."

Therefore, Medea's words about motherhood and crime can be interpreted from a metaliterary perspective as well (48–50):

> **levia memoravi** nimis;
> haec virgo feci. **gravior** exsurgat dolor:
> **maiora** iam me scelera post partus decent.

Seneca's new tragedy involves a plot "greater" (*maiora*) than the deeds recounted in a "lighter" (*levia*) genre such as the elegiac world of the *Heroides*.[129] In the following act, Medea claims that only "light pain can admit advice and hide itself" (*levis est dolor, qui capere consilium potest / et clepere sese*, 155–6) and indicates to the Nurse that she is planning something worthy of the heavier grief (*gravior...dolor*, 49) she feels. Indeed, the word *levis* continues to be important throughout the play to indicate the difference between past and present, elegy and tragedy. For instance, after destroying Creon and Creusa, Medea remarks on her need to discover a new type (genre?) of punishment (*poenarum genus*, 898), because "light is the revenge which pure hands perform" (*vindicta **levis** est quam ferunt purae manus*, 901).[130] Note that Ovid claims in his *Tristia*, "Tragedy defeats every genre in the weight of its writing" (*omne genus scripti **gravitate** tragoedia vincit*, 2.381); thus we can see that the *gravior dolor* Medea mentions denotes the impending tragedy.[131] The heaviness of pregnancy and imagery of childbirth that Seneca stresses in his *Medea* indicates the generic change from elegy to tragedy.

Medea's memory of previous crimes also alludes to the beginning of *Heroides* 12 and reinforces the new authorship of the tragedy. There, Ovid's Medea wrote, "I remember that I, the queen of Colchis, made time for you" (*At tibi Colchorum, **memini**, regina vacavi*, 1). Hinds, drawing upon the work of Conte, finds that words referring to memory can be used to mark a specific allusion, and here we can view how Seneca reworks the elegiac tradition of the *Heroides*.[132] In both works, Medea finds herself in a creative dialogue with her past, but now the "light" themes of the elegiac past are unsuitable for her tragic grief. Similarly, in the *Heroides* she is unable to change: "She has no hope of persuading Jason: she can simply tell, and tell again, how and why she has earned his gratitude, addressing the story, uselessly, to his deaf and ungrateful ears."[133] In Seneca's *Medea*, the

---

[129] Cf. *Am.* 3.1.41–2 where Elegy says, "I am light, and my darling, Cupid, is light with me; / I am not stronger than my subject matter" (*sum levis, et mecum levis est, mea cura, Cupido; / non sum materia fortior ipsa mea*). Also note the "lightness" of elegy at *Am.* 1.1.19 and *Rem.* 379–80. Cf. James (2003) 112–3 for the elegiac *puella's levitas*.

[130] Cf. *Med.* 905–7 for her view that her previous crimes, even those in the play, are *levia*.

[131] Cf. Kelly (1993) 8–10 for more on the *gravitas* of Roman tragedy.

[132] Hinds (1998) 3–4 and bibliography ad loc.

[133] Verducci (1985) 72–3.

potential for change exists (and is, in essence, the plot of the tragedy), and Medea can redefine herself by turning away from her maternal and marital relationships, and embracing the darker powers embodied by her magical ability.

Further supporting such an interpretation, Seneca's Medea claims she will not bluster futilely (26–8):

>**querelas** verbaque in cassum sero?
>non ibo in hostes? manibus excutiam faces
>caeloque lucem.

>Do I compose complaints and blather in vain?
>Shall I not attack my enemies? I will shake the torches from their hands
>And the light from the sky.

The term *querelae* appears elsewhere in the elegiac poetry of Propertius and Ovid's *Heroides* to be shorthand for the genre of elegy as a whole.[134] Seneca is shaping his Medea into a figure who will transcend the genre of elegy and will commit deeds worthy of tragic *gravitas*. While Seneca's Medea still identifies herself as Jason's wife and a mother to his children, the imagery surrounding the opening speech reveals how Seneca subverts these roles and foreshadows future crime.

Seneca's new interpretation of wedding imagery and elegiac themes continues in the first choral song where he reworks a moment found in Ovid's *Heroides* and points to similarities between the young Medea and Jason's new bride. This gives further background to Medea's state of mind in Seneca's drama while also granting the chorus's song metaliterary implications. This choral song attempts to reappropriate nuptial language (which Medea has perverted in the prologue) and celebrate the upcoming wedding of Jason and Creusa.[135] As Costa comments, "Seneca has written a dramatically effective incident, which thrusts the knife further into M[edea]'s wounded heart, and gives an unusually organic role to the chorus, which here at least is by no means the conventional passive commentator."[136]

While this choral ode may lack strong verbal links with Ovid, it emphatically stages a moment found in *Heroides* 12. In this way, Seneca wishes to "complete" Ovid's work and give a poetic account of the hymn mentioned there (135–58).

---

[134] Cf. Prop. 1.18.29–30, Ovid *Her.* 1.69–70, Ovid *Her.* 3.5–6. Cf. Baca (1971) for more on *querela* and *lacrimae* in Ovid's *Heroides*.

[135] Cf. Ahl (1985) 159–60, who calls attention to wordplay within the stellar imagery of the chorus.

[136] Costa (1973) ad loc.

This is a fine example of an intertextual moment in the work that is not primarily a verbal allusion, as Seneca adds dramatic touches to the scene in order to indicate his supplementation of Ovid's material.[137] The scene as a whole responds to the epithalamium that Medea could only report in the epistolary framework of the *Heroides*.[138] Ovid's Medea writes (12.137–42):

>ut subito **nostras Hymen** cantatus ad **aures**
>   venit, et accenso lampades igne micant,
>tibiaque effundit socialia carmina vobis,
>   at mihi funerea flebiliora tuba,
>pertimui, nec adhuc tantum scelus esse putabam;
>   sed tamen in toto pectore frigus erat.

>When suddenly the chant of Hymen came to my ears,
>   And torches glimmer with their kindled flame,
>Flutes poured out songs prosperous to you,
>   But for me a song more tearful than the funeral horn,
>I feared, but I did not yet believe such a crime;
>   But nevertheless there was a cold shudder in my entire breast.

Seneca presents these *socialia carmina* in the words of the chorus who sends forth the joyous song (*mittite carmina*, 108). Seneca responds to Ovid's song by composing an original version of an epithalamium.[139] Seneca's choral ode points out the differences in perspective between the chorus and Medea, and reveals that one aspect of the play's conflict is the dispute over language itself. While the chorus praises the power of marriage, Medea attempts to free herself from her previous roles (wife and mother) and soon will posit her revenge as a novel type of marriage ceremony ("I am looking upon new kind of wedding," *nuptias specto novas*, 894), identifying the connection between her past love for Jason and the revenge she will enact.

Signaling a metaliterary response to Ovid, Seneca's Medea reappears on stage and comments on the chorus that she has just heard (116–20):

---

[137] Seneca writes a song in lyric meters (minor Asclepiadean and Glyconics) that cannot be accommodated to the elegiac distich. Cat. 61 is in Glyconic strophes while Cat. 62 and Theoc. 18 are in dactylic hexameter.

[138] This poetic "completion" of another author's work also can be compared to episodes such as Vergil's description of Achaemenides' life on the island of the Cyclopes after Odysseus left (*Aen.* 3.588ff.).

[139] The inclusion of references to Bacchus' son Hymen and fescennine verse also indicates the metadramatic interests of Seneca, as Bacchus was the patron god of drama and fescennine verses were theorized to be its origin (cf. Liv. 7.2.7).

Occidimus: aures pepulit **hymen**aeus **meas**.
vix ipsa tantum, vix adhuc credo malum.
hoc facere Iason potuit, erepto patre
patria atque **regno** sedibus solam exteris
deserere durus?

> I am done for: the wedding song has struck my ears.
> Scarcely do I believe so great an evil has happened.
> Was Jason able to do this to me, who has lost
> My father, my homeland, and my rule? Is he so harsh
> To desert me alone in foreign parts?

Medea's first line recalls the Ovidian Medea's description of the wedding song in *Heroides* 12. Seneca points the reader back to the *Heroides* at the close of his original hymn to signal his literary completion of the Ovidian text and to indicate what such an epithalamium should contain. While this is occurring at a metaliterary level, Seneca is also appropriating language from both the *Heroides* and the *Metamorphoses* to construct the following lines. When Medea indignantly asks, "Was Jason able to do this to me?" (*hoc facere Iason potuit*, 118), she mirrors language she used as a young girl in Ovid's *Metamorphoses* (7.40–3):

> ut per me sospes sine me det lintea ventis
> virque sit alterius, poenae Medea relinquar?
> si **facere hoc** aliamve **potest** praeponere nobis,
> **occidat** ingratus!

> [Shall I save him] in order that he may sail away without me,
> Become the husband of another, and desert me, Medea, for punishment?
> If he is able to do this or to prefer another to me,
> Let the ungrateful man perish!

In the *Metamorphoses*, her love for Jason, the oaths uniting them, and Jason's good looks persuade Medea that he would never betray her (*Met.* 7.43–7), but Seneca's Medea has learned what sort of man Jason truly is. Seneca repeats language from the *Metamorphoses* that muses on one possible future scenario for Medea and Jason, one that we will see enacted (for the most part) in Seneca's play.[140] Seneca's Medea will thus embody the anger foretold by Ovid's Medea (*occidat ingratus*), but will find a novel way to punish Jason. Medea's exclamation

---

[140] While he does not perish in the play, he does abandon Medea for another woman and leave Medea behind for punishment, in this case exile from Corinth.

"I'm done for" (*occidimus*, 116) can be seen to ironically point to her future revenge against Jason, a revenge worse than death.[141]

Seneca's language also parallels that of the *Heroides*, where Medea laments her position without Jason: "I am forsaken, having lost my kingdom, fatherland, home, and husband, who alone was everything to me" (***deseror** amissis **regno patriaque** domoque / coniuge, qui nobis omnia solus erat*, 12.161–2). This is Medea at her most elegiac. The trope that the beloved is "everything" to the lover is common throughout elegiac poetry.[142] Seneca emphasizes this elegiac representation of Jason by claiming that he is "harsh" (*durus*), another elegiac commonplace.[143] Through these generic connections with elegy, Seneca adds depth to Medea's character that the lines might not carry on their own. Thus, this passage indicates how Seneca's tragic Medea blends the young Colchian princess of the beginning of *Metamorphoses* 7 and the spurned lover of *Heroides* 12. Both intertextual passages highlight Medea's love for Jason. As Seneca's Medea says in summing up her actions up to this point in her life, "I have done no crime out of anger: my unlucky love raged" (*et nullum scelus / irata feci: saevit infelix amor*, 135–6).[144]

Seneca's Medea: Mother and Wife (Becoming "Medea")

Medea's love is transformed into anger in the course of the play, but it is not a simple, linear development.[145] Medea debates her feelings and the implications of her anger towards Jason. The intertextual relationship of Seneca's *Medea* to Ovid's *Heroides* as well as those sections of the *Metamorphoses* that describe Medea's passion stress the emotional background of Medea's love of Jason. Seneca highlights the internal conflict that Medea feels through her multiple soliloquies, and the intertexts add emotional intensity and clarity to her personae. The personae of Senecan tragedy, at their best, offer a multifaceted investigation of the

---

[141] Seneca's Medea styles Jason as *ingratus* in her dealings with him (*ingratum caput*, 465; *ingrate Iason*, 1021).

[142] E.g., Prop. 1.11.23: "You alone are my home, you, Cythnia, alone are my parents, / you are all the moments of my happiness" (*tu mihi sola domus, tu, Cynthia, sola parentes, / omnia tu nostrae tempora laetitiae*), and Richardson (1976) ad loc.

[143] Cf. D. F. Kennedy (1993) 31ff. for a discussion about *durus/mollis*, gender, and Latin love elegy.

[144] While I am concerned with Ovidian intertexts exclusively in this chapter, this line obviously recalls *Aen.* 4.532 (*saevit amor*). Vergil's description of Dido influences Seneca's characterization of Medea. See Fantham (1975) for more instances.

[145] Contra Shelton (1979) 61, "Seneca's Medea is already at the height of her anger when the play opens, and she remains at this emotional peak throughout the play." Medea's emotions are excessive throughout the play, but she is not the one-dimensional figure of *ira* that Shelton and Cleasby (1907) believe.

individual both within the mise-en-scène and in the larger rhetorical, literary, and societal context. Seneca's Medea finds herself hesitating to assign blame to Jason, and only after she hears of her exile from his lips does she brace herself to commit her revenge.

In the second act, Medea argues with her Nurse about the proper course of action to take against Jason. This passage, together with its intertextual model, shows how Seneca's Medea will progress in the play. Medea cleverly responds to the Nurse's objections, which results in a quick staccato exchange (168–71):

Nut. Rex est timendus. Me. Rex meus fuerat pater.
Nut. Non metuis arma? Me. Sint licet terra edita.
Nut. Moriere. Me. Cupio. Nut. Profuge. Me. Paenituit fugae.
Nut. **Medea**—Me. **Fiam.**

Nurse. The king must be feared. Medea. My father was a king.
Nurse. You do not fear arms? Medea. Not even if they sprung from the earth.
Nurse. You will die. Medea. I want to. Nurse. Flee! Medea. I regret my flight.
Nurse. Medea— Medea. I shall become her.

Medea deftly shrugs off the Nurse's pleas, and her responses reflect her own past deeds, all of which were done to aid Jason. She had left her father, the king of Colchis, and had helped Jason defeat the sown soldiers.[146] She will not flee or give in to Creon and his demands.[147] Critics have noted that the two-word phrase *Medea—fiam* recalls the words of Ovid's Hypsipyle, who imagines Jason returning with Medea to Lemnos (*Her.* 6.149–51):[148]

paelicis ipsa meos implessem sanguine vultus,
   quosque *veneficiis* abstulit illa tuos.
Medeae Medea forem!

I would have filled my eyes with the sight of your mistress's blood,
   And your eyes, which she stole away by magic.
I'd have been a veritable Medea to Medea!

---

[146] Cf. Ap. Rhod. *Argon.* 3.1026ff.; Ovid *Met.* 7.1–148.

[147] Before this exchange, Medea notes that she is strong enough to handle all opponents: "Medea remains: here you see sea, land, steel, fire, the gods, and thunderbolts" (*Medea superest: hic mare et terras vides / ferrumque et ignes et deos et fulmina*, 166–7).

[148] Cf. Tarrant (1995) 223. For more on "becoming Medea" cf. Schiesaro (2003) 213, Littlewood (2004) 50, Bartsch (2006) 258–62, and Star (2012) 76–82.

Here, Hypsipyle laments that Medea has enchanted Jason and wishes she could punish Medea by becoming like Medea herself.[149] Hypsipyle knows of Medea's reputation as both a seductress and a witch, and yearns to become as savage as the Medea who has replaced her in Jason's heart. When Seneca's Medea responds to the Nurse's cry of "Medea" by claiming, "I will become [Medea]," the reader is forced to recognize the intertextual flourish that has occurred. In Seneca's play, Medea will live up to her reputation, destroying Jason's mistress by means of her magic (*venenis*, 737, 833, recalling *veneficiis* above). In one word (*fiam*), Seneca emphasizes that Medea will perform the very actions for which she is known throughout her literary and mythological history, and that she will come to embody what was for Hypsipyle only a threat. Medea erases the doubt inherent in Hypsipyle's imperfect subjunctive *forem* by replacing it with the concrete future, *fiam*, and near the conclusion of the play one finds the present tense as Medea states, "Now I am Medea" (*Medea nunc sum*, 910).[150] Seneca's tragedy concerns itself with Medea's self-definition, and that definition is contingent on her previous mythological and intertextual qualities. Both Medea and Hypsipyle are angry that another woman has charmed Jason away, but Medea will fulfill the wish that Hypsipyle uttered and carry out a Medea-like revenge on the other woman, in this case Creusa.[151] Seneca's Medea becomes "Medea" in the course of the tragedy, and she already identifies, at this early point in the play, the role that she will eventually endorse and enact in the tragedy.[152]

After commenting on her previous deeds done to benefit Jason, Medea softens her anger and sympathizes with Jason. She considers these actions to be her dowry to Jason and links her marriage to Jason with her crimes. Medea places the blame firmly on Creon, saying (137–43):

> Quid tamen Iason potuit, alieni arbitri
> iurisque factus? debuit ferro obvium
> offerre pectus—melius, a melius, dolor
> furiose, loquere. si potest, **vivat meus,**
> **ut fuit, Iason; si minus, vivat tamen,**

---

[149] Knox (1995) ad loc. gives this translation of the phrase and explains that the wordplay is possible because "by [Ovid]'s day the name of Medea was a by-word for a sorceress and seductress."

[150] Discussed in more detail below.

[151] Hypsipyle utters a curse near the end of *Heroides* 6 that will come true in Seneca's *Medea*: "As bitter a sister to her brother and daughter to her sad father, so bitter may she [Medea] be to her children and her husband" (*Quam fratri germana fuit miseroque parenti / filia, tam natis, tam sit acerba viro*, 159–60).

[152] Can Medea only be "herself" in tragedy? Seneca finds features of her character worth exploring that are *not* found in other existing tragic accounts, and the spirit of Senecan tragedy is to transcend previous accounts (or, at the very least, transform them) in order to amplify Seneca's concerns.

memorque nostri muneri parcat meo.
Culpa est Creontis tota.

> What was Jason able to do, subject to
> The power and law of another? He should have
> Offered his chest to the sword—No, speak better,
> Better, raging sadness. If it is possible,
> Let my Jason live, as he was; if not that, nevertheless
> Let him live, and, mindful of me, let him enjoy
> The life I gave to him. The blame is entirely Creon's.

Exploring another facet of her personality, Seneca now posits that Medea, despite her anger towards Jason, does not wish him to suffer on her behalf.[153] She hopes that he lives and remembers that he owes his life to her (*muneri…meo*). Medea's tender feelings suggest similar passages in both Ovid's *Heroides* and *Metamorphoses*. In the *Heroides*, Ovid's Medea also compares her actions to a gift, namely, her dowry to Jason. Explaining that the Golden Fleece, the survival of the Argonauts, and, finally, Jason's survival are all her doing, Ovid's Medea concludes (12.205–6):

> **Quod vivis**, quod habes nuptam socerumque potentis,
>   Hoc ipsum, ingratus quod potes esse, **meum est**.

> That you live, that you have a powerful bride and father-in-law,
>   And even this, that you are able to be ungrateful, are owed to me.

Medea questions whether Jason should live and recognizes that she is responsible for his continued existence, although it has not benefited her. Likewise, in the *Metamorphoses*, a young Medea soliloquizes about her love for Jason, and wishes for his survival: "Whether that man lives or dies is in the hands of the gods; yet let him live!" (***vivat** an ille / occidat, in dis est;* ***vivat tamen***, 23–4). Seneca's Medea debates the culpability of Jason and the fittingness of punishment by utilizing the Ovidian intertexts to show the conflict brewing deep in Medea's heart.[154] As Seneca's Medea is tossed between anger and love, so, too, do the intertexts vacillate. Medea's desire that Jason live and be mindful of her is a far cry from her earlier wish that he live (*vivat*, 20) only to be punished.

When Medea enters the third act of the play, she claims, "If you ask yourself, miserable woman, what limit you should place on your anger, imitate your love"

---

[153] Note the description of her pain, *dolor furiose*, and its verbal connection with the Fury.

[154] Seneca repeats the hortatory subjunctives *vivat* (140, 141) from the *Metamorphoses* and signposts the allusion with the appeal to his memory (*memorque*, 142).

(*si quaeris odio, misera, quem statuas modum, / imitare amorem*, 397–8). By pointing to her previous love, Medea connects the two emotions that define her character in the Seneca's play as well as indicating the possible extent of her revenge. Her anger, like her love, will have no limit, and she will outstrip the violence of monsters, the turbulent sea, or windswept flames in her rage.[155] Medea exhibits the extremes of all emotions, and, in her mutability, it is not surprising that she still questions Jason's involvement in her exile, only to conclude now that he is guilty (415–9):

> **Timuit** Creontem ac bella Thessalici ducis?
> **amor timere** neminem verus potest.
> sed cesserit coactus et dederit manus:
> adire certe et coniugem extremo alloqui
> sermone potuit—hoc quoque **extimuit** ferox;

> Did he fear Creon and wars with Thessaly's king?
> True love can fear no man.
> But even if he was compelled to comply and surrender:
> Surely he was able to approach and to tell his wife
> This final message—yet the fierce hero even feared to do this!

Medea spits out this final sarcastic phrase with the venom of a woman undervalued, underappreciated, and underestimated. Medea knows the difficulty in making decisions influenced by fear and love, as she herself chose to follow Jason and betray the love of her family (especially in killing Apsyrtus). In *Heroides* 12, Ovid's Medea debated this very decision: "On one side is love, on the other, fear; yet the fear increases my love" (*hinc* **amor**, *hinc* **timor** *est; ipsum* **timor** *auget* ***amorem***, 12.61). The intertext points out that the young Medea found that her fear intensified her love for Jason and casts doubts on whether Seneca's Jason exhibits "true love" (*amor…verus*, 416). The young, elegiac Medea of Ovid's work comes to Jason's aid and helps him in his toils, but this older Medea recognizes Jason's love as a flimsy thing indeed. Jason himself will reckon that it is actually his *pietas* towards his children, and not fear, that influences his decisions (*non* **timor** *vicit fidem, sed trepida pietas*, 437–8). While Seneca's Medea hesitates and hopes Jason will show some resolve, she recognizes that he is a mere shell of a hero, and his "ferocity" (*ferox*, 419) will be seen to be paper-thin against Medea's own rage (*ferox*, 442) and fury.[156]

---

[155] *Med*. 407–14.

[156] Most recently emphasized when Medea states, "my passion for punishment will never cease" (*numquam meus cessabit in poenas furor*, 406). Medea often takes on Fury-like attributions in the play

Although Seneca's Medea is interested in reformulating and strengthening her relationship to Jason, Jason expresses no affection towards her and only shows concern when their children are mentioned. Medea notes this dedication, so different from what he has shown her, remarking, "Does he love the children so much? Good, that's it, that's the place to strike" (*sic natos amat? / bene est, tenetur, vulneri patuit locus*, 549–50). Earlier in the play, Seneca foreshadowed the possibility of a revenge involving the children, but it is only here that Medea decides to use the children to retaliate against Jason.[157] After Jason exits, Medea exclaims (560–5):

> Discessit. itane est? vadis oblitus mei
> et tot meorum facinorum? **excidimus** tibi?
> numquam **excidemus**. hoc age, omnis **advoca**
> vires et **artes**. fructus est scelerum tibi
> nullum scelus putare. vix fraudi est **locus**:
> timemur.

> He has left. Is it true? Do you make your way
> Forgetful of me and all my deeds? Have you forgotten me?
> You will never forget me. Come on then, summon all your
> Strength and art. The reward of your crimes is that you think nothing
> A crime. There is barely space for deception:
> I am feared.

Here Seneca ingeniously reworks a line from Ovid's *Heroides*.[158] In its original context, Ovid's Medea tells of the place where she met Jason and his promise to marry her, then asks, "Do you know the place or have you forgotten places along with me?" (*noscis? an* **exciderunt** *mecum* **loca**? 12.71). Ovid's Medea bases her trust on her marriage with Jason and the temple where they were married. Seneca places similar language in the mouth of his Medea not only to show the discrepancy in Jason's character but also to give these words a sinister overtone. *Heroides* 12 utilizes Jason's faulty memory (*immemor*, 16)

---

as she avenges herself (*vultum Furoris cerno*, 396). Medea was also deemed *ferox* by Creon (*fert gradum contra ferox* 186).

[157] Arcellaschi (1996) 185–6 sees this as the turning point of the tragedy.

[158] Hinds (2011) 28 expresses this as a mock rejoinder by Medea, in which she says, "Can you *still* not remember (as a husband, as a reader…) all that I am to you, how the *topoi* of our story are shaped? Well then, let me repeat the lesson, and perhaps this time it will stick." He notes how this passage also activates the Contean idea of poetic memory; cf. Conte (1986) 57–69, passim.

as a spur for many of the complaints she provides in the course of the letter.[159] Seneca's Jason should not forget (*oblitus*, 560) Medea's past so readily, for if there is a "place to wound" (*vulneri...locus*, 550), there is also a "place for crime" (*fraudi...locus*, 564).[160] Concomitantly, Seneca weaves in a moment from the *Metamorphoses* with the expression *advoca... artes*. When Jason faces the sown men, Medea, fearing for his life, "sings a helpful spell and calls forth secret arts" (*carmen / auxiliare canit secretasque* **advocat artes**, 7.137–8).[161] This is exactly the sort of deed that Jason has forgotten (*oblitus... meorum facinorum*), and the strong Ovidian *figura etymologica* (*carmen... canit*) leaves no doubt that Medea's revenge will spring from her magical ability (staged in the following act). In fact, in her incantation, Medea seems to recall intratextually this very passage when discussing the fire that Prometheus gave her (and which will presently consume Creusa, Creon, and Corinth): "He taught me how to hide its strength with my art" (*docuit condere* **vires** / **arte**, 823–4). If before her magic was used to help Jason (*auxiliare carmen*), now the reverse is true.

The love that Medea has for Jason and for their children defines her actions through the first half of Seneca's *Medea*. Medea's self-conception springs from her roles of mother and wife, and she attempts to come to terms with the results of Jason's desertion. The intertextual source material gives background information to Medea's past relationship with Jason and shows how he has betrayed her love. Medea's anger causes her to pervert both nuptial and maternal language in order to presage the revenge that will be enacted onstage.[162] The imagery also points to the generic escalation that Seneca is performing in his tragedy. Medea's deeds must transcend those described in elegy, and Seneca's language cleverly points to the character she will become in the course of the play (*Medea...fiam*, 171). But, before the murder of her children, Medea must punish Creusa and Creon, and in order

---

[159] During Medea's pretended reconciliation, she bids Jason to remember the "better me" and "erase those things given over to anger" (*haec irae data / **oblitterentur***, 556–7). Here memory is figured like a text that can be "erased." This happens also at 466 where Medea bids Jason "unroll his memory" (*revolvat animus*) and proceeds to give information that can be found in the *Metamorphoses* (7.141–58) and *Heroides* (12.93–108). Cf. *Ep.* 72.1 where Seneca compares his memory to a book roll (*explicandus est animus*) and *Ep.* 28.4: *sed modo, inquis, hunc librum evolvere volo, modo illum*.

[160] Medea calls upon the gods of marriage at the play's opening to call attention to Jason's abandonment (*Di coniugales*, 1).

[161] Jakobi (1988) 56 points out that the phrase *vires advocare* "ist gut senecanisch."

[162] The chorus understands the power of spurned love: "No force of fire or swollen wind or hurled missile is to be feared as much the way a spurned wife burns and hates" (*Nulla vis flammae tumidive venti / tanta, nec teli metuenda torti, / quanta cum coniunx viduata taedis / ardet et odit*, 579–82).

to do so she assumes the persona of witch, a side of her character that Jason seems to have forgotten.

Seneca's Medea as Witch

Seneca focuses on Medea's persona of witch in the fourth act of his *Medea*, lavishly detailing her supernatural powers. In doing so, he responds strongly to Ovid's description of Medea's magical rites in the *Metamorphoses*, and emphasizes how he moves beyond Ovid's portrayal. In addition, the language of the incantation recalls descriptions of Medea and the Argonauts from earlier in the play, and these connections indicate how Medea has now gained control of the dramatic action. There can be little question of the efficacy of her magic as Seneca stresses not only the transformative nature of her power (as found in Ovid's scene) but also its ability to inflict pain and suffering upon others.

In the beginning of the act, the Nurse explains that she has seen Medea's past witchcraft and that her mistress's current state of anguish will lead to some greater evil. As she had done in the third act, the Nurse describes Medea's actions, which are then enacted on stage. Boyle comments, "Each of these descriptions distances both the Nurse and the audience from Medea, transforming the Nurse herself into an audience to Medea's theatre of magic."[163] Medea no longer appears as a character to whom the Nurse can appeal (as in the second act), but she has separated herself from the human realm. The Nurse declares (673–5):

> vidi furentem saepe et aggressam deos,
> caelum trahentem: **maius** his, **maius** parat
> **Medea monstrum**.
>
> I have often seen her raging and attacking the gods,
> Drawing down the sky: Medea is preparing something
> Greater than this, something more monstrous.

This claim resonates both in language and sound pattern with the chorus's earlier description of Medea as an evil "greater than the sea, a reward worthy of the first ship" (***maius**que mari **Medea** malum, / merces prima digna carina*, 362–3). Medea herself claims that she is more frightening than Creon and Acastus: "There is an even greater fear than these: Medea" (*est et his **maior** metus: / **Medea***, 516–7). Seneca stresses that Medea's name indicates her essential character, both when

[163] Boyle (1997) 130.

Medea refers to herself in the third person and when it appears in the comments of other characters.[164] Charles Segal writes of the connection between Medea's name and her characterization in the play, "The sound-plays between *Medea / monstrum* or *Medea / malum* on the one hand... and *Medea / mater* on the other hand reflect in the microcosmic structure of phonic patterns the tension between monstrosity and maternity that constitutes the central dynamic force of Medea's tragedy."[165] The use of the word *maius* in the Nurse's description of Medea points to Seneca's attempt to surpass Ovid's previous representation of her magical abilities, just as previously it indicated the "greater crimes" that suited the mature, tragic Medea.[166] It may also recall the incantation from the *Metamorphoses* where uses of *maius* bookend the spell that Medea casts to rejuvenate Aeson.[167] Thus, the Nurse's comment specifies the grandiose nature of Medea's planned revenge and, as an intertextual marker, indicates that this act will continue to give a tragic spin on Ovid's works.

Seneca stresses Medea's magical abilities, devoting an entire scene to the Nurse's description of Medea's magic and then giving Medea's polymetric incantation in her own words.[168] This spell owes much to descriptions of witches in Augustan literature and the portrayals of Medea in Ovid's poetry.[169] The Nurse catalogues the snakes that Medea has summoned and the preparations of Medea's spell (675–739). In doing so, Seneca once again has recourse to Ovid's *Amores* 3.1 and the metapoetic choice between the personifications of elegy and tragedy in that poem. The Nurse reports Medea's peroration, in which she claims, "Now, yes, now it is time to stir up something more impressive than ordinary

---

[164] Medea refers to herself in the third person at 171, 524, 934. Note especially the implications of such formulations as *Medea...fiam* (171). Cf. Fitch and McElduff (2002) 27n25: "Because self-construction takes place largely through language, the process by which the *dramatis personae* 'write themselves', and write themselves *anew*, is akin to that by which the author rewrites their stories."

[165] Segal (1982a) 241. The wordplay occurs, e.g., at 171, 266–8, 288–90, 362–3, 683–4, 908–10, 933–4, and 947–8. Note the Nurse's description of "the whole crowd of evils" (*omnem...turbam malorum*, 628–9) that Medea conjures.

[166] Cf. *Med.* 50: *maiora iam me scelera post partus decent* and the discussion of generic ascent from *Heroides* 12 above. See also Schiesaro (1994) 200 and Hinds (2011) 23–6.

[167] Medea plans to give Jason a "greater gift" (***maius***... *munus*, 7.175) and after she mixes the drugs in her cauldron, Ovid comments that she has finished her "more than mortal purpose" (*propositum...mortali...**maius***, 7.276).

[168] Hine (2000) 175 comments on the dramatic surprise of Medea's appearance: "The audience would be used to long messenger speeches reporting what has happened indoors.... In this act the Nurse appears to be reporting in a similar way on the actions M[edea] has performed indoors, when suddenly M[edea] is heard and then seen coming on stage herself."

[169] Cf. Verg. *Ecl.* 8; Hor. *Epod.* 5; Ov. *Met.* 7.179–293, *Her.* 6.83–94. Cf. Ogden (2009) 115–45 for witches in Latin literature as a whole.

crime" (*iam iam **tempus est** / aliquid **movere** fraude vulgari altius*, 692–3). This statement recalls Tragedy's admonishment to Ovid: "It is time that you be stirred up, stricken by a heavier thyrsus" (***tempus erat**, thyrso pulsum graviore **moveri**,* 3.1.23). This impulse to transcend a common crime is paradigmatic of Seneca's criminal masterminds, and the statement here indicates even more emphatically that Seneca is preparing something special, and particularly "tragic", for the reader in this act.

The Nurse's extended catalogue of snakes and poisonous herbs reveals the universal pull of Medea's magic. The Nurse characterizes Medea as an artist of crimes (*scelerum **artifex**,* 734), who can change the world through her magic (737–9):

> addit venenis verba non illis minus
> metuenda.—Sonuit ecce vesano gradu
> canitque. mundus vocibus primis tremit.
>
> She adds words, no less frightening than those poisons.
> Behold! The sound she makes with maddened foot
> And she sings. The world trembles at her first words.

Littlewood comments on the similarities between Medea's power as a witch and poetry: "Poetry does not simply charm, but fashions its material and creates a world. Magic is thus a fine image for grand poetic projects and sublime art."[170] The trembling of the world at Medea's words shows her control of this dramatic world, and the Nurse's description of her magic proves its potency. The Nurse relates Medea's domination of nature as she summons serpents from the Arctic and the Libyan desert, from the earth and the heavens, finally bringing the mythological scourge of Python and the Colchian serpent who guarded the Golden Fleece.[171] The herbs she gathers come from similarly disparate locations, from the blood-stained crags of the Caucasus to the rich stream of the Hydaspes and were cut during each season.[172] Within this section there are no less than four marked intertexts to Ovid's *Metamorphoses* as well as the situational similarity of the incantation. Seneca verbally unites his wakeful Colchian serpent to Ovid's; the locations from which Medea picks her poisons expands Ovid's geography; and her method of gathering those poisons

---

[170] Littlewood (2004) 158.
[171] *Med.* 680–704.
[172] *Med.* 705–30.

likewise mimics Ovid's works.[173] Seneca surpasses Ovid's description of Medea by doubling the accounts of her enchantment (both her own and the Nurse's), elaborating Ovidian details, and increasing the sway of Medea's power. In the *Metamorphoses*, Medea collects her herbs only from Greece, whereas Seneca's Medea has covered the known world in her collection. The stress on the songs that summon the serpents, help aid in the collection of poisonous plants, and ultimately shake the world calls attention to both the language of the Nurse's speech itself and the poetic fabric of the play. As the Nurse explains Medea's control over the poetic world, Medea herself appears onstage to enact the power that has been described.

When Medea surprisingly emerges from the house, she delivers a polymetric magical song that invokes the gods of the Underworld and Hecate, details the favorable signs given to her, recounts the preparation of the poisoned gifts, and concludes by sending the poisoned gifts to Creusa.[174] If the Nurse's speech focused on the emulation of the comparable Ovidian passage with intertextual echoes linking the works, Medea's song primarily works intratextually to connect this spell with earlier sections of the play. This is not to say that it lacks the characteristic intertextual play of Seneca *tragicus*, but the echoes are further strengthened through intratextual links that highlight Medea's control of the play. Seneca stresses the poetic aspect of magic: Medea's previous feats of magic were accomplished by her song (*cantu*, 760), by the order of her voice (*vocis imperio meae*, 767), and by her chants (*cantibus*, 769). In the *Metamorphoses*, Ovid's Medea likewise stresses the vocal component of her spell, and her travels through Greece result in a series of mini-metamorphoses, suitable to the themes of transformation and renewal found in the *Metamorphoses*.[175] Seneca complicates his lengthy *aemulatio* of the Ovidian passage (Ovid's Medea speaks for twenty-seven lines (7.192–219); Seneca's for 108 lines (740–848)) by breaking up Medea's song into a variety of meters that change according to the topics of the song.[176] Such metrical *variatio* is possible in the tragic genre but cannot be

---

[173] These are detailed in Jakobi (1988) 58–9. The serpent is vigilant (*pervigil*, 703; *pervigilem*, Met. 7.149), before yielding to sleep (*sopite*, 704; *sopire*, Met. 7.149). Seneca includes mountains which Ovid's Medea has traversed (720–1; cf. Met. 7.224). Medea picks poisonous grasses (*mortifera carpit gramina*, 731) as did Ovid's (*carpsit...vivex...gramina*, Met. 7.232) and uses a similar scythe or fingernail (*cruenta falce*, 722, *ungue...cantato*, 730; *cantata...falce*, Her. 6.84).

[174] Hine (2000) ad loc. admirably organizes the sections of the song.

[175] *Cantus* (195), *cantu* (201), *vocoque* (202), *verbis et carmine* (203), *iubeo* (205), *carmine* (208). Note also the power of song describing Medea's spell at Ovid's Met. 7.167—"What can songs not do?" (*quid enim non carmina possunt?*)—and the stress on her spells at the conclusion of his treatment at Met. 7.424: "She fled death by her spells" (*effugit illa necem ... per carmina*). As Wise (1982) 21 has noted, "The relation of language to the magician's powers of metamorphosis connects Medea's incantations with poetic activity."

[176] Cf. Hine (2000) 184.

achieved in the dactylic hexameter of epic and, much like the wedding hymn earlier in the play, provides evidence of Seneca's desire to compose an original song that would be impossible in the Ovidian source. Medea's song, not the optimistic epithalamium of the first chorus, will come true in the course of the play, and her magical skill is stressed through the length and metrical complexity of the incantation.

Through linguistic parallels, Seneca links Medea's spell with the chorus's description of her and the fates of the other Argonauts (mentioned in the third choral ode directly preceding this act). The chorus had compared Medea's power to that of the swelling Danube (*torrens Hister*, 584–5), but now Medea claims she even has controlled the Danube (763–4):

> et Hister, in tot ora divisus, truces
> compressit undas omnibus ripis piger

> And the Danube, branching out in so many mouths,
> Held back its harsh waves, now slowly washing its banks.[177]

Medea claims that Hecate has helped her to control the seasons (*temporum flexi vices*, 759), the weather (*evocavi nubibus siccis aquas*, 754), and the harvest (*coacta messem vidit hibernam Ceres*, 761), as well as the stars (768–70) and the seas (755–6, 765–6).[178] Medea can control the winds (*tacente vento*, 765) for which Tiphys, the Argo's helmsman, dared to write laws (*legesque novas scribere ventis*, 320), and she has shattered the cosmic law ("The law of earth and heaven were mixed up at the same time," *pariterque mundus lege confusa aetheris*, 757). The means by which the Argonauts perished (articulated in the third chorus 616–69) will aid Medea's revenge on Jason, as she employs elements of their destructive quality against Creusa and Creon. She adds Nessus' poison (775–6), ash from Hercules' pyre (777–8), and the torch of Althaea (779–81) to her spell, which recalls the deaths of Meleager and Hercules described earlier.[179] The Corinthian chorus had stressed the power of a wife bereft of her marriage (579–82):

> Nulla vis flammae tumidive venti
> tanta, nec teli metuenda torti,
> quanta cum coniunx viduata taedis
>   ardet et odit.

---

[177] Seneca's delineation of the various rivers expands upon *Met*. 7.199–200: "The rivers returned to their springs" (*amnes / in fontes rediere suos*).

[178] Most of these deeds are also found at *Met*. 7.192–219.

[179] Hercules' death (639–42), Meleager's death (644–6). Medea's use of the same poison and Hercules' ash foreshadows a similar fate for the recipient of the gift.

No power of fire or swelling wind is so great,
Nor is the hurled spear to be so feared,
As much as when a wife has been deprived of her wedding torch,
   She burns and she hates.

Seneca's Medea literally enacts the chorus's words in summoning a fiery destruction upon Jason's new bride and father-in-law.[180] In leaving behind her role as Jason's wife and assuming the power of a sorceress, Medea further asserts her ability to manipulate the action of the play. Medea's spell delineates the particular revenge that Medea intends while the language and imagery reverberate with Ovid's accounts and the previous acts of the play.

In detailing specific intertexts with Ovid's *Metamorphoses*, one finds Seneca often uniting past instances of Medea's support for Jason with her current desire to cause him pain and suffering. Seneca's Medea snatches the flames that once issued from the bulls of Aeetes, which she herself had helped Jason to tame ("I have flames ripped from the singed throat of the bull," *habeo **flammas usto** tauri / **gutture** raptas*, 829–30). Ovid's bulls were similar: "So did the bull's chests and singed throats resound with confined flames" (*pectora sic intus clausas volventia **flammas** / **gutturaque usta** sonant, Met.* 7.109–10). Medea herself had earlier mentioned these same bulls to Jason when confronting him for his ingratitude: "Let your mind remember the fiery breath of the bull" (*revolvat animus igneos **tauri** halitus*, 466). While Jason faced this foe with magical aid from Medea, his new wife will not be so lucky. Once again an intertext combined with an intratext strengthens this parallel. Seneca's Medea declares that Creusa's fate is to outshine the wedding torches, in a literal sense (837–42):

   stillent artus ossaque fument
   vincatque suas flagrante coma
      nova nupta faces.
   Vota tenentur: ter latratus
   audax Hecate dedit et sacros
   edidit ignes face luctifera.

Let her limbs dissolve and her bones smoke;
Let the new bride defeat her own torches
   With her burning hair.
   The prayer is being granted: bold Hecate
Barked three times and gave forth holy flame
From the grief-granting torch.

---

[180] Creusa is set ablaze (836–9) and her ashes are mixed with her father's (*cinere permixto*, 880).

This passage combines Ovidian allusion with imagery from earlier in the play to deepen the sense of dread and pathos inherent in the situation.[181] The phrase "new bride" (*nova nupta*) was likewise used by Ovid to describe Creusa in the section of the *Metamorphoses* when he summarizes the events of this very play ("But after the new bride burned because of Colchian poisons," *sed postquam Colchis arsit **nova nupta** venenis, Met.* 7.394). Although Ovid passes over the events in Corinth in a mere four lines, Seneca intertextually recalls this line through this violent elaboration of Creusa's impending demise. By recalling this particular line, Seneca thus signals that he is staging the events that Ovid elides. In addition, Seneca wishes to call attention to a threat of Ovid's elegiac Medea, who hopes Creusa "will cry and, burning, will defeat my fires" (*flebit et ardores **vincet** adusta meos, Her.* 12.180). In the *Heroides*, Ovid's Medea figures her love to be like an uncontrollable fire, but, when transferred to Creusa, the metaphorical fires become real. Seneca lingers on the scene and adds details germane to the context of the play.[182] Torches have appeared throughout the play both as an attribute of the Furies (15) and within the wedding context (27, 67, 398). Medea's spell has benefited from Althaea's torch (779); she has used a torch in her preparations (800); and the emission of fire from the torch of Hecate (842) promises that Medea's spell will be effective.[183] The reported death of new bride (*nova nupta*) also gives rise to Medea's claim "I look upon a novel wedding" (***nuptias specto novas***, 894) at the beginning of the next act.[184] Thus Seneca finds a way to incorporate more fully the Ovidian intertexts in the poetic fabric of his tragedy and emphasize the way that wedding imagery has been perverted to designate the horrific death of Creusa.

The various intratextual connections with the Argonautic chorus as well as earlier sections of the play underline how Medea is both the result of the Argo's journey and the cause of future calamity.[185] Thus the tragedy of the play can be viewed as a consequence of the violation of natural boundaries and as another entry in the catalogue of the "punishment of the Argonauts," detailed in the previous chorus. Medea herself becomes the instrument of that revenge, like the

---

[181] The pointed juxtaposition of death and marriage is found in epigrams from the *Greek Anthology* that discuss the death of a young bride (*A.P.* 7.487, *A.P.* 7.710). Rehm (1994) discusses the similarity of funeral and wedding imagery in Greek drama.

[182] This description gives the information that we might expect from the messenger speech. Seneca's elaboration is nowhere near as gruesome as Euripides' (*Med.* 1186–96).

[183] Hecate's light (as Luna) is also compared to a pale torch (793). In the *Heroides*, Medea claims her first love for Jason burned like a torch (12.33–4). Her love, figured as fire, cannot be extinguished: "I, who repelled fierce flames with my learned salves, am not able to flee my own fires," *quaeque feros pepuli doctis medicatibus ignes, / non valeo flammas effugere ipsa meas* (12.165–6).

[184] Also note her cry "O wedding day!" (*O nuptialem!*, 986) when going through with the infanticide.

[185] Cf. 361–4 where Medea, styled "an evil greater than the sea" (*maiusque mari Medea malum*), is called the reward (*pretium*, 361) of the mission.

women who rip apart Orpheus, the poisoned robe that consumes Hercules, Althaea, and the snake that destroys Idmon.[186] Hecate will help Medea as she breaks the bonds of the cosmos and devises a revenge that can be placed within the Argonautic context and the larger world of the play.

In the incantation scene, Seneca creatively responds to previous representations of Medea in the works of Ovid to emphasize the power of her magic and to indicate that his own Medea will transcend the presentation of Ovid's Medea in the *Heroides* and, especially, the *Metamorphoses*. In doing so, he characterizes his Medea as a witch who can transform the world and directs her wrath towards Jason's new bride and family. Seneca also stresses the metaliterary aspects of the spell as the language, length, and meter signal his attempts to outstrip Ovid's representation of Medea. The imagery of the spell unites the punishment of Jason with the deaths of the Argonauts (detailed in the third chorus) as well as further elaborating wedding motifs (torches, *nuptias novas*), and the destructive power of fire. The results will be seen in the final act of the play, but Seneca's characterization of Medea has not yet attained its final manifestation.

Seneca's Medea: A new Medea?

In the concluding act of his *Medea*, Seneca explores Medea's varying personae and places them in dialogue with one another as Medea contemplates infanticide and the proper revenge against Jason. Medea's characterization as a witch and her magical prowess distance her from the human world yet, at the same time, Medea seems all-too-human in her emotional response to the wrongs inflicted by Jason. We have seen how Ovid's *Metamorphoses* emphasizes Medea's magical ability, and how the *Heroides* provides background to Medea's self-conception as Jason's wife. The *Heroides* also stresses Medea's love for her children, but Medea's self-conception as a mother has been altered by her hatred for Jason.[187] In the fifth act, intertextual references to Ovid give the reader a more complete view of her volatile personae and her role as a surrogate poet. At the close of the play, Medea ascends the heavens in her dragon-drawn chariot, clearly surmounting the mortal world by her actions, yet she considers herself still, in

---

[186] Each of these fates can be related to Medea: Orpheus' death recalls Medea's portrayal as Maenad (382, 806), and Medea's magic can be seen as the flip side of Orpheus' song (405, 762–70); the poisoned robe of Hercules to Medea's gifts for Creusa (775–6); Althaea killed her son for the sake of her brother (1005); Medea soon enchants serpents from those same Libyan sands where Idmon died (682). Cf. Hine (2000) ad loc. for the problematic mythology behind parts of this catalogue.

[187] Cf. *Med.* 23–5, 171; 925–6: "Children, once mine, you pay the penalty for your father's crimes" (*liberi quondam mei, / vos pro paternis sceleribus poenas date*).

some way, Jason's wife.[188] Her love for Jason, excessive from its inception, now curdles to bitter hatred, and in this act Medea points to her romantic tie to Jason and her role as spurned wife as the motivating factor in the tragedy. Medea's character is realized in this act, and Seneca points out how he has manipulated the plurality of the intertextual tradition of Ovid's Medea(s) in the creation of his own tragic Medea.

The intervening chorus wonders what character Medea will manifest: a sorceress as she has just appeared, or some other persona? The chorus comments that Medea lacks self-control (866–9):

>   Frenare nescit **iras**
>   Medea, non **amores**;
>   nunc **ira amor**que causam
>   iunxere: quid **sequetur**?

>   Medea does not know how
>   To control her anger, or her love;
>   Now anger and love have united,
>   What will follow?

Throughout Seneca's tragedy, Medea's love has often recalled the emotion displayed by the characters in the elegiac letters of Ovid's *Heroides*.[189] Her anger, too, has been expressed through intertextual references to the *Metamorphoses* as well as allusions to the potential violence found in the laments and threats of the *Heroides*. This passage may also reference Medea's famous conflict between reason (*mens*) and passion (*cupido*) in the *Metamorphoses*, where she explains, "I see the better and endorse it, but I follow the worse" (*video meliora proboque, / deteriora sequor*, 7.20–1).[190] Both anger and love are now etched on Medea's face, and Seneca shows the results of such emotional turbulence (there is no place for reason in this play). That such a combination of emotions may lead to tragedy can be seen in the preceding stanza, because the chorus exclaims (863–6):

>   **huc fert** pedes et **illuc**,
>   ut tigris orba natis
>   cursu furente **lustrat**
>   Gangeticum **nemus**.

---

[188] Cf. Walsh (2012) 90 for Medea's divinity and removal "from her human state."

[189] It is significant that the plural *amores* is used at 867, because it can also signify elegiac poetry, as both Gallus' and Ovid's works were entitled *amores*. Cf. Prop. 2.1.1, Ov. *Am*. 1.12.21.

[190] This line surely influenced *Phd*. 177–9. See discussion above. It is an imitation of Medea's famous line in Euripides' play (*Med*. 1078–80).

> She moves here and there,
> Like a tigress who has lost her young
> Wanders the groves of the Ganges
> With maddened pace.

Line 863 resembles one of the two extant passages of Ovid's lost tragedy, *Medea* (*feror huc illuc, vae, plena deo,* Fr. 2 Ribbeck), a line probably spoken by Medea.[191] Seneca alludes to this line in order to show that such a mixture of excessive love and hate will lead specifically to a tragedy. Seneca also offers an intratextual comment on this line through the repetition of words from Medea's spell. In her incantation, Medea states that she wanders with bare feet through secluded groves in honor of the goddess Hecate (*tibi...secreta nudo **nemore lustravi** pede,* 752–3). That the tigress wanders in similar groves (*lustrat...nemus*) can be seen as a poetic way for Seneca to claim that Medea's spell has been fulfilled.[192] She *is* full of a god(dess), Hecate, and her vengeful curses will be realized in the tragic genre.

The final act is notable for the lengthy monologue that Medea delivers in which she deliberates whether she should kill her children. Instead of the typical messenger speech, Seneca prefers to show the actions of Medea, her emotional debate, and the murder of her children.[193] She has been the central concern of the play, dominating the actions and manipulating the other characters. Gill says of Medea's monologue and her separation from the other characters, "This conflict centers on Medea's thinking about herself (turning on the question of whether she can sustain her image of herself as the perpetrator of ultimate evil) rather than on her responses to others."[194] Now Medea takes her place, center stage, and reveals what she has become. She has committed a crime worthy of her poetic and mythological reputation, and she emerges in this scene as a complex combination of mother, witch, and scorned wife.

In the final act, Medea's love for her children and anger at Jason push her to debate whether she should act as a mother or as a wife.[195] Here we see the results

---

[191] Cf. Eur. *Med.* 1342 and Cleasby (1907) 61, who points out other parallels to Ovidian poetry (*Met.* 6.636ff.; *Met.* 13.547ff.; *Fast.* 4.457–62). This quote is preserved in Sen. *Suas.* 3.7 and illustrates Ovid's debt to a lost Vergilian phrase *plena deo*. It appears that it was a very well-known case of allusion, which leads me to posit this connection between this line and Ovid's fragment. Cf. Costa (1973) ad loc. in support of this interpretation. Hine (2000) ad loc. is more skeptical.

[192] At *Met.* 7.32, the young Medea claims she should be the child of a tigress (*de tigride natam*) if she allows Jason to die against the fire-breathing bulls. Seneca's Medea now *is* a tigress and wants Jason to suffer something worse than death.

[193] Seneca does utilize messenger speeches in other plays, e.g., *Phd.* 1000–1114.

[194] Gill (1987) 36.

[195] Cf. *Med.* 943–4: "Anger puts affection to flight / affection now drives my anger away. Yield, pain, to affection" (*ira pietatem fugat / iramque pietas. cede pietati, dolor*).

of Medea's multiple personae, which have been created throughout the play, as Medea questions her motivation for revenge (924–30):

> liberi quondam mei,
> vos pro paternis sceleribus poenas date.
>   Cor pepulit horror, membra torpescent gelu
> pectusque tremuit. ira discessit loco
> **mater**que **tota coniuge** expulsa redit.
> egone ut meorum liberum ac prolis meae
> fundam cruorem? melius, a, demens furor!

> Children, once my own,
> You are to pay the penalty for your father's crimes.
>   Terror has gripped my heart, my limbs grow cold,
> And my chest trembles. My anger has gone
> And my motherly feelings return with the wife utterly banished.
> Shall I shed the blood of my own children and race?
> Ah! Think better, mad rage!

Medea weighs the differences between acting like a mother (*mater*) and acting like a spurned wife (*coniuge*), and at this moment her love for her children takes precedence. This temporary change of heart, however, will not last. Since the start of the play, Seneca has carefully associated motherhood with crime, and here, near the close of the play, such language appears again. In her debate, Medea claims that all crimes accomplished when she was younger must be bettered (905–8):

> hoc age! en faxo sciant
> quam **levia** fuerint quamque vulgaris notae
> quae commodavi scelera. prolusit **dolor**
> per ista noster.

> Come on then! I will do this and see to it that
> They understand how light and common were the crimes,
> Which I committed on his behalf. My pain practiced through those.

Medea recalls her crimes as she did at the start of the play, where she also considered them to be too light for the mature mother Medea (*levia...nimis*, 48).[196]

---

[196] Cf. *Med.* 901: "It is a meager retribution which pure hands commit" (*vindicta levis est quam ferunt purae manus*). Likewise note that her earlier deeds would be bettered because "a heavier bitterness arises" (***gravior exurgat dolor**, 49*).

The metapoetic implications explored there hold valid in this passage as well, because Medea wishes to surpass both her previous actions and previous elegiac representation. Once spurred to revenge she realizes she has not produced enough children to sate her vengeance (954–7):

> utinam superbae turba Tantalidos meo
> exisset utero, bisque septenos parens
> natos tulissem! sterilis in poenas fui –
> fratri patrique quod sat est, peperi duos.

> Would that the throng of proud Niobe left my womb,
> And I would have been the parent to fourteen children!
> I was too sterile to punish in an appropriate manner.
> But there is enough for my brother and father; I gave birth to two.

Now motherhood is a means for revenge, and Seneca's Medea indicates that the intimations of infanticide found earlier in the play will come to fruition.[197]

Medea comes to focus more on her role as wife and her previous erotic connection with Jason as the final scene progresses. Seneca calls attention to this characterization of Medea by alluding to Ovid's *Heroides*, which underscores the elegiac background to Medea's anger. Seneca's Medea reworks one of the final comments of the Medea of the *Heroides*, "Where anger leads, I will follow" (*quo feret **ira**, **sequar***, 12.209), as she states, "The ancient Fury seeks again my reluctant hand. / Anger, where you lead, I do follow" (*repetit invitam manum / antiqua Erinys. **ira, qua ducis, sequor***, 953).[198] The sentiment is the same, only the tense has changed. This allusive pattern mirrors Medea's claim that she "is now Medea" (*Medea nunc sum*, 910) after her earlier promise, "I will become Medea" (*Medea...fiam*, 172).[199] Ovid's elegiac Medea hopes to punish Jason and Creusa in the future; Seneca's Medea is in the process of doing so now. Furthermore, whereas Ovid's Medea worries she may regret her future actions, saying "Perhaps I shall regret my action" (***facti fortasse pigebit***, *Her*.12.209), Seneca's Medea finds pleasure in her deeds (990–2):

---

[197] Cf. *Med*. 25–6: *parta iam, parta ultio est: / peperi*. Her desire to extinguish any maternal connection with Jason is further emphasized when she asserts "if any pledge now hides in the mother, I will scour my womb with the blade and draw it forth" (*in matre si quod pignus etiamnunc latet, / scrutabor ense viscera et ferro extraham*, 1012-3).

[198] It is notable that *ira* defines tragedy for Ovid at *Rem*. 375: *tragicos decet **ira** cothurnos* ("Anger befits the tragic buskin").

[199] The differences in tense call attention to the differences in genre and to Medea's self-formation in the play.

> quid, misera, **feci**? Misera? **Paeniteat** licet,
> **feci**. voluptas magna me invitam subit,
> et ecce crescit.

> Miserable woman, what have I done? Miserable?
> Although I may regret it, I have acted. A great pleasure arises in me,
> and, lo! [she sees Jason] increases.[200]

Seneca's Medea has become something greater than the elegiac Medea of Ovid's *Heroides*, but these allusions point back to the motivation for her actions. Her anger springs from her past love for Jason. Medea states that she is "following" her anger, and this corresponds to previous uses of the verb *sequor* in the play. The chorus had wondered what would follow the union of Medea's love and anger ("What will follow?" *quid **sequetur**?*, 869), and Medea earlier had postulated that she would leave her husband as she followed him ("In what manner do you leave your husband? In the same way you followed him" *quo virum linquis modo? / hoc quo **secuta es**,* 53–4). Seneca utilizes this verb to signpost Medea's transformation into an agent of revenge, and the final allusion to Ovid's *Heroides* 12 specifies that she is continuing the persona elucidated in that poem. Seneca's Medea reveals how the destruction of her previous love for Jason has impelled her acts of revenge.[201]

Seneca stresses that his Medea outstrips previous representations, as she becomes an amalgam of witch, spurned wife, and mother in the play. His intertextual relationship with Ovid allows him to carefully delineate and interrogate Medea's various personae while simultaneously commenting on the poetry of his tragedy. At the close of the play, allusions to Ovid's Medeas diminish, and Seneca works to show how *his* Medea now takes control of events onstage.

The language Seneca employs to describe Medea's possible revenge can also be seen as a comment on Seneca's version of events. Seneca's Medea addresses her grief: "Seek new material, grief: you will bring a practiced right hand to every crime" (*quaere materiam, dolor: / ad omne facinus non **rudem** dextram afferes,* 914–5). The use of *materiam* points to both the means of revenge and the way in which this telling of the Medea story is to be rendered.[202] Medea acts like a skilled (*non rudem dextram*) declaimer who must win over the audience through her rhetorical skill, or a poet who writes his work in a sophisticated manner.

---

[200] Note how forms of *facio* and verbs of regret (*pigebit / paeniteat*) are used in both descriptions.

[201] Note Medea's language after learning of Creusa's and Creon's fiery demise (*Med.* 895): "Why, soul, do you stop? Follow your auspicious start" (*quid, anime, cessas? **sequere** felicem impetum*).

[202] *OLD* s.v. *materia* 6, 7. *Materia* can be used to describe the subject matter of a speech or poetry. Cf. *Ep.* 79.6, Ov. *Tr.* 2.382, Quint. *Inst.* 3.7.3, Tac. *Dial.* 35.4. See Littlewood (2004) 265, 277–8 for the metaliterary use of *materia* in the *Phaedra*.

Seneca's Medea claimed earlier that the hands of a girl could not cause sufficient damage: "What great deed were unpracticed hands able to dare? What was the fury of a girl able to do?" (*quid manus poterant **rudes** / **audere** magnum, quid puellaris furor?*, 908–9).²⁰³ In the *Heroides*, Ovid's Medea, in writing her letter, also fixates on the power of her hands and the difference between writing and killing: "What my right hand dared to do it does not dare to write" (*quod facere **ausa** mea est, non audet scribere **dextra**, Her.* 12.115).²⁰⁴ Hypsipyle, however, knows what Medea is capable of doing with her hands, as she suggests "Medea's hands are capable of every crime" (*Medeae **faciunt** ad **scelus** omne **manus**, Her.* 6.128). In pursuing her complete vengeance against Jason, Seneca's Medea realizes this is the time to be the "Medea" that Hypsipyle feared: "Go, your crime is complete—but your punishment is not: continue, while your hands are capable" (*vade, perfectum est **scelus**— / vindicta nondum: perage, dum **faciunt manus**,* 986–7). Now, at the conclusion of the play, her hands will compose a sufficient plot against Jason.

Seneca uses language that emphasizes Medea's role as the creator of the action, and she comes to resemble the artist who expresses himself through his work. As Boyle states, "Medea's language is used in the play not only to evoke the powers of darkness but to realize Medea's own dramatic myth."²⁰⁵ When Jason enters the scene and urges his troops, "Let us capture the very author of this fearful crime" (*ipsam sceleris **auctorem** horridi / capiamus,* 988–9), the words ring true for the reader who understands Medea's control of events on stage. Medea wants to display her new position, and rejoices when Jason appears (992–4):

> derat hoc unum mihi,
> spectator iste. nil adhuc facti reor:
> quidquid sine isto fecimus sceleris perit.

> This alone was lacking to me,
> That man as a spectator. I count nothing done as yet:
> Whatever crime we accomplished without him was wasted.

Medea feels that she must prove her power to Jason and the world, and that she needs this audience in order to do so.²⁰⁶ She will kill her remaining son with

---

²⁰³ Ovid's Medea also defines herself as a simple girl (*puellae / simplicis, Her.* 12.90–1) when she first met Jason.

²⁰⁴ Earlier in that poem, she designates her marriage with Jason as the intermingling of right hands (***dextrae dextera*** *iuncta meae*, 12.90).

²⁰⁵ Boyle (1997) 132.

²⁰⁶ Seneca strongly marks the theatrical spectators at the deaths of Asyanax and Polyxena in the *Troades* (cf. 1078–87, 1118–64). The Fury of the *Thyestes* wants Tantalus to be present as spectator

Jason watching (*te vidente*, 1001), and she wishes she had more children to truly express her pain: "Even if I kill two, the number is too small for my pain" (*ut duos perimam, tamen / nimium est dolori numerus angustus meo*, 1010–1). Near the close of the play, Medea asks Jason, "Do you recognize your wife? I am accustomed to flee in this way" (*coniugem agnoscis tuam? / sic fugere soleo*, 1021).[207] This stresses the persona of wife, which has incited Medea to action, as well as her literary and mythological past. Bartsch calls attention to the use of *agnoscere* in antiquity for the recognition of allusion and this sense may lurk behind the word here.[208] Medea is accustomed to flee in this manner in previous literary accounts such as Ovid's *Metamorphoses* when she escapes Pelias' daughters.[209] As Boyle states, "The metatheatrical sense (here irresistible) is that this is how Medea always leaves her play.... If 'this Medea has read Euripides', this Jason has not."[210] She mocks the tragic *anagnorisis* and reveals near divine powers of sorcery as her serpent-drawn chariot appears. Her last words place her among the heavens, to Jason's dismay (1025–7):

> ego inter **auras** aliti **curru vehar**.
> IA. Per alta vade spatia sublime aetheris,
> testare nullos esse, qua veheris, deos.

> I will be carried aloft in my winged chariot.
> JASON. Go through the high spaces of lofty heaven,
> Bear witness that, where you are carried, no gods exist.

Medea has become godlike in her ability to change the world, and Seneca characterizes her as an authorial figure in order to foreground her ability to create change and direct the action. Earlier in the play, she addressed the sun: "Allow me to be drawn through the air on my ancestor's chariot" (*da, da per **auras curribus***

(*spectante te*, 66). Mowbray (2012) 400 comments on the brutality of killing both children onstage: "Medea, in fact, revels in the victimization of her 'captive', Jason, who is both target of her revenge and the ultimate *intended audience* of her drama."

[207] Cf. *Thy.* 1005–6. Cf. Bartsch (2006) 260–5 for the various ways of reading Medea's recognition.

[208] Bartsch (2006) 262, citing Seneca the Elder's story of Ovid's borrowings of Vergil (*Suas.* 3.7).

[209] *Met.* 7.350–1: "But if she had not gone through the air on her winged serpents, / she would not have been free from punishment" (*quod nisi pennatis serpentibus isset in auras, / non exempta foret poenae*). Likewise, she "flees the arms of Jason" (*Iasonis **effugit** arma*, 7.397) at the conclusion of the condensed version of the tragedy in the *Metamorphoses*.

[210] Boyle (1997) 132. Also cf. Bartsch (2006) 261: "The result of the drama's attention to the question of recognition is that *personal* self-recognition and *literary* recognition necessarily coalesce here."

*patriis **vehi**,* 32), and such a prayer has been answered.²¹¹ The strong ring composition of the play, beginning and ending with "gods" (*Di,* 1; *deos,* 1027), encompasses a godlike figure in Me**dea**.²¹² She remains tied to her literary tradition, but Seneca has offered a fruitful manner of commenting on that tradition both through his intertextual play with Ovid and through his strong characterization of Medea's various roles in the play.

Seneca's Medea emerges from the play as a complex intertextual heroine. She has come to realize the potential that was implied in the laments and complaints of Ovid's elegiac Medea (the Medea of the *Heroides*) as well as the powerful transformative ability of Ovid's epic Medea (the Medea of the *Metamorphoses*). Throughout the play, Seneca utilizes these intertexts in order to comment on the behavior of his heroine; his tendency to include language from these intertexts throughout the play indicates his active redefinition of terms. Thus marriage imagery and maternal language come to indicate violence and revenge. Metapoetics play a major role in the *Medea* (and *Phaedra*), for Seneca points out the way in which his adaptation continues, completes, and amplifies Ovid's previous versions. Seneca crafts his Medea to emerge as a quasi-divine figure at the close of the play as well as an active manipulator and creator of her own character.

Seneca creates his characters of Medea and Phaedra in part through these echoes of Ovid. While I concentrated primarily on Ovidian Medeas in my investigation of Seneca's Medea, one could also bring in additional intertexts from Ovid (or Vergil, or Horace). In both of these plays Seneca utilizes intertextuality to question the roles these characters assume in the course of their plays. By returning these tragic heroines to their proper genre, Seneca exposes the generic limitations found in the Ovidian accounts. His tragedies draw attention to characteristics and language found in Ovid, but now figured in the larger tragic context to uncover meanings more at home in the fiery remains of Corinth or the incestuous royal palace of Athens.

---

²¹¹ Moreover these lines recall the story of Phaethon; cf. Costa (1973) ad loc., Littlewood (2004) 156–7, 168–9 for Phaethon in the *Medea*, and Ker (2009) 123 for Phaethon in Seneca's prose works.

²¹² Cf. Ahl (2000) 166–9 for the possible wordplay.

3

Intertextuality and Plot

"I'm a writer who likes to be influenced."
—Kenneth Koch

"It's not where you take things from, it's where you take them to."
—Jean-Luc Godard

One would come to Seneca's tragedies with certain prejudices (in Gadamer's terminology) or expectations as to their form and function.[1] But how would a reader (or spectator) know that the work presented is a tragedy, and not a comedy or an epic poem? The distinguishing features of tragedy (and what was acceptable for tragedy) were debated seemingly from its inception in Greece and could be seen in flux on the stage of the Theater of Dionysus in Athens.[2] Part of its allure to early Greek literary critics possibly derives from the very peculiarity of this genre "that polymorphically juxtaposed all earlier and contemporary poetic genres, and hence was itself visibly obsessed, already from the earliest evidence to which we have access, by the question of its own generic status."[3] Of course, there is a great dis-

---

Epigraph: The Kenneth Koch quote is taken from Lethem's (2011) essay "The Ecstasy of Influence," which is partly composed of intertexts from a wide variety of writers (he explains each of the unattributed quotes in a handy key at the conclusion of the piece). Senecan tragedy exhibits a similar celebration of his influences.

[1] Cf. Gadamer (1975) 271–9 on prejudice and 297 (in a discussion of contemporary works of art):

> Obviously we approach such creations with unverifiable prejudices, presuppositions that have too great an influence over us for us to know about them; these can give contemporary creations an extra resonance that does not correspond to their true content and significance. Only when all their relations to the present time have faded away can their real nature appear, so that the understanding of what is said in them can claim to be authoritative and universal.

[2] Issues such as the acceptability of staging historical events such as in the *Persians*, the importance of the didactic function of tragedy (debated in Ar. *Ra.* 1005–88), and even the number of speaking roles were all subject to change.

[3] Most (2000) 19.

tance between Greek tragedy and Roman tragedy, and between Seneca and Sophocles, but the formal aspects of what "makes up" a tragedy are relatively consistent: mythological tales or "slices from Homer" (as Aeschylus deemed his tragedies) presented with grandeur in heightened language,[4] featuring choral songs that break up and comment on the action of the play, and the resulting emotional punch of watching (or reading) such events. Both Aristotle and Horace analyze what makes a tragedy a tragedy and issue directives about the suitability of themes, plot arcs, and language—many critics still hearken back to their edicts when looking at Senecan tragedy.[5] In this vein, some may protest that Seneca's Medea kills her children "onstage" (blatantly ignoring Horace's advice, "Let Medea not slaughter her children in the open"[6]) and therefore has written a flawed tragedy. The debate whether Seneca's tragedies were meant to be performed is indicative of the larger question of Seneca's tragic style, as most of the judgments against staging boil down to aesthetic criteria that reflect the critics' own taste more than that of the audience of Seneca's Rome.[7] Seneca's conception of the proper elements of tragedy (including messenger speeches, the chorus, iambic dialogue) is formed from his understanding of the Greek and Roman theatrical tradition, but enlivened by his response to the poetry of the previous generation.[8] In this chapter, I investigate certain formal elements of Seneca's tragedies—the prologue speaker, choral songs, and messenger speeches—in order to reveal how intertextuality influences these components. Close examination reveals that intertextual references can be seen to color or even control the plot of the play, while larger generic features help to shape these very elements. For instance, Horace's lyric poetry finds renewed expression in Seneca's choral odes; both the meters and the themes of Horace's *carmina* prompt Seneca's choice of topics, meter, and language.[9] Messenger speeches, always in some sense moments of "epic" narrative within the tragic genre, are likewise influenced by

---

[4] Goldhill (1997) 127 notes that "already, in the classical polis, 'the tragic' has become synonymous with a certain grandeur of expression, high-flown periphrasis and even heroic posturing.... There is a style and vocabulary proper to the genre." Cf. Hor. *Ars* 81–98 for the correct diction of tragic figures. Seneca's own bombast and rhetorical style, while indicative of his time, should not be looked upon as something completely different from what was found in classical Athens.

[5] Staley (2010) seeks to recover an Aristotelian reading of Seneca's tragedies.

[6] Hor. *Ars* 185: *ne pueros coram populo Medea trucidet.*

[7] While I will not discuss this in detail, cf. Zwierlein (1966) for the fundamental statement of Seneca's *Rezitationsdramen* and G. W. M. Harrison (2000) for a collection of essays that show both how and why Seneca's tragedies can be staged. Cf. Kohn (2013) for the dramaturgy of individual plays.

[8] This, in itself, is not anything new, and one can find Euripides attempting to include and comment on the works of his predecessors, as well as Ennius producing poetry that he believed was innovative and representative of his time; cf. Hinds (1998) 63–74. Note Tarrant (1995) 225 on the importance of the Augustan poets to Senecan tragedy: "Another possible inference would be that Seneca's conception of tragic poetry owed at least as much to Augustan ideas of literary genre and generic innovation as to the form of classical Greek tragedy."

[9] See Davis (1993) for the Senecan chorus in general.

the epics of Vergil and Ovid as well as by the rhetoric of the time.[10] A reading of the messenger speech of the *Phaedra* as well as Talthybius' report in the *Troades* (164–202) indicates Seneca's interest in manipulating epic tropes and evaluating the pose of the epic narrator within the generic confines of tragedy.

Prologue Speakers

The use of a prologue speaker to set the scene and give the pertinent background information to the audience was common in Greek tragedy and can be found especially often in the works of Euripides.[11] Seneca's plays show variation in the structure of the prologue, from the protagonist explaining the troubled situation (*Medea, Oedipus*) to a dialogue between infernal figures (*Thyestes*) and even a lyric song (*Phaedra*).[12] The prologues can be integrated seamlessly into the action of the play (as in the *Troades*) or stand somewhat apart (Juno of *Hercules Furens*), but regardless of their narrative integration, the information given in the prologues is fundamental to the development of the play's action. Senecan prologues provide the first instance of important imagery, motifs, and themes that resound throughout the respective tragedies (e.g., the marriage/wedding motif of the *Medea* examined in the previous chapter). The intertexts found in the prologues often reappear later in the tragedy: an ominous echo of Actaeon's demise in the *Phaedra* foreshadows Hippolytus' dismemberment, and recognition of a line from the first *Eclogue* in the speech of Thyestes' ghost sways its application later in the *Agamemnon*.[13] Here I examine two diverse examples of the prologue speaker: Juno (*Herc. F.*) and Oedipus (*Oed.*). These figures not only provide the expected information but also reflect upon their position as both interpreters and instigators of the action. Juno's character is heavily drawn from moments of the *Aeneid* in which she jump-starts the action of the epic, and her own *furor* eventually infects Hercules with his characteristic frenzy. Seneca, always interested in exploring the psychology of anger and madness, provides a view of *furor* that is self-directed and suitable for a hero whose only injury can come from his own hand. The prologue

---

[10] Cf. J. Barrett (2002) 23–55. While intertexts with epic works can happen anywhere in Senecan tragedy, the messenger speeches are moments in which one character takes on the role of "epic" narrator and presents a report of events that the other characters have not experienced.

[11] A point Euripides makes to counter Aeschylus' obscurity at Ar. *Ra.* 945–7. For more on Seneca's treatment of the prologue, see Tarrant (1976) 157–61.

[12] Littlewood (2004) 269–301 explores the copious intertextual echoes of *Phaedra*'s prologue.

[13] Cf. Littlewood (2004) 296–8 for the implications of *Phd.* 83–4 and *Met.* 3.334–5. Tarrant (1976) ad 37 points out the echo of *Ecl.* 1.27–9. Seneca cleverly picks up the subject of the Vergilian line ("freedom," *libertas*) at the moment Agamemnon returns and Cassandra ironically claims that "freedom is here" (*libertas adest*, 796) pointing out "popular philosophical ideas of freedom and servitude; the liberty referred to is of course that of death" (Tarrant (1976) ad loc.).

of the *Oedipus* offers the reader the first glimpse of Oedipus as problem solver and mirrors the structure of the play with its series of poetic riddles to be solved. While Oedipus recognizes his guilt from the play's outset, intertextual parallels stress that his previous intellectual ability will not avail him in this crisis, and that the diseased world around him is an expression of his own internal corruption.

Juno *Furens*

Hercules Furens opens at night. Juno enters and her wrath swells as she scans the constellations, each one the catasterism of an affair of Jupiter. If his mistresses and bastard children hold such places of eternal honor, she must inhabit the earth, because "whores hold heaven" (*paelices caelum tenent*, 5).[14] Seneca focalizes Juno's perspective of the universe to indicate her own (warped?) view of the cosmos, in which every star seems to be mocking her powerlessness against Jupiter's frequent affairs. For instance, Juno heaps abuse on figures such as Orion and Ariadne although they are not traditionally grouped among Jupiter's lovers or illegitimate children.[15] Such a distorted view befits Juno's own incipient madness and points to her tenuous sanity at the play's start, which parallels Hercules' own fragile emotional and psychological "health." Juno has persecuted Hercules (the son of Alcmene and Jupiter) throughout his life, but his famous labors now appear to be coming to an end. The goddess, however, rouses herself to attempt another foray against Hercules (27–9):

> non sic abibunt odia: vivaces aget
> violentus iras animus, et **saevus dolor**
> **aeterna bella** pace sublata **geret**.

> My hatred will not end in this way:
> My violent spirit will enact everlasting wrath,
> My savage pain will wage eternal war, with peace banished.

These lines contain reminiscences of the representation of Juno at the beginning of the *Aeneid*, where she will not forget her hatred of the Trojans (*necdum etiam causae irarum **saevique dolores** / excidderant animo*, *Aen.* 1.25–6), is fixated on the "wound" they have given her (***aeternum*** *servans sub pectore vulnus*, *Aen.* 1.36),

---

[14] The opening salvo comes from Ovid's *Metamorphoses* (cf. Hinds (2011) 15), although the overall picture seems particularly Vergilian (see below). Ovid's Juno may already be understood as his reading of Vergil's (cf. Prauscello (2008)).

[15] See Fitch (1987a) ad loc. for the curious inclusions among the catalogue of Jupiter's infidelities.

and continues to wage war against them (***bella gero***, *Aen.* 1.47).[16] Seneca recalls the frightening figure of the *Aeneid* and implicitly suggests a similar rationale for Juno's hostility. In the *Aeneid*, Juno's hatred of Aeneas springs from Paris' judgment in favor of Venus, the Trojan descent from Dardanus (a bastard son of Jupiter, like Heracles), and Ganymede's honors.[17] Seneca's Juno here will "wage eternal war" but also "enact everlasting wrath," and the verb *ago* may point to the theatricality of this moment because it can also denote "to play the part of, act as."[18] The verbal connections between the Juno of the *Aeneid* and that of the *Hercules Furens* suggests that Seneca wishes the two figures to be read in conjunction—but to what end? For Putnam, "the opening monologue of Juno... carefully echoes the initial lines of the *Aeneid* with phraseology... to such a degree that it often resembles a powerful dramatization, in soliloquy, of what Virgil leaves implicit in his third-person narrative."[19] In his dramatization of her character, Seneca provides the reader a much more nuanced view of the inner workings of Juno's mind and her eventual discovery of a method of revenge (while Vergil's opening book includes a fourteen-line monologue, it is dwarfed by Seneca's 124-line speech).[20] The *Aeneid* intertexts clearly signal the continuation of her characteristic *furor* and *ira* from that epic work, but now directed at a new target and with fearful implications for her own psychological profile.

Seneca's Juno is obsessed with Jupiter's past infidelities and with her own inability to punish Hercules suitably, both notable topics for poets such as Ovid, as well as fundamental to her similar obsessive hatred of Aeneas in the *Aeneid*.[21] That Seneca may be interested in developing or modifying previous accounts can be seen in Juno's pronouncement "I complain too late about things that happened long ago" (*vetera sero querimur*, 19) as well as "I complain of things too trifling"

---

[16] Fitch (1987a) notes the parallels ad loc.

[17] *Aen.* 1.26–8. In addition to her general support of the Greeks against the Trojans (*Aen.* 1.24), these more personal reasons appear to be operative in her continued persecution of Aeneas and his men.

[18] *OLD* s.v. *ago* 26. For the role of *ira* as a generic marker of tragedy, cf. Ovid *Rem.* 376. *Vivax* will appear later in the play when Amphitryon reacts to the deaths of his grandchildren (*cernere hoc audes, nimis / **vivax** senectus?* "Do you dare to see this, too long-lasting old age?," *Herc. F.* 1026–7).

[19] Putnam (1995) 254. Such a dramatizing impulse on Seneca's part can be seen behind many of his intertextual nods (e.g., the wedding hymn of the *Medea*, discussed in Chap. 2).

[20] As the speech continues, prominent echoes of *Aen.* 7 appear as well, so we can see the conflation of these two Juno-inspired moments of the *Aeneid* in Seneca's opening. Seneca may point to the transference to the tragic genre by making his Juno focus on Thebes as a locus for her hatred, since she has been "made a stepmother" so often by this city (*quotiens novercam fecit!* 22). Cf. Zeitlin (1990) 130–67 for Thebes as a tragic topos, "in both senses of the word: as a designated place, a geographical locale, and figuratively, as a recurrent concept or formula, or what we call a 'commonplace'" (131).

[21] Cf. *Met.* 2.508–30, 9.176–204 where Hercules repeats his labors and identifies Juno as *novercam* (181).

(*levia sed nimium queror*, 63).²² Both of these outbursts are analogous to Seneca's belated authorial position: as Juno hints at the need for novelty in the production of a plot equal to Hercules, so Seneca seeks to rejuvenate the tragic story of Hercules' madness. After this second outburst, Juno elaborates her true fear that Hercules will seek the heavens now that he has "conquered" the other realms. This fear, in fact, is validated later in the play when Hercules desires to ascend to the heavens (and, of course, his transformation into a god is part of the mythological tradition).²³ By representing Hercules' "destined" apotheosis from Juno's viewpoint and crafting a dramatic monologue for Juno, Seneca finds a fresh manner of representing Juno and the ramifications that her anger will have for Hercules.

In this prologue, Seneca has combined the two primary appearances of Juno from the *Aeneid* (in the first and seventh books—both notable moments of "prologue" activity) as a way to show the *labor* involved in persecuting Hercules and to investigate the nature of *furor* itself.²⁴ His Juno takes on the anger and pain from both of these sections of the *Aeneid* to become a more fearful composite that haunts the resulting action of the tragedy. After a number of false starts, which serve to illuminate Hercules' *virtus* and her own paradoxical position as the cause of his fame ("I have provided the place for his glory," *gloriae feci locum*, 36), she finally decides to call upon the Furies. While the Underworld is the locus for such figures, it is not enough to sic a Fury on Hercules, as he has already conquered the Underworld (50–63), and Juno fears that this will be an insufficient source of punishment.²⁵ No monster can overcome Hercules, "nobody except himself: let him now wage wars with himself" (*nemo est nisi ipse:* **bella** *iam secum* **gerat**, 85). This fulfills Juno's earlier, and intertextually marked, call to arms (*aeterna* **bella**...**geret**, 29), but now, notably, with Hercules acting against himself. To cause Hercules to turn on himself, Juno needs the Furies. In so doing, she parallels her actions in the seventh book of the *Aeneid*, in which she sum-

---

²² E. Wilson (2004) 99 claims, "Juno's frustrations are parallel to those which impel the Senecan text to struggle against the pressure of a dominating literary tradition, and with the pressure of everyday bloodshed in imperial Rome." Juno's claims are similar to Medea's complaints (*querelas*, 26) in her prologue speech.

²³ Of course this expressed desire for assaulting heaven occurs when he is maddened: "The heaven is untouched, a labor worthy of Hercules" (*immune caelum est, dignus Alcide labor*, 957). Hercules' plot to lead the Giants against the Olympian gods is called "the crazy impulse of a maddened heart, although grand" (*pectoris sani parum, / magni tamen...dementem impetum*, 974–5).

²⁴ By "prologue" activity, I am signifying the way in which the appearance of Juno acts to impel the action of the epic forward from these two starting points. Juno instigates the action in *Aen.* 1 with her visit to Aeolus' cave, and in *Aen.* 7 when she rouses the Fury from the Underworld to punish the Trojans and create a suitable casus belli (*flectere si nequeo superos, Acheronta movebo*, 7.312).

²⁵ Juno claimed that his return from Hades was "trifling" (*parum est reverti*, 49), pointedly reversing the Sibyl's belief in the difficulty of reemergence from the Underworld (*Aen.* 6.126–9), cf. E. Wilson (2004) 99–100.

mons the Fury Allecto from the depths of the Underworld to goad Amata and Turnus into battle. Fitch has chronicled the similarities of language, but one point needs further clarification.[26] When Juno urges the Furies, "Arouse the heart" (***concutite pectus***, 105), the clear parallel is Juno's call to Allecto to "arouse your fruitful heart" (*fecundum **concute pectus***, *Aen.* 7.338). While in the *Aeneid*, the line clearly refers to Allecto, it is unclear here if the *pectus* should be Juno's, the Furies', or even Hercules' in this section. Seneca writes (104–6):

> hoc agite, poenas petite violatae Stygis;
> **concutite pectus**, acrior mentem excoquat
> quam qui caminis ignis Aetnaeis furit.

> Do it, seek revenge for the desecrated Styx;
> Arouse the breast, let a flame fiercer
> Than that which rages in the forges of Aetna broil the mind.

The very indeterminacy of the attribution points to the problematic nature of such fury—it spreads like fire, and everyone who comes into contact with it will manifest its rage.[27]

I believe that the surrounding context helps to determine that, in fact, the breast is that of the Furies and therefore directly parallels the situation from *Aeneid* 7.[28] While it is not uncommon in the play, the word *pectus* also becomes representative of Hercules' madness (*pectoris sani parum*, 974; *pectus o nimium ferum*, 1226), discussions of Amphitryon's suicide (1312), and the union between father and son (1320).[29] This repetition indicates that the arousal of the Furies' breast will lead to Hercules' subsequent madness and suffering. Seneca modifies the Vergilian tradition by indicating that Juno herself must suffer insanity in order to conceive of a worthy plot against Hercules (which, in turn, will involve his own madness). Whereas in the *Aeneid* Juno charges Allecto with instilling madness in others, in order to indicate the severity of her anger towards Hercules, Seneca's Juno must first be struck by the Furies' goad. Juno's speech becomes more and more frenzied as it unfolds, because Juno herself enacts the fury that she wishes to inflict upon Hercules. For Seneca, the impulse to rage must not be external but rather internal; Juno reveals the necessary quasi-rational assent to anger. This follows one of Seneca's insights about *furor* found in his

---

[26] Fitch (1987a) ad loc.

[27] Littlewood (2004) 117 believes this may be "ambiguous by design."

[28] Tarrant (1985) 100 notes that a similar use of *concute...pectus* in the *Thyestes* "is used...of stirring up one's own potential for disorder." In that case Tantalus is stirred up to infect his ancestral home, whereas here the Furies act as one step in Juno's own descent into *furor*.

[29] The word appears eighteen times in the play.

De Ira, namely, that it always directed in some sense against the agent who wields it.[30] Therefore, if Juno comprehends that the only one that can defeat Hercules is Hercules himself, madness is the perfect conduit for her revenge because it too is self-directed ("Fury, always armed against itself," *in se semper armatus Furor,* 99). While in the *Aeneid* Juno can summon Allecto and have her inflict others with fury,[31] in the *Hercules Furens,* Juno feels she must rage first in order for Hercules to do so (107–112):

>   ut possit animum captus Alcides agi,
>   magno furore percitus, nobis prius
>   insaniendum est: Iuno, cur nondum furis?
>   me me, sorores, mente deiectam mea
>   versate primam, facere si quicquam apparo
>   dignum noverca.

>   In order that Hercules, captured in his mind, may be driven,
>   Enflamed by great furor, first I must be made frenzied:
>   Juno, why do you not rage yet?
>   Sisters, first turn against me, scatter my wits,
>   If I am preparing to do something worthy of a stepmother.

It is at this moment, after she has made the decision to suffer insanity that she is able to foretell the grim homecoming that Hercules will endure.[32] Schiesaro comments, "Juno's words do not describe reality as much as they in fact create it: she envisages Hercules' challenge, and—behold—the challenge really takes place shortly thereafter. In this respect she embodies the creative power of the author, and the plot that she conceives is the tragedy which happens."[33] By focusing on a moment that recalls Juno's own appearance in *Aeneid* 7, Seneca acknowledges that Vergil had an

---

[30] Seneca elucidates this self-destructive quality in the first paragraph of his *De Ira*: "This emotion, provided it harm another, gives no thought to itself, and rushes onto its own weapons, so eager for vengeance it drags the avenger down with it" (*dum alteri noceat sui neglegens, in ipsa inruens tela et ultionis secum ultorem tracturae avidus,* 1.1), and repeats it often in the work (1.5.2, 1.7.4, 2.35.5, 3.1.5, 3.28.1).

[31] In the *Aeneid*, Allecto is hated even by the other spirits of the Underworld (*Aen.* 7.327–8). Amphitryon finds Hercules' hyperbolic desire for punishment (*Herc. F.* 1202–18) indicative of his *furor*: "He rages against himself, which is the very quality of fury" *quoque habet proprium furor, / in se ipse saevit, Herc. F.* 1220–1).

[32] Cf. Zwierlein (1986b) ad loc. for more on the text of *Herc. F.* 108–14 and his choice of *nobis* over *vobis* at 108. Zwierlein also notes the similarity in sentiment to Horace's *Ars* 101–3, where he discusses the actor's emotions as a way to incite the audience to similar emotions. Linguistic parallels point to Hercules' own later madness (**dignus** Alcide labor, 957; vota persolvi libens / te **digna**, 1037–8; pectoris **sani** parum, 974; pelle **insanos** fluctus animi, 1092).

[33] Schiesaro (2003) 186. Staley (2010) 98–100 discusses Seneca's use of the Fury in this scene.

"archetypal role as a poet of *furor* (and *nefas*)" and that he will continue to emphasize the destructive nature of *furor* for those whom Juno torments.³⁴

After summoning the Furies, she realizes that the only way to do something "worthy of a stepmother" is to change her tactics (*vota mutentur mea*, 112). At this point, Juno essentially rehearses what will occur later in the play—her own madness presages the madness that Hercules will endure and the destruction that he will wreak upon his family (118–23):

> stabo et, ut certo exeant
> emissa nervo tela, librabo manu,
> regam furentis arma, pugnanti Herculi
> tandem favebo—scelere perfecto licet
> admittat illas genitor in caelum manus.
> **Movenda** iam sunt **bella**.

> I will stand, and I will influence his hand
> So that the released arrows will leave the string without error;
> I will rule the arms of that one raging and, at last,
> I will favor Hercules in his fight—once the crime is committed,
> Then, let his father admit those hands into heaven.
> Now wars must be begun.

These lines sketch Hercules' future destruction of his family, and Seneca is careful to echo the language found in Juno's prologue later in his tragedy to indicate the fulfillment of the fury that Juno has unleashed within both Hercules and herself.³⁵ In this passage, Juno focuses on how the actions of her hand (*manu*, 119) will lead to bloodshed at the hands of Hercules (*illas...manus*, 122), which may make his deification problematic. When Hercules acknowledges that he has murdered his family (a recognition brought about by seeing the blood on his hands, 1192–3), he identifies his hands as the very hands of Juno (*o novercales manus*, 1236), nicely conflating the metaphorical sentiment with Juno's actual hands, which have directed the arrow. Near the conclusion, Amphitryon embraces Hercules right hand (*hanc manum amplector libens*, 1319), indicating his forgiveness. The plot that the Fury has provided is to make Hercules the very instrument of revenge against himself, and Juno's directive that *movenda sunt bella* recalls her similar response in the *Aeneid*, "I will move Acheron" (*Acheronta*

---

³⁴ Schiesaro (1992) 61 discusses how the *Thyestes'* intertextual connections to *Aeneid* 7 (in part the use of *concute...pectus*) point to thematic, ethical, and metapoetic connections with the second half of the *Aeneid*.

³⁵ Amphitryon describes the discharged (*emissa*, 993) arrow whistling through the body of Hercules' son. Additional language from this section of the prologue is echoed at *Herc. F.* 990–1 and 1171–2.

movebo, 7.311), as well as Vergil's own, "I am beginning a greater work" (*maius opus moveo*, 7.44). As Vergil's Juno instigates the action of the *Aeneid*, so Seneca's Juno shows how fury infects the characters of the *Hercules Furens*, and that the end result of such madness is self-destruction. Intertextual connections with the figure of Juno from the *Aeneid* point to broader thematic parallels between the two works and metapoetically hint at Juno's role as an author or director of the action, while also delineating Seneca's psychological focus in his tragedy.

In addition to the prologue's dramatization of Juno's character, one can detect additional connections between the dramatic design of the *Hercules Furens* and the plot of the *Aeneid*. If Juno's hatred here can be paralleled with her representation in the *Aeneid*, can the figures of Hercules and Aeneas and their sufferings be paralleled as well? It is my contention that this is one of Seneca's reasons for presenting Juno as prologue speaker and that the similar plot scenarios (Juno searching for a way to destroy those who are hateful to her) enable the reader to see broad similarities between the two works as a whole. In this reading Hercules is similar to Aeneas, who likewise attempts to make his way "home" after undergoing a series of labors brought about through the hatred of Juno (including trips to the Underworld), and whose homecoming is further destabilized through wars that must be waged as well as the suffering these wars produce.[36] In fact, Vergil employs Hercules as a model for Aeneas' own behavior, especially in *Aeneid* 8.[37] In the *Aeneid*, the toils of Hercules can be seen as the mythical paradigm for Juno's persecution of the Trojans, and Vergil points out how Hercules endured "thousands of harsh labors...by the will of unjust Juno" (*duros mille labores...fatis Iunonis iniquae*, *Aen.* 8.291–2).[38] In the *Aeneid*, Hercules acts as a model for Aeneas' heroism, but also evokes specific problems.[39] One may wonder if the rage that Aeneas feels at the close of the epic ("burning with rage and terrible in his anger," *furiis accensus et ira terribilis*, 12.946–7) can be read

---

[36] Note that the description of Hercules' *katabasis* is signposted by a reference to the *Aen.*1.203: "Perhaps it will be pleasing at some point to remember these things" (*forsan et haec olim* **meminisse** *iuvabit*) when Amphitryon urges Theseus to recount what they suffered: "What was difficult to endure, it is sweet to remember" (*quae fuit durum pati,* / **meminisse** *dulce est*, 656–7). Seneca's description of the Underworld, as well as other portions of the play, borrows much from the *Aeneid* as well; cf. Fitch (1987a) passim.

[37] Cf. Putnam (1995) 256: "Critical opinion generally sees Hercules as an allegorical prefiguration of a sequence of Roman greats from Aeneas to Augustus, a sequence well illustrated in book 8 itself as we progress in our mind's eye from Evander's primitive Palatine to the snowy threshold of the newly dedicated Apollo temple, agleam in Luna marble."

[38] Gransden (1976) ad loc. points out that the phrase *fatis Iunonis iniquae* recollects the *odiis Iunonis acerbae* at 1.668, "where the reference is to Aeneas. Both heroes suffered at Juno's hands."

[39] Putnam (1995) 256–7 cautions that the portrayal of Hercules in the *Aeneid* features madness (*furens animis*, *Aen.* 8.228) and anger (*fervidus ira*, *Aen.* 8.230). Galinsky (1988) views these echoes differently.

into Hercules' own fury in Seneca's play.⁴⁰ If so, Seneca continues the tale beyond the ending of the *Aeneid* by dramatizing Hercules' response to the madness that consumed him earlier. Theseus and Amphitryon both encourage Hercules to acknowledge that he was not at fault for the events of the play and that his *virtus* must now consist of renouncing anger (*Herculem irasci veta*, 1277).⁴¹ His family and friends will stand by Hercules, but one wonders if Hercules himself will be prone to murderous rage even after the events of this tragedy.⁴² For the Roman reader, the intertextual references both encourage recognition of the similarities in plot and comment on Seneca's reception of Vergil's national epic. Seneca's prologue emphasizes the consistency in the characterization of both Hercules and Juno from work to work and era to era, but adds his own psychological expansion of the effects of *furor* on both Juno and Hercules.⁴³

Seneca points to the infectious quality of *furor* as it spreads from the Fury to Juno and finally consumes Hercules, leading to the destruction of his family and his traumatized attempts to come to terms with his crime. Seneca repeats language found in Juno's prologue later in the play in order to point to the violence that springs from her wrath (***ira**que nostra fruitur*, 34; *perge,* ***ira****, perge*, 75). If a goddess can succumb to madness, so can a hero. The intertextual engagement with the *Aeneid* in the opening of the *Hercules Furens* leads the reader not only to envision Juno in a similar light as in that epic but also to map the action of Seneca's play onto the epic events of the *Aeneid*. While Vergil's *Aeneid* concludes ambivalently with the death of Turnus at the hands of Aeneas, Seneca is interested in exploring the final denouement of Hercules attempting to cope with his rage and anger after the slaughter of his family. In so doing, Seneca formulates Hercules' rage in a different manner. While the characters surrounding him (i.e. the internal audience) may forgive the results of his madness, Hercules himself can only look at his survival as

---

⁴⁰ Amphitryon groups these emotions together after Hercules' long death-wish speech (1202–18), indicating that he has not changed his anger (*mutavit iras*, 1220) and still shows the signs of *furor* (1220).

⁴¹ When observing his dead wife and children, Hercules claims, "My anger rushes against all" (*ruit ira in omnis*, 1167). In following his father's advice, Hercules addresses his *virtus*: "Yield, heroism, endure the command of your father" (*succumbe, virtus, prefer imperium patris*, 1315).

⁴² E. Wilson (2004) 111 questions any redemptive reading of the conclusion: "The play ends abruptly, so that Hercules' last words remain his despairing, half-funny realization that even Hades knows him all too well....A journey to Athens means something very different for Seneca as a Roman. It is a regressive move, back to the past, and even the past can offer no hope."

⁴³ This play can be seen as an expansion of Hercules' character from *Aen.* 8—there are parallels in motivation, as pointed out by Putnam (1995) 257: "Rather, as we ponder the intricacies of Virgil's delineation of the Greek hero's progress through Pallanteum, we can with equal fairness claim him as spiritual ancestor of Seneca's Hercules, contemplating suicide and observing in the mirror of his psyche 'a monstrous form, impious, savage, inexorable, wild' (*monstrum impium saevumque et immite ac ferum*, 1280)." Both Fitch (1987a) and Putnam find in Hercules' character an unswerving hubris and predilection for violence.

another in the long line of his heroic labors: "Let this labor also be added to Hercules' labors, let me live" (*eat ad labores hic quoque Herculeos labor: / vivamus*, 1316–7). At the conclusion of the play, Hercules, almost in spite of himself, gives in to the advice of his father and makes his way to Athens for absolution. One wonders if he will be able to forgive himself for his actions or if his brand of heroism necessitates the rage and anger problematized in the tragedy.[44]

Oedipus' Plague

Seneca's *Oedipus* begins with the world suffering from plague. The sun is dim, heat blasts the fields, rivers are reduced to dust, horses and cattle fall dead, and the populace wretchedly wastes away. Racked with fear and guilt, Seneca's Oedipus laments the imperial power he has "stumbled into" (*in regum incidi*, 14) and fears everything around him. Indeed, when the play begins Oedipus dreads that the plague is of his making and claims, "I've made the sky noxious/guilty" (*fecimus caelum nocens*, 36). Seneca lavishes detail on the plague, a description that exhibits such a density of literary reminiscences that it has led one critic to deem it a "textually transmitted disease."[45] Thucydides, Lucretius, Vergil, and Ovid are responsible for many of the details, but Seneca reinvigorates these elements by continuing to stress the language and imagery of the plague throughout the play, and by identifying the sufferings with Oedipus himself. Oedipus explains the results of the plague (52–6):

> Nec ulla pars immunis exitio vacat,
> sed omnis aetas pariter et sexus ruit,
> iuvenesque senibus iungit et gnatis patres
> funesta pestis, una fax thalamos cremat,
> fletuque **acerbo funera** et questu carent.

> No part is left immune from destruction,
> But every age and sex is ruined equally,
> The deadly plague joins youths to elders and fathers to children,

---

[44] The wide-ranging readings of this play fall broadly into similar "pessimistic" and "optimistic" camps, as with the conclusion of the *Aeneid*. For an overview cf. Hine (1987) 257: "There remains an ambivalence in Hercules' character, traces of wanton violence and arrogance as well as heroic grandeur."

[45] Slaney (2009) 58. She provides further examples of the intertextual echoes: "It is clear, however, just how convoluted the spread of this particular trope has been, and how messy the question of sources" (58). Jakobi (1988) points out eight possible intertexts with Ovid's plague at Aegina, and Töchterle (1994) notes echoes from authors such as Lucretius, Manilius, Vergil, and Thucydides.

> One torch turns newlyweds into ash,
> And funerals lack bitter weeping and mourning.

Here, the universality of the blight is stressed in language reminiscent of the plague at Aegina described in Ovid's *Metamorphoses* (7.611–3):

> qui lacriment desunt indefletaeque vagantur
> natorumque patrumque[46] animae iuvenumque senumque,
> nec locus in tumulos, nec sufficit arbor in ignes.

> Mourners are lacking, and the unlamented souls of children,
> Fathers, young men, and elders wander about,
> There is no space for tombs, no wood for pyres.

Once again mourners and tears are lacking, and the plague has now left the souls of those affected to wander without the necessary funerary rites.[47] In the mouth of Oedipus, however, such language also attains unexpected significance and irony. Wedding imagery (*iungit, fax, thalamos*) can be read as an indictment of Oedipus' marriage to his mother,[48] and the chiastic line that joins young and old, fathers and children (*iuvenesque senibus iungit et gnatis patres*) is representative of Oedipus himself, who as a young man killed an elder and as a son killed his father.[49] In fact, this is exactly how Oedipus describes the event later in the play when he remembers "when the haughty old man first pushed me, a youth, aside with his chariot" (*cum prior **iuvenem senex** / curru superbus pelleret*, 770–1). In addition, Oedipus himself can be seen as plague-like: as the plague destroys families, so his incest obliterates normative family categories (he is father to his brothers, son to his wife, etc.).[50] As in the *Hercules Furens*, the prologue's intertexts offer an initial expression of the themes and narrative arc that will continue to inspire the action of the play. While Juno is able to rehearse the plot that will come to pass, Oedipus' confused agony about the situation indicates the upside-down world of his plague-ridden Thebes. It is a world where "nature has been reversed" (*natura versa est*, 371; cf. *Natura in uno vertit Oedipoda*, 943), and every examination, whether that of

---

[46] Following Heinsius' emendation.

[47] One can find a similar description of those impacted by the plague at *Met.* 7.589–92. Both of these parallels are noted by Jakobi (1988) 91.

[48] After Oedipus has blinded himself, he screams, "At last I have discovered a night suitable to my marriage bed" (*inventa **thalamis** digna nox tandem meis*, 977).

[49] Cf. Laius' description of Oedipus (634–5, 638–40): "But the bloody king, who possesses the scepter, the reward of vicious murder and resides in the foul bedroom of his father" (*sed rex cruentus, pretia qui saevae necis / sceptra et nefandos occupat **thalamos patris***, 634–5; also cf. 638–40).

[50] Both Frank (1995a) 124, and Busch (2007) 258–9 have noted this parallel.

Manto ("let's investigate" *scrutemur*, 372) or Oedipus (*scrutatur*, 965) uncovers the foul crime (*nefas*, 373) lurking just below the surface.

Seneca accumulates the plague accounts of previous poets in order to exaggerate the seriousness of his Theban plague, and to bind their language into the larger poetic context of his *Oedipus*.[51] In doing so, he magnifies elements from their accounts and comments on their applicability to his particular rendition. Thus, Oedipus' figuration of the funerals lacking mourning (*fletuque **acerbo funera** et questu carent*, 56) echoes Vergil's *Aeneid* and his account of the souls of children who died before their time, "whom the black day of death stole from their mother's breast and submerged in untimely death" (*ab ubere raptos / abtulit atra dies et **funere** mersit **acerbo***, Aen. 6.428–9).[52] Seneca's repetition of Vergilian language not only calls attention to the pathos of the funerals of plague victims, but it also implies that the plague caused the deaths of infants and includes them among the victims (although they are not noted specifically in the text). One may also see such elements as part of the "hell on earth" of the *Oedipus*' opening, as this passage comes from Vergil's description of the Underworld.[53] These Vergilian and Ovidian intertexts reveal how Seneca can provide additional dramatic irony in his phrasing of the plague or supplement the plague depiction to be even more all-encompassing than it initially appears. Seneca attempts to create a plague that surpasses his predecessors' works, while enlivening their language and hinting that Oedipus is the cause of the plague itself.

Oedipus' Sphinx

As the prologue continues, Jocasta calls upon Oedipus to remember that he is the leader of Thebes and must show courage in the face of adversity. Oedipus claims that he is courageous, as his interaction with the Sphinx proves, and that his intellect provides the foundation for his heroism.[54] When Creon returns with a difficult oracle from Delphi, Oedipus says, "Speak, although it may be

---

[51] For instance, the chorus's plaintive song notes the deaths of animals in a way similar to Vergil's plague at Noricum (*G*. 3.478–566), while also restating the human cost (found also in Oedipus' prologue). In addition, the famous seven gates of Thebes are not able to handle all the dead (*non satis septem patuere portae*, 130), which pointedly recalls Ovid's account ("since the gates were not sufficient for so many funerals" *neque enim capiebant funera portae*, Met. 7.607). Seneca has combined the human and animal plagues of Lucretius and Vergil, and dismissed the possible regeneration of Aeacus' Myrmidons (although he owes much to Ovid's plague, Met. 7.522–613).

[52] I owe this observation to Luca Grillo. This Vergilian passage also influenced Seneca when he describes the deaths of Hercules' children (*in primo/ limine vitae*, Herc. F. 1131–2), as Vergil wrote of children who expired *in limine primo... / dulcis vitae*, Aen. 6.427–8. Cf. Austin (1977) ad loc.

[53] The opening chorus stresses how Thebes has become Hades-like, with Cerberus wandering the land and ghosts flitting around the groves (*Oed*. 171–5). The word *funus* appears prominently (seven times) in the opening scenes.

[54] For more on Seneca's representation of the Sphinx and the Sphinx in mythology, cf. Töchterle (1994) ad loc. and Ahl (2008) 75–9.

uncertain: it is granted to Oedipus alone to understand ambiguous matters"
(*Fare, sit dubium licet: / ambigua soli noscere Oedipodae datur*, 215–6).[55] Oedipus'
ability (verified by the bilingual etymological pun between *nosco* and οἶδα)[56]
is graphically explored in the final section of the prologue when Oedipus relates
how he solved the riddle of the Sphinx (92–102):

> nec Sphinga caecis verba nectentem modis
> fugi: cruentos **vatis** infandae tuli
> rictus et albens ossibus sparsis solum;
> cumque e superna rupe iam praedae imminens
> aptaret alas verbera et caudae movens
> saevi leonis more conciperet minas,
> **carmen** poposci, sonuit horrendum insuper,
> crepuere malae, saxaque impatiens morae
> revulsit unguis viscera expectans mea;
> nodosa sortis verba et implexos dolos
> ac triste carmen alitis **solvi** ferae.

> Nor did I flee the Sphinx, weaving her words in dark ways:
> I stood up to the bloody grimace of that foul poetess
> And the ground strewn white with scattered bones;
> She threatening her prey from her high cliff
> Spread open her wings, and roused her battle spirit
> By lashing her tail like a savage lion.
> I asked for the riddle. She screamed horribly from above,
> Her jaws creaked, and impatiently she tore at the stones
> With her claws in anticipation of my guts.
> I untangled the knotted words and devious tricks of that oracle
> And I solved the grave riddle of the winged beast.

This is one of the longest extant descriptions of the Sphinx from antiquity, and
its details are important to the play as a whole.[57] The Sphinx appears here as a
murderous monster, but also a singer, whose horrifying (*horrendum, triste*) riddle

---

[55] It is notable that Creon actually quotes the oracle in dactylic hexameters. Tragedy can encompass different meters for a variety of reasons—the hexameter was the accustomed meter of oracular pronouncements.

[56] This bilingual pun stresses that Oedipus' intellect is his most important quality, and forms of *noscere* appear often in the text; cf. Boyle (2011) ad loc.

[57] A fragment of Euripides' *Oedipus* (540) also describes the Sphinx in language that Seneca may be imitating (the Sphinx's wings and tail are described in Euripides' play, and his Sphinx also may "grind down" something (text uncertain) as Seneca's tears up the stones of the cliff. Busch (2007) 239–40 also connects Euripides' description to Seneca's description of the rainbow.

must be solved (*solvi*) by Oedipus.⁵⁸ Seneca's description also recalls Ovid's rendition of this event, but he fleshes it out with the grim elaboration characteristic of his tragedies (*Met.* 7.759–61):

> **carmina** Laiades non intellecta priorum
> **solverat** ingeniis⁵⁹, et praecipitata iacebat
> inmemor ambagum **vates** obscura suarum;

> The son of Laius, using his wits, had solved the riddle
> Which had deluded others, and the dark prophetess threw herself
> Headlong from the cliff, forgetful of her own tricks.

Ovid's three lines are expanded into an eleven-line description that further entangles the Sphinx within the literary fabric of the play. For instance, Oedipus himself will be labeled as *cruentus* by Laius (*rex cruentus*, 634, 642); Oedipus will rage like a lion (*quasi…leo*, 919–20) when searching for a fitting punishment, and will use his own claw-like fingernails to blind himself (*unguibus*, 968). Mastronarde comments on the system of motifs (kinship, incest, destruction) expressed through these verbal connections, "This one too tends to create a unity out of Oedipus' crime, the monstrous Sphinx, the plague, etc.—a unity in which the abnormal is normal, *natura versa est*."⁶⁰ While Ovid famously avoids the Oedipus tale in his Theban history, Seneca pointedly reinserts Oedipus into a decidedly Ovidian Thebes where transformation is ever-present.⁶¹

This Ovidian intertext emphasizes the Sphinx's poetic aspect, and her riddle (*carmina*) is very much like a complex poem that needs to be interpreted. Seneca repeats Ovid's description of the Sphinx as a *vates*, a term resuscitated by the Augustan poets to describe themselves.⁶² Seneca presents his Sphinx as poetic figure, high on her cliff, weaving words (*verba nectentem*, 92), like a murderous

---

⁵⁸ The whitened bones on the ground are reminiscent of those surrounding other monstrous singers, Vergil's Sirens: "The cliffs of the Sirens were white with the bones of many victims" (*scopulos Sirenum…multorum* **ossibus albos**, *Aen.* 5.865).

⁵⁹ Note that later in the play, when searching for a suitable punishment, Oedipus addresses himself, *utere ingenio, miser* (947) and repeats forms of *solvere* (*poenas…solvis*, 937; *solvendo non es*, 942). The *ingenium* of Oedipus can be seen as symbolic for the "inborn" literary tradition that he embodies and his "solution" leads to his suffering.

⁶⁰ Mastronarde (1970) 305.

⁶¹ Note especially the second and third choral odes. See Hinds (2011) 10–14, and the discussion of the *Oedipus* in Chap. 4.

⁶² E.g., *Aen.* 7.41, where Vergil addresses the Muse Erato: "You, goddess, you, advise your poet" (*tu vatem, tu, diva, mone*), and Hor. *Carm.* 4.6.44: *vatis Horati*. For more on Vergil as *vates*, cf. Gildenhard (2007) 86–92. For the use of *vates* by the Augustan poets, cf. Newman (1968), and Ahern (1990). For the term proem-in-the-middle, cf. Conte (2007) 219–31.

Muse that must be approached and conquered.[63] This sets the precedent for much of the action of the play in which Oedipus must act as the interpreter for a series of reported events and is placed in a similar position to the reader of the play.[64] The Sphinx's riddle foreshadows the Delphic oracle given by the Pythia, and she will be styled in language similar to the Sphinx (*imminens*, 228; *vates*, 230). Oedipus' skill at decipherment encourages his identification with a reader willing to see behind the meaning of words and notice the "clues" that Seneca offers in his construction of the plot. Miller notes the resemblance of Oedipus to a detective trying to understand the given evidence: "The perennial success of the story of Oedipus may lie more in its powerful narrative presentation of the *problem of narration* than in any solution it presents to the question of man's origin and nature."[65] Oedipus' unraveling of the meaning of the riddle leads to the death of the Sphinx as well as his elevation to kingship. But this new position only leads to trouble, as he becomes a stand-in for the Sphinx and the problems that she once brought to the city. Oedipus has a premonition of this at the end of the prologue (106–8):

> ille, ille dirus callidi **monstri** cinis
> in nos rebellat, illa nunc Thebas lues
> perempta perdit.

> The accursed ashes of that clever monster
> Wage new wars against us; now that scourge,
> Although killed, ruins Thebes.[66]

The ghost of Laius underlines this identification when he calls Oedipus a "tangled evil, a monster more riddling than his Sphinx" (*implicitum malum / magisque* **monstrum** *Sphinge perplexum sua*, *Oed*. 640–1).[67] It would appear that Oedipus'

---

[63] The use of *necto* to indicate the composition of poetry can be seen at Ov. *Pont*. 4.2.30: *nec numeris* **nectere verba** *iuvat*, and Sen. *Ben*. 1.4.5; *modis* can be indicative of meter (cf. *OLD* s.v. *modus* 7). Does Seneca figure his poetic predecessors as a sort of Sphinx whose poetic output must be "solved" for his own poetry to be able to be understood?

[64] Cf. my discussion in Chap. 4.

[65] J. H. Miller (1990) 74 (my emphasis), who also understands the character of Oedipus as "both detective and murderer in this aboriginal detective story."

[66] The use of *callidus* often is used of Muses (*callida musa Calliope*, Lucr. 6.93) or, famously, poetic phrases (Horace's *callida...iunctura*, *A.P.* 47–8). Boyle (2011) ad loc. notes, "Later Oedipus sees the necromancy of Act III as a 'devious' (*callidi*, 668) plot which he can solve, as he did the riddle of the 'devious' Sphinx."

[67] Creon styles the Sphinx as an object of fear (244), as is her song (*nefandi carminis tristes minae*, 246). In his *Phoenissae*, Seneca has Oedipus claim that he should sit on the Sphinx's abandoned cliff as a *monstrum...maius* (*Phoen*. 122) and ask questions about his fortune, which none will solve. Additionally, the use of *lues* for the Sphinx recalls its previous use of the plague (29) and connects the

foreboding is not unfounded and that he acts as a surrogate Sphinx for Thebes. The intertexts with Ovid's *Metamorphoses* here (and later in the text) encourage the reader to note this transformation, as Oedipus is the conduit for the *pestis* that ravages Thebes and another in a long series of monsters (*monstra*, 724) native to Thebes.[68] The prologue of the *Oedipus* introduces pervasive imagery and language found in the play and highlights Oedipus' desire to make sense of the world around him. Intertexts with the Augustan poets allow Seneca to comment on the diseased state of Thebes and point to Oedipus' own role in the outbreak. Seneca finds ways to connect these echoes with the larger mood and themes of the play intratextually, creating a "tightly-knit complex of associations."[69] As we readers attempt to untangle the various intertexts and understand their significance for the tragedy, so Oedipus approaches the various events with an eye to resolving the crisis at hand. Although Oedipus fails to understand the implication of the various narratives that are presented to him (the *extispicium* scene, the necromancy), Seneca shows how the failed pursuit of such knowledge can be the very stuff of tragedy.

Choral Songs

Seneca's use of the chorus to comment on the action of the play, engage in dialogue with characters, and introduce new themes corresponds with its traditional role in fifth-century Greek tragedy. The lyric chorus has often been considered the foundation of tragedy, as choral songs on mythical themes or dithyrambs gradually incorporated dialogue between the chorus leader and additional characters.[70] Tarrant has noted that additional features of Seneca's conception of the chorus probably derive from postclassical tragedy (e.g., their presumed absence during certain acts).[71] Seneca's choral songs can be integrated with the action in a remarkable manner, such as the call-and-response action of the chorus of captive Trojan women (*Tro.* 67–163), or seemingly detached in the manner of the

---

Sphinx to Oedipus' own feverish suffering (*lue*, 859) due to his characteristic "swollen feet" (857–9; note *pedes* and *innatus tumor* concluding successive lines). In doing so, Boyle (2011) ad loc. proposes, "Seneca suggests verbally the origins of the Theban plague in the wounds of Oedipus."

[68] This mention of Oedipus and the Sphinx comes outside of the Theban books of the *Metamorphoses*, during a speech of Cephalus in which he describes the monstrous fox that ravaged the Theban countryside after the Sphinx. Ovid uses the word *pestis* to describe the fox, a word used to denote the plague in Seneca's *Oedipus* (4, 55, 93, 152, etc.).

[69] Mastronarde (1970) 305.

[70] Cf. Csapo and Slater (1994) 89–101, 349–68 for the origin of tragedy as well as the use of the chorus. For more on Seneca's conception of the chorus, cf. Davis (1993) and D. E. Hill (2000).

[71] Tarrant (1978) 221–8.

stock songs (*embolima*) of Agathon.⁷² Seneca's choral songs exhibit marked *variatio* in both subject matter and meter, and should be analyzed within the context of their tragedies. While Seneca includes numerous intertexts with the Greek and Latin literary and philosophical tradition in crafting his choral songs, I will focus on his use of Horace because Seneca's choral songs embody one of the final flowerings of Horatian lyric in the classical world.⁷³ The presence of Horatian intertexts in Seneca's choral songs indicates Seneca's interest in employing Horatian meters as well as the language, imagery, and themes from Horace's poetry. Seneca looked back to Horace as *the* lyric poet of Rome and expected his readers to understand the complete context of his model.⁷⁴ By placing Horatian lyric in a tragic context, Seneca encourages the reader to understand how he has reinterpreted Horace's poetry from this novel point of view. At times a tension arises when Horace's lines are put in the mouths of the chorus members, or are given a "tragic" spin in the dramatic context, yet at other times we can observe how Seneca may have found the seeds of such troubling interpretations in the Horatian original and its lyric perspective.

It is important to note that one can find Horatian echoes in all of Seneca's choral odes and that these intertexts often point to parallels in themes, imagery, and mythological details.⁷⁵ On a thematic level, choral songs on the mutability of fortune are common in Senecan tragedy (*Herc. F.* 524–91, *Phd.* 959–88, *Phd.* 1141–8, *Oed.* 987–94, *Ag.* 57–107), often drawing upon Horatian odes that are likewise concerned with this issue, especially *Carm.* 2.10. Thus, when the preliminary chorus of the *Agamemnon* sings of the propensity for great things to be destroyed (i.e., "the bigger they are, they harder they fall"), it relies on a series of exempla culled from Horace *Carm.* 2.10, such as the fact that lighting strikes high hills (***feriunt** celsos **fulmina** colles*, 96; cf. ***feriunt**que summos / **fulgura** montis*, *Carm.* 2.10.11–2), and the need to trim one's sails in a stiff wind (***vela** secundis inflata Notis / **ventos nimium** timuere suos*, 90–1; cf. *sapienter idem / contrahes **vento nimium** secundo / turgida **vela***, *Carm.* 2.10.22–4). Seneca is careful

---

⁷² Cf. Csapo and Slater (1994) 349–50, 354 for more on *embolima*. Critics have viewed the ode to Bacchus at *Oed.* 403–508 as the most representative culprit of such disregard for the dramatic context, but this may be overstated, since the ode touches upon scenes of metamorphosis from Bacchus' mythical history that present him as a fitting precursor to the tragic transformations that plague Thebes—his hometown and the site of his own tragedy, *Bacchae*, which lies behind much of the action of Seneca's play.

⁷³ Statius *Silv.* 4.5 and 4.7 are also imitations of Horace in Horatian meters.

⁷⁴ Tarrant (1995) 223–4 points out that Seneca gives more weight to his Latin allusions and, citing his references to Vergil, Catullus, and Cicero in the *Apocolocyntosis*, remarks that in all of these "the reader *must supply the original sense or context* in order to appreciate the irony of the citation" (n35, my emphasis).

⁷⁵ Spika (1890) finds references in every choral ode. Horatian intertexts also appear in other scenes as well, but not in such density as in the choral songs.

to find Horatian echoes that fit into the larger subject matter of his play, so, for instance, lightning and sailing imagery are prevalent in Eurybates' messenger speech in the *Agamemnon*.[76] In a similar manner, the use of Horatian imagery such as the beauty of Glycera, who "shines more brightly than Parian marble" (*splendentis* **Pario marmore** *purius, Carm*.1.19.6), can be applied to Hippolytus' face in Seneca's *Phaedra*: "It will shine more clearly than Parian marble" (*lucebit* **Pario marmore** *clarius*, 797).[77] In addition, mythological details such as the use of mountains in the Gigantomachy (*Ag.* 342–7; cf. *Carm.* 3.4.49–52) and Icarus' faulty employment of Daedalus' wings (*Oed.* 896–8; cf. *Carm.* 4.2.2–4) owe verbal elements to Horace's lyric poetry. In the examples below, I focus on representative Horatian intertexts to investigate how Seneca's reading of Horace acts as a commentary on the Horatian poem as a whole or on Horace as a poet.

How Troy Falls: The Captive Chorus of *Agamemnon* and *Carm.* 3.3

Seneca's choruses vary in meter and concern. While Seneca utilizes anapests most commonly, he employs additional lyric meters such as Asclepiadean, Sapphic, and Glyconic.[78] In two plays, *Agamemnon* and *Oedipus*, Seneca experiments with polymetric songs that exploit the rhythmic variety of lyric meters and often vary from line to line. Seneca's *Agamemnon* features two polymetric choruses (589–636, 808–66) that are built from Horatian metrical cola, but without the standard stanzaic units of Horace's lyrics. These songs are strikingly original, and by dividing Horatian forms into cola, Seneca is able to combine different meters, although in these odes he shows a preference for Alcaic, Sapphic, and Asclepiadean.[79] Such metrical virtuosity indicates Seneca's interest in exploring the possibilities of lyric verse and provides the most obvious indication of his innovative fusion of Horatian material in order to create his distinctive poetry.

The first of these polymetric choruses appears after Clytemnestra learns of Agamemnon's return to Mycenae in the *Agamemnon*. A chorus of Trojan

---

[76] Cf. the calm before the storm (*deserta* **vento vela**, 466), the paradox that sailors enjoyed the light of lightning, *fulmen*, during the storm (495), Pallas' attack on Ajax with Jove's lightning bolt (*fulmine*, 528; *fulmen*, 535). See Baertschi (2010) for more on this messenger speech, which focuses "exclusively on the voyage and the destruction of the fleet."

[77] The importance of *Carm.* 1.19 for Seneca's conception of desire in the *Phaedra* has not been fully explored, but it also informs the chorus's view of Venus and Cupid (*Phd.* 274–8 ~ *Carm.* 1.19. 1–4).

[78] Fitch (1987b) offers a study of Seneca's anapests.

[79] Tarrant (1976) 372–81 breaks down each of the polymetric cantica of the *Agamemnon* and explains the metrical principles at work. See Leo (1878) 110–34 on the polymetric choruses in general.

captives enters and sings of their current plight and the fall of Troy. It is a song that blends moments of Horace's *Carm.* 3.3 with Vergil's *Aeneid*, but from the point of view of alternative Trojan survivors—instead of Aeneas, the enslaved female prisoners. Seneca has altered the optimistic theme of apotheosis found in the original Horatian lyric, which speaks of Augustus' future place among the gods of Olympus because of his steadfastness and sense of justice. Seneca places Horace's language on the lips of these newly subjugated women in order to point out that an individual who is prepared to die is likewise equal to the gods (*par superis erit*, 609). Horace claims (*Carm.* 3.3.1–8):

> Iustum et tenacem propositi virum
> non civium ardor prava iubentium,
>   non vultus instantis tyranni
>   mente quatit solida neque Auster,
>
> dux inquieti turbidus Hadriae,
> nec fulminantis magna manus Iovis;
>   si fractus illabatur orbis,
>   impavidum ferient ruinae.
>
> Neither the eagerness of the mob urging crime
> Nor the face of the threatening tyrant,
> Nor the stormy Auster
> (the turbulent overseer of the violent Adriatic)
>
> Shakes the just and steadfast man from his firm resolve,
> Not even the immense hand of Jupiter when hurling lightning;
> Even if the whole world, cracked, should fall upon him,
> The ruins will strike him without fear.

In the face of such cataclysmic destruction, the courageous man will remain calm, cool, and collected, and by such an art (*arte*, 9) various gods attained divinity (Pollux, Bacchus, Hercules). Politically speaking, Augustus is to be praised because of his steadfastness and strong-willed commitment to restoring Roman values; thus he deserves deification.[80] Seneca's chorus recalls Horace's language, but with a near reversal in meaning as the captive women praise the finality of

---

[80] Cf. Günther (2013) 388: "He is persistent in resisting any temptation to alienate the Roman people from the path assigned to them by their divinely willed destiny; he is the man to redirect their path once and forever toward the conditions under which the divine will granted their founder Romulus to become the deified patron of a nation destined to rule eternally over the world."

death, a death that Horace's figures are able to transcend.[81] The chorus sings of death's tranquility, which offers refuge and is figured as a harbor (*Ag.* 593–603):[82]

> nullus hunc terror nec impotentis
> procella Fortunae movet aut iniqui
>   flamma Tonantis.
> pax alta nullos civium coetus
> timet aut minaces victoris iras,
> non maria asperis insana Coris,
> non acies feras pulvereamve nubem
> motam barbaricis equitum catervis,
> non urbe cum tota populos cadentis
> hostica muros populante flamma
>   indomitumque bellum.

> [This harbor] is untouched by fear;
> Neither the storm of fierce Fortune,
> Nor the thunderbolt of an angry Jupiter disrupts it.
> That deep peace fears no hordes of citizens,
> No threatening anger of the vanquisher,
> No wild seas stirred up by harsh Corus,
> No fierce battle lines nor a cloud of dust
> Stirred up by the hooves of barbarian cavalry divisions,
> No populations falling (city and all) as the enemy fires
> Destroy the walls, no unrestrained war.

Seneca's language evokes the catalogue of troubles that will not shake the resolve of Horace's protagonist even if the actual verbal parallels are slight (***civium** ardor / **civium** coetus; vultum instantis tyranni / minaces victoris iras; Auster, dux inquieti turbidus Hadriae / maria asperis insane Coris; fulminantis magna manus Iovis / iniqui flamma Tonantis*).[83] Seneca's chorus, however, is contemplating death with a directness that is far removed from the world of Horace's ode. For Horace, the actions of Augustus or Hercules on earth will allow them to become divine, but Seneca's chorus can only choose death as an escape from life's agony.

---

[81] Seneca also has these Horatian lines in mind at *Thy.* 358–62 when describing how neither thunderbolts nor a wind-strewn sea will frighten a true king. Cf. Tarrant (1985) ad loc.

[82] It is appropriate for these survivors of an epic storm-at-sea (described by Eurybates from 421–578) that death would be thought of as a peaceful harbor (*portus...placidus*, 592).

[83] Cf. Tarrant (1976) ad loc., who remarks, "For Horace's final trial, the *fractus orbis*, Seneca substitutes several lines on war and the sack of cities, suiting the circumstances of his chorus and leading to the narrative section which follows."

Death's tranquil harbor cannot be disturbed by the turmoil of the world at war, and the individual who is able to accept death serenely may become equal to the gods, but there is no sense that one of these Trojan prisoners of war could become a god. Seneca's chorus has effectively imitated Horatian language and themes in order to contrast their perspectives on death. In addition Seneca makes the imagery found in Horace's ode both more concrete and more resonant with the dramatic situation because the chorus has just escaped a storm featuring all the winds (*Ag.* 474–84), plenty of lightning (*fulmine irati Iovis*, 528), and the destruction of their homeland (*ruinas*, 669,708). The world of these mortal captives has come to an end because of the sack of Troy, and their subsequent song stresses what they endured during Troy's final hours. There is, however, another reason why Seneca may have thought of this particular poem in his depiction of the fall of Troy.

As Horace's poem continues, the action moves (curiously?) to Olympus, where Juno discusses her rationale for granting divinity to Quirinus and stresses that her love for Rome hinges on Troy's permanent obliteration.[84] This speech comprises the majority of the poem (18–68) and reasserts that Troy must remain in ruins for Roman power to flourish unabated and, if it should rise again, Juno would destroy it for a third time. Such a speech provides a dash of epic coloring to Horace's poem, as assemblies of the gods are common in epic, and Ennius' *Annales* featured a parallel scene discussing Quirinus' apotheosis.[85] Horace provides Juno's rationale for the fall of Troy, and one can see that her anger still burns when she discusses the causes of her "heavy wrath" (*gravis iras*, 30–1) and the ruins of Troy, where now "cattle amble over the tombs of Priam and Paris / and wild beasts, untroubled, hide their young" (*dum Priami Paridisque busto / insultet armentum et catulos ferae / celent inultae*, 40–2).[86] In addition, Horace's Juno tells of the doom awaiting Troy, should it be rebuilt out of misplaced piety (*nimium pii*, 58) by the Romans, concluding with the image of wives weeping once again for their lost husbands and children (*ter uxor / capta virum puerosque ploret*, 67–8).

In the *Agamemnon*, Seneca provides the human counterpoint to Juno's speech and engages in the same synthesis of epic and lyric material as Horace. The personal view of these survivors (*vidimus*; 611, 625) demonstrates that they believe the cause of Troy's demolition to be a cowardly act of trickery (*furto*, 624), certainly

---

[84] For a survey of opinions on Horace's rationale for including Juno's speech after the opening praise of justice and steadfastness, cf. Nisbet and Rudd (2004) 35–8. S. J. Harrison (2007b) 184–8 discusses the different generic registers included in the poem.

[85] As did Vergil (*Aen.* 12.808–28) and Ovid (*Met.*14.812–6); both of these passages are based on Ennius' *Annales* 54–5 (Sk.). Cf. Feeney (1991) 125–7. At the poem's conclusion, Horace comments on the inappropriate nature of this digression for his lyric poetry (69–72).

[86] S. J. Harrison (2007b) 187 stresses that this image incorporates "the discourse of hexameter prophecy as a further strategy of generic elevation."

nothing divine. The reader attuned to the initial Horatian intertexts may expect a similar rationale for Troy's destruction, but Seneca gives the Trojan perspective to events as they describe the Trojan horse, their last night in Troy, and the death of Priam. These epic events are indebted to the second book of the *Aeneid*. Intertexts to Vergil's work stress the dramatic highpoints in the narrative: when the Trojan horse crossed the threshold of Troy (***limine in ipso** sonipes, Ag.* 630 ~ *quarter **ipso in limine** portae / substitit, Aen.* 2.242–3), the celebration of the Trojans (*Ag.* 638–9; cf. *Aen.* 2.238–40), and the rage of Pyrrhus (*Ag.* 656–8; cf. *Aen.* 2.499).[87] Horace's inclusion of epic material in his lyric song leads to an "apology" at the poem's close, but Seneca follows his lead unapologetically.[88] Seneca expects the reader to remember the whole of *Carm.* 3.3, while offering a different epic formulation of Troy's fall and doing it in a polymetric lyric song. If the chorus is doomed to further lamentation, slavery, and death, they are able to approach it with the Stoic resolve that Seneca applauds in his philosophical works.[89] Their perspective on Troy's destruction may be distant from the partisan view of Juno, but they have also learned from their suffering how to die ("O how miserable it is not to know how to die!" *o quam miserum est nescire mori!,* 610), and this knowledge makes them a match for the gods (*par superis,* 609). Seneca explores the human experience that Juno downplays and gives voice to the laments of the captive women. In doing so, Seneca has found an innovative way of integrating the two sections of Horace's poem in his tragic chorus. While Juno's speech about the fall of Troy presages the future power of Rome, Seneca chooses to dramatize the reaction of Trojan women to their city's annihilation but hints that their trials have given them the insight and perseverance to view death in the correct manner.[90]

Eternal Death?: *Carm.* 3.30 in Troy

The *Troades* concerns the final hours of the Trojan women (it can be seen as a prequel to the *Agamemnon*'s chorus of survivors discussed above), and the themes of death and dissolution unite the action of the play.[91] While Troy

[87] Cf. Tarrant (1976) ad loc. for more on these recollections.

[88] Horace complains that his lyric Muse should not render the "speeches of the gods" and reduce "great things to small measures" (*referre sermones deorum et / magna modis tenuare parvis, Carm.* 3.3. 71–2).

[89] Cf. T. D. Hill (2004) 145–82 for more on Seneca's ideas about suicide in particular. Nisbet and Rudd (2004) 36 acknowledge that the primary theme of the ode, firmness of purpose, "was a virtue particularly prized by the Stoics."

[90] An apposite echo of this ode can be found at *Thy.* 360–2, where it once again describes the chorus's idealized view of death. Tarrant (1985) ad loc. discovers ironic intent within the context of the *Thyestes*.

[91] See Lawall (1982), Colakis (1985), and Shelton (2000) for discussions of death in *Troades*.

smolders in the background, the Greeks capture and kill Astyanax and Polyxena in spite of the attempts of Hecuba and Andromache to save these final remnants of Priam's family line. In the second choral ode (371–408) the Trojan women dismiss any possibility of the afterlife, in direct conflict with both their previous sentiments about Priam and Hector in the Elysian fields (156–60) and the reported appearance of Achilles' ghost demanding the death of Polyxena (181–202).[92] This ode has been faulted for this seemingly contradictory stance, but Seneca often provides various perspectives on an event or philosophical point, and while he may sacrifice unity, he gains the opportunity to provide multiple perspectives on particularly fertile subjects.[93] The transition from a belief in the afterlife rich in mythological detail to the certainty of total annihilation after death ("Do you ask where you lie after death? Where things unborn lie." *Quaeris quo iaceas post obitum loco? / quo non nata iacent*, 407–8) may also be motivated by the action of the play and the chorus's attempt to deny any truth to the sacrifice demanded by Achilles' ghost.[94] After questioning what may happen after death, the chorus concludes that death is the absolute end of one's life, and, as in the ode of the *Agamemnon* discussed above, such a view encourages a positive connotation of death as a refuge from the struggles of life.[95] A reading of the chorus that takes into consideration its Horatian intertexts leads to the conclusion that the dead may still influence the protagonists in the play, although in a less "dramatic" way than the ghosts and dreams that appear in the *Troades*.

The chorus begins with a series of questions addressing the truth of the story (*fabula*, 371) that some part of the soul survives death. This evocative opening stresses the realistic details of the burial ceremony, including the unsettling touch of the cremating torch against one's bare side (*nudum tetigit subdita fax latus*, 381). As part of the questions posed, the chorus states (376–80):

> non prodest animam tradere funeri,
> sed restat miseris vivere longius?
> an **toti morimur nullaque pars** manet

---

[92] Andromache will later dream that she sees Hector's ghost (438–60), and imagines she can see it when fighting for Astyanax's life (683–5).

[93] Cf. Littlewood (2004) 93: "In addition to representing the same force of necessity in different modes *Troades* represents images of reality which are clearly not to be reconciled with each other." Rosenmeyer (1989) 33–4 briefly discusses this passage among other vacillations in Seneca's prose and poetry.

[94] Cf. Busch (2009) 272: "The second ode responds to this rebuttal by suggesting that the dead do not enjoy any afterlife at all; they simply cease to exist and, by implication, require no sacrifices."

[95] As Fantham (1982) ad loc. recognizes: "The speakers are serenely confident in both personal and cosmic annihilation, seeing the certainty of total death as a comfort and argument for abandoning earthly hopes and fears."

nostri, cum profugo spiritus halitu
immixtus nebulis cessit in aera?

Is there no benefit to handing over the soul to death?
Do the miserable have to live even longer?
Does all of us die and no part of us remain,
When, with a final sigh, the spirit has mixed with the mist
And disappeared into the air?

The meter of this choral song is the lesser Asclepiadean, the same meter as three of Horace's most important programmatic odes about poetry and the immortality conferred upon a poet through his poetry (*Carm.* 1.1, 3.30, and 4.8).[96] While Seneca's choice of meter may not indicate independently that he has in mind these poems, his phrasing (*an toti morimur nulla que pars manet / nostri*) is surely indebted to Horace *Carm.* 3.30.[97] In this concluding poem to his first three books of odes, Horace writes of his poetic achievement as something everlasting and immune to the ravages of time or decay. As such, he does not question his immortality (*Carm.* 3.30.6–9):

non omnis **moriar**, multaque **pars mei**
vitabit Libitinam: usque ego postera
crescam laude recens, dum Capitolium
scandet cum tacita virgine pontifex.

Nor will I completely die, and a great part of me
Will avoid Libitina. In time to come my fame will flourish,
Ever-refreshed, for as long as the priest climbs the Capitoline
Together with the silent Vestal virgin.

Although the chorus wonders if we wholly die or a part of us remains, Horace confidently asserts that he will continue to "live" as long as his poems are read and Roman power survives. The chorus expands upon its initial questioning to stress that everything in the universe will come to an end and that "greedy time and void consume us" (*tempus nos avidum devorat et chaos*, 400). At this moment in the drama, the chorus wants to encourage this point of view, even though this scene is sandwiched between appearances of Achilles' ghost (168–202) and the ghost of Hector (in Andromache's dream, 443–60). The play contemplates various views of death, from Helen's "The best death is to die without fear of death" (*optanda mors est sine metu mortis mori*, 869) to Andromache's hope to die and be reunited with Hector (*nam mori votum est*

---

[96] Other Senecan choral odes in this meter include *Herc. F.* 524–91, *Thy.* 122–75, and *Med.* 56–74.
[97] Pointed out by both Fantham (1982) ad loc. and Boyle (1994) ad loc. but with little discussion.

mihi, 577). If Andromache followed the chorus's lead, it is possible that she would not have betrayed Astyanax, for Ulysses' threat that a "savage death was awaiting him" (***mors manebat** saeva*, 621) causes her to tremble in fear.[98]

The chorus urges us to believe that the stories of the Underworld, therefore, are only stories, equivalent to a bad dream (*par sollicito fabula somnio*, 406), and should be unheeded because after death there is nothing.[99] In the same way that the chorus mentions the monsters and features of Hades (Cerberus, Dis' threshold) only to deny their existence, so the words of Horace are echoed, only to deny their truth. In appropriating Horace's language, however, Seneca's chorus also validates Horace's claim about the power of his poetry and its timelessness. As the *fabulae* surrounding the characters of the play ultimately influence their behavior and their self-conception (nowhere more so than Ulysses), so Seneca may be pointing out the literary nature of the play itself, likewise often rendered with the word *fabula*.[100] Wilson expands upon the importance of these stories to the characters of the play:

> In the *Trojan Women*, ghost are reported to have appeared, but none are seen on stage as in other tragedies; for death must remain ambiguous and enigmatic.... However, the nearness of the dead is felt by the living characters constantly and deeply. Is Hector nothing to Andromache? Is Priam nothing to Hecuba? Or Achilles to Pyrrhus.... The dead and the past dominate the drama: Hector's tomb; the reported apparition of Achilles; Andromache's dream of her husband; the funeral rites of the first chorus; Agamemnon's memory of his daughter.[101]

The literary tradition that lurks behind the play's design, both in its mythological pedigree and its poetic intertexts, can grant insight into the actions or psychology of the characters, and with this intertext Seneca highlights the variable views on death. The recollection of Horace's meter and words comes to embody the undying influence of poetry, and, seeing as the previous act has been especially dependent on various moments of the *Iliad*, one can see how poetry (and the fame granted to individuals through poetic song) is still very alive for understanding these characters.[102] While the chorus hopes to deny the soul's immortality

---

[98] This intratextual connection is further strengthened by Ulysses' claim, "This is the part that must be examined by me" (*hac **parte** quaerenda est mihi*, 625).

[99] Death is a single act (*individua*, 401) destroying both the body (*corpori*, 401) and soul (*animae*, 402).

[100] E.g., Hor. *Ars* 190, 320, 339. Cicero identifies *fabula* with tragedy at *Inv.* 1.27. In Seneca's prose he often denotes dramatic works as (*Ep.* 76.31, 77.20).

[101] M. Wilson (1983) 51.

[102] The debate between Pyrrhus and Agamemnon is rife with allusions to scenes from the *Iliad*. Cf. the comments of Fantham (1982) 254: "The accusations bandied between Agamemnon and the

(hence the appearance of Achilles' ghost must be a fabrication), the intertext works against their sentiment.¹⁰³ Poetry is immortal, and, as the tragedy continues, one can see the various ways that the characters, in this play possibly more than any other of Seneca's, are unable to escape their previous manifestations in literature and are doomed to repeat the past.¹⁰⁴

Versions of Orpheus: Reading *Carm.* 1.12 with Medea and Hercules

Seneca utilizes the figure of Orpheus as a useful foil to characters such as Medea and Hercules, and, although the rationale for Orpheus' appearance may differ, in each case Horatian intertexts strengthen the literary and thematic connections.¹⁰⁵ Both Orpheus and Medea harness the power of the sung word in order to change the world around them (*carmina, cantus: Med.* 229, 356, 358; 684, 688, etc.), while Orpheus and Hercules both live to tell the stories of their sojourns in the Underworld.

In his descriptions of Orpheus, Seneca has recourse to language found in Horace's *Carm.* 1.12, a poem that indirectly raises Orpheus to a position equal to (if not above) the other praiseworthy figures of Horace's encomium.¹⁰⁶ While ultimately the purpose of this ode is to assert Augustus' divinity, it is important to note the position of Orpheus in this work.¹⁰⁷ Horace begins the poem asking what man, hero, or even god his Muse should celebrate. This Pindaric opening leads to Horace's description of the echo (*imago*) resounding among the mountains where Orpheus once plied his trade.¹⁰⁸ Orpheus' power over nature is stressed (1.12.7–12):

---

son of Achilles depend closely on the abuse exchanged between Agamemnon and Achilles in the first book of the *Iliad*; in general Agamemnon fights Pyrrhus with criticism of his father, but one episode from the *Iliad*, Achilles' acceptance of Priam's supplication and return of Hector's body, is used instead to reproach Pyrrhus with falling away from his father's standards."

¹⁰³ Another possible intratextual recollection of these lines occurs when Astyanax is being led to his death and a "great part" of the crowd observes (*magna pars*, 1128) followed closed by the Trojan survivors seeing the "last part of falling Troy" (**partem** *ruentis ultimam Troiae*, 1131).

¹⁰⁴ For the problematic intertextual repetition of Andromache's character see Zissos (2008).

¹⁰⁵ Cf. Segal (1983) and Littlewood (2004) 156–66 for more on Orpheus in Seneca's tragedies.

¹⁰⁶ One can find additional echoes of this ode at *Phd.* 748 and 972 so it would appear to be a Horatian poem that Seneca admired.

¹⁰⁷ Feeney (1998) 113: "Augustus is now not just a man who is the heir of Republican tradition, and not just a son of a god like Romulus, but one who enjoys a unique relationship (verging at times on identification) with the supreme god himself."

¹⁰⁸ Nisbet and Hubbard (1970) 140–6 note the Pindaric echoes. While Horace will use the same terminology, *iocosa...imago*, at 1.20 to discuss a literal echo, there may be some intertextual

> unde **vocalem** temere insecutae
> Orphea **silvae**,
> arte materna rapidos morantem
> fluminum lapsus celerisque **ventos**,
> blandum et auritas fidibus canoris
> ducere quercus?
>
> On which [mountains] the forests once followed
> Melodious Orpheus headlong,
> He who was delaying the white-water river rapids
> And the quick winds by means of his mother's craft,
> He was persuasive enough even to lead the attentive oaks
> With his tuneful lyre.

Horace finds a way to mention Orpheus first, as representative of the first poet, in his song that celebrates famous figures and even the gods (Jupiter will be the next subject of praise). The mention of Orpheus in this position can be seen as self-reflexive and indicative of Horace's own ideas about the importance of poets. While not stressing that poetry and song are *equal* to the deeds of gods and heroes, by praising Orpheus' abilities initially in his catalogue, Horace has cleverly elevated the poet's role and praises his ability to affect the natural world on par with the gods.[109] Orpheus' ability to shape the world through his song as well as his position as one who blurs the line between hero and god are also important for Seneca's reading of this poem in his tragedies.[110]

The praise of Orpheus' singing ability can be seen in both Seneca's *Hercules Furens* as well as his *Medea*, but in each case the tragic context points to the insufficiency of such power, effectively subverting the praise and power with which Horace had imbued the poet. In the *Medea*, the third choral ode specifies the various forms of suffering that the Argonauts have endured because of their transgression of the natural world (*exigit poenas mare provocatum*, 604), and, in the midst of this catalogue, Orpheus is the second figure mentioned (625–33):

> Ille **vocali** genitus Camena,
> cuius ad chordas modulante plectro

---

signposting here to Pindar, as Horace is actually repeating his language. Horace will later allegorize Orpheus at *Ars.* 391–3 and make him *sacer interpresque deorum* (391).

[109] Horace's Jupiter (1.12.15–6) and the Dioscuri (1.12.29–32) are notable for their power over the elements.

[110] Feeney (1998) 111 notes, "As the poem moves to its climactic evocation of Augustus as the one who straddles all three categories at once, it reveals the porosity of the divisions constructed by the Greek and Roman traditions."

> restitit torrens, siluere **venti**,
> cum suo cantu volucris relicto
> adfuit tota comitante **silva**,
> Thracios **sparsus** iacuit per agros,
> at **caput** tristi fluitavit Hebro:
> contigit notam Styga Tartarumque,
>   non rediturus.
>
> The famous son of melodious Camena,
> At the sound of whose picked strings
> The rushing river came to a stop, the winds hushed,
> Birds, ceasing their own songs, came to him,
> With the whole forest attending,
> He has died, torn apart on Thracian fields,
> His head floated down the sad Hebrus River;
> He has reached the familiar Styx and Tartarus,
> But he will not return this time.

Seneca echoes the language of Horace's poem (*vocalem/vocali*; *venti/ventos*; *silvae/silva*) as well as the wonders of Orpheus' song, but he grimly emphasizes his dismemberment and his final destruction (not found, naturally, in Horace's poem). Medea's voice (*vox*) is often stressed in the play, notably for its power over the same natural world that is associated with Orpheus: note how the seas rise without wind (*tacente **vento***) at the command of Medea's voice (***vocis*** *imperio meae*) at 765–7.[111] Orpheus' dismemberment evokes Medea's murder of her brother, Absyrtus, whose body she scattered in the sea (***sparsum****que ponto corpus*, 133) and who will later figure in her self-assertion as an avenger figure ("Now I am Medea: my genius has grown through my evils. / It is pleasing, (yes!) pleasing, that I ripped off my brother's head," *Medea nunc sum: crevit ingenium malis. / iuvat, iuvat rapuisse fraternum **caput***, 911–2).[112] Within the course of the play, the beneficial "magic" of Orpheus' song will be surpassed by Medea's spells, which can likewise influence the woods, rivers, and animals.[113] It is her power of song that is truly effective in Seneca's tragic world and that will prove to

---

[111] The winds and trees associated with Orpheus are marked in Seneca's *Medea* as being particular to Orpheus (*silva*, 229—the only other appearance of this word in the play), or for issues such as transgression (Tiphys dares "to write new laws for the winds" (*ventis*, 319–20)) or Medea's wrath (579).

[112] Cf. Littlewood (2004) 165–6 for more on how "Orpheus' death foreshadows a future crime."

[113] Segal (1983) explains: "When Medea exerts her power over the lower world (740ff.) and over earth, sea and sky (752ff.), she releases rather than calms nature's violence.... *Torrens*, 'rushing stream,' for example, describes both her wrath in 584 and the snake she calls forth in 694."

be the driving force behind the revenge she enacts. In addition to these ties to the tragic context, the final hope for return (*rediturus*) is snatched away from Orpheus, although this was the expressed desire of each Argonaut earlier in the ode (*raptor externi* **rediturus** *auri*, 613).

Horace *Carm.* 1.12 also influences the chorus of the *Hercules Furens*, who sing with assurance of Hercules' ability to surmount the toils of Hades, precisely because Orpheus himself was able to do so. Once again details of the ode hinge on Horace's poem (*Herc. F.* 572–6):

> quae **silvas** et aves saxaque traxerat
> **ars**, quae praebuerat fluminibus **moras**,
> ad cuius sonitum constiterant ferae,
> mulcet non solitis vocibus inferos
> et surdis resonat clarius in locis.

> Whose art had controlled the woods, birds, and rocks,
> And had caused delays in streams,
> And at whose song the beasts had stood still,
> He charms the ghosts with his unaccustomed songs
> And his voice resounds clearly in those regions devoid of sound.

Seneca recalls Horatian language (*silvas/silva, ars/arte materna, moras/morantem*) and stresses Orpheus' potential for success. If Orpheus is as powerful a singer as Horace and Seneca's chorus would have us believe, then he may return victorious from the Underworld. Unfortunately, his return journey will be marred by the loss of Eurydice, and it is this loss that foreshadows Hercules' own difficulties in spite of his return. Orpheus loses his beloved Eurydice in part because of his inability to wait until they have reached the upper world ("True love hates and does not endure delay: / When he hurries to discern his prize, he loses her," *odit verus amor nec* **patitur moras**: / *munus dum properat cernere, perdidit*, 588–9). A similar impatience governs Hercules' character, and his attempt to conquer the Underworld by force is narrated in similar terms ("The son of Alcmena did not endure any delay / he overcomes the ferryman and restrains him with his own pole," *non* **passus** *ullas natus Alcmena* **moras** */ ipso coactum navitam conto domat*, 772–3).[114] The inability of Orpheus to achieve his goal hints at the future failure of Hercules when his madness ravages his family and himself. As Fitch states, "Orpheus did not in any real sense overcome the realm of death. He appeared to have rescued Eurydice, but shortly thereafter destroyed her in error; the parallel with

---

[114] The verb *propero* is repeated nine times in this play and defines Hercules' propensity for action.

what will happen to H[ercules] and his family is too close to be missed."[115] The chorus may hope that "the regions which were able to be conquered by song will be conquered by strength" (*quae vinci potuit regia carmine, / haec vinci poterit regia viribus*, 590–1), but the poetic context challenges this possibility.

In both moments of reception, Seneca recalls Horace's ode to question Orpheus' true power. Horace makes him a stand-in for the creative power of the poet and poetry, essentially likening himself to Orpheus as he pronounces Augustus' near divinity.[116] Figures such as Hercules, mentioned only briefly in Horace's poem (*dicam et Alciden*, 1.12.25), who have become gods are similar to Orpheus, but Seneca casts a cynical eye on their successes and accentuates their failures (the loss of Eurydice, the destruction of Hercules' family). Medea becomes an even more effective poet-figure and one responsible for her own self-creation and quasi-divine immortality. Her own fusion of love and hate is shown to be stronger than Orpheus' true love.[117]

The Limits of Horatian Choral Lyric?: *Carm.* 1.3 and Vergil

The second choral ode of Seneca's *Medea* focuses on the audacity that Tiphys displayed in first setting forth on the waters without knowledge of the constellations (309–15) or the winds (316–7), and in such a novel craft (302). The invention of navigation, however, is not necessarily a good thing. While it can bring together different peoples and promote colonization and trade, it also signals the end of the Golden Age when (331–4)

> sua quisque piger litora tangens
> patrioque senex factus in arvo,
> parvo dives, nisi quas tulerat
> natale solum, non norat opes.

> Each man, in ease kept to his own shores
> And grew old on his father's land,
> Rich in little, he knew no wealth,
> Except that which his ancestral soil brought forth.

---

[115] Fitch (1987a) 253.

[116] Cf. Feeney (1998) 114: "Power and immortality are the quintessential marks of ancient divinity, and the power and immortality of Augustus were both bound up with the representations of poetry."

[117] Note the chorus's opening words about the power of a woman who "burns with hatred" (*ardet et odit*, *Med.* 582) and *Med.* 867–70.

Such a sentiment is also found in *Carm.* 1.3, in which Horace composes a *propempticon* for Vergil, who is sailing to Greece. The Horatian ode clearly influences Seneca's chorus in both its language and its themes, beginning with Seneca's figuration of the first ship as "such a fragile craft" (*rate tam fragili*, 302), clearly recalling Horace's *fragilem...ratem* (1.3.10–1). Seneca comments on the excessive daring of Tiphys (*nimium audax*, 301; *ausus*, 318; *audax*, 346), which parallels the intrepid spirit of the first helmsman found in Horace *Carm.* 1.3.9–16 (*illi robur et aes triplex*).[118] In doing so, Seneca also specifies his name, which Horace omits. For Horace, such courage becomes indicative of man's audacity and his desire to surpass the limits of the natural world (*Carm.* 1.3.25–8):

> **audax** omnia perpeti
> gens humana ruit per vetitum nefas.
> **audax** Iapeti genus
> ignem fraude mala gentibus intulit.

> Rashly enduring everything
> The human race rushes to forbidden crime.
> Rashly the son of Iapetus
> Brought fire to mankind by wicked theft.

Through the Horatian recollection, Seneca equates the audacity that leads Tiphys to first try the waves with mankind's rashness and propensity for crime. Both poets believe that setting off to sea for the first time leads quickly to the destruction of the natural boundaries that god established (*Carm.* 1.3.21–4; *Med.* 335–9).[119] Whereas Horace ends by generalizing that such criminal action keeps Jupiter's thunderbolts busy (*Carm.* 1.3.37–40), Seneca specifies the results of the first sea voyage (360–3):

> Quod fuit huius pretium cursus?
> aurea pellis
> maiusque mari Medea malum,
> merces prima digna carina.

> What was the price of this journey?
> The Golden Fleece and Medea,

---

[118] The focus in this ode on excessive daring (*nimium* 301, 326) parallels the excessive curses of Medea (812), and spurs on her infanticide (*nimium est dolori numerus angustus meo*, 1011). Likewise, Medea is figured as the punishment for anyone who touched the oars of the "daring ship" (*audacis...carinae*, 607).

[119] Cf. Spika (1890) 16–7 on these echoes.

An evil worse than the sea,
A worthy reward for the first ship.

Seneca's chorus thus caps Horace's list of "heroic" figures that transcend the natural bonds of the world (Daedalus, 34; Hercules, 36) with Medea, who is more dangerous than the sea itself (*maiusque mari Medea malum*—an alliterative line in the best tradition of Roman tragedy).[120] She recognizes this fact in her self-identification: "Medea remains: here you behold sea and land / sword, fire, the gods, and the thunderbolt!" (*Medea superest: hic **mare** et terras vides / ferrumque et ignes et deos et fulmina*, 166–7). Part of the aim of Seneca's tragedy is to show how Medea is a worthy recompense for the transgressions of the Argonauts, and Seneca delights in exhibiting how much greater her powers truly are.[121] As Medea embodies and surpasses the evils wrought by the first navigator, so Seneca surpasses the reach of Horace's poem by showing Medea's propensity for evil in his tragedy.

Horace's poem, however, has struck many critics as a curious *propempticon*. After all, a poem that hopes to send off a friend on a dangerous journey should be full of prayers for safety and not damning indictments of mankind's naval daring. Some readers, seizing on this poem's peculiarity, have postulated that it may indicate Horace's generic stance vis-à-vis Vergil and may offer a criticism of Vergilian "mimesis" (in Pucci's terminology).[122] In this reading, the odd turn (for a *propempticon*) to the dangers inherent in sea travel is indicative of Horace's warning to Vergil that an epic endeavor such as that undertaken in the *Aeneid* may lead to trouble.[123] But does Horace's critique of Vergilian epic continue to resonate in Seneca's reception and reuse of Horatian language in this choral ode? I believe it

---

[120] Cf. Hinds (2011) 23 for alliteration with Medea's name and the comment of Hine (2000) ad 14: "Seneca uses alliteration sparingly (in contrast to Republican tragedians), so it is the more striking when it occurs."

[121] In the incantation scene, Medea utilizes materials that have been figured in the deaths of various Argonauts (ash from Hercules' pyre, the torch of Althaea) and ends with her belief that *audax Hecate* (841) has granted her prayer.

[122] Pucci (1992). The bibliography for this poem is immense, and its basic stance on Horace's attitude towards Vergil vacillates with the different schools of thought (cf. ibid. n5 for a survey).

[123] Cf. Cairns (1972) 231–6 for Horace's use of the generic elements of a *propempticon* and encomium. Pucci (1992) 672 comments on the epic hazards:

> In attempting to achieve his epic vision—a vision grounded in a fundamentally negative view of the world—Virgil had achieved, according to Horace, only a vision of darkness that highlights mankind's inability to know his world entirely or even clearly. Virgil, in a poetic sense, as an artist, had sought heaven itself, and the consequences, so Horace suggests in this ode, do not bode well for mankind in general as readers of Virgil or for Virgil in particular as a poet.

Cf. Putnam (2006) 109 for the allegorical warning to Vergil in this poem.

does and suggest that the final coda encourages us to think of the critical implications of Seneca's reception of this Horatian poem. The conclusion of Seneca's chorus is unique in its own right, because it appears to refer to contemporary time and not the days since the Argo first set sail. In disrupting the dramatic timeframe of the play, the chorus voices the concerns of a Roman living in the first century CE and does so in markedly *Vergilian* language (364–79):

> Nunc iam cessit pontus et omnes
> > patitur leges:
> non Palladia compacta manu
> regum referns inclita remos
> > quaeritur Argo—
> quaelibet altum cumba pererrat.
> Terminus omnis motus et urbes
> muros terra posuere nova;
> nil qua fuerat sede reliquit
> > pervius orbis:
> Indus gelidum potat Araxen,
> Albin Persae Rhenumque bibunt—
> venient annis saecula seris,
> quibus Oceanus vincula rerum
> laxet et ingens pateat tellus
> Tethysque novos detegat orbes
> nec sit terris ultima Thule.

> Now the sea has yielded and endures
> All our laws: no famous Argo is needed,
> Constructed by Pallas' hand and rowed home by kings—
> Any skimpy raft roams freely over the deep;
> Every boundary has been removed,
> Cities have established walls on uncharted lands;
> The world, now easily traversed, has left nothing in its former place:
> The Indian drinks from the Araxes,
> Persians gulp the Elbe and the Rhine—
> The age will come in later years,
> When Ocean will release the fetters of the world
> The lands will be wide-open and Tethys will uncover new countries
> Far-off Thule will no longer be the boundary.

In this finale, Seneca opens up the concerns of the play to his contemporary Roman world, and intertexts with all three of Vergil's canonical works display the generic enrichment found in his choral odes.[124] While Horace's ode may criticize Vergil's epic concerns, Seneca finds that Vergil is the best exponent of a larger worldview, as he includes intertexts with the *Eclogues, Georgics,* and *Aeneid*. This is also a strong turn away from Seneca's obsessive concern elsewhere in the *Medea* with embodying "the power of the past over the present and the future."[125] Vergil's works create a link to the contemporary world because each of these intertexts draws on moments that specifically mention Octavian/Augustus or Roman imperium.

Seneca states that the seas, now navigable, have lost their power to separate different peoples, which leads to the possibility of Persians and Indians drinking the rivers of Europe. This is a pointed reversal of an *adunaton* ("impossibility") found in Vergil's first *Eclogue*, when the shepherd Tityrus claims that he will always remember the face of Octavian (1.59–63):

> ante leves ergo pascentur in aethere cervi
> et freta destituent nudos in litore pisces,
> ante pererratis amborum finibus exsul
> aut Ararim Parthus bibet aut Germania Tigrim,
> quam nostro illius labatur pectore voltus.

> Nimble stags will pasture in the sky
> And the sea will abandon its bare fish on the shore,
> And the exiled Parthian will drink the River Saône
> Or the German will drink the Tigris,
> Before the face of that man would fade away from my heart.

While Seneca's language does not specifically reference any of Vergil's terms here, the sentiment is similar and likewise features the identification of seeming impossibilities through the drinking of distant rivers. What is featured as unattainable in Vergil is now plausible in Seneca's *Medea* because of navigation, and may in fact have been part of the irony of this passage in the first *Eclogue*.[126] Although Tityrus will be able to live happily, the exile and migrations that he believes to be

---

[124] See S.J. Harrison (2007b) for more on generic enrichment (the way that the various Augustan genres confront and react with one another) in Vergil and Horace.

[125] Schiesaro (2003) 211. Schiesaro finds a strong contrast between the teleology of epic and the regressive nature of Senecan tragedy, in which "Senecan characters stage a rebellion against the notions of law and order represented by time's unerring flow.... The desire to turn back the clock on history, personal and otherwise, finds its most poignant expression in the emphasis placed on the past, which slowly bulges out of proportion as it invades the present and conditions the future."

[126] Cf. Putnam (1970) 55: "Tityrus considers that his words could never find fulfillment, and associates these good things... with the face of the young god in Rome. For Meliboeus, the 'impossible' horrors have become true."

impossibilities are a reality for Meliboeus because of the civil wars.[127] If, however, the world is turned upside down (as in Seneca's play), Tityrus may forget the face of Octavian, and thus such a miracle could be a double-edged development. Fyfe comments on the political ramifications, "Seneca's allusion to this passage intensifies the sense of the unnatural disorder caused by the Argonautic expedition, and associates that displacement with the unmythical world of Rome."[128] As so often in Seneca's reading of Vergil's corpus, he has found a way to indicate that he already noted possible negative connotations for Vergil's poetry, in this case that the civil discord vexing the world of the first *Eclogue* can be a reflection of his own (*nunc*, 364) times.

Such imperial concerns continue in Seneca's coda as he next echoes Vergil's *Aeneid*. Jupiter's famous prophecy of Roman dominance acts as the model for Seneca's phrasing "in distant years to come" (*venient annis / saecula seris*), when Vergil's Jupiter states (1.283–5):

> veniet lustris labentibus aetas
> cum domus Assaraci Pthiam clarasque Mycenas
> servitio premet ac victis dominabitur Argis.
>
> The age will come in distant years
> When the royal house of Assaracus will yoke Phthia and
> Famed Myceneae in slavery and will rule over defeated Argos.[129]

Roman dominance links both passages, although the Senecan chorus speaks more universally about the dispersal of obstacles for exploration and the opening up of new lands. Those lands may be thought of as possible routes for the expansion of the Roman Empire itself. Seneca's ode concludes with new lands being exposed beyond "far-off" (*ultima*) Thule, which Vergil had utilized in the *Georgics* when speaking of Octavian's future divinity (1.29–31):

> an deus immensi venias maris ac tua nautae
> numina sola colant, tibi serviat **ultima Thule**,
> teque sibi generum Tethys emat omnibus undis;

---

[127] Cf. Meliboeus' comment at *Ecl.* 1.4: "We are fleeing our fatherland" (*nos patriam fugimus*).

[128] Fyfe (1983) 87. Such thoughts may also reveal Seneca's "anxieties of imperialism" (cf. Benton (2003)).

[129] Seneca also echoes this passage in his *Troades* when Hecuba highlights Troy's destruction with the fact that the "whole home of Assarcus billows with smoke" (*omnisque late fumat **Assaraci domus***, 17). Zissos (2008) 193 claims, "Such attenuated allusion is characteristic of Seneca's strategy of engagement, registering the *Aeneid* as a kind of 'shadow text' or intertextual foil for the implied reader."

> Whether you would become a god of the wide sea and sailors worship
> Your divinity alone, far-off Thule would serve you,
> Tethys would make you her son-in-law with all the waves as dowry.

This Vergilian *contaminatio* indicates Seneca's interest in creatively imitating Vergil's language in this coda and bridging the world of the *Medea* with that of contemporary Rome. If the choral ode as a whole responds to Horace's poem, this final section would seem to point to the importance of Vergil's poetry in Seneca's own lyric creations.[130] Each instance of intertextuality involves passages focused on the power of Rome, especially as embodied in Augustus himself. Seneca observes the continuity from the principate of Augustus to the Julio-Claudian emperors under whom he wrote, and, in speaking of his contemporary era, the intertexts indicate Seneca's possible political reading of Vergil's works. In doing so, the intertexts help to "Romanize" the *Medea*, juxtaposing the mythical past with the present day.[131] While the new world order of Rome allows for the free exchange of peoples, it may also open the doors to a Medea-like figure.[132] However, it is difficult to read this passage with complete pessimism. The pride that the chorus feels in the current "age of exploration" can also be mapped onto the inherent freedom of Seneca's literary travels through the Augustan poets. In responding to Horace's warning to Vergil about writing epic poetry, Seneca reveals his poetry's ability to encompass different genres, and through these Horatian and Vergilian intertexts, he embodies his own self-conscious poetics that exults in combining and supplementing the Augustan poets for his own literary purposes.

Horace clearly influences Seneca's choice of theme, meter, and language in his choral odes, but each ode is subsumed in the larger tragic context. Words and images from the choral odes, like tendrils of a vine, reach into the tragic context and are interpreted within it. Intertexts to Horace's *carmina* show that Seneca was a careful interpreter of Horace. Indeed, often the purpose of the intertext is contingent on his reading of the complete Horatian poem and his overall interpretation of that poem (and its poetics). In these cases, metapoetic intent is probable, revealing Seneca's interest in creating dramatic poetry that updates what is acceptable or customary for Horace's lyric creations.[133]

---

[130] A similar move from Horatian to Vergilian intertexts can be seen in the *Agamemnon* ode analyzed above.

[131] Cf. Tarrant (1995) for Roman elements in Senecan tragedy: "His sense of the world as a geopolitical entity is clearly linked to his experience as a citizen of Rome under the last Julio-Claudians" (229–30).

[132] See Littlewood (2004) 168: "However, even as the tragedy follows this inevitable trajectory of decline and even as the national epic is inverted in Medea's victory, there is celebration of the flawed sublimity of an empire which refuses to observe Virgilian and Augustan boundaries."

[133] See Rosenmeyer (1989) 37 on the generic limits of lyric: "In their abstracted forms... neither the epic nor the lyric builds on issues of incremental questioning or thrusts the contestants into a position of role-playing. That is left to the drama."

Messenger Speeches

If his choral odes offer a personal and lyric point of view on the action of the play, Seneca's messengers are closer to epic poets whose omnipresent reporting of offstage events permits Seneca to try his hand at epic narrative.[134] While all give information about events taking place offstage, Seneca varies the characteristic messenger scenes by experimenting with their placement in the plays (as early as the second act in the *Troades*), the personality of the messengers (revealing nuances and biases), and even the length (the description of the storm in the *Agamemnon* reaches over 150 lines, while the messenger of the *Medea* delivers his speech in a clipped eleven-line dialogue with the chorus). This variety of length, placement, and character reveals Seneca's interest in surprising his readers in these narrative sections.[135] The messenger speeches, at their best, crystallize the themes and motifs of the tragedy as a whole from yet another point of view.[136] Seneca recognizes the importance of messenger speeches as a fundamental component of tragedy that allows the tragic poet to include an essentially epic element in the work. As such, these speeches should not be considered tacked on or divorced from the primary concerns of the play, although Seneca can sometimes seem to get carried away in detailing the action and setting of these episodes.[137] The messenger has a status that bridges both the dramatic and epic genres, because he functions as a character in the drama but provides details unknown to those on stage and provides an eyewitness account, tantamount to the position of an epic poet. Barrett explains these two roles:

> This double status, then, defines a central aspect of the conventional messenger, as he speaks with a voice that must negotiate the tensions that result from his ambiguous position. His narrative not only forms part of Aristotle's *mimesis*; it also claims—and to an appreciable degree functions as though possessing—an extradiegetic status.[138]

---

[134] Amoroso (1981), Larson (1994), Garelli-François (1998), and Baertschi (2010) offer valuable studies of the Senecan messenger speech. See Schiesaro (2003) 121–32 for the messenger speech in *Thyestes* and Mowbray (2012) 407–16 for the final messenger speech of the *Troades*.

[135] E.g., Medea's nurse offers a description of Medea's magic spell that acts as a substitute for a messenger speech (670–739), but then Medea herself comes on stage and enacts the spell (740–848).

[136] Larson (1994) 31–42, 63–70, passim focuses on the importance of messenger speeches for Seneca's descriptive style and narrative mode. She believes, however, that "the Senecan messenger-speech stands, therefore, as a piece which is entirely separable from the dramatic context in which it occurs" (70), which unfairly limits their importance to the play as a whole.

[137] Cf. Tarrant (1976) 249 on the messenger of the *Agamemnon*: "What follows is less impressive, and comparison with Virgil, Ovid, and Lucan is to Seneca's disadvantage. Perhaps the traditional character of the subject and his knowledge of earlier poetic treatments worked to his harm, leading to a comprehensive but uninspired manipulation of familiar topics and inhibiting his own talents for allusiveness and compression." Baertschi (2010) finds that such "hyper-epicizing" is intentional.

[138] J. Barrett (2002) 73.

Seneca exploits the epic features of messenger speeches in order to provide an extended narrative that often provides an authoritative (and authorial) view of events. However, the significance of the messenger's tale is invariably questioned by the surrounding dramatic context and the characters' own perspectives on what happened offstage and how it impacts them. Through this internal response to the narrative or events described, one can see these speeches as subsidiary tragedies in their own right, mirroring the action of the play and presenting their own audience or reader who questions the events reported.[139]

In these speeches, intertextuality can serve a variety of functions. For example, the messenger's report of the great storm at sea of the *Agamemnon* cannot help but remind the reader of similar storms in Ovid and Vergil, and Seneca infuses his speech with details found in his predecessors' narratives in order to portray an even fiercer storm.[140] Vergilian intertexts such as the winds falling upon the sea (***incubuere*** *mari totumque a sedibus imis / una **Eurusque Notusque** ruunt, Aen.* 1.84–5) are elaborated with an eye to poetic rivalry (*Ag.* 474–6):

> undique **incumbunt** simul
> rapiuntque pelagus infimo **eversum** solo
> adversus **Euro** Zephyrus et Boreae **Notus**.

> On every side the winds fall upon the sea
> And simultaneously seize the waters churned up from their bed
> Zephyrus opposing Eurus and Notus contrary to Boreas.

Seneca not only repeats language from Vergil's passage but also adds to the number winds involved, placing four winds in the same line, a feat that recalls attempts of previous poets, from Homer to Ovid.[141] The destructive quality of each storm matches the anger of the gods against the fleets, but, in addition, Seneca relates this storm to the larger themes of reversal in the play and even the destruction of Agamemnon's royal line, as Electra later states, "The home has been completely overturned" (***eversa*** *domus est funditus*, 912).[142] Likewise, when

---

[139] Cf. Garelli-François (1998) 27: "Le récit de messager ne s'offre ni comme une imitation du drame, ni, véritablement, comme un morceau de théâtre dans le théâtre: il dramatise et théâtralise, comme peut le fair, à l'occasion, la poésie épique ou le récit historique." Mowbray (2012) characterizes the "captive audience" of the *Troades*' final messenger speech as "a *mise-en-abyme* of embedded audience- and actor-figures whose responses multiply and refract off each other as they negotiate the two 'performances' of murder-sacrifice" (394).

[140] See Baertschi (2010) for this speech as a whole.

[141] Cf. Tarrant (1976) ad loc. for the conventional contest of the winds, and Seneca's unique ability to place four winds in one line.

[142] The verb *verto -ere* and its cognates are used frequently in the *Agamemnon* to indicate the themes of reversal and reciprocal destruction (see next chapter).

Cassandra looks forward to giving her own messenger speech to the dead, she utilizes similar language to relate "the sea full of overturned ships" (*repletum ratibus **eversis** mare*, 1006). The language of the messenger speech both looks back to previous literary accounts (and attempts to surpass those accounts) and resonates within the dramatic context. Seneca effectively points out how the storm at sea presages the storm awaiting Agamemnon on his return.

In the messenger speeches, intertexts to epic sources may give further support to their epic role in the fabric of the play. Because these messengers offer narratives from their own point of view, they can play the role of poets in their own right, and some of the messengers relish telling their horrific tales (e.g., the messenger of *Thyestes*).[143] The first example of this chapter reveals how epic tropes and intertexts lend credence to the ghost vision of Achilles in the *Troades* and forcefully indicate the immanent violence that threatens the Trojan women. This is also a relatively modest example of a messenger speech, length-wise, yet it hits upon many of the fundamental characteristics of the Senecan messenger speech. The second example analyzes the messenger speech of the *Phaedra* as a response to Ovidian and Vergilian epic in which Seneca creates a horrific epyllion that questions the literary tradition behind the death of Hippolytus.

The Return of Achilles

The second act of the *Troades* features Talthybius' report of the appearance of the ghost of Achilles and his demands for a human sacrifice (Polyxena) in order for the Greeks to sail home. Although the idea of Achilles' ghost demanding Polyxena's sacrifice is part of the mythological tradition, Seneca's description of the emergence of the ghost at Troy, his speech, and the reaction of the natural world at his arrival further emphasize the devastation he will cause for the surviving Trojans.[144] Seneca has Talthybius announce that he has been the eyewitness of omens stranger than truth (*maiora veris monstra.../ vidi ipse, vidi*, 169–70), which strike him with fear (*pavet animus, artus horridus quassat tremor*, 168).[145] Talthybius describes the earthquake that coincides with Achilles' arrival

---

[143] Tarrant (1985) 180 comments, "From an initial state of nearly speechless horror, the Messenger grows steadily more involved with his narrative, becoming at last almost buoyant in displaying his powers of description. By the latter part of the scene he has absorbed Atreus' flair for the ironic retort, and in his final lines he sounds as jubilantly confident as Atreus himself that the crime can no longer be suppressed."

[144] Other versions of Achilles' ghost include Eur. *Hec.* (37–41), Soph. *Polyxena* frag. 523 (Lloyd-Jones), and, especially important for Seneca's account, Ovid *Met.* 13.439–48.

[145] The fearful nature of the events to be reported is a topos in Seneca's messenger speeches (cf. *Phd.* 991–5, *Ag.* 416–8, *Thy.* 634–40, *Tr.* 1956–9, *Med.* 670). For Talthybius' fear, cf. Garelli-François (1998) 25.

from the Underworld and symbolizes the war's destruction of the Trojan landscape.[146] Troy's sacred groves (*lucus sacer*, 174) and mountains (175) crack and crumble in the upheaval, opening a way for Achilles' ghost to approach through his grave (*tumulum levat*, 180). The messenger sets the reader up to expect a marvelous narrative, and one way in which the tale reflects its grandeur (*maiora*) is through the variety of epic intertexts that help to place Achilles in his proper generic and mythological context.[147]

Indeed, Talthybius' very horror at the sight may remind the reader of Aeneas' feelings of horror as he relates a similar ghost encounter in the third book of the *Aeneid*. After Aeneas and his men leave Troy they soon arrive at the tomb (*tumulus*, 3.22) of Polydorus in Thrace, where Aeneas attempts to gather wood to make a sacrifice. However, he witnesses an astonishing and chilling marvel (*horrendum et dictu video mirabile monstrum*, 3.26) as blood flows from the broken soil, and Aeneas states, "Cold fear shakes my limbs and my blood congeals with dread" (*mihi frigidus horror / membra quatit gelidusque coit formidine sanguis*, 3.29–30). While the language recalls Talthybius' response (*artus horridus quassat tremor*), there are many expressions of fear similar to this in Senecan tragedy and even in the *Troades* itself.[148] This Vergilian intertext, however, is particularly appropriate to Talthybius' speech because of the centrality of the tomb for both Seneca's Achilles (*tumulum*, 180, 196) and Vergil's Polydorus (who will receive a proper tomb at *Aen.* 3.63), as well as the link between this episode and the larger context of the *Troades*.[149] Seneca's play has long been seen as a *contaminatio* of two Euripidean plays, *Troades* and *Hecuba*, and the visitation of Polydorus' ghost is central to Euripides' *Hecuba*.[150] Seneca has pointed to a moment of Vergil's own appropriation of Euripidean tragedy and reclaimed it as part of the

---

[146] Cf. Larson (1994) 31–8 for the way in which such descriptions reveal Seneca's interest in "accumulating details to make a picture of one stage in this chain of events" (34).

[147] Note the interaction between Talthybius and the chorus at the opening of the scene on the question of "delay" (*mora*, 164, 166). This is one of the primary motifs of the play, and the messenger's description of the *monstra* provides an explanation for the current delay. The chorus's response to the appearance of Achilles' ghost is essentially given in the choral ode analyzed above. Staley (2010) has examined the uses of *monstrum* in Senecan tragedy, finding that "they are ... both the kind of kataleptic impressions that Stoic tragedy should present, as well as occasions for interpretation and judgment that model cognition and encourage understanding" (120).

[148] *Tro.* 623–4: "My soul left my limbs, they are shaken and weakened / my blood congeals, frozen with cold," (*Reliquit animus membra, quatiuntur, labant / torpetque vinctus frigido sanguis gelu*). Cf. *Agam.* 5: "Lo! My soul quakes, fear shakes my limbs" (*en horret animus, et pavor membra excutit*).

[149] Note how one "fierce spectator" (*ferus spectator*) uses Hector's tomb (*tumulo Hectoreo*, 1087) for a good view of the sacrifices of Astyanax and Polyxena. Astyanax's mangled body will not be collected for burial (*tumulo*, 1110), and Polyxena is put to death on Achilles' funeral mound (*tumulumque Achillis*, 1121), which savagely "drinks" her blood (*saevusque totum sanguinem tumulus bibit*, 1164).

[150] The ghost of Polydorus gives the prologue of *Hecuba*, and the first half of the play is concerned with the death of Polyxena.

tragic genre.[151] In placing a similar reaction to a ghost in the mouth of Talthybius, Seneca calls attention both to the epic/tragic background of this type of infernal manifestation, while subtly marking the differences between the two accounts. Aeneas, his men, and the surviving Trojan women (*Iliades*, 3.65) perform the correct ritual for Polydorus (which involves animal sacrifice—*sanguinis*, 3.67). The Trojan women of Seneca's play, however, can only powerlessly lament when the ghost of Achilles drinks the blood of Polyxena (*saevusque totum sanguinem tumulus bibit*, 1164) in a horrible perversion of funerary and marriage ritual.[152] In the *Aeneid* only the voice of Polydorus escapes the grave, but Seneca renders his Achilles as a frighteningly huge figure who flashes forth to issue his commands, in a manner similar to ghosts emerging from trapdoors on the Roman stage.[153] Seneca recognizes that Vergil's Aeneas is acting as a narrator in much the same way as his Talthybius, and points to a similar event in the aftermath of the Trojan War, but one with disparate outcomes for those involved.[154]

The Vergilian intertext bridges the different accounts of Trojan survivors and foreshadows the demand for Polyxena's death, but Seneca also has in mind the thirteenth book of Ovid's *Metamorphoses* as he rewrites the appearance of Achilles' ghost found there (13.339–48).[155] Ovid's ghost resembles the representation of Achilles at the beginning of the *Iliad* when he began to draw his sword against Agamemnon (*ferus infesto petiit Agamemnona ferro*, 13.444). Seneca expands Ovid's brief account and adds details that recall Achilles' notable prowess in war from episodes that span Achilles' roles in the epic cycle (181–9):

> emicuit ingens umbra Thassalici ducis,
> Threicia qualis arma proludens tuis
> iam, Troia, fatis stravit aut Neptunium
> cana nitentem perculit iuvenem coma,
> aut cum inter acies Marte violento furens
> corporibus amnes clusit et quaerens iter

---

[151] Cf. Panoussi (2009) 149: "The figure of Polydorus constitutes yet another connection between the Vergilian narrative and Euripides' play: just as *Hecuba* opens with the appearance of the ghost of Polydorus requesting burial (47–50), so Book 3 of the *Aeneid* begins with Aeneas violating the tomb of Polydorus."

[152] For more on the perversion of ritual in *Troades*, cf. Panoussi (2005) 422–6.

[153] Cf. Cicero's mention of the ghost of Pacuvius' *Iliona* emerging onstage through a trapdoor (*Sest*. 126).

[154] For the use of *ipse...vidi*, cf. Austin (1964) 29, who describes the similar phrase in *Aeneid* 2: "The whole Book is a personal narrative, an eyewitness account of the fall of Troy, told by a survivor. Virgil has adapted to Epic the technique of the Messenger's speech in Greek Tragedy." This Vergilian scene concludes with the "lands and cities fading in the distance" (*terraeque urbesque recedunt*, 3.72), a phrase that fascinates Seneca (cf. *Ep*. 28.1.6, 70.2.3, and a possible intertext at *Ag*. 444–5).

[155] The numerous recollections are listed by Jakobi (1988) 23–4.

> tardus cruento Xanthus erravit vado,
> aut cum superbo victor in curru stetit
> egitque habenas Hectorem et Troiam trahens.

> The great ghost of the Thessalian leader flashed forth,
> Such as when he prepared for your downfall, Troy,
> By devastating Thracian arms, or when he defeated
> The son of Neptune notable for his white hair,
> Or when boiling with berserker rage among the battle lines
> He blocked rivers with corpses and the Xanthus,
> Sluggish with bloody waves wandered from its banks,
> Trying to find a path around the carnage;
> Or when he stood victorious on his high chariot handling the reins
> Dragging Hector and Troy behind him.

Seneca's messenger fashions an Achilles who recalls his early military exploits, but always with an eye towards the fall of Troy (*Troia*, 183; *Troiam*, 189). The long simile (*qualis*, 182) recalls the use of epic similes, but instead of a comparison with a force of nature, his ghost reveals the qualities of his mythical past.[156] Talthybius adds details known from the epic tradition such as Achilles' choking of Cycnus (found in Ovid, *Met.* 12.70–145), blocking the Xanthus with bodies (*Il.* 21.1–221, Cat. 64. 357–60), and dragging Hector's corpse (*Il.* 22.396–405, *Aen.* 1.483).[157] Seneca exploits the literary accounts of Achilles in order to flesh out his heroic résumé and to make this ghost a more imposing figure than Ovid's. Seneca does this because the majority of the remaining act is comprised of a debate about the propriety of Polyxena's sacrifice, during which the worth of Achilles' deeds is disputed.[158] In the figure of Achilles, Seneca can encapsulate the entire epic tradition, and a further echo of the Homeric tradition points out how Seneca continues to vie with Ovid's account.

Continuing to act like an epic narrator,[159] Talthybius presents the words of Achilles' ghost as direct speech (191–6):

> ite, ite, inertes, debitos manibus meis
> auferte honores, solvite ingratas rates

---

[156] Cf. Garelli–François (1998) 22 for the messenger's use of "comparaisons homériques."

[157] The ghost of Achilles also recalls his appearance at *Ody.* 11.473–540.

[158] Pyrrhus believes Achilles deserves the sacrifice (245–9), while Agamemnon opposes such violence on the grounds that Troy has suffered enough and it is uncustomary (286–91, 298–9). Eventually the decision falls upon Calchas, whose proclamation that Polyxena must be sacrificed echoes, in part, Talthybius' speech (cf. *umbra Thessalici ducis*, 182; *Thessali busto ducis*, 361).

[159] Cf. Kirk (1990) 28–35 for speeches in Homer: "Nearly half of the *Iliad* consists of direct speech" (28). Seneca uses it often in messenger speeches; cf. *Med.* 690–704, *Oed.* 926–34, *Ag.* 517–26, 545–52, passim. Direct speech not only implies impartial reporting but also enlivens the narrative.

> per nostra ituri maria. non parvo luit
> **iras Achillis** Graecia et magno luet:
> desponsa nostris cineribus Polyxene
> Pyrrhi manu **mactetur** et tumulum riget.
>
> Go ahead and leave, cowards! Take away the honors
> Owed to my hands and release the thankless ships,
> Soon to travel over my seas. Greece paid a high price
> For Achilles' anger and will pay greatly again:
> Let Polyxena as a bride to my ashes be sacrificed
> By Pyrrhus' hand and besprinkle my tomb.

Seneca expands the four-line speech of Achilles in Ovid's *Metamorphoses* (13. 445–8), where he likewise demands the sacrifice of Polyxena (*mactata Polyxena, Met.* 13.448).[160] The language from this description is highlighted in Seneca's account (*mactetur*) and stressed throughout this play to underscore the perversity of such a human sacrifice (248, 361, 943, 1002, 1063). In his description of Achilles' ghost, Ovid claims he looked similar (*similisque minanti*, 13.442) to his first appearance in the *Iliad*, when he threatened "unjust Agamemnon with his sword" (13.443–4). Seneca strengthens the connection to the Homeric epic tradition of Achilles by focusing on his *ira*. Seneca's *iras Achillis* is a gloss on the first line of the *Iliad*, where it is the μῆνιν...Ἀχιλῆος that causes Greek suffering.[161] His wrath is central to his character and to epic song; a later choral ode even notes how Chiron would "sharpen Achilles' vast rage by singing of battle" (*ingentes acuebat **iras** / bella canendo*, 834–5).[162] This nod to the epic tradition also may be seen as a way for Seneca to better Ovid's depiction, as he not only looks back to the beginning of *the* major epic detailing Achilles' wrath (and a moment 190 lines before Achilles threatens Agamemnon) but also indicates another justification for the later troubles of the Greek fleet, as Achilles' words foreshadow the many difficult homecomings of heroes such as Agamemnon, Ulysses, and Menelaus. As Fantham notes, "Seneca's public will refer the prophecy not to the mere sacrifice of a captive princess but to the fatal storm and murderous homecomings after the fleet departs from Troy."[163] Because Ovid had

---

[160] Cf. Boyle (1994) ad 191ff. "*manibus* (with a short a), 'hands', picks up the final word of Ach.'s speech, *manes* (with long *a*), 'shades', *Met.* 13.448, while at the same time translating *virtutis nostrae*, 'my valour,' of *Met.* 13.446." Jakobi (1988) adds further parallels of language or sense.

[161] Talthybius points to his epic representation as *iratus Achilles* when describing his voice (*irati sonus*, 190).

[162] Also note how Horace claims that Achilles' rage (*iracundus*) is central to his *dramatic* characterization (*Ars* 120–2).

[163] Fantham (1982) 238.

included this scene in his *Metamorphoses*, Seneca relies on the reader's recognition of Ovidian details that he has elaborated. In order to point to the importance of this speech for the action of the *Troades*, Seneca cleverly has Hecuba pick up on Achilles' first words (***ite, ite***, 191) directly after Astyanax and Polyxena have been killed, saying, "Go on, go, Greeks, now seek your homes safely" (***ite, ite***, *Danai, petite iam tuti domos*, 1165). Hecuba's bitter response indicates how now the war can finally be considered over (*bellum peractum est*, 1168), but not through the deaths of famous warriors like Achilles—only through the slaughter of these two young defenseless Trojans (*concididt virgo ac puer*, 1167). Achilles' name and actions haunt the characters of play, with his anger ultimately transferred even to his final victim—Polyxena falls onto his tomb "with an angry blow" (***irato impetu***, 1159).[164] Seneca's emulation of Ovid's scene shows how he attempts to surpass Ovid's epic through the inclusion of additional epic intertexts that extend the scope of Achilles' heroic deeds and by exploring the suffering caused by Achilles' demand in the course of his *Troades* (by contrast, the *Metamorphoses* breathlessly moves from Achilles' ghost to the immediate death of Polyxena).

Talthybius closes his speech by zooming out to incorporate the reaction of the natural world to Achilles' disappearance back into the netherworld (199–202):

>   immoti iacent
> tranquilla pelagi, ventus abiecit minas
> placidumque fluctu murmurat leni mare,
> Tritonum ab alto cecinit hymenaeum chorus.
>
>   The tranquil sea lies motionless,
> The wind has abandoned its threats and
> The calm sea murmurs with light waves;
> A chorus of Tritons sang a wedding hymn from the deep.

The calm winds recall the initial obstacle facing the Greek fleet at Aulis, but the break in the weather also allows Talthybius to hear the singing of a wedding song in honor of Achilles and Polyxena.[165] This exceptional detail is further embellished by both the poetic craft of these lines (note the density of Greek words as well as the enclosing word order of the final two lines) as well as the recollection of another wedding song that also discussed Achilles and Polyxena, namely

[164] Although Achilles is not a proper dramatis personae, his name appears over twenty times in the play.

[165] Note how Hecuba's threatening language to Ulysses reverses this calm scene and indicates the storm about to trouble the Greek forces: "My fates will follow me and no tranquil peace will come to the sea; the deep will rage with winds" (*me mea sequentur fata non* **pelago** *quies /* **tranquilla** *veniet, saeviet* **ventis mare**, 994–5).

Catullus 64.[166] Within the course of Catullus' epyllion about the marriage of Peleus and Thetis, the Fates sing an epithalamium concerned with Achilles' life and deeds (*egregias virtutes claraque facta*, 348).[167] Catullus' description involves three witnesses (*testes*) to Achilles' deeds: mourning mothers (349–51), the Scamander river (357–60), and Polyxena (362–4, 368–70). Gaisser has examined the various internal narrators and audiences of this poem and concludes: "Their testimony, each more terrible than the last, does not challenge the *veridicos cantos* of the Parcae nor yet the valor of Achilles. The witnesses attest to the deeds prophesied by the Parcae but pronounce them horrible."[168] In the *Troades*, Seneca provides similar "witnesses" to Achilles' deeds both in this messenger speech and in the opening and closing of the play (when another messenger tells of Polyxena's death). The mourning of mothers is central to the *Troades*, and actions such as the loosening of hair (*incultum... solvent crinem*, 64.350) and beating of the breast (64.351) are described in detail in the first choral exchange between Hecuba and the Trojan women (*Tr.* 83–129 involves mourning for Achilles' most famous victim, Hector).[169] The remaining two witnesses to Achilles' actions are found in Talthybius' speech, as he provides his own account of the bodies that choke the river and the future sacrifice of Polyxena on Achilles' tomb. Catullus proclaims the tomb will receive the white limbs of the wounded maiden (*niveos **perculsae** virginis artus*, 64.364), a choice of language that may have influenced Seneca's report of Cycnus' death (*perculit*, 184). Catullus further describes the death of Polyxena in particularly gruesome language: she will be beheaded like an animal in order to drench the tomb with blood (*alta Polyxenia madefient caede sepulcra*, 64.368). The death of Polyxena can be seen as the end of the Trojan War, and the wedding of Peleus and Thetis can be seen as its beginning. Seneca recollects Catullus 64 in Talthybius' speech to indicate that his *Troades* will provide its own conclusion to Achilles' wrath. Seneca's chorus of Tritons sing a wedding song (*hymenaeum*, 202) for Polyxena and Achilles, but behind their words one may remember the nuptial occasion described in Catullus (*hymenaeos*, 64.20). Seneca provides an interpretation of Catullus 64 much like Curran's: "Transcending the fundamental antithesis in the poem, that between the heroic past and the degenerate present, is a vision of a tragic constancy in human nature,

---

[166] While Catullus does lie outside the scope of the majority of my study, this detail seems particularly germane to the discussion.

[167] Note that Pyrrhus will claim he enjoys recounting the famous praise and renowned deeds of his father (*inclitas laudes iuvat / et **clara** magni **facta** genitoris sequi, Tr.* 236–7).

[168] Gaisser (1995) 612.

[169] While mourning activities are relatively consistent, there may be a recollection of Catullus' language during the repeated calls to loosen hair (*solvite crinem*, 84; *solvimus... crinem*, 98–99) and beat the breast (93–4; *iam nuda vocant pectora dextras*, 106; *pulsu pectus tundite vasto*, 114; *tibi maternis ubera palmis / laniate patent*, 120–1).

stated in mythological terms, which contradicts the antithesis and reveals evil and suffering lurking beneath the surface of the brilliantly enameled picture of the Age of Heroes."[170] For Seneca, writing about the death of Polyxena, the pessimism and harsh details of Achilles' "heroism" found in Catullus' poem would have seemed to anticipate his role in the *Troades*. The fates (*fata*, 64.321, 326) that the Parcae spun out are the same fates that figures such as Hecuba, Polyxena, and Pyrrhus must confront or fall victim to in Seneca's play.[171] Talthybius, an epic narrator, recalls previous epic versions of Achilles in his messenger speech, highlighting the interplay between such narrative sections and the tragedy as a whole as well as Seneca's reception of these accounts of Achilles' life and deeds.

The Messenger Speech of the *Phaedra*

If Talthybius' opening speech of the *Troades* provides a small-scale version of the epic tropes found in messenger narratives, the messenger speech of the *Phaedra* shows Seneca at his most "hyper-epic."[172] The messenger discloses Hippolytus' manner of death, and his speech (991–1122) synthesizes the actions and concerns of the play from his point of view. Similes, long ecphrases of the landscape and the monster, and intertexts to the works of Vergil and Ovid lend the narrative its epic feel.[173] Ovid's tale of Hippolytus' death and rebirth (*Met.* 15.492–546), the story of Phaethon (*Met.* 2.103–328), and specific moments from the *Aeneid* further delineate the horrific nature of Hippolytus' death, the motivation for Theseus' curse, and place Hippolytus' heroic action in the dramatic context. The allusive play between Seneca and Ovid also reveals how Seneca utilizes intertextuality to comment on the nature of tragedy as opposed to the epic world of the *Metamorphoses*. Epic poetry, especially Ovid's *Metamorphoses*, is built upon the speeches of different characters, and these narrators each bring their own

---

[170] Curran (1969) 191. For more on Achilles in Catullus 64, cf. Putnam (1961) 192–5 and Fitzgerald (1995) 162–3.

[171] Cf. the words of Calchas: "Fate grants a way for the Greeks with the accustomed price: / a virgin must be sacrificed on the tomb of the Thessalian chief" (*Dant **fata** Danais quo solent pretio viam: / mactanda virgo est Thassali busto ducis*, 360–1) and Boyle (1994) 23–5 for the importance of fate in this play.

[172] Cf. Janka (2004) 49, 54.

[173] Gahen (1988) and Jakobi (1988) document the pervasive number of intertexts. Commentaries by Boyle (1987), Coffey and Mayer (1990), and Casamento (2011) are also informative. Cf. Larson (1994) for more on these descriptions as ecphrases and Bartsch (2007) for ecphrasis in Seneca in general. Erasmo (2004) considers this scene an example of Seneca's rhetorical expansion of Ovidian material.

personae and biases to their tales.[174] Ovid has Hippolytus himself, resurrected as Virbius, describe his own death—clearly revealing his own uniquely subjective view of the situation. In spite of his status as quasi epic poet, Seneca's messenger also gives a partial view, clearly sympathizing with Hippolytus and verifying facts that Virbius reported; subtle touches in his speech indicate his disgust at Theseus and his curse.[175] The messenger speech clearly acts as a climax for many of the themes and motifs of the play, which Seneca indicates by manipulating language from these intertexts in the surrounding scenes.[176] The multiplicity of verbal and situational allusions must be viewed both against the literary tradition and also within the context of the play itself.

The Epic Messenger

In *Metamorphoses* 15.492–546, Ovid's Virbius describes his death to Egeria in the first person, and in doing so he reveals himself to be a questioning narrator who probes the circumstances of his death and is interested in expressing the pathos of his story as a quasi-*consolatio* to Egeria.[177] Seneca's messenger speech responds to details from Ovid's account, and accentuates its imagery to correspond to themes of the *Phaedra* as a whole. For instance, Virbius describes the turbulent sea as follows (*Met.* 15.508–10):

> cum mare surrexit cumulusque inmanis aquarum
> in montis speciem curvari et crescere visus
> et dare mugitus summoque cacumine findi.

---

[174] Cf. Barchiesi (2002) 181: "With Ovid we can go further and say that the poem is 'mostly *about* narrative', if we consider the strategic importance of telling stories for the plot. The poet narrates, the characters, when they have an occasion to speak, tend to become narrators."

[175] Cf. Baertschi (2010) 253, summarizing the work of Barrett and de Jong: "By assuming the voice of the epic poet the messenger thus liberates his account from the partiality that defines the speech of the other characters onstage. Simultaneously, the affiliation with epic enhances his credibility, establishing his voice—as is essential for his role—as authoritative in the many competing claims to truthfulness." Note how the messenger laments over Hippolytus (*heu me*, 997), refers to Hippolytus as Theseus' son (*gnatus*, 1064) in spite of Theseus' claim ("I, as father, know my son died long ago" *gnatum parens obisse iam pridem scio*, 998), and cross-examines Theseus at the close of the speech (1118–22).

[176] Cf. Most (1992) for general analysis of this scene: "It is evident that Seneca has gone far beyond his Ovidian inspiration, not only by lengthening and elaborating the details of his own narrative, but above all by repeatedly reminding the viewer... of Hippolytus' dismemberment throughout the rest of the play" (393).

[177] Cf. Virbius' question "Was it more from fear of discovery or offence at my repulse [that Phaedra brought evidence against me]?" (*indiciine metu magis offensane repulsae?*, *Met.*15.503). This question gets at the heart of the tragic dilemma that Seneca explores in his tragedy. Virbius believes his tale will help ease Egeria's suffering, while the messenger believes Theseus deserves to suffer for his actions. See Segal (1984) 314 for features of Ovid's tale as *consolatio*.

> When the sea swelled, and the huge mass of water seemed
> To be curved in the shape of a mountain and seemed to grow
> And to bellow and to be split at the top of its wave.

Here Virbius describes his personal view of the situation focused on what seemed (*visus*) to have happened. Seneca's messenger provides a similar description of the sea's tsunami-like wave and describes it as follows (*Phd.* 1025–7):

> Haec dum stupentes sequimur, en totum mare
> **immugit**, omnes undique scopuli adstrepunt;
> **summum cacumen** rorat expulso sale...

> While we follow marveling at these things, the whole sea bellowed,
> All the cliffs on every side shout in response;
> The top of the wave drips with emitted spray...

The verbal reminiscences (*mugitus/immugit, summo cacumine/summum cacumen*) show that Seneca is responding to Ovid, but the messenger also provides the spectators' response to these shocking events (*stupentes*).[178] This shows the stunned state of mind of the messenger and his comrades, and supports Virbius' impression of these miraculous events, which he claims will amaze Egeria (*mirabere*, 15.499). The bellowing of the sea is likewise tied into the imagery of the *Phaedra*, for the choral ode on love mentions that peaceful deer bellow when struck with desire (*mugitu*, 343). Additionally, Phaedra believes that Hippolytus' body could have been mangled by the Minotaur (*taurus biformis*, 1172), who fills the Daedalian maze "with immense bellowing" (*vasto... **mugitu***, 1171). This not only fits in with Phaedra's focalized view of her desire as analogous to her mother's but also references the courageous deeds of Theseus, whose heroism spurs Hippolytus to action ("It's my father's task to defeat bulls," 1068).[179] This is just one example of the copious references to Ovid's tale, but it shows how Seneca finds additional ways to make the intertextual language resonate in the tragic context.[180]

As Seneca's messenger continues to tell his tale, he practices the *contaminatio* that Senecan tragedy embodies by merging Ovid's death of Hippolytus with the

---

[178] *Sequimur* is a disputed reading. Cf. Zwierlein (1986b) ad loc. Other possible readings include *quaerimus* (Coffey and Mayer support) and *querimur* (Boyle). Note Ovid's Virbius' similar reaction to Egeria's metamorphosis: *Amazone natus / haud aliter **stupuit*** (15.552–3). Forms of *stupeo* appear earlier in the play to describe Phaedra's desire (607) and the Nurse's denunciation of Hippolytus (719).

[179] Cf. Paschalis (1994) for more on this imagery in the play. It is notable that the only moment of direct speech in this messenger's account highlights Hippolytus' belief in his heroic lineage vis-à-vis Theseus.

[180] Jakobi (1988) finds over twenty recollections of Ovid's account in this section.

Metamorphoses' account of the death of Phaethon.[181] In this particular case, the messenger clearly marks his epic view of the situation by mentioning Phaethon in an epic simile replete with Ovidian allusions. Ovid's Virbius describes how he was thrown from his chariot and his body suffered dismemberment (*Met.* 15. 527–9):

> ossa gravem dare fracta sonum fessamque videres
> exhalari animam nullasque in corpore partes,
> noscere quas posses, unumque erat omnia vulnus.

> You would have seen my broken bones give a hard snap,
> And my tired soul finally expire. There were no parts of my body
> Which you would be able to recognize, all was one wound.

As he catalogues his destruction, he places the Nymph Egeria at the scene and claims she would have seen (*videres*) his last breath, but would be unable to recognize (*noscere*) any part of his bloodied body.[182] Seneca's messenger, unlike Egeria, *was* present at Hippolytus' death, and his language mimics Virbius' while adding details important to the interpretation of Seneca's tragedy. Both accounts focus on the physical rending of his body and Hippolytus' final wounded appearance. The messenger relates how the chariot team ran wherever fear led them (1090–6):

> talis per auras non suum agnoscens onus
> Solique falso creditum indignans diem
> Phaethonta currus devium excussit polo.
> Late cruentat arva et inlisum caput
> scopulis resultat; auferunt dumi comas,
> et ora durus pulcra **populatur** lapis
> peritque **multo vulnere** infelix decor.

> Just as the chariot team of the Sun, not recognizing his weight,
> Was indignant that the day had been entrusted to a false Sun and
> Shook out Phaethon from a remote part of the sky.
> He bloodies the fields far and wide and his crushed head

---

[181] See Littlewood (2004) 104–10, 121–34, passim for Phaethon in the tragedies.

[182] The question of recognition is important for the final scene of the play when Theseus attempts to reassemble Hippolytus' body. While he may recognize his crime (*crimen* **agnosco** *meum*, 1249) and certain pieces (*laevi lateris* **agnosco** *notas*, 1260), at the end we may question how much knowledge he has gained of himself and his role in the tragedy (cf. Boyle (1987) 26).

> Bounces from the rocks, bushes carry away his hair,
> The hard stone devastates his beautiful looks
> And his unlucky beauty perishes in many a wound.

The messenger's Phaethon simile comes on the heels of numerous intertexts with Ovid's Phaethon story such as Hippolytus' headlong fall (*praeceps*, 1085 ~ *Met.* 2.320), the horses' struggle with the yoke (*luctantur iugo / eripere*, 1083–4 ~ *Met.* 2.315), and their subsequent headlong flight (*qua timor iussit runt*, 1089 ~ *Met.* 2.202–4).[183] Seneca's messenger mentions the Phaethon story so prominently not simply because both involve horses careening out of control, but because of the motif of wishes gone awry and the complications between fathers and sons.[184] Both Phaethon and Hippolytus wish to perform deeds similar to their fathers, but both are shown to be woefully incapable. In the case of Hippolytus' death, the relationship is further complicated because Theseus' wish to his father, Neptune, culminates in Hippolytus' demise. Both Theseus and the Sun ultimately regret that their wishes were granted and lament the deaths of their sons (*Phd.* 1213–43, *Met.* 2.381–93).

Seneca ties this speech into the fabric of the play as a whole through language that picks up from both the Phaethon and the Virbius sections of Ovid's *Metamorphoses*. The idea that Hippolytus' beauty perishes in "many a wound" (*multo vulnere*, 1096) is Seneca's *variatio* of the idea found in "Everything was one wound" (*unumque erat omnia vulnus, Met.* 15.529).[185] Seneca weaves this phrase throughout his play: in the opening hunting song, the boar is known for inflicting "many a wound" (***vulnere multo*** *iam notus aper*, 30), and at the close, Theseus picks up a piece of Hippolytus' body rendered unidentifiable by the damage (***multo vulnere*** *abruptum undique*, 1266).[186] The messenger's use of *populatur* resonates in the play with similar uses at 280 and 377, both referring to the effects of desire on the body.[187] The chorus uses this verb to indicate the violent flame of passion (*igne furtivo populante venas*, 280); the Nurse describes how lovesickness ravages Phaedra (*populatur artus cura*, 377); and the messenger relates this verb to the destruction of Hippolytus' beauty.[188] This word itself may derive from

---

[183] Jakobi (1988) details each of these instances and the various verbal recollections.

[184] Note also that both stories draw attention to the collection of the shattered body for burial (*Met.* 2.333-9; *Phd.* 1105-10, 1256-79).

[185] Both Phaedra (*quo tuus fugit* ***decor***? 1173) and Theseus (*huc cecidit* ***decor***? 1270) comment on Hippolytus' resultant disfigurement.

[186] Theseus goes on to say, "I do not know what part of you it is, but it is part" (*quae* ***pars*** *tui sit dubito; sed* ***pars*** *est tui*, 1267), recalling the context of Ovid's version (*nullasque in corpore* ***partes***, 15.528).

[187] Boyle defends both readings while Zwierlein brackets both passages. Boyle (1987) 23 finds the repetition shows "*natura vindex* in triumphant and irresistible operation."

[188] Hippolytus' beauty has been stressed throughout the play, especially in the second choral ode, but even there it is deemed an "unreliable good": *anceps forma bonum mortalibus* (761). Cf. Most (1992) 394–5.

Ovid's account of Phaethon's death, where his hair is ignited by "devastating fire" (*flamma **populante**,* Met. 2.319).[189] The reader of the play moves from the general mention of desire as a cosmic force to its specific destructive effects on Phaedra and Hippolytus.

Seneca's messenger continues to lavish detail on the death of Hippolytus, and depicts the event as a sexualized *sparagmos* (1098–1102):

> tandemque raptum truncus ambusta sude
> medium per inguen stipite ingesto tenet;
> [paulumque domino currus affixo stetit][190]
> haesere biiuges vulnere—et pariter moram
> dominumque rumpunt.

> Finally a tree stump with burned stake
> Holds him with its stalk thrust through the middle of his groin;
> [the chariot stopped for a moment with its master fastened]
> The team was detained by the wound—and at the same moment
> They break their delay and their master.

The gruesome physicality of this description has been read as a symbolic result of Hippolytus' repressed sexuality and an inversion of his hunting prowess: "Diana's kingdom of field, rock, bramble, bush and tree tears his flesh and his body apart in a grotesque and unambiguous orgy of sexual violence."[191] At the same time, with these words, Seneca's messenger is correcting and elaborating a line of Virbius' account: "My muscles are held on a sharp stake and part of my limbs are snatched" (*nervos in stipe teneri / membra rapi partim,* Met. 15.525–6). Here the messenger responds to the general account of Ovid's Virbius by casting light on a detail Virbius (purposefully?) elided. The word *nervus* can mean "sinew, muscle" but also "penis."[192] While Ovid's Virbius shies away from stating what actually occurred, the Seneca zooms in on the impact of a stalk "through the middle of his groin" (*medium per inguen **stipite** eiecto **tenet**)*. In doing so, Seneca's messenger emphasizes the sexual violence resulting from the unchecked passion

---

[189] Additional language from this section that recalls the Phaethon episode includes the focus on recognition (Met. 2.161: *leve pondus erat, nec quod **cognoscere** possent*) and the chariot (*currus*) coursing through the air (Met. 2.202, 205). The verb *excutere* also figures in Virbius' telling of his destruction (*excutior curru,* Met. 15.524).

[190] Zwierlein (1986a) follows Axelson and deletes 1100, but it is retained by Coffey and Mayer (1990). See their discussion ad loc.

[191] Boyle (1987) 23.

[192] *OLD* s.v. *nervus* 1b. Cf. Adams (1982) 38 and D. F. Kennedy (1993) 59, who interprets Ov. *Am.* 1.1.17–8 in a similar manner.

of Phaedra and the blind rage of Theseus. Here, Seneca corrects Ovid's ambiguous language to portray Hippolytus' violent end, an end that accentuates the frustrated passions of Phaedra and Hippolytus.[193]

But what exactly did the supernatural monster from the sea look like? Why does Seneca's messenger vividly depict the monster in such heightened rhetoric? Coffey and Mayer hit upon the reason in their commentary: "The description is self-indulgently long and belongs rather to epic tradition."[194] The epic elements of Ovid's *Metamorphoses* and Vergil's *Aeneid* actively influence Seneca's creation.[195] If Hippolytus' death unites two Ovidian accounts, now Seneca features both Augustan epic poets in order to create a magical beast that expands imagery and themes from the play. It is not enough for the monster to be, like in Ovid, simply a bull (*Met.* 15.511–3):

> corniger hinc **taurus** ruptis expellitur undis
> pectoribusque tenus molles **erectus** in auras
> **naribus** et **patulo** partem maris evomit ore.
>
> From here a horned bull is driven from the broken waves
> And, raising its chest to the light breezes, spits out water
> From its nostrils and gaping mouth.

In Virbius' telling, the miraculous appearance of a bull from the sea is startling enough to spook his horses and cause his demise. Seneca's messenger, however, elaborates his description of the bull and, in doing so, comments on the cause of its appearance. His hybrid bull/whale shares characteristics with Virbius' figure (*taurus*, 1036; *erexit*, 1037; *naresque hiulcis haustibus patulae fremunt*, 1043), but is given much more detail (1036–49), and this rhetorical expansion ties the appearance of the monster to an earlier moment of the play in addition to adding elements from Vergil's poetry.

---

[193] Cf. Segal (1986) 75: "The bull that destroys Hippolytus is a distorted emanation of his own repressed sexuality, a monstrous projection of his own violent hatred of a part of himself. It is also a symbol of Phaedra's expressed sexuality and therefore a manifestation of the tragic impossibility of the bond between himself and Phaedra, the point of precarious, unstable juncture between her fantasies and his terrors."

[194] Coffey and Mayer (1990) ad loc. Is it the character or Seneca who is being self-indulgent? Hutchinson (1993) 126 issues a more sympathetic assessment: "The poet has attacked his extravagant narrative with immense and exhilarating gusto; but strangeness, wit, and organization have complicated the extremity and made the passage as a whole not facile bombast but alert, lively, and imaginative poetry."

[195] DeJong (1991) has considered the Euripidean messenger speech to be an example of epic narrative. Coffey and Mayer (1990) ad loc. comments on the similarity between the messenger's use of Ovid's *Metamorphoses* and Eumolpus' transformation of Vergil *Aen.* 2 into a messenger speech on the death of Laocoön (Petron. *Sat.* 89). Both accounts reveal the appropriation of epic material in a "dramatic" context.

Seneca's monster embodies the violence lurking under the surface of passion, and intertextual echoes both expand and complicate the literary ramifications of his monster. Intertextuality adds nuance and metaliterary significance to Seneca's description of the sea monster, which blends the portrayal of Laocoön's sea serpents in the second book of the *Aeneid* with the actions of the bull-in-love of his *Georgics*.[196] Seneca's monster becomes a metapoetic emblem for the *contaminatio* Seneca practices in his writing as its hybrid shape attempts to embody the horrific violence of epic. Verbal similarities between the *Aeneid* and the *Phaedra* hint at the monster's power as well as its size (*Phd.* 1036–7, 1046–8):

> caerulea taurus colla sublimis gerens
> **erexit** altam fronte viridanti **iubam**....
> tum **pone tergus** ultima in monstrum coit
> facies et ingens belua **immensam** trahit
> squamosa **partem**.

> The bull lifting its blue neck high bore
> A lofty crest from its green forehead....
> Then, behind its back, the hindquarters of the monster
> Are drawn together and the huge scaly beast drags a large tail.

The snakes of the *Aeneid*, sent by a god to destroy Laocoön, resemble Seneca's beast with their crested heads aloft (***arrecta iubae***, *Aen.* 2.206) while "the rest of their body skims the water behind and twists their huge back in coils" (***pars** cetera pontum / **pone** legit sinuatque **immensa** volumine **terga**,* 2.207–8). Seneca's monster transcends Vergil's in form, and the focus on its back (*terga*) recalls beasts such as those Diana hunts (*Phd.* 64) or Jupiter's transformation into a bull to transport Europa (*stravit sua terga*, 304). In each case, the uncanny and deadly manifestation of the divine dramatically manifests the wide divide between the gods and mortals.[197] The Vergilian intertext also strongly sympathizes with the victims of the serpents, and, as the snakes wind around their defenseless victims, so Hippolytus' reins are drawn taut as he struggles with his bonds.[198]

---

[196] Cf. Segal (1984) 320–1, who concludes: "Whereas Virgil humanizes the bull, Seneca depersonalizes it into a murderous machine. This creature becomes terrifyingly and pitilessly Other." There are additional intertextual resonances with *Georg.* 3 and the first choral ode. See Boyle (1987) ad loc.

[197] Seneca's *Phaedra* notably does away with the divine "framing" of Aphrodite and Artemis in Euripides' *Hippolytus*. Seneca chooses to focus on the damage caused by human agency throughout his play; this "divine" punishment is sanctioned by Theseus alone.

[198] *Aen.* 2.215 (*implicat*) and *Phd.* 1085 (*impliciut*); *Aen.* 2.217 (*ligant*) and *Phd.* 1087 (*ligat*); *Aen.* 2.220 (*nodos*) and *Phd.* 1087 (*nodos*). Seneca strongly marks how the immense shape (*facies*) and tail (*partem*) of the beast leave Hippolytus in pieces (*partem*, 1104; *partes* 1258, 1278). Cf. Staley (2000) for more on this passage.

The epic snakes from the sea befit the heroic tone of the messenger's speech, but, as the narrative continues, it also focuses on a specific moment of Vergil's poetry that can be found in both the *Aeneid* and the *Georgics*.[199] The description of the bull in the *Georgics* is part of a larger discussion of passion and its negative impact on the animal world (*G.* 3.232–4):[200]

> et **temptat** sese atque **irasci** in cornua discit
> arboris obnixus trunco, ventosque lacessit
> ictibus, et sparsa ad pugnam **proludit** harena.

> He spurs himself and learns to focus his anger in his horns;
> Sparring with a tree trunk, he tears the winds with blows,
> And rehearses the fight on the scattered sands.

Seneca's monster underscores the *ira* that passion can manifest (*Phd.* 1059-61):

> hic se illa moles acuit atque **iras parat**.
> ut cepit animos seque prae**temptans** satis
> **prolusit irae**, praepeti cursu evolat.

> Here that monster sharpens and prepares his anger.
> When it has roused its strength and tested itself enough
> In its rehearsal of anger, it flies forth headlong.

The *Georgics* passage details how a bull, strongly personified as a frustrated lover, rouses his anger before returning to defeat his rival. Here, the intertext is appropriate because of the passion of Phaedra for Hippolytus, and the bull imagery unites many strands of the mythic history of Minos, Pasiphae, Theseus, Ariadne, and the Minotaur.[201] This same description of the bull, however, is also used as a simile for Turnus in the *Aeneid* (12.101–6). Seneca finds a moment that is common to both Vergilian works in order to comment on the power of figurative language in the creation of his phantasmagorical monster.[202] Clearly, Vergil is

---

[199] Cf. Introduction pp. 13–5 for another moment in which Seneca focuses on a Vergilian passage that is common to the *Georgics* and the *Aeneid*.

[200] Cf. *G.* 3.209–11, where Venus is considered to be the greatest danger for the care (*industria*, 209) of the farmer. Cf. Thomas (1988b) ad loc. for more on the human dimension of this description.

[201] Paschalis (1994) discusses such imagery in the play as a whole. When Phaedra sees Hippolytus' body, she asks, "What fierce minotaur with horned head ripped you apart?" (*quis...taurus biformis ore corniger ferox / divulsit?*, 1170–3).

[202] The repetition of this scene in both works may have led to Seneca's recollection of these lines.

calling attention to the similarity between Turnus' wrath (esp. considering the lost "heifer," Lavinia) and the anger of the bull, which is inspired by desire. Turnus' love for Lavinia causes him to "burn more for arms" (*ardet in arma magis*, 12.71), and, in his frenzy, "fiery sparks shoot from his whole face and fire sparkles in his eager eyes" (*totoque ardentis ab ore / scintillae absistunt, oculis micat acribus ignis*, 12.101–2). The monster's eyes also "emit flames" (*flammam vomunt*, 1040), which the messenger explains are characteristic of "the leader of a fierce herd" (*feri dominator…gregis*, 1039). In the *Georgics*, after the defeated bull gathers his strength for one more attack, Vergil compares his onrush to a breaker gathering momentum at sea. This destructive wave echoes the conditions that Seneca's messenger describes that produced the monster.[203] Whereas the figurative possibilities are central in Vergil (the wave as a simile for the bull, the bull as a simile for Turnus' passion/rage), Seneca makes both concrete expressions of the power of Venus ("goddess born from the rough sea" *diva non miti generata ponto*, 274) and the curse of Theseus. The overall context of the *Georgics* passage, from its opening warning against Venus (3.209–11) to its final crashing wave, features in Seneca's creative reworking of its particulars to depict his monster. These intertexts work to emphasize the ferocity and background "motivation" of the monster as a divine scourge meant to punish the false "passion" of Hippolytus (i.e., the rape that he has been accused of) or the true passion of Phaedra. Vergilian touches indicate Seneca's larger literary concerns—his tragic view consumes the imagery and language of competing genres and creates something suitably frightening and grand.[204]

In addition, this section of the messenger's speech strongly responds to the first choral ode of the *Phaedra* and the depiction of desire found there.[205] Verbal parallelism links the two passages. Zeus, assuming the form of a bull, dominates the waves (**pectore** *adverso* **domuit** *profundum*, 307). In the messenger's speech, the bull is described as "the leader of a fierce herd" (*feri* **dominator**…*gregis*, 1039), and his chest and dewlap are mottled with green clinging moss (*musco tenaci* **pectus** *ac palear viret*, 1044).[206] Likewise, the monster's amphibious nature

---

[203] Common words include *fluctus* (G. 3.237, Phd. 1013, 1018, 1030), *pontus* (G. 237, Phd. 1015, 1033), *ex alto* (G. 3.238, Phd. 1007), *sinus* (G. 3.238, Phd. 1012, 1019), and forms of the verb *volvo* (G. 3.238, Phd. 1019, 1097—where it is used to describe the wheels of the chariot rolling over Hippolytus).

[204] Cf. Schiesaro 2003 225: "From this perspective the vast mass of circumscribed intertextual points of contacts with previous poets, especially Virgil and Ovid, becomes in *Thyestes*, and in Senecan tragedy at large, a source of *horror* and at the same time a reiterated—if imperfect—apology for its legitimation." Note that the messenger claims this *monstrum* is an "evil greater than fear" (*malum / maius timore*, 1032–3).

[205] See my discussion in Chap. 2.

[206] In seeing the remains of Hippolytus' body, Phaedra addresses Neptune as the "savage leader of the deep" (*profundi saeve* **dominator** *freti*, 1159) and wants him to attack her with "monsters of the blue sea" (*monstra* **caeruli** *maris*, 1160).

is stressed in Seneca's account, and his cobalt neck (*caerulea*, 1036) and eyes flash flame or are notable for their blue color (*caerula*, 1041). This description mimics the effects of love on the inhabitants of the sea, where the chorus informs us of the reach of Cupid's arrows (336–7):

> **caerulus** undis grex Nereidum
> flammamque nequit relevare mari.
>
> The sea-blue group of Nereids
> Is unable to relieve their flame by the sea.

The metaphoric flames of love in the Nereids have become real flames in the eyes of the messenger's monster. This extended description allows Seneca to tie the monster into the tragedy's theme of the destructive power of love. The beast (*belua*, 1047) acts as a metaphor for the desire of Phaedra, which will tear apart Hippolytus as surely as love has power over gods and animals alike (351–3):

> amat insani **belua** ponti
> Lucaeque boves: vindicat omnes
> natura sibi, nihil immune est.
>
> The beast of the wild sea loves, even elephants love:
> Nature claims all for itself,
> Nothing is immune.

The messenger's description of the monster combines elements of *Metamorphoses* 15 and Vergil's poetry, as well as strong intratextual nods to the previous choral description of the power of desire. In this way, Seneca grants the monster additional relevance to the world of the play and shows the danger of excessive emotion, especially sexual desire. Because of the density of intertextual material in this section, Seneca encourages the reader to view his messenger as an interpreter of the Augustan epics in his own right. Seneca emulates Vergil and Ovid and transcends the violent monsters they created in order to stress the tragic ramifications of desire and misunderstanding for all the protagonists of the play. Although Virbius could be reborn in the *Metamorphoses*, this will not be an option for Seneca's Hippolytus in the face of a monster that dwarfs Ovid's measly bull from the sea.[207] The messenger's epic monster represents Seneca's response

---

[207] The question of Hippolytus' survival as Virbius seems to have been a matter of debate among the Augustan poets; cf. *Aen.* 7.761–82; *Fast.* 3.261–6, 6.733–62; and *Carm.* 4.7.25–8. Echoes of *Met.* 15 dealing with Virbius' rebirth are found scattered at other points of the *Phaedra* (820–4 ~ *Met.* 15.

to the Augustan epic tradition—a monster that embodies the various forces of passion, savagery, and lust that plague the protagonists of the play.

Conclusion

From Juno's Vergilian prologue to the messenger speech of the *Phaedra*, one can see how Seneca manages to blend his intertextual engagement with the Augustan poets into the themes and concerns of his tragedies. Imagery and language from the intertexts frequently appear in the mouths of different characters, which provides multiple views of the material and guides the reader to recognize the importance of these intertexts for the play as a whole. Prologue speakers set the mood of the play with intertexts reinforcing the major motifs and concerns to be dramatized. Choral odes provide lyric analysis of the tragic action, and reflect and refract Horace's philosophical and metapoetic concerns. The messenger acts as an epic poet who is able to proclaim authoritatively and (almost) omnisciently the events happening offstage. Intertexts to epic sources, much like epic similes, help to expand the scope of the event being described and force the reader to bridge the divide between tenor and vehicle, or, in this case Senecan *aemulatio* and his Ovidian (or Vergilian) model.[208] Goward remarks on how these formal elements work together, "Tragedy's markedly hybrid form is one of its great strengths, since at each juncture between different modes and different focalisations the audience are freshly re-engaged in their struggle to discover meaning."[209] Seneca brings together different genres through intertexts to their Augustan practitioners and finds ways to amplify, flout, or theatricalize his models. The incest theme of Oedipus and the bizarre monster from the sea of the *Phaedra* can be seen as representations of Seneca's intertexual *contaminatio* that attempt to reflect his reception of various Augustan poets. The three formal features of tragedy investigated in this chapter offer a suggestive panorama of the ways intertextuality works hand in hand with Seneca's tragic poetics to interrogate the very meaning of the language itself.

538–40; 847–8 ~ *Met.* 15.531–2). These, combined with Theseus' own return from the Underworld, could lead the reader to believe that Seneca is preparing for a conclusion in which Hippolytus is reborn, but the extensive damage to his body, replete with the echo of Horace *Sat.* 1.4.62 (*disiecti membra poetae*) in Hippolytus *disiecta...membra* (1256), proves that his death is final in Senecan tragedy. Cf. Most (1992) 406–8 and Staley (2010) 116 for discussion of the Horatian echo.

[208] Cf. Conte (1986) 52–7 for discussion of how allusion functions as metaphor.
[209] Goward (1999) 11.

4

Intertextuality, Writers, and Readers

> That poet seems to me to be able to walk the tightrope,
> Who, by illusions, stirs up, troubles, calms, and fills my heart
> With empty terrors. He's like a magician,
> Who can transport me now to Thebes, now to Athens.
> —Horace *Ep.* 2.1.210–3

As can be seen from characters such as Medea and narratives such as the messenger speech of the *Phaedra*, studies of Senecan intertextuality illuminate the intersection of at least two literary works in dialogue with one another. At times the original genre and context of the source material exerts overwhelming influence and gives a strong Vergilian or Horatian feel to Seneca's text. More often, however, the "new" tragic view of the model (now contextualized in Seneca's dramatic works) offers a contradictory or challenging interpretation of the model text. Repetition of the intertextual language elsewhere in the play frequently rebrands the original material with tragic repercussions. Because of its hybrid nature, the tragic genre allows the various intertextual sources to be presented and transformed by their new context. Seneca compiles material from a variety of poetic genres (epic, lyric, didactic, etc.) in his tragedies and such material enriches the work by bringing into play the traditional associations of those genres. As Edmunds states, "Intertextuality demands the interpretation of at least two texts,"[1] and the tragedies offer ways in which Seneca, qua reader and writer, interprets the works of Vergil, Ovid, and Horace. His tragedies offer paradigms of readership and authorship as various characters are positioned as surrogate poets (Medea) and readers (Oedipus). In this chapter I offer readings of additional moments in which Seneca seems interested in offering a view of his poetics through the intertextual critique of his precursors.[2] In order to illustrate how he develops his poetics by manipulating the theories of his predecessors,

---

[1] Edmunds (2001) xviii.
[2] Previous metapoetic readings can be found in Chaps. 2 and 3.

I examine Seneca's recollections of two seminal statements of Augustan poetics: the proem of the third book of Vergil's *Georgics* and Horace's *Ars Poetica*. The parallels with Horace's *Ars Poetica* also allow Seneca to comment critically on Horace's dramatic principles and offer a corrective view of his tragic poetics. After these examples of Seneca's critical thought developing *through* the past, I analyze the figure of Cassandra, who acts as a surrogate poet in the *Agamemnon*. As such, she provides versions of the events at Troy that are developed from works such as Vergil's *Aeneid*, Ovid's *Fasti*, and Horace's *Ars Poetica*, but often with an eye to the future. Seneca gives Cassandra two speeches about the death of Agamemnon to exploit the poetic potential inherent in tragedy as a mélange of diverse genres and to stress the motif of repetition in the *Agamemnon*. Finally, I discuss another moment in which Seneca combines various genres in order to provide a reading of his poetic predecessors as well as problematize the act of reading itself. The *Oedipus* provides a series of responses to signifying events and poetic pronouncements (*extispicium*, the Delphic oracle) that act as paradigms for the act of reading. However, most of the readings done in the play are shown to be inexact, incomplete, and ill-advised in the tragic context. This hermeneutic model culminates in the necromancy scene (530–658), in which Creon's messenger speech to Oedipus allows Seneca to question the immortal legacy of the Augustan poets. Although their works survive, they may not provide their original message in the upside-down world of Seneca's *Oedipus*.

Seneca's *Georgics*

The *Georgics* offers Seneca disparate material for reflection. Quotations from the *Georgics* appear in his prose works with some frequency: he employs the description of the bee society to illustrate the importance of a just leader to the Roman people (*Clem.* 4.1), validates Vergil's choice of the old-fashioned word *asilus* to describe the gadfly (*Ep.* 58.2), and muses on his picturesque lines describing the rivers Larius and Benacus in a passage discussing the beauty and benefits of nature (*Ben.* 5.3).[3] In general, Seneca's pronouncement that "Vergil did not want to teach farmers, but to delight his readers" (*nec agricolas docere voluit, sed legentes delectare, Ep.* 86.15) appears operative in the varied use of this work across Seneca's corpus because the didactic element of the *Georgics* is downplayed. Intertexts to the *Georgics* in the tragedies likewise provide a rich variety of interpretative material, and thus far we have seen how the *Georgics* can be seen lurking behind descriptions of work and kingship (Chap. 1) and passion

---

[3] Cf. Henderson (2004) 147–8 for Seneca's view of Vergil's gadfly and passim for additional interactions between the letters and Vergil's *Georgics*.

(Chap. 2), as well as indicating the expanse of the known world (Chap. 3). Verbal "borrowings" from the *Georgics* appear frequently in the tragedies (Coffey and Mayer count over sixteen instances in the *Phaedra* alone),[4] and, as with all intertextual analysis, the question is whether such moments are significant for the interpretation of the play. Seneca often indicates the significance of such intertexts by manipulating the language of that intertext throughout the tragedy in which it appears. In the following discussion, I show how Seneca recalls one passage of the *Georgics*—namely, the proem of the third book—at moments when questions of poetics are concerned. This proem offers Vergil's "most extensive, and most complex, programmatic statement" in the *Georgics*, looks forward to the epic project of his *Aeneid* (the metaphorical depiction of a temple celebrating Octavian), and reinforces the poetic parameters of his Callimachean *Georgics*.[5] Seneca echoes certain segments of this passage in order to place the dramatic action in a similar poetic framework, validate the poetics at work in his play, and to question the generic implications of the forthcoming tragic conflict.

Vergil's *Medea* and *Oedipus*

The beginning of Seneca's *Medea* presents a vision of Medea contemplating her position as a mother, a wife, and an imminent avenger.[6] Medea believes that she must accomplish more heinous crimes than those previously done if Jason actually leaves her (51–55):

> accingere ira teque in exitium para
> furore toto. paria narrentur tua
> repudia thalamis: quo virum linques modo?
> hoc quo **secuta es. rumpe iam segnes moras**:
> quae **scelere** parta est, **scelere** liquenda est domus.

> Gird yourself with anger and prepare to destroy them,
> With fury fully aroused. Let your divorce match the story
> Of your marriage: How will you leave your husband?
> In the way you followed him. Now break your sluggish delay:
> The house was gained by crime; it must be left by crime.

These are the final lines of Medea's prologue speech and reveal that she is planning great crimes against Jason and that she, in some sense, knows that such a

---

[4] Coffey and Mayer (1990) 197–203.
[5] Thomas (1988b) 30.
[6] See above pp. 97–101 for more on the opening of the *Medea*.

revenge will be the subject of songs to come (*narrentur*, 52). Medea's haste ("Now break your sluggish delay") parallels Vergil's own call to action near the close of his proem (*G.* 3.40–3):

> interea Dryadum silvas saltusque **sequamur**
> intactos, tua, Maecenas, haud mollia iussa:
> te sine nil altum **mens** incohat. en age **segnis**
> **rumpe moras.**

> Meanwhile let us follow the woods and untouched groves of the Dryads,
> Following your difficult orders, Maecenas:
> Without you, my mind begins nothing great. Come on then,
> Break your sluggish delay.

While the collocation *rumpe moras* appears twice in the *Aeneid* (4.569, 9.13) and is featured in Seneca's *Troades* (*rumpe fatorum moras*, 681), the repetition of these three words together is unique to the *Georgics* and *Medea*. In addition, Seneca plays on language found in this passage, as his Medea will follow (*secuta es*) her own precedent in devising a revenge, while Vergil will follow (*sequamur*) the topics relevant to the *Georgics*, and not the epic themes he has just rehearsed.[7] If Vergil's mind "begins nothing great" without Maecenas, Medea's "mind stirs up within" (***mens*** *intus agitat*, 47) when contemplating her past actions.[8] In the following lines, Vergil claims he will gird himself (*accingar*, 3.46) to sing of the fiery battles of Caesar in the future, while Medea does something similar with her anger (*accingere ira*, 51). But why would Seneca wish the reader to remember Vergil's call to resume the subject matter of the *Georgics* at this point in his *Medea*?[9] The broad parallels place Medea in an analogous position to Vergil himself and point to her position in the play as a poet figure who can create/control the tragic scenario through her own language (especially her magical ability). At this point in the play, the type of revenge Medea will enact is still hazy, although she wishes to bring about even greater crimes (*maiora ... scelera*, 50) than previously (55). It is notable that the connection between delay (*mora*) and crime (*scelus*) will also appear at the close of the play, when Jason essentially asks Medea to complete her revenge (and kill their child). He states, "At least do not delay my punishment" (***moram***que *saltem supplicis dona meis*, 1015), only to have Medea respond, "Enjoy your crime slowly, grief, do not rush it; / this day is

---

[7] See my discussion of *sequor* in the *Medea* in Chap. 2.

[8] Medea claims she will "costume her mind with the Caucasus" (*Caucasum* ***mente*** *indue*, 43).

[9] Hine (2000) ad loc. comments that the Vergilian phrase "may remind the reader that, parallel to Medea's ambition to equal her previous actions, there runs the poet's ambition to equal his predecessors' poetry."

mine" (*perfruere lento **scelere**, ne propera, dolor / hic meus dies*, 1016–7).[10] While at the start of the play she urges herself to begin the revenge plot, by the play's end she relishes the time she spends in torturing Jason and performing the crime. The language found in Seneca's account reappears at the close of the play to indicate the particular plot she has followed and to stress her position as an authorial figure in her own right. In looking back to Vergil's *Georgics*, Seneca positions his Medea to be a poetic figure, capable of wreaking vengeance comparable to her previous feats, but also intimating that something more impressive is on the way.

Vergil's proem is a complex pronouncement, however, in which he claims that the neoteric mythological poetry of his age has become too commonplace and that he will create something greater in the future (*G.* 3.3–12). This future endeavor is metaphorically figured as a temple, but accentuated by triumphal as well as Epinican imagery and alive with allusions to contemporary history.[11] How much of this additional information is necessary for understanding the possible ramifications of this passage in Senecan tragedy? Is Seneca setting up his tragedies in the vein of the *Georgics* project or as the more grandiose future endeavor that Vergil anticipates? While it may be safer in the *Medea* to simply suggest a correspondence between Vergil's poetic persona and the powers of Medea herself, in the *Oedipus* the passage as a whole acquires even further significance.

The *extispicium* episode of Act 2 offers symbolic representations of Oedipus' future and emphasizes the gulf in knowledge between the audience and the characters. When Manto, Tiresias' daughter, describes the tumultuous events of the perverted sacrifice, her language becomes somewhat muddled, but what is clear is that this is an ominous event.[12] The bull and heifer fall with wounds prefiguring those of Oedipus and Jocasta (341–50), the liver has two "heads" (359–60, indicating the future discord between Oedipus' two sons), an embryonic calf is found in the unmated heifer, which slowly comes to its feet and attacks the priests (372–80). These disruptions are indicative of the tragic world of Oedipus' (and Seneca's) Thebes, where, "order has been changed" (*mutatus ordo est,*

---

[10] A further intratextual link is Medea's self-address "Shall this day go by without action?" (***segnis** hic ibit dies*, 399), revealing how she continues to spur herself utilizing language from the Vergilian intertext.

[11] The bibliography for this passage is vast, but Miles (1980) 166–81, Thomas (1983), Hardie (1986) 48–51, and the commentaries of Thomas (1988b) and Mynors (1990) are foundational.

[12] The allegorical interpretation of the events can be found in Pratt (1939) 93-9, but Busch (2007) finds that the confusing language is itself indicative of the disruption of nature's laws found in the *Oedipus*, and undermines possible symbolic meanings. In general, the *sympatheia* between all aspects of nature (in this case, the plague, Oedipus, the animal world, etc.) is stressed through the repetition of language and imagery of disorder in this act (cf. *Nat.* 2.32.4).

366) and "nature has been reversed" (*natura versa est*, 371).[13] As at the beginning of the sacrifice, where an intertextual connection with Ovid's description of a rainbow helps foreshadow later developments,[14] so at the close of the episode, the intertextual *contaminatio* of Ovid's *Metamorphoses* and the proem of *Georgics* 3 provide insight to the results of the sacrifice. Tiresias, flummoxed at the information he has been given, claims (390–2):

> Nec alta caeli quae levi pinna secant
> nec **fibra vivis rapta pectoribus** potest
> ciere nomen[15]; **alia temptanda est via**:

> Neither the vault of heaven which birds cross on light wing
> Nor the entrails ripped from living breast are able to summon the name;
> Another way must be tried.

Neither Tiresias nor Oedipus can understand what the signs (*signa*, 384) have meant, and Tiresias admits here that augury and *extispicium* are ineffectual for the current crisis. The failure of the *extispicium* is emphasized further through the Ovidian intertext. In the final book of the *Metamorphoses*, Pythagoras denounces eating meat (Pythagoreans were vegetarians because of their belief in the transmigration of souls), and derides man's sacrificial practices (*Met.* 15.136–7):

> protinus **ereptas viventi pectore fibras**
> inspiciunt mentesque deum scrutantur in illis;

> Thence they inspect the entrails ripped from the living breast
> And inspect the will of the gods in those entrails.

This Ovidian passage concludes Pythagoras' argument that traditional modes of divination are rubbish, and that the process itself is cruel and unnecessary.[16] Seneca recalls Ovid's words in order to strengthen the impression that the sacrifice is

---

[13] The Ovidian stress on change and mutation is notable for Seneca's Thebes and places the action of the play in a post-*Metamorphoses* setting; cf. Hinds (2011) 9–21.

[14] Cf. Chap. 1 pp. 46–51.

[15] This phrase could be an intertext in its own right as Ovid uses similar language when Ceres searches for Persephone in his *Fasti*, calling out to her by name or simply as "daughter" ("and she shouts either name in turn" *alternis **nomen** utrumque **ciet***, 4.484). The reader will recall Persephone, like Laius, must be roused from the Underworld.

[16] Ovid's pathetic description of the cattle sacrificed (15.120–42) culminates in Pythagoras' view that eating beef is the equivalent of eating one's "fellow laborer" (*colonos*, 142). Note also the use of *scrutemur* at *Oed.* 372 and *scrutatur* at *Oed.* 965. Pythagoras believes "all things are changing" (*omnia mutantur*, 15.165) and is a fitting (Ovidian?) voice for the transformations endemic in Oedipus' Thebes.

deceptive and misleading for those involved. It is notable, however, that the sacrifice is relatively clear for the reader/audience who knows the specifics of this mythological tale and pays close attention to the signs offered.[17] This increases the dramatic irony of the situation and may lead some to question Oedipus' skill at deciphering riddles, especially those related to his own life.

In addition, Palmieri has pointed out the importance of *alia temptanda est via* (392) as a response to Vergil's programmatic statement in book 3 of the *Georgics*: "A way must be tried, by which I may be able to lift myself from the ground and victoriously fly on the lips of men" (***temptanda via est****, qua me quoque possim / tollere humo victorque virum volitare per ora*; G. 3.9–10).[18] This proem offers a variety of literary antecedents, which Vergil recalls even as he asserts his modern poetics. As Gale states, "The lines simultaneously proclaim and illustrate the poet's mastery of tradition: Virgil paradoxically celebrates his originality in language appropriated from Pindar, Callimachus, Ennius, and…Lucretius."[19] A similar strategy is at work with Seneca's appropriation of Vergilian and Ovidian language at this moment, as Seneca signals an awareness of the poetic tradition and his own need to move past previous accounts. Whereas Vergil rejects the neoteric topics popular among poets of his time and searches for a novel way to ensure his poetic immortality, Tiresias indicates his need to search for truth among the dead (and in this action, Seneca will recall the *katabasis* of Vergil's *Aeneid*).[20] Schiesaro notes how this Vergilian allusion marks Seneca's "analogous intention to innovate," but fails to stress that much of the innovation of the upcoming necromancy scene is dependent on intertextual resonances with Vergil's *Aeneid* (as well as other Augustan poetry).[21] Through this intertext to Vergil's programmatic proem, Seneca can make his Tiresias into a rival poet figure, who must search for his own manner of revealing the truth, which happens to be partly through the utilization of the works of dead poets. From Seneca's belated position, the *Georgics* proem with its epic overtones of desiring to build a temple to Octavian (G. 3.13–6), singing "the fiery battles of Caesar" (*ardentis…pugnas / Caesaris*, G. 3.46–7), and preserving his name for future generations would

---

[17] Tiresias may have figured out the *extispicium*, because his words (*his invidebis quibus opem quaeris malis*, 387) seem to imply his knowledge that there is something rotten in Thebes.

[18] Palmieri (1989) stresses Seneca's differences from the Sophoclean account, in particular the importance of Laius' pronouncement from the Underworld. Cf. Thomas (1988b) ad loc. and Hinds (1998) 52–56 for the important metapoetic terms and intertexts of the Vergilian proem. Oedipus becomes victorious (*victor*, 974) after he blinds himself.

[19] Gale (2000) 11.

[20] Discussed below pp. 215–31.

[21] Schiesaro (2003) 226–8. His virtuoso reading of the scene does note the shocking nature of poetry to explore the depths of the psyche: "Poetry is to be the medium which enables Underworld and upper world to communicate, and in so doing transgresses the semiotic and ethical boundary which should guarantee the separation of those worlds and protect the living from pollution" (227).

have called to mind the *Aeneid*.[22] In a sense, Seneca's own reading of the *Georgics* proem can be seen in the way the way in which he looks forward to the *Aeneid*'s epic *katabasis* with his own similar scene. When Creon relates Tiresias' necromancy in an epic messenger speech, he even recalls this language in claiming that the earth groaned either because Acheron was outraged at the invasion (***temptari***, 577) or because of the new path made for the dead (*daret functis **viam***, 579). Therefore, when searching for a "new way" Seneca marks his debt to Vergil by paralleling language found in the *Georgics*' metapoetic proem, but also includes a scene in his play which corresponds to the *Aeneid*'s descent into the Underworld.[23] These two scenes of *extispicium* and *katabasis* are the most shocking additions for readers accustomed to Sophocles' *Oedipus Tyrannus*, and Seneca points to their novelty by looking back to Vergil's proem of *Georgics* 3. Seneca's Oedipus, however, discovers a far different lesson from his father than that of Vergil's Aeneas, as the ghost of Laius threatens him in language recalling Tiresias' statement "Let him crawl, uncertain of the way, trying the sad path before him with an old man's staff" (*reptet incertus **viae**, / baculo senili triste prae-**tempt**ans iter*, 656–7). Seneca foreshadows his Underworld scene by recalling the larger context of the prologue to the *Georgics*, and this scene becomes the conduit through which Oedipus' punishment is pronounced. He will not find a path to "lift himself from the ground" but rather will be damned to limp his way, blind, on the novel path that Seneca has granted him.

Ars Tragica

Although it may come as a surprise that Seneca aligns himself to Vergil's poetic principles, it should come as no surprise that Seneca would look back to Horace's *Ars Poetica* in developing his understanding of poetics.[24] After all, this is *the* Latin treatise on dramatic poetry, written by one of the most famous poets of the Augustan period. Quintilian, writing in the generation after Seneca, certainly found Horace's *Ars* worthy of respect, and foregrounds it in the preface of his *Institutio Oratoria*.[25] That being said, one finds that the *Ars Poetica* is not

---

[22] Thomas (1988b) 36–7.

[23] Note that both Oedipus (*quaeratur **via** / qua nec sepultis mixtus et vivis tamen / exemptus erres*, 949–51) and Jocasta (*mortis **via** / quaeratur*, 1031–2) utilize similar language when thinking about their method of self-punishment.

[24] See my Introduction for more on the way Horace's *Ars Poetica* influences Senecan poetics.

[25] Laird (2007) n1 mentions that Quintilian "quotes this single poem on eight occasions—more frequently than any other single poem of Horace, and almost as many times as he quotes from all four books of the *Odes*." Cf. Brink (1963) and his commentary (1971) as well as Rudd's (1990) for more about the *Ars* as a whole.

mentioned often in recent discussions of Senecan tragedy, in part because it is a difficult work in its own right.[26] It has features of both a letter and a *sermo*, is discursive and prone to apparent digressions, and, being poetry about poetics, also occasionally embodies the poetic principles it expounds.[27] In fact, this would be *the* Horatian poem in which the echo of Horatian language by a later author would imply a metapoetic dimension. Approximately one third of the *Ars Poetica* is concerned with drama specifically,[28] but the work also provides a general panorama of poetic principles: the necessary unity of a poem as well as the appropriate meter and style for the subject matter, the particulars of tragedy and comedy (characterization, number of actors, etc.) and even satyr plays,[29] the qualities of the poet himself, and, finally, his quest for wisdom (the fount of good writing). How did Seneca read this work? An investigation of the intertextual dialogue between Horace's *Ars Poetica* and Seneca's tragedies reveals that Seneca manipulates the tenets of Horace's text to indicate the ways in which his tragedies transcend the advice given there.[30] It will be shown that Seneca often has the larger Horatian context in mind, and the lines he echoes often come from particular moments of the *Ars* in which Horace has tragedy in mind. If Horace's work gives a glimpse of the poetics he endorses and practices in the *Ars* itself, so Seneca's tragedies are representative of his own concept of dramatic poetry and offer commentary on Horace's precepts.

One example of the intertextual dialogue established by Seneca is found in his *Medea*. In the final choral ode, the chorus describes Medea's manic behavior (857–62):

>   quis credat exulem?
>   Flagrant genae rubentes,
>   pallor fugat ruborem.
>   nullum vagante forma
>   **servat** diu **colorem**.
>   huc fert pedes et illuc.

---

[26] Cf. Schiesaro (2003) 65, 120, 132; Littlewood (2004) 246n138; Staley (2010) 38, 102, 152n11.

[27] As Russell (2006) 328 states, "It is difficult to write a sentence about the *Ars*, especially one which claims to paraphrase it, without acute diffidence. Problems posed, solved or dissolved by four centuries of scholarship have resulted in a neurotic confusion unexcelled even in classical studies."

[28] Cf. Brink (1963) 220–24 on the special place of drama in the *Ars*: "Once the content of verse comes to the fore, Horace's true concern is the poetic forms in which a large subject has to be organized, drama and to a lesser degree epic." *Ars* 153–294 concentrates on drama in particular, but dramatic poetry is referenced throughout the poem.

[29] Cf. Wiseman (1988) for more on the existence of the satyr play in Rome and Horace's attempts to pull it back into classical parameters from its more untamed iterations.

[30] Additional echoes of the *Ars* include *Med.* 27 (*verba...sero*) and *Ars* 46 (*in verbis...serendis*) as well as *Tr.* 441 (*somnus obrepsit*) and *Ars* 360 (*obrepere somnun*).

> Who would believe Medea to be an exile?
> Her ruddy cheeks burn,
> A pallor puts the blush to flight.
> She preserves no color for long,
> Her appearance keeps changing.
> She strides to and fro.

While the chorus wonders what will happen *next* if Medea's love and hatred join forces (866–9), the language recalls an apposite moment from Horace's *Ars Poetica*, when he is summarizing the standards of diction in poetic genres (86–8):

> descriptas **servare** vices operumque **colores**
> cur ego si nequeo ignoroque poeta salutor?
> cur nescire pudens prave quam discere malo?
>
> Why am I greeted as a poet, if I don't know how (or am unwilling)
> To adhere to the established varieties and tones of poetic genres?
> Why do I, in false shame, prefer to be ignorant than to learn?

Horace muses on his position as a poet who will know the proper literary styles and observe them (*servare*) if he is worth his salt. Goldberg notes that the word *color* also recalls the world of Roman declamation: "Those schooled in rhetoric, which most assuredly means Seneca and his audience, would also hear in *color* its technical sense, that is, the kind of plea a speaker makes, the line of argument, the 'complexion' he puts on the case at hand."[31] Brink notes that for Horace's audience "these are not the *colores* known from the Elder Seneca," but Seneca recasts the term to give it the rhetorical implications as well.[32] If Seneca is looking back to Horace at this moment, then his language acquires metapoetic potential: Is his Medea following the tenets set out for tragedy at this moment, and what "complexion" will Medea assume? It turns out that the larger context of the Horatian passage aids our interpretation, because it is at this moment that Horace first turns to drama and especially to tragedy to elucidate the different styles of diction (and this is the initial moment that the reader may intimate the importance of drama for Horace's *Ars*).[33] The position of this intertext in the *Medea* assumes additional significance, because this is the moment in which Medea takes on a more tragic *color* herself. She has just sent the poisoned

---

[31] Cf. Goldberg (1997) 172. For more on this scene and the influence of Seneca the Elder, cf. Trinacty (2009) 269–71.

[32] Brink (1971) ad loc. "The 'colouring' here is the 'tone' or 'style' appropriate to different genres of poetry."

[33] For Brink (1971) ad loc. *Ars* 89–118 focuses on "styles of diction exemplified by drama."

gift to Creusa and the smell of smoke is in the air. If one is listening for it, the following line of Seneca's chorus, "She strides to and fro" (*huc fert pedes et illuc*, 862), continues to insist upon Medea's transformation into the tragic Medea the audience expects, because this line recalls one of the fragments of Ovid's *Medea* (and apparently a famous one), "Alas, I am carried to and fro, inspired by the god" (***feror huc illuc****, vae, plena deo* (fr. 2 Ribbeck).[34] Seneca signposts that he is interested in "adhering to the established varieties and tones of poetic genres" by first recalling the Horatian line from the *Ars* and then further supporting it by an intertext with the most famous previous Latin tragedy on the Medea theme. His rhetorical poetics, however, causes Medea's *color* to have declamatory overtones and stresses her ability to create a persona all her own.

These intertextual connections make Seneca's *Medea* the culmination of a way of thinking about tragedy from Horace through Ovid, but the language also operates intratextually to point to the difference between the Medea at the opening of the play and her assumption of the role of a tragic avenger at the close. This is especially seen in the repetition of forms of *servo -are* in the play. When Medea speaks to Creon earlier, she stresses that she was the savior of the Argonauts (225–8):

> Solum hoc Colchico regno extuli,
> decus illud ingens Graeciae et florem inclitum,
> praesidia Achivae gentis et prolem deum
> **servasse** memet.

> From the realm of Colchis, I brought only this:
> That mighty honor and famous flower of Greece,
> The defense of the Achaeans and the race of the gods,
> I saved them!

Another line, possibly spurious, continues this identification, as Medea states, "It doesn't trouble me to have saved the honor of so many kings" (*non paenitet **servasse** tot regum decus*, 243).[35] However, her ability to save the Argonauts, and Jason, stemmed from her magical powers, and instances of the word *servare* come to assume a more sinister tone when she plots her revenge. Twice in her great incantation (and no more than thirty lines away from the initial reference discussed above) she mentions preserving ingredients for destruction

---

[34] See the discussion above pp. 119–20.
[35] Cf. Fitch (2004b) ad loc. for rejection Hine (2000) ad loc. for acceptance.

("I commanded them to preserve their silent evil" *tacitum iussi* **servare** *malum*, 832; "Preserve the seeds of fire hidden in my gifts" *donisque meis semina flammae / condita* **serva**, 834). There is a narrative arc from Medea as past savior to Medea as current figure of tragic *ira*, and the repetition of this verb displays Medea's transformation from acting out of love for Jason to acting in the throes of wrath against him. These are the only instances of the word in the play and seem to be leading up to the moment in which Medea assumes her "proper" role as tragic heroine, crystallized in the choral ode (and endorsed by the Horatian intertext).

Another example indicates how the tragic context influences Seneca's reception of Horace's *Ars Poetica*. Near the conclusion of his work, Horace writes of the "mad poet" (*vesanus poeta*, cf. 455), a caricature of a poet, full of *ingenium* but lacking in *ars*, whose foolish behavior may indicate a desire to commit suicide.[36] While Horace's tone is mocking in this section, it is the close of the work as a whole and offers a striking portrait of a man, head in the clouds, belching forth verses until he falls into a pit or well (*sublimis versus ructatur... decidit auceps / in puteum foveamve*, 457–9). Horace cautions the reader against saving him, because, he reasons, he may be like Empedocles and therefore wish to commit suicide (464–6).[37] Horace continues with the sarcastically solemn statement, "Let it be permitted for poets to die. / He who saves one unwilling to be saved might as well kill him" (*sit ius liceatque perire poetis. / invitum qui servat idem facit occidenti*, 466–7). This is precisely the case because he will continue to try to commit suicide even if saved (468–9), and he is so deranged (*certe furit*, 472) in his continual composing that Horace implies his condition is a curse caused by urinating on his father's ashes (471) or sacrilegiously (*incestus*) disturbing a sacred locale.

Brink comments on line 467, "The verse seems to be imitated in a serious context by Sen. *Phoen.* 100 *occidere est vetare cupientem mori*; but at *Ben.* II.14.4 the Stoic moralist argues against this permissiveness."[38] In the *Phoenissae* (an incomplete tragedy that concentrates on events after Seneca's *Oedipus* and the civil war between Eteocles and Polynices), Seneca's Oedipus urges Antigone to let him commit suicide (98–102):

>   qui cogit mori
> nolentem in aequo est quique properantem impedit;
> [occidere est vetare cupientem mori]

---

[36] For a similar reception of Horace's "mad poet" (and the *Ars* in general), see Hooley (1997) 26-63 on Persius 1.

[37] N.b. the remembrance of this moment in *Ep.* 79, mentioned in the introduction.

[38] Cf. Brink (1971) ad loc.

nec tamen in aequo est: alterum gravius reor:
malo imperari quam eripi mortem mihi.

> He who compels
> The unwilling man to die does the same thing
> As he who hinders the man hurrying to die;
> [To forbid one who desires to die is to kill him]
> But it is not the same thing: I think one is worse:
> I would prefer my death to be sentenced than to be taken away from me.

While Zwierlein brackets the line that recalls Horace's *Ars* as spurious, scholars such as Frank and Fitch argue for its inclusion.[39] I believe the line should remain—in part because of the reference to Horace's *Ars*, and because this line is later echoed by Antigone as she argues against her father's death wish, saying, "That man who has trampled on fate...who has need of no gods, why should that man desire or seek death?" (*qui fata proculcavit...cui deo nullo est opus, / quare ille **mortem cupiat** aut quare petat?*, 193–6).[40] In addition, the contexts are similar, even if the tone is not. Oedipus is the very embodiment of impiety (*nefandus **incestificus** exsecrabilis*, 223) and full of rage (*furor*, 353), although he is not the comic figure of Horace's *Ars*. Oedipus' madness at this moment in the *Phoenissae* causes him to wish for death and also reveals the "florid repetitiveness characteristic of declamation."[41] The force of the sentiment holds, however, and is a fitting sententia for Oedipus' plight. Seneca further elaborates the Horatian sententia with the following line, "I would prefer my death to be sentenced than to be taken away from me," showing how Seneca tries to one-up Horace in a game Seneca knows well (namely, the rhetorical use of sententiae).[42] One may wonder if we should find some humor in the application of the mad poet's predicament to that of Oedipus (or is Oedipus to be viewed as a poet in his own right?), but what is obvious is that Seneca recalls Horace at this moment in order to unveil his own more effective version of the idea. A similar impulse can be seen when Seneca's Cassandra recalls Horace's sentiments in the *Agamemnon*.

---

[39] Cf. Leo (1878) 209–10 for rejection and Fitch (2004b) 67 for discussion.

[40] The following lines also have forms of *cupio* and *mors* to emphasize its repetition. The phrase "desire to die" appears elsewhere in Senecan tragedy; cf. *Herc. F.* 116, *Ag.* 996, and *Med.* 170. Oedipus mentions the shared word *occidere* in two other places (35, 261).

[41] Frank (1995b) ad loc. Cf. Sen. *Contr.* 8.4.1: *non magis crudeles sunt qui volentes vivere occident quam qui volentes mori non sinunt*, and *Herc. F.* 513 for similar sentiments.

[42] Note how the Latin of the sententia (*malo imperari quam eripi mortem mihi*) is further elaborated later in Oedipus' speech: *ubique **mors** est. optume hoc cavit deus: / **eripere** vitam nemo non homini potest, / at nemo **mortem**; mille ad hanc aditus patent* (151–3).

Intertextuality and Metapoetics

The following sections discuss scenes from the *Agamemnon* and *Oedipus* in which Senecan characters act as metapoetic figures. In the first case (Cassandra), Seneca presents varying interpretations of the death of Agamemnon, and the intertexts of the accounts vary accordingly. These intertexts give us alternative thematic and poetic contexts in which to view Agamemnon's death and point to the contrasting registers Seneca's poetry can achieve. Although Cassandra's curse is to be misunderstood by the characters around her, she emphatically provides a Trojan interpretation of Agamemnon's death that Seneca elaborates with his characteristic erudition in order to stress the theme of repetition in the play. The second example offers another metapoetic account as Creon describes to Oedipus the necromancy that Tiresias performed to raise Laius from the dead. This necromancy unites passages from Vergil and Ovid (among other poets) that resonate within the dramatic context of the *Oedipus*. Seneca, however, complicates the position of the reader because Oedipus misunderstands the information given him by Creon. The distancing of such perspectives (Oedipus'/our own) helps to distinguish Oedipus' view of the situation as separate from that of the external reader, and this separation adds to Oedipus' feelings of isolation as well as the dramatic irony of the play.

Cassandra as (Falsa?) Vates

The *Agamemnon* derives much of its power from its stark message of the inescapability of fate and revenge. From the initial scene of the ghost of Thyestes pronouncing doom upon the house to the final words of the play when Cassandra tells Clytemnestra, "A madness will come upon you too" (*veniet et vobis furor*, 1012), the characters in the play are caught in a network of talionic violence without much hope for change.[43] As Boyle states, "The human denizens of *Agamemnon*'s world are yet simply that through which history's cycle of crime and punishment take place."[44] This play is notable for the variety of viewpoints offered, and the lack of a centralized viewpoint allows Seneca to explore the positions of Greeks and Trojans, avengers and victims.[45] Cassandra's role in the play

---

[43] One does not get the sense that this play could be the start of a trilogy ending with the *Eumenides*, and Tarrant (1976) 10 points out that this play does not seem to be based on Aeschylus' *Agamemnon*, stating, "Nothing in Seneca's play requires direct knowledge of Aeschylus." For more on *furor* in the *Agamemnon*, cf. Paschalis (2010).

[44] Boyle (1983) 205.

[45] Fitch (2004a) 118–19 explains, "None of these ways of understanding appears authoritative, in the sense of excluding others. This situation corresponds to the fact that none of the dramatis personae is central or dominant in the play.... Authority is decentered both in the events of the play and in ways of understanding them."

has been interpreted in a variety of ways. Whether one views her as a sadistic spectator (Littlewood), a paradigm of the repetition of past *nefas* (Schiesaro), or a model of "death's freedom" (Boyle, Shelton), it is clear that her character fascinated Seneca.[46] The final two acts are united by her presence and her intricate speeches provide two separate, but overlapping, views of Agamemnon's death and the rationale for his assassination. Seneca ties these speeches into both the fabric of this play as well as the Augustan poetic tradition in order to explore varying ways to represent Agamemnon's death. When under the influence of Phoebus, Cassandra provides an imagistic and fevered view of Agamemnon's death. In this moment her narrative is much like a choral ode, incorporating intertexts from Horace as well as Vergil in detailing her near-hallucinatory view of the future. In the final act, however, her tone is more measured, and her description of the events in the palace stands in for a messenger speech with epic elements and a notable intertext to Horace's *Ars Poetica*.[47] Cassandra can be seen as a surrogate for the tragic poet, and her different renditions of this single event reveal Seneca's exploration of varying poetic registers and source material for his tragedies. Seneca utilizes Cassandra to highlight aspects of intertextuality, metatheater, and metapoetry through her unique position as both *vates* and quasi-messenger. In her final speech, Cassandra has become, if not the voice of truth, the closest approximation possible.

Cassandra appears at the beginning of the fourth act and engages in a dialogue with the chorus about her own sufferings and the torments of Troy, before she is possessed by Phoebus and gives her inspired speech. She claims that the chorus need not include her in their laments, because she will express her own suffering: "Remove your lamentation from my troubles, I will be equal to my own troubles" (*cladibus questus meis / removete: nostris ipsa sufficiam malis*, 662–3). The chorus responds with an anapestic song, noting that it is best to mourn with others (*lacrimas lacrimis miscere iuvat*, 664; *iuvat in medium deflere suos*, 667). This repetition of *iuvat* is important to the play as a whole, as characters from Eurybates (434–5) to Cassandra (750–1, 1011) restate this word in order to mark strongly personal views of Troy's fall. The chorus provides a catalogue of birds lamenting alone (who once, pre-metamorphosis, were women) and forge a strong connection with contemporary Rome by mentioning followers of the Magna Mater;[48] their language focuses on the singing ability of these figures

---

[46] Cf. Littlewood (2004) 215–26; Schiesaro (2003) 202–8; Boyle (1983) 206–9; Shelton (1983) 179.

[47] A transition noted by Littlewood (2004).

[48] Cf. Tarrant (1976) ad 686ff. for more on Cybele and the *Galli*. Seneca connects the Trojan captives with this cult because it originated in the east before being introduced to Rome in the late third century BCE, cf. Beard et al. (1998) 96–8, passim.

to suggest Cassandra's aptitude for song and lament.[49] The chorus concludes, recalling its opening words, with the statement (691–2)

> non est lacrimis, Cassandra, **modus**,
> quia quae patimur vicere **modum**.

> There is no limit, Cassandra, to our lamentation
> For Because the things we endure have surpassed limit.

While Cassandra notes that the Trojan sufferings will be the subject of song for time eternal—"Restrain the tears which every age will request" (*Cohibete lacrimas omne quas tempus petet*, 659)—she takes upon herself the task of singing about her own misery. The repetition of *modus/modum* at the end of paired lines not only shows the polyptoton that Seneca adores[50] but also hints at the additional metrical variety of this section of the play with two polymetric choruses bookending Cassandra's intriguing song. In fact, *modus* can mean "meter" in Latin, and Seneca here is emphasizing the fact that no single meter suffices for tragedy.[51] In her mantic state, Cassandra will include a lyric song, and her switch from *senarii* to iambic dimeters in midspeech is an unusual feature of her discourse.[52] Through this focus on features of song/poetry, Seneca indicates that he is interested in exploring various poetic registers in this section of his play (replete with pertinent intertexts).

In her first speech, Cassandra exhibits the madness and raving that is common to the literary tradition (eyes rolling, violent trembling, hair standing on end, etc.).[53] Cassandra, however, seems indignant that she would still suffer such bouts of mantic prophecy, and asks the god why he still troubles her after Troy's fall (720–5):

> Quid me furoris incitam stimulis **novi**,
> quid **mentis** inopem, sacra Parnasi iuga,
> **rapitis**? recede, Phoebe, iam non sum tua;
> extingue flammas pectori infixas meo.

---

[49] Cf. *mobile carmen* (670), *cantat* (671), *in varios modulate sonos* (672), *lugere* (676), *leviter plangente sonent* (682).

[50] Cf. Canter (1925) 160–1.

[51] *OLD* s.v. *modus* 7. Cf. Ov. *Am.* 1.1.2 *materia conveniente modis*.

[52] Cf. Tarrant (1976) ad loc.: "This is the only certain example in the authentic play of a change from trimeters to a lyric meter within a speech, but *Pha.* 1199–200 should probably be assigned to Theseus (with E), thus producing a parallel."

[53] In her frenzy, she resembles the Sibyl of Cumae, and intertextual parallels help hammer home this identification; cf. Tarrant (1976) ad 710ff.

cui nunc vagor vesana? cui **bacchor** furens?
iam Troia cecidit—falsa quid vates **ago**?

Holy heights of Parnassus, why do you snatch me
Roused by pricks of new madness, and out of my mind?
Phoebus, withdraw, I am no longer yours;
Douse the flames fastened to my heart.
For whom do I now wander in my madness?
For whom do I rage as a Bacchante? Troy now has fallen—
What business have I as a failed prophet?[54]

Now that she has been given to Agamemnon as his slave, Cassandra notes that she is no longer Phoebus' (*iam non sum tua*), and therefore he should not be able to control her behavior any longer. If her previous prophecies centered on the coming destruction of Troy, now that Troy has fallen (*iam Troia cecidit*), she wonders what else she can rant about. But would Cassandra always consider herself a *falsa...vates* because she is continually misunderstood and disbelieved by the Trojans, or if there is something more to her words? There certainly is irony here, because she has been proved to be a true prophet (Troy did fall), but she takes up the identification of a "false prophet," one that is suitable to this dramatic situation. After all, she is "playing the part" (*ago*), and this part additionally draws upon two intertextual sources to indicate her suitability not only as a poet figure but also as a dramatis persona in her own right.[55]

The intertextual references and parallel subject matter (namely, the production of poetry through divine inspiration) suggest that Seneca wishes us to think of Horace's *Carm.* 3.25 — an ode to Bacchus that touches upon the poetic power of Horace to praise Augustus. Commager remarks on Horace's perspective, "Although Horace claims that it is his new attempt to immortalize Caesar that inflames him, he seems captivated less by Caesar's 'immortal glory' than by his own power to create it."[56] Whereas Horace aims to sing the glory of Caesar, Cassandra is singing of the death of a king, Agamemnon, but it is really the power of poetry to "evoke the sensations of creation" that both songs target.[57]

---

[54] Cf. Fitch (2004b) 168–9 for the text and translation of *falsa quid vates ago*.

[55] OLD s.v. *ago* 26 for the translation "To play the part of, act as, behave as."

[56] Cf. Commager (1962) 347. Connor (1971) and Batinski (1991) 372–4 also focus on the poetics of this ode.

[57] Commager (1962) 347. Nisbet and Rudd (2004) 299 remark on the disconnect between topic and expression in *Carm.* 3.25: "Here, although the celebration of Augustus is the avowed purpose of the ode, that is not its most striking feature; indeed a Maenad's ecstasy makes an odd analogy for political commitment, however fervid. What one takes away, rather, is some sense of the mysterious phenomenon of poetic possession."

This section is strongly marked as lyric through the Horatian echo, although it is in the standard meter for spoken dialogue (iambic senarii). Horace's position as *vates* in Rome is contrasted to Cassandra's identification of herself as a *falsa vates*, and Seneca will supplement this view with additional intertextual references to Vergil in order to point out the importance of this tragic vision.[58]

Horace begins *Carm.* 3.25 in a manic state not unlike Cassandra's own (1–8):

> Quo me, **Bacche, rapis** tui
> plenum? quae nemora aut quos **agor** in specus
> velox **mente nova**? quibus
> antris egregii Caesaris audiar
> aeternum meditans decus
> stellis inserere et consilio Iovis?
> dicam insigne recens adhuc
> indictum ore alio.

> Where are you snatching me, Bacchus?
> I am full of you. Into what groves or caves am I being driven
> Swiftly with a new mind?
> In what caverns will I be heard practicing to place
> My immortal praise of famous Caesar
> In the stars and in the council of Jupiter?
> I will sing of a noble deed, recent,
> Until now unspoken by another's lips.

Cassandra's words echo the first three lines of Horace's lyric with the repetition of forms of *rapio, ago, novus, mens*; the incessant questioning; and terms referring to Bacchus (his name in Horace and *bacchor* in Seneca). For Horace, *Carm.* 3.25 allows him to explore the parallels between Bacchic possession and poetic inspiration with a Maenad standing in for Horace himself.[59] Seneca takes up this identification, with Cassandra now acting like a poetess herself, and certainly like a Maenad.[60] Horace rejoices in being able to sing a novel and lofty song "not trifling or humble, not even mortal" (*nil parvum aut humili modo, / nil mortale,*

---

[58] For more on Horace as *vates*, cf. Nisbet and Hubbard (1970) ad 1.1.35.

[59] For more on the identification of Horace with the Maenad and what this portends for the subject of this poem, cf. Nisbet and Rudd (2004) 296–9.

[60] The chorus calls attention to this in the words directly preceding this speech (*clause male / custodit **ore maenas** impatiens dei*, 718–9).

C. 3.25.17–8),⁶¹ and Cassandra's words provide a strong example of just such a song. While it is Phoebus who ostensibly causes Cassandra's madness, the strong Bacchic overtones bring to mind the Horatian references in this ode, in addition to the traditional identification of Bacchus as both the god of madness and, more importantly, the god of the theater.⁶² Because of this aspect of his divinity, the following intertext assumes further significance since Seneca draws upon an intertextual connection within the *Aeneid* that references the tragedy most associated with Bacchus, namely, Euripides' *Bacchae*.

As Cassandra lapses into her maddened state, she asks (*Ag.* 726–7):

> Ubi sum? fugit lux alma et **obscurat** genas
> **nox** alta et aether abditus tenebris latet.

> Where am I? The nourishing light has fled and deep night
> Darkens my eyes; the heavens hide, covered in shadows.

Intertextual parallels of this passage link Cassandra's madness with that of Dido, and prominent features of their characterization may also be paralleled through such an identification (both are driven mad, prophecy revenge, and welcome death).⁶³ In the fourth book of the *Aeneid*, Dido herself tells how, "when dark night holds the lands" (***nox** cum terras **obscura** teneret*, 4.461), nightmares of Aeneas "drive her mad" (*agit…furentem*, 4.465), and Seneca echoes this language in the passages cited above (*cui bacchor **furens**?…falsa quid vates **ago**?*, *Ag.* 724–5). The following lines further strengthen the metaliterary aspects of this identification as Seneca hints at the importance of such madness in the theatrical paradigm of this play.

Cassandra continues to describe her vision in language that calls to mind both the *Aeneid* and the *Bacchae* as she suffers from double vision (two suns! two Argoses!), which points to the "madness" of seeing Argos as new Troy as well as indicating the generic propriety of such a moment. She claims (728–30):

---

⁶¹ Batinski (1991) notes the Callimachean overtones in Horace's poem, with Bacchus' influence mirroring that of Apollo in Callimachus: "This selection of an unexplored theme echoes Apollo's injunction to Callimachus that he avoid the well-trodden path. Bacchus, who had swept Horace off to these isolated places, has encroached on Apollo's domain.… The poet is entering uncharted territory" (373).

⁶² Nisbet and Rudd (2004) 297 point out, "Bacchus was the patron of dithyramb and drama, and his status as a poetic god was enhanced in the Hellenistic and Roman periods."

⁶³ I owe this observation to Amanda Wilcox. Cassandra is able to map onto a variety of characters through intertextual connections with them. Cf. Pobjoy (1998) for Vergil's tragic imagery in the Dido story and Panoussi (2009) 133–4 for the maenadism of Dido (*bacchatur*, 4.301) and discussion of the theatrical nature of this section of the *Aeneid*.

> Sed ecce **gemino** sole praefulget dies
> **geminum**que **duplices** Argos atollit domus.
> Idaea cerno nemora?

> But look, daylight shines from doubled suns,
> Doubled Argos raises up twin homes.
> Do I look upon the groves of Ida?

In the *Aeneid*, Vergil recalls the *Bacchae* and Pentheus' description of two suns in his portrayal of Dido's madness (4.469–70):

> Eumenidum veluti demens videt agmina Pentheus
> et solem **geminum** et **duplices** se ostendere Thebas...

> Just as maddened Pentheus saw the legions of Furies
> And a twinned sun and Thebes doubled...

Vergil's simile breaks the dramatic time of the epic and recalls a moment from the theatrical tradition of Greece and Rome. This moment of Vergil's epic is, in the words of Austin, "the only direct allusion in Virgil to stage-representations... but there is nothing stagy about the lines, and any Roman reader familiar with Greek tragedy would find them a terrifyingly real picture of Dido's condition."[64] Seneca has seized upon this line because of its strong associations with both madness and the theater, he but also wishes his reader/audience to remember the full context of the Vergilian quote, which continues as follows (4.471–3):

> aut Agamemnonius scaenis agitatus Orestes,
> armatam facibus matrem et serpentibus atris
> cum fugit ultricesque sedent in limine Dirae.

> Or Orestes, Agamemnon's son, hounded over the stage,
> When he fled the spirit of his mother, armed with torches
> And black serpents, and the avenging Dirae sitting on his doorstep.

Seneca's own *Agamemnon* provides the backstory for these lines, and Seneca recalls this particular passage because of the larger Vergilian context. This description of the Furies' persecution of Orestes for the death of Clytemnestra is particularly appropriate for Cassandra because she is not only calling attention

---

[64] Cf. Austin (1955) ad loc.

to the resemblance of events in Argos with events in Troy but also pointing to the future destruction of Clytemnestra.[65] The cycle of revenge will not end with the death of Agamemnon that Cassandra is predicting, but will continue (and the later scene showing Orestes' rescue indicates Seneca's own interest in indicating the future consequences).[66] In the lyric sequence of Cassandra's speech, she sees the Furies and provides a grim picture of these goddesses, describing them in language common to the fourth and seventh books of the *Aeneid*.[67] In addition, a reader who connects Cassandra's double vision with Dido's will understand the strong theatrical associations of Dido at that moment, and will find in its appropriation a clever indication of Seneca's desire to reclaim this definitive theatrical moment of the *Aeneid* for his own tragedy. Seneca recognizes the fusion of *furor* and theatricality that Dido embodies in the *Aeneid* and exploits her portrayal for his Cassandra (perhaps Dido's own power of prophecy (*Aen.* 4.612–29) as well?). If Dido's madness is the textual antecedent of Cassandra's, Seneca indicates that it is more at home in the tragic genre, where the larger context of the Vergilian simile befits the dramatic events being staged.

As Cassandra's speech continues, she offers a series of equivalencies that indicate the similarities between what happened at Troy and what is happening at Argos. Cassandra questions whether she is looking upon the groves of Mount Ida (730), and notes that a *furtivum genus* (732) must be feared, whether it is Paris or Aegisthus.[68] This leads to the further vision that the shades of her ancestors are calling her, which contains sustained echoes of the *Aeneid*. In this section of her speech (741–58), Cassandra addresses various members of her family, and the accounts of figures such as Hector and Deiphobus have clear intertextual nods to the *Aeneid*.[69] Her vision of the Underworld parallels the beginning of the play when the ghost of Thyestes comments on the future revenge, but now with an added Trojan emphasis.[70] Whereas Thyestes believes Agamemnon's murder

---

[65] Panoussi (2009) 136 comments on the ramifications of Dido's maenadism, "Dido herself is earlier portrayed as a Fury (4.384–7; Hardie 1993: 41). The fury of maenadism and the *furor* inflicted by Furies and other such creatures are thus closely linked."

[66] As does the final line of the play: CLYTEMNESTRA: Mad woman, you will die. CASSANDRA: A fury will come upon you as well (CL. *Furiosa, morere.* CA. *Veniet et vobis furor*, 1012).

[67] Cf. *Ag.* 759–64 and Tarrant (1976) ad loc.

[68] Could these *Idaea nemora* remind the reader of the *nemora* where the poet Horace is driven (*C*. 3.23.2)?

[69] For Hector cf. *Aen.* 2.272–6; for Deiphobus cf. *Aen.* 6.494–534. Littlewood (2004) 218–9 finds that "Seneca reverses the Vergilian narrative in having Cassandra respond to the apparition of Deiphobus with a prayer that Hell open to allow the Trojans to look on the destruction of Mycenae and with the apparition of figures like Tisiphone."

[70] Thyestes considers Aegisthus' sole purpose in life to be the killing of Agamemnon ("The reason for your birth, Aegisthus, is here," *causa natalis tui, / Aegisthe, venit*, 48–9) and draws upon his own crimes and punishment as the backdrop to the play's action ("I, Thyestes, shall surpass all by my crimes. Shall I be surpassed by my brother?" *vincam Thyestes sceleribus cunctos meis. / a fratre vincar?*, 25–6).

befits the house of Tantalus, for Cassandra it is retribution for the fall of Troy and the horrors endured by the Trojans. For this reason, she repeats the injunction *te sequor* ("I follow you," *Ag.* 742, 747) before mentioning members of her family (Priam, Hector, Troilus, and Deiphobus), but one must also understand that Seneca is *following* Vergil's *Aeneid*.[71] Seneca's adaptations of each of these Vergilian accounts are particularly noteworthy (exhibiting the condensation or elaboration typical of Senecan intertextuality) and evocative of their individual context in the *Aeneid*. For instance, after stating "I follow you" (*te sequor*) Cassandra mentions Troilus, *nimium cito / **congresse Achilli** Troile* ("Troilus, you who met with quick Achilles too soon," *Ag.* 747–8). Here, Seneca abbreviates Vergil's stirring report of Troilus' downfall (*Aen.* 1.474–8):

> parte alia fugiens amissis Troilus armis,
> infelix puer atque impar **congressus Achilli**,
> fertur equis curruque haeret resupinus inani,
> lora tenens tamen; huic cervixque comaeque trahuntur
> per terram, et versa pulvis inscribitur hasta.

> In another part Troilus is in flight with weapons left behind,
> Unlucky boy and no match to meet with Achilles,
> He is carried off by his horses and, bent backward,
> Clings to the empty chariot, still holding the reins;
> His neck and hair are dragging in the dirt,
> The dust is inscribed by the point of his spear.

Seneca marks his own "following" of Vergil by incorporating a famous Trojan death from the *Aeneid* that also draws attention to itself as a *written* account. The writing motion of the spear in the dust is emblematic of the process of engraving (if we are meant to think of these scenes as a relief in the bronze doors) or even the composition of a work of poetry.[72] Each victim of Cassandra's report

---

[71] Peirano (2013) 85 positions *sequi* as part of the Roman vocabulary of *imitatio*. Cassandra knows full well that in "following" Hector, Priam, et al. she is moving towards her own death (cf. *Ag.* 752–4). Seneca uses language of "following" for his philosophical ideas: *Non ergo **sequor** priores? Facio, sed permitto mihi et invenire aliquid et mutare et relinquere* ("Do I then follow no predecessors? I do, but I permit myself to discover something new, to change, to forsake" (*Ep.* 80.1). For the literary ramifications for "following" Vergil, cf. Stat. *Theb.* 12.816–7: *nec tu divinam Aeneida tempta, / sed longe **sequere** et vestigia semper adora* ("Don't test the divine *Aeneid*, but rather follow far behind and always honor its footsteps").

[72] As Putnam (1998) 31 elucidates:

> Concomitant with this creative tension [between ekphrasis and epic narrativity] is the irony lodged in perusing verbal description about an act of writing located in painting. Useless "writing" is inscribed climactically in brilliant words about art, as if to underscore

represents an important moment of Vergil's epic, whether the dream of Hector in Book 2 or the discussion of the fall of Troy with Deiphobus in Book 6. As a condensed response to the Trojan victims of the *Aeneid*, Seneca's Cassandra positions herself as an Aeneas-like figure who will likewise visit the Underworld. Cassandra, however, ironically enjoys (*iuvat* is repeated at the beginning of lines 750 and 751) her tour among the dead, as she knows Agamemnon will soon join the Trojans in Hades. Seneca continuously mines Vergil's epic in this speech in order to give his own interpretation and his own *color* ("spin") to the remnants of the house of Priam. While Vergil followed the surviving members of the Trojan line by centering his epic on the figure of Aeneas, Seneca counters this optimism by focusing instead on Cassandra. In the Underworld, Aeneas will see the future greatness of Rome, while Cassandra and the dead Trojans will take delight in the destruction of Agamemnon. In a story where acts of revenge merely fuel subsequent retributive acts, this is the best one can hope for.

While Seneca connects this scene to Vergil's *Aeneid*, he also incorporates it within the tragic context of this play through the repetition of language and imagery found earlier in the *Agamemnon*. Cassandra's review of the figures of the Underworld recalls the speech of Thyestes' ghost from the prologue, but with a different motivation. There, the ghost remarks (10–2):

> Libet reverti. nonne vel tristes lacus
> incolere satius? nonne custodem Stygis
> trigemina nigris colla iactantem iubis?

> I want to return. Is it not better to inhabit
> The grim lakes, to live near the watchdog of Styx
> Tossing his threefold neck with its black mane?

While Thyestes' ghost wishes to return to the shades to avoid being a spectator to the destruction of Agamemnon, Cassandra relishes her ability to review the figures of the Underworld and call upon them (and the deceased Trojans) to observe the coming slaughter (750–2):

> iuvat per ipsos ingredi Stygios lacus,
> iuvat videre Tartari saevum canem
> avidique regna Ditis!

the inseparable union in ekphrasis between what is seen and the medium through which sight is imagined. Ekphrasis here fosters such a collusion, of writing in war and writing of war, of dust and permanence, of the "turns" on which linear writing depends that also both mimic the reversals, and therefore portend the ultimate moment of mortality, which fate brings even to the young.

> It is pleasing to approach the Stygian lakes;
> It is pleasing to see the savage hound of Tartarus
> And the kingdoms of greedy Dis!

In using similar language (descriptions of the Stygian lake and Cerberus), Seneca parallels the characters of Cassandra and Thyestes' ghost in order to point to the future vengeance; but for Cassandra the killing of Agamemnon is in recompense for the Greek actions at Troy, *not* familial bloodshed. Cassandra situates herself as a Thyestean figure, but now her call "The fates are turning themselves back" (*fata se **vertunt retro**,* 758) hints at the Trojan rationale for Agamemnon's death, in contrast with Thyestes' cry, "Nature has been turned back" (***versa** natura est **retro**,* 34), in describing his incestuous relationship with his daughter.[73] This turn backwards to the past and the deceased befits Cassandra, whose eyes roll back in her head during the onset of her madness (***versi retro** / torquentur oculi,* 714–5). Past actions return to haunt the present, like waves churning back against themselves, during the messenger's description of the storm (*vento resistit aestus et ventus **retro** / aestum revolvit,* 488–9). It would appear there can be no escape from the cycle of revenge, and the language of Cassandra's speech hinges upon past wrongs, and past writings, to point to the future vengeance to come.

It is after this injunction (*fata se vertunt retro,* 758) that Cassandra begins to sing in iambic dimeters, and this section of her speech continues her view of the Underworld and looks back to the very origins of the family lines whose paths are crossing in this play. The Furies are evoked here not only because they are spirits of vengeance but also because of their associations with both Cassandra (who is subject to *furor;* cf. 720, 724) and the description of Allecto in the *Aeneid.*[74] The idea of "the fates turning back" is brought into stark focus with Cassandra's vision of Tantalus and Dardanus (769–74):

> Et ecce, defessus senex
> ad ora ludentes aquas
> non captat oblitus sitim,
> maestus futuro funere.
> exultat et ponit gradus
> pater decoros Dardanus.

---

[73] Thyestes' cry is particularly Senecan and resounds with similar cries in the *Oedipus.* Cf. Rosenmeyer (1989) 140: "Strictly speaking, it makes no sense to distinguish between a natural order and an overturned order; there is, in Seneca's frightening world, no uninfected, unimpaired nature to be inverted. The formulation *versa natura est* is dictated by the need of language to describe change and process as starting from a standard position."

[74] Tarrant (1976) ad loc. notes the parallels with *Aen.* 7. Hardie (1993) 41–2 sees Allecto as a version of the furious Dido with whom Cassandra has already been identified.

> And behold! The tired old man,
> Forgetful of his thirst,
> Does not try to capture the water
> Playing about his mouth,
> Saddened by the future funeral.
> But father Dardanus leaps and dances,
> Setting down graceful steps.

Tantalus is described in language that is reminiscent of the play's prologue (*senex*, 22; the description of the water lapping before his lips, 19–20), but now he mourns for the coming death of his great-grandson Agamemnon. Dardanus (the founder of Troy and Cassandra's own great-great-grandfather) celebrates the coming destruction of Agamemnon as a proper recompense for the fall of Troy.[75] In general, this opening speech of Cassandra continuously recalls the mythological past of Troy as a way to explain Agamemnon's imminent murder.[76] Seneca positions Cassandra as a *falsa vates*, but a *vates* nonetheless, who can sing the truth, even if it is not understood, and who can channel the power of madness into song much like the Horatian ode.[77] By placing material from the *Aeneid* in his tragedy and intertextually "signposting" its transfer (e.g., with Cassandra's use of the "two suns" line from the *Aeneid*), Seneca grants Cassandra special importance to the aftermath of the Trojan War, and makes her an interpreter of the tradition of the *Aeneid*. Her own "reading" of the fall of Troy may be indicative of Seneca's understanding of the *Aeneid*, and we can see how he manipulates the material to suit his own tragic project. Seneca's Cassandra now can take comfort from the deaths and mutilations of her family, knowing that Agamemnon's retribution is nigh and that Clytemnestra is sharpening her axe.

The second speech of Cassandra likewise comments on itself through intertextual echoes, but whereas the first speech looks back again and again to the *Aeneid*, this narrative finds inspiration in other sources, especially Horace's *Ars*

---

[75] Tarrant (1976) ad loc. mentions that "Seneca's picture of Tantalus and Dardanus reacting to the fortunes of their respective descendants may owe something to the words of Ovid's Althaea…; Seneca's use of the idea, however, is unmistakably his own, particularly the grotesque detail of Dardanus dancing a jig of triumph."

[76] This may also make the reader think back to Cassandra's own appearances in the *Aeneid* and recognize that her position as *vates* is utilized by Anchises (*Aen.* 3.183–7) and Juno (*Aen.* 10.68) to verify Aeneas' decision to sail to Italy. Juno also uses Cassandra's reputation as a seer in order to cause the burning of the boats in Sicily (*Aen.* 5.636). Seneca's strong interest in Cassandra as *vates* indicates the importance he saw in her character in that epic, although she does not appear very frequently.

[77] Cassandra's position as *vates* may also recall the "many previous warnings of seers" (*multa… **vatum** praedicta priorum*, *Aen.* 4.464), which horrified Dido preceding her comparison to Pentheus and Orestes.

Poetica. Cassandra enters after a choral ode on the exploits of Hercules and states (867–70, 872–5):

> **res agitur** intus magna, par annis decem.
> eheu quid hoc est? **anime**, consurge et cape
> pretium furoris: *vicimus victi Phryges.*
> bene est, *resurgis Troia*....
> Tam clara numquam providae mentis furor
> ostendit **oculis**: video et intersum et fruor;
> imago visus dubia non fallit meos:
> **spectemus**!

> A great deed is being done inside, worthy of those ten years.
> Alas! What is this? Rise up, my soul,
> And seize the reward of your madness!
> We, the defeated Trojans, have won.
> Good, you rise again, Troy....
> The frenzy of my prophetic mind has never shown
> Such clear thing to my eyes. I see it, I am there, I enjoy it;
> The sure image does not deceive my eyes.
> Let us watch!

Cassandra opens by intimating her suspicion that something important is occurring inside the palace and utilizes language found in Horace's *Ars Poetica*, when Horace proscribes the suitable scenarios for a messenger speech (*Ars* 179–182):

> aut **agitur res** in scaenis aut acta refertur.
> segnius irritant **animos** demissa per aurem,
> quam quae sunt **oculis** subiecta fidelibus et quae
> ipse sibi tradit **spectator**.

> Deeds either happen onstage or are reported there.
> Things only heard stimulate the souls more slowly,
> Than those which are perceived by the sharp eyes and
> Those which the spectator grasps for himself.

The repetition of *res agitur* in both passages as well as Cassandra's belief that this vision she has received is crystal clear (note the repetition of *oculis*; Cassandra calls upon her *anime*; and Horace refers to *animos, spectemus/spectator*) and shows Seneca's adaptation of the language of Horace's treatise. For

Horace seeing is believing, and he appears to favor showing to merely telling.[78] Seneca, however, positions his Cassandra as a messenger figure, who is reporting the sort of information that is appropriate for these speeches. Although she may invite those around her to "watch" what is happening inside, her narrative of the events is a more vivid way of representing the action. Note how in her earlier speech she also bid the ghosts of the Trojan dead to "watch" (*spectate*, 757).

Seneca provides two narratives with differing literary antecedents to establish Cassandra as a tragic poet who has to write in differing generic registers throughout the play. As in the Vergilian intertext of Dido's double vision, the larger context of the Horatian passage is important. The *Ars* offers the most comprehensive view of dramatic conventions in Horace's age, and Seneca wishes to update the poetics described there by showing them in action on the tragic stage. Horace will go on to speak about the propriety of events to be staged instead of reported such as Medea's murder of her children or the feast of Thyestes (*Ars* 185–6), both scenes that Seneca stages in his *Medea* and *Thyestes*. Seneca wants to indicate that his version can be as evocative as a visual representation, and that he attempts to surpass Horace's rather dry injunctions through stressing that Cassandra's vision is clear and transports her (and us) to the very dinner table. Seneca points to the pleasure that such *furor* can cause by pairing *furor* and *fruor* at the conclusion of subsequent lines—the anagram surely indicates Cassandra's focalization of the events and transforms her *furor* into something pleasant.[79] If her *furor* earlier in the play aligned her with Horace (720, 724) and the production of lyric poetry, now she can enjoy the reward of that madness (*pretium furoris*, 868) in a messenger speech.[80] Seneca employs Horace's own language against him as he points out the efficacy of poetic language for expressing Cassandra's own experience of Agamemnon's murder. The passage as a whole is evocative of the power of language to show a more precise "picture" than can be achieved merely through the eyes, as Cassandra creates a speech emblematic of Senecan poetics in its precise portrayal of Agamemnon's murder and in its *aemulatio* of the Augustan poets.

---

[78] Cf. Brink (1971) ad loc. "Action on the stage is the most vivid presentation and H. describes it by using the terminology that rhetoricians had developed for their *evidentia*. Dramatic presentations *oculis subiecta* are therefore more vivid than *demissa per aurem*."

[79] Staley (2010) 62. Ahl (2000) 166–70 on Senecan wordplay concludes: "Seneca, like Chaucer, uses wordplay as an integral part of his poetic composition. It is an interweaving of meaning and form, not simply gratuitous decoration which the chastening eye of scholars or translators should relegate to a cautious footnote or expunge in the interests of 'taste'" (169–70).

[80] Cassandra's speech features an epic simile (*ut…hispidus…aper*, 892) and the very detail of the description (note especially the gruesome death stroke of the axe, 901–3) mimics what is found in traditional messenger speeches.

Furthermore, in this passage, Seneca "verifies" the words of Cassandra through an additional intertextual echo to the first book of Ovid's *Fasti*.[81] When writing about the Carmentalia (and Ovid makes sure to stress the etymology with *carmen*, 467), he gives Evander's wife, Carmentis, an inspired speech as she sees the future site of Rome, including the lines (523–4)

> **victa** tamen **vinces** *eversa*que, **Troia, resurges**;
> obruit hostiles ista ruina domos.

> Although defeated and destroyed, you will overcome, Troy, and rise anew;
> Your very ruin will wreck the homes of your enemies.

Beyond merely being the source of Seneca's *vicimus victi Phryges... resurgis Troia*, the larger context once again highlights the very message of Cassandra's speech. Cassandra sees the death of Agamemnon as being tantamount to a Trojan victory, while the intertext also points to an alternative "victory" for Troy in the future founding of Rome. While Cassandra may be focusing on the present revenge, the future is also embedded in her words intertextually, and this fits her role as a prophetess. Senecan intertextuality often will provide a variety of views on an event, in the same way that different characters may interpret an action in their own idiosyncratic manner. So Cassandra continually posits the death of Agamemnon as recompense for the horrific Greek actions at Troy, while also pointing out the similarities between Agamemnon and Priam.[82] In this quasi-messenger speech, Cassandra finally recognizes that "the fates have come" (*venere fata*, 885), which responds to her earlier pronouncement that "the fates are turning themselves back" (*fata se vertunt retro*, 758).[83] When Electra appears after Cassandra's speech, she comments that "the house is completely overturned" (*eversa domus est funditus*, 912), picking up on this motif, which is likewise rooted in the Ovidian intertext (*eversa*, 1.523).[84] Cassandra herself claims, at the play's conclusion, that she will willingly die in order to act as a messenger to her Trojans (*nuntium Phrygibus meis*, 1005). At this point, one understands that the substance of this speech is exactly what she will report. In order to relate

---

[81] For more on this scene in general, cf. Green (2004) ad loc.

[82] Cf. the stichomythia at 791–9 and the description of Agamemnon's feast (875–80). Agamemnon is even dressed in Priam's clothes (880).

[83] This speech also acts to reify what the ghost of Thyestes foresees, including the final meal (*epulae*, 875 ~ *epulis*, 11), the sun's possible reversal (908–9 ~ *nocti diem*, 36), and the response of the ghost and Cassandra (5 ~*horreo atque animo tremo*, 883). Cassandra, however, may be trembling with expectation and not necessarily fear in the same way as Thyestes' ghost.

[84] This event is foretold in Cassandra's earlier speech, "That wild foster son will overturn the home" (*agrestis iste alumnus* ***evertet domum***, 733).

the news, she is happy to have survived Troy's destruction ("Now, now it is pleasing to have outlived Troy," *iam, iam iuvat vixisse post Troiam, iuvat*, 1011). The repetition of *iuvat…iuvat* recalls her first speech (750–1), where she imagined a tour of the Underworld—a tour to be undertaken very soon (if we are to believe Clytemnestra). Seneca weaves together this language to point to earlier moments of the play and not only increase the impression that what was fated has come to pass (note the *paria fata* at 1008) but also indicate the revenge yet to come (*veniet et vobis furor*, 1012).[85]

This analysis of Cassandra's speeches points to her importance as a character who can evoke different poetic registers in her speeches and provide metapoetic or alternative views of the poetry of Horace, Vergil, and Ovid. Seneca is careful to interlace Cassandra's language with the rest of the play, but also to draw upon the Augustan literary tradition in defining her roles as *vates* and messenger. In the fourth act, she resembles an inspired lyric poet (à la Horace *Carm.* 3.25) as well as an interpreter of the *Aeneid*, as she parallels the future death of Agamemnon and his mutilated corpse with the deaths of Trojans such as Hector, Troilus, and Deiphobus. In the fifth act, she becomes a messenger and hopes to provide an account to her kinsmen in the Underworld—an account that will resemble the speech that she relates at the start of this act. Intertextual echoes with Horace emphasize that Cassandra's speech attempts to surpass traditional messenger speeches by providing an individual view of events offstage (note her ironic enjoyment of the message instead of the traditional messenger's fear) and stressing the rhetorical and poetic power of Seneca's language. As we look at these two passages, we find Seneca musing upon tragedy itself by including references to the most "theatrical" moment of the *Aeneid* as well as Horace's *Ars Poetica*. He reclaims Dido's madness for tragedy and shows Horace that a messenger speech can be as evocative as a visual spectacle.

Oedipus the Reader

Cassandra can be seen as a poet in her own right, who relates her tale that will never be fully understood by those around her, even as she modifies it and attempts to render it in different language. Her tragedy, in part, is this curse—to be aware of the future but unable to change it, or even express it clearly to those she loves. Cassandra operates as a surrogate poet for Seneca, and reveals how the intertextual incorporation of Horace, Vergil, and Ovid can offer a glimpse of his theatrical use of their poetry. Oedipus offers a different type of tragic figure. He

---

[85] The final revenge of Orestes over Clytemnestra is further expressed as a madness (*furor*, not only an "avenging agent"), which Clytemnestra herself reciprocally deserves (she was *furens* in striking down Agamemnon at 897).

is someone who takes pride in his ability to understand the riddling world around him, but eventually his investigations lead to his downfall. While Seneca's Oedipus cuts a rather fearful figure compared to Sophocles' cocksure protagonist, he still believes that he will be able to harness the truth through a series of divinatory events specific to Seneca's version (Delphic oracle, *extispicium*, necromancy). In Chapter 1, I examined how the intertextual clues of the *extispicium* point to situational similarities between Oedipus and Arachne, while the Callimachean touches indicate the similar learned poetics shared by Ovid and Seneca.[86] The intertext with Vergil's *Georgics* examined earlier in this chapter indicated Seneca's desire to produce a novel work of poetry that embraced moments from both the *Georgics* and the *Aeneid*. In this section I examine Seneca's necromancy episode and then the reaction of Oedipus to this narrative. The information provided to him is in the form of poetry, and this poetry has an intertextual component. In this scene both Creon and Tiresias act as poet figures; Creon describes the liminal setting for the necromancy, and Tiresias, styled as *vates* (552, 571), issues a "magic song" (*carmen...magicum*, 561) that unlocks the Underworld itself.[87] By styling Oedipus as an interpreter, albeit a flawed one, Seneca encourages the external reader to look into the riddling nature of this account and recognize the hidden messages at play. If Oedipus is a quasi-detective, then the reader must try to assemble the clues given by the text, even those inaccessible to Oedipus (such as intertexts) to formulate an interpretation that befits the dramatic irony and ultimate message of Seneca's *Oedipus*. Seneca crafts the necromancy scene, in part, as a series of interactions with Augustan literature and as an examination of the liminal position of the poet who seeks to create something new and alive from the language of the dead.

Necromancy

After the inconclusive attempts to alleviate the plague through consulting the Delphic oracle (221–38) and then the *extispicium* of the second act, Tiresias claims that the ghost of Laius must be questioned to uncover the name of his murderer (*caedis auctorem indicet*, 394).[88] When Creon returns from the necromancy to reveal the results to Oedipus, he fears the king's anger. Oedipus attempts to force Creon to reveal the secrets, threatening torture, "unless you

---

[86] Cf. pp. 46–51 above. It should be clear that Seneca is a worthy heir of the Callimachean poetics of the Augustan poets.

[87] Well explored in Schiesaro (2003) 8–12: "With different degrees of power and knowledge, these three characters all embody a desperate search for truth, the very search that motivates the tragedy from its inception" (11). For an opposing opinion see Braund (2002) 217–9.

[88] Seneca's account does follow many of the traditional rites for raising the dead; cf. Ogden (2001) 169–70, 173–6, and passim.

reveal your secrets from the ritual" (*arcana sacri voce ni retegis tua*, 522), a statement that recalls the language used earlier about the secretive nature of the Delphic oracle and the *extispicium*.[89] This language as well as the description of the necromancy itself once again highlights the interpretative paradigm at hand, namely, Oedipus must listen to another's story and deduce the meaning of the tale (and this could be extended back in time to his encounter with the Sphinx). And what a tale it is! Creon's long messenger speech detailing the rite of necromancy is a poetic tour de force that incorporates previous portrayals of Hades but focuses on an ecphrasis of the locale, the song of the seer, and the resulting catalogue of nefarious figures. In each of these segments, Seneca manipulates intertextual echoes to the Augustan poets in order to grant those passages negative connotations that further stress how their placement in the diseased world of Thebes transforms their original Augustan context.

The opening ecphrasis specifies the features of the grove where the act of necromancy will take place. This *locus horridus* reflects the tragic world of Thebes, but also acts as a liminal zone where the dread figures of the Underworld may mingle with the living.[90] As such, it may not be surprising that elements of the locale resemble *Aeneid* 6, but additional echoes of the *Georgics*, *Eclogues*, and Ovid's *Metamorphoses* indicate Seneca's interest in exploiting the full corpus of Augustan poetry to create his tragic scenario.[91] Seneca begins his ecphrasis of the dark forest (530–6):

> Est procul ab urbe lucus **ilicibus niger**
> Dircaea circa **vallis** inriguae loca.
> cupressus altis exerens silvis caput
> virente semper alligat trunco nemus,
> curvosque **tendit quercus** et putres situ
> annosa **ramos**: huius abrupit latus
> edax vetustas;

---

[89] Creon claims the Delphic oracle "hides its secrets in tangled ambiguities" (*ambage flexa…/ arcana tegere*, 214–5), and the confused flame of the altar "hides the anger" (*iras tegunt*, 333) of the gods, and Oedipus demands Tiresias tell him what the "signs of the terrifying rite portend" (*sacri signa terrifici ferant*, 384).

[90] Cf. Schiesaro (2006) 430–6 for more on the features of the *locus horridus* and its ability to articulate "the relationship between landscape and dramatic action" (434). Aygon (2004) 214–8, 413–5 points out descriptive elements and their possible significance in the play. Hinds (2011) 9–21 highlights the "geopoetical" implications of this post-Ovidian Thebes.

[91] Details such as the cave with its dark pool and shadows can be traced to Verg. *Aen.* 6.237–8, as can the list of personified evils (*Oed.* 590–4; *Aen.* 6.274–81). For more on this see the discussion in Chap. 1.

> There is a grove, dark with holly, far from the city,
> Around the watery vale of Dirce.
> Cypress trees thrust their heads from the lofty woods
> Eternally bounding the grove with their verdant trunks;
> The ancient oak stretches its branches, now weak with rot:
> Devouring old age has torn away its side;

The ancient wood appears numinous, but, on closer inspection, it is shown to be decaying from old age and rotting from within.[92] This is in stark contrast to (one of) its models. This passage incorporates features from a beautiful "pastoral" moment found in the third *Georgic* where shepherds are encouraged to rest in the midday heat (3.330–4):

> aestibus at mediis umbrosam exquirere **vallem**,
> sicubi magna Iovis antiquo robore **quercus**
> ingentis **tendat ramos**, aut sicubi **nigrum**
> **ilicibus** crebris sacra **nemus** accubet umbra.

> But in midday heat let them seek out a shady vale,
> Where the great oak of Jove may stretch out huge branches
> With aged strength, or where a grove, dark with crowded holly,
> Reclines with blessed shade.

This moment from the *Georgics* describing a respite from the summer heat is a pleasing vision of the shepherd and his flock delighting in the noontime shade. Here Seneca underscores how even a seemingly idyllic model is given negative connotations as the heat brought on by the plague is greater than any summer day: "The sun increases the flames of the searing Dog Star" (*sed ignes auget aestiferi canis / Titan*, 39–40), and the shady grove is only sought for raising the dead (indeed, the flocks were the first to feel the force of the plague).[93] An understanding of the larger context from the *Georgics* may encourage further reflection on the effects of plague, as Thomas elucidates, "The pastoral element is heightened... partly as a prelude to the treatment of the Libyan herdsman, but partly as an evocative but *ultimately ominous prelude to the plague*, which will destroy the

---

[92] Seneca writes about the majesty of old forests at *Ep.* 41.3 and finds them worthy of veneration (a passage inspired by a quotation from the *Aeneid* about the religiosity of groves, *Aen.* 8.352–3).

[93] Cf. *Oed.* 132–3: *prima vis tardas tetigit bidentes: / laniger pingues male carpsit herbas* ("The pestilence first affected the slow sheep: / the wooly one weakly plucked the rich grass"). In itself, this echoes Verg. *G.* 3.465, where they "more slowly plucked the grass tops" (*summas carpentem ignavius herbas*).

pastoral existence and set the notion of a pastoral golden age on its head."[94] Vergil's description of the plague at Noricum influenced Seneca's earlier description of the plague at Thebes,[95] and Seneca read this moment of the *Georgics* as an anticipation of the coming plague. In a sense, the reader glimpses the before and after by this intertextual connection, as we may recall the pastoral bliss in Vergil, but even then the plague was on the horizon. Now, in a plague-ridden Thebes we see the results of the sickness on the human and natural world. Seneca's glade is a worthy spot for summoning the dead as it recalls, in part, the restful, numinous (*sacra*, 334) forest of the *Georgics*, but now tainted by deadly associations with the plague.[96] Seneca's perceptive reading of the *Georgics* already hinted at the plague lurking behind the most pleasing pastoral description, and his intertext aims to direct the reader to such a "hidden" meaning.

Continuing the associations of this glade with a lost pastoral ideal, Seneca's cypress trees, like those found in Vergil's first *Eclogue*, tower over their surroundings (*Ecl.* 1.24–5):

verum haec tantum alias inter **caput ex**tulit urbes
quantum lenta solent inter viburna **cupressi**.

But this city [Rome] towers above other cities
As much as cypress trees are accustomed to tower over low-lying shrubs.

Seneca has manipulated the Vergilian comparison in order to make the cypress trees, associated with death in Roman thought, one of the principal features of his grove.[97] Whereas the funerary connections were downplayed in Vergil's *Eclogue*, Seneca features them as part of his grim *locus horridus*, a place where the shade so delightful for the bucolic poet is transformed into a harmful force. Seneca will go on to describe the *umbra gravi* (542), an indication both of the perversion of the pastoral ideal and of the suitability of environment for the ghosts (*umbras*, 584) that will come to the spot.[98] It is notable that when Laius finally appears, he "raised his shameful head" in language that echoes these

---

[94] Thomas (1988b) 102 (my emphasis). Also see Thomas (1987) 235, where he shows how Vergil himself is deriving his information from Varro but contextualizing it into the *Georgics*: "In effect the technical passage of Varro has become a bucolic poem of 17 lines, elegantly structured and self-contained, but at the same time setting up a contrast with one of the chief themes of *Georgics* 3—the subsequent annihilation of pastoral existence."

[95] Cf. Boyle (2011) ad 37–70 for an overview.

[96] Both Seneca (*Oed.* 187) and Vergil (*G.* 3.566) describe the plague as a *sacer ignis*.

[97] Cf. Boyle (2011) ad loc. for the funereal aspects of the cypress.

[98] Cf. Schiesaro (2006) 431–2 for Seneca's negative use of *umbra* and its Lucretian and Vergilian antecedents.

very trees (*pudibundum* **extulit** / **caput**, 620), both uniting the imagery of the locale and the denizens of the Underworld and calling attention to Seneca's creative reuse of Vergil's language.

In a similar vein, Seneca writes of the "devouring old age" (*edax vetustas*, 536), which has withered the oak's trunk and made it dependent on the surrounding forest for support (536–7). This formulation echoes Ovid's *Metamorphoses*, where the poet writes of his epic's ability to survive his own death (15.871–2):

> iamque opus exegi, quod nec Iovis ira nec ignes
> nec poterit ferrum nec **edax** abolere **vetustas**.
>
> And now I have completed my work, which neither the anger of Jove
> Nor fire, nor iron, nor devouring old age will be able to destroy.

Coming near the close of the *Metamorphoses*, these lines express Ovid's hope that his poem's fame will enable his own immortality (*vivam*, 15.879).[99] Here Ovid is revisiting a previous claim about the ravages of time expressed earlier in the speech of Pythagoras, "Time the devourer of things and you, hateful old age, you destroy everything" (*tempus* **edax** *rerum, tuque, invidiosa* **vetustas** / *omnia destruitis*, 15.234–5). Seneca's use of *edax vetustas* points out two different implications of this intertext, in effect it provides readings of both moments from the *Metamorphoses*. Ovid overcomes this grievous force through his own rewriting of it in his final coda and the expression of his immortality through his poetry. For Seneca, "devouring old age" befits the landscape and adds to the despondency of the scenario (in this way strongly supporting the sentiment from 15.234–5), but it can also be seen as a textual marker for discussions of poetic immortality and, conveniently, is placed on the border between the world of the living and the world of the dead.[100] Seneca thus endorses Ovid's intimations of immortality through the recollection of his language. He calls the reader's attention to the ramifications for a description of the Underworld—this is (poetic) ground that has been traveled before, but he will attempt to grant it a novel twist, especially through the use of intertexts from a variety of sources, or from conspicuous language found in one source (Ovid's *edax vetustas*).[101]

---

[99] For more on this *sphragis*, cf. Wickkiser (1999).

[100] The fact that the *sphragis* is a close reworking of Horace's *Carm*. 3.30 simply adds to the poetic significance of such an intertext and its implications for poetic immortality.

[101] To hammer home the poetic pedigree of this scene, he ends the description, "Cold water pools in eternal icy; a muddy swamp encircles the dripping spring" (*restagnat umor frigore aeterno rigens; limosa pigrum circumit fontem palus*, 546–7), which seems to echo the description of the Underworld in both the *Georgics* (4.478–80) and the *Aeneid* (6.438–9).

Into this landscape strides Tiresias as *vates* (553), intending to rouse the dead by means of his ritual and song. His garb recalls that of Vergil's Charon, and he is fulfilling a similar purpose in providing passage to the figures of the Underworld (although in Seneca's play the souls are released to the upper world and there is not the traditional descent). In the *Aeneid*, Charon is an old man (*senior*, 6.304), of horrible squalor (*terribili squalore*, 6.299), with a wizened beard (*canities*, 6.300) and foul garb (*sordidus…amictus*, 6.301). Tiresias plays the part well in being a sorrowful old man (*maestus…senex*, 554) with white hair (*canam comam*, 555), a befouled countenance (*squalente cultu*, 554), and a funereal robe (*funesto…amictus*, 551–2). In addition, adjectives such as *squalida* and *maestum* are significant for the play as whole, initially appearing to describe the shuttered light of the sun (*nube maestum squalida…iubar*, 2), and point to the "uniformity of mood" pervasive throughout the *Oedipus*.[102] After filling a ditch with firebrands stolen from funeral pyres (550–1) and sacrificing animals in a holocaustic ritual (556–8), Tiresias calls upon the dead (559–63):

> Vocat inde manes teque qui manes regis
> et obsidentem claustra Lethaei lacus,
> carmenque magicum volvit et rabido minax
> decantat ore quidquid aut placat leves
> aut cogit umbras;

> Thence he summons the shades and you, who are their lord,
> and the one who guards the barrier of the lake of Lethe,
> He unrolls the magical song, and, terrifying in his frenzied speech,
> He chants out whatever may please or gather the light shades.

Tiresias beckons the forces of the Underworld to reveal themselves, and his magical song (*carmen…magicum*) attempts to harness the resulting roll call of personified evils, Theban figures, and other inhabitants of Hades. His song "with frenzied speech" (*rabido…ore*) parallels Vergil's description of the Sibyl's voice when possessed by Apollo (*os rabidum*, *Aen.* 6.80; *rabida ora*, *Aen.* 6.102). Seneca stresses that the charm has poetic qualities (*carmen, decantat*) and, further, that it has to be repeated in order to gain efficacy (*canit…rursus*, 567–8; *graviore…voce et attonita*, 568). Details from *Aeneid* 6 point to the *katabasis* context, while the reader notes that Tiresias' song is doing the same thing as Seneca's passage—in both cases there is a desire to repeat as well as amplify the previous

---

[102] The phrase is Mastronarde's (1970) 294. He finds that "these words of gloom and sorrow draw together sections of the play and aspects of its imaginary world—Oedipus' state of mind, the condition of the heavens, the dead, the necromancy and his contact Laius" (295).

accounts.¹⁰³ As one reads of Tiresias' magical chant, one also reflects on Seneca's own poetry and his own desire to bring "the dead" back to life, and, indeed, this section of Creon's speech results in a breech between the borders of the two worlds (571–3):

> "audior" vates ait,
> "rata verba fudi: rumpitur caecum chaos
> iterque populis Ditis ad superos datur."

> "I am heard," the prophet says,
> "My words have been fulfilled: the dark gulf is burst
> and a way to the upper world is given to the populations of Dis."

If a poet's words are heard, magic can occur and his successful incantation leads to further poetry.¹⁰⁴ The provided way (*iter*, 573; *viam*, 579) allows Seneca to stress the impact of the world (and words) of the dead on the living, and leads to a long catalogue of the horrors released from Hades. Since this scene follows upon Tiresias' cry "Another path must be tried" (*alia temptanda est via*, 390), it acts as the responding novel "path" in the search for the murderer's name.¹⁰⁵ As such it assumes the epic tone (*graviore voce*, 568) of Vergil's *Aeneid*, and reworks aspects of Vergil's *katabasis* that are germane to the themes and imagery of the *Oedipus*.

After Tiresias reveals the Underworld to Creon, he observes various infernal figures including the sown warriors who comprised Thebes' first population, the Erinys (placed early in the list because of the tragedy's concern with familial bloodshed), and "whatever the eternal shadows create and conceal" (*quidquid aeternae creant / celatque tenebrae*, 591–2). This initial catalogue of personifications repeats many of the ills Vergil's Aeneas found near the entrance of Dis' realm, including Luctus (*Aen.* 6.274, *Oed.* 592), Morbus (*Aen.* 6.275, *Oed.* 593), Senectus (*Aen.* 6.275, *Oed.* 594), and Metus (*Aen.* 6.276, *Oed.* 594).¹⁰⁶ What is more surprising and specific to the *Oedipus* is the addition of the current plague

---

¹⁰³ Seneca writes that the "dogs of Hecate bark" (*latravit Hecates turba*, 569), echoing the idea found in the *Aeneid*: "Dogs seemed to howl as the goddess [Hecate] approaches through the shadows" (*visaeque canes ululare per umbram / adventante dea*, *Aen.* 6.257–8).

¹⁰⁴ Cf. Schiesaro (2003) 12: "The uncontrolled fear that pushes Seneca's Oedipus to search for explanations (unlike his Sophoclean counterpart) eventually leads him to discover in the song of Laius the truth he was afraid to know. Passion leads to poetry, and poetry is the revelation of truths carefully hidden from the upper world of reason and power." The phrase *rata verba* derives from Ovid *Met.* 4.387, where the prayer of Hermaphroditus is granted.

¹⁰⁵ Cf. the discussion above pp. 190–3.

¹⁰⁶ Cf. the discussion above pp. 33–9.

ravaging the city among such evils (*avidumque populi Pestis Ogygii malum*, 589). In supplementing these personifications, Seneca finds a way to adapt the locus classicus of Underworld evils to the world of his play, linking the language of the plague to Vergil's description as well as the themes of the *Oedipus*.[107]

After noting his own reaction to the vision ("My spirit left me," *nos liquit animus*, 595), Creon composes an epic simile to describe how Tiresias, bold and fearless, calls forth the legions of souls (600–7):

> non tot caducas educat frondes Eryx
> nec vere flores Hybla tot medio creat,
> cum examen arto nectitur densum globo,
> fluctusque non tot frangit Ionium mare,
> nec tanta gelidi Strymonis fugiens minas
> permutat hiemes ales et caelum secans
> tepente Nilo pensat Arctoas nives,
> quot ille populos vatis eduxit sonus.

> Eryx does not bring forth so many falling leaves
> Nor, in the middle of spring, does Hybla produce so many flowers,
> When the bees swarm together in a close-knit mass,
> Nor does the Ionian Sea break so many waves,
> Nor do so many birds, fleeing the threats of the icy Strymon,
> migrate and, cutting a path through the sky, replacing
> Artic snows for the warm Nile,
> So many were the souls the sound of that prophet brought forth.

The comparison of the number of souls in the Underworld to events on earth is a common topos, and Seneca shows himself equal to the task as he expands three famous Vergilian passages.[108] In the *Georgics*, Orpheus descends to Hades and sees the souls of the dead (*G*. 4.473–4):

> quam multa in foliis avium se milia condunt,
> Vesper ubi aut hibernus agit de montibus imber...

> As many as the thousands of birds who hide themselves under leaves,
> When evening or a winter storm drives them from the mountains...

---

[107] Cf. Boyle (2011) ad 410–1, "*Avidus* is a thematic epithet of this play, linking the plague (4, 589), death (164), and Oedipus' blinding (965) as markers of 'fate's lust' (411)." Earlier the chorus equated the plague with *malum*: "All things have felt our evil" (*omnia nostrum sensere malum*, 159).

[108] Cf. Boyle (2011) ad loc. for additional literary antecedents.

In his *Aeneid*, Vergil expands upon the number of the deceased (*Aen.* 6.309–12):

quam multa in silvis autumni frigore primo
lapsa cadunt folia, aut ad terram gurgite ab alto
quam multae glomerantur aves, ubi frigidus annus
trans pontum fugat et terris immittit apricis.

As many as the leaves which fall in the forest at the first frost of autumn,
Or as many as the birds which gather landwards from the deep tossing sea
When winter puts them to flight across the water
And sends them to sunny lands.

Seneca has crafted sections of his "epic" simile from these two descriptions of the vast number of dead souls in Hades and rejuvenates the topos through his inclusion of additional metaphorical language. For Seneca, the leaves of autumn and the migrating birds of winter also call to mind the springtime flowers of Hybla and the bees swarming at that time. We can see how Seneca develops the notion of infinity, adding further comparisons that comment on other seasons (spring), and including elements such as ring composition (*educat*, 600; *eduxit*, 607) to display his artistry.[109] While some may believe such additional elements are redundant (and unwanted), their inclusion shows Seneca's further interest in combining elements of the *Georgics* and *Aeneid*. The idea of the number of waves in the sea can be found (in a similar comparative context) at *Georgics* 2.108, and the specification of birds fleeing the River Strymon also appears in the *Aeneid*.[110] One element that is missing from Seneca's account is the presence of the souls of young men and maidens, mothers and husbands, and heroes, lines common to both the *Georgics* and *Aeneid* passages.[111] Seneca elides these souls from his description because it is his desire to focus on the mythological heroes and villains of Theban genealogy and because he already mentioned the human suffering in his opening plague descriptions. In Seneca's Underworld, one will not find the souls of normal folk, but only those of tragic Theban figures.

One further intertext must be noted. The bees of Seneca's simile recall a further Vergilian Underworld description, when Aeneas and his father, Anchises,

---

[109] The four comparisons vary in length from one line to two lines, then one, followed by a three-line comparison. See Fraenkel (1957) 427: "We have simply to state that the duplication of similes in parallel sentences or clauses was employed by several Augustan poets as a means of stressing the importance of a passage by adding to its stylistic weight."

[110] *Aen.* 10.264–6. Cf. Tochterle (1994) ad loc. for more on these two additional intertexts.

[111] *Aen.* 6.306–8 = *G.* 4.475–7: *matres atque viri defunctaque corpora vita / magnanimum heroum, pueri innuptaeque puellae, / impositique rogis iuvenes ante ora parentum*. The repetition of these lines in both of Vergil's works makes Seneca's neglect of them significant.

reach the banks of Lethe and observe the souls of future Roman greats (*Aen.* 6. 706–9):

> hunc circum innumerae gentes populique volabant;
> ac veluti in pratis ubi apes aestate serena
> floribus insidunt variis et candida circum
> lilia funduntur, strepit omnis murmure campus.

> Around this river, countless races and peoples flit about;
> Just as when, during the calm summer, bees settle on various flowers
> In the meadows and stream around bright lilies,
> The whole plain hums with their buzzing.

Anchises is thrilled to relate the future deeds of these souls, and the pleasant simile of the bees indicates the optimistic prophecy about to be revealed. While Seneca seems to focus more on the swarming of the bees, the repeated terms and the situational similarity may indicate his indebtedness to Vergil.[112] Seneca's *contaminatio* of these Vergilian passages, however, colors the possibly positive connotations of the bee simile, as the Theban dead that are summoned indicate the tragic history of the city and the inescapable fate that Oedipus must face. While including a variety of Vergilian material relating to the Underworld in this simile, Seneca exhibits his idiosyncratic manner of combining this material in order to reflect the matter at hand. In this case, the next catalogue will not consist of famous Romans, but rather of famous Thebans who are paraded in a grim succession of tragic figures.

This collection of mythological figures such as Amphion, Niobe, Agave, and Pentheus not only associates them thematically with the Oedipus tale but also indicates their close association with tragedy and tragic themes.[113] Niobe and Agave highlight extreme perversions of the *maternus amor* (630) that Laius pronounces as the underlying cause of Thebes' torments in addition to connecting their plights to Jocasta and Oedipus. Tiresias, through his song (*vatis…sonus*, 607), brings forth past tragic figures, but his language throughout this episode continually evokes his Augustan predecessors. Such an amalgamation of Greek and Roman is typical of Seneca's tragedies, where the topics of Attic drama are

---

[112] Boyle (2011) ad loc. believes Seneca had this Vergilian passage in mind as "the shades of future Romans 'fly about' (*volabant*) like 'bees' (*apes*) in the cloudless summer, lighting upon dappled 'flowers' (*floribus*)."

[113] See Schiesaro (2003) 9n3 for more on the tragic lineage of these Theban figures, while Boyle (2011) ad 608–12 notes, "Their [Zethus' and Amphion's] story and that of their mother…and of Amphion's wife, Niobe, were the subject of several tragedies, including Sophocles' *Niobe*, Euripides' *Antiope*, Pacuvius' *Antiopa*."

dressed up in the textual sophistication of post-Augustan poetry. In this section, Seneca utilizes the figure of Tiresias to comment on writing tragedy; both the sort of stories to tell and the way in which to tell them. Bringing forth the dead acts as a trope for intertextuality, in which the author combs through the stories told by previous authors until discovering an evocative line, image, or theme to be redeployed.

When the ghost of Laius appears, he looks much like Tiresias himself,[114] and therefore we should expect his speech to be no less emblematic of Seneca's poetry, and it does not disappoint, as it strongly exhibits Seneca's trademark rhetorical sophistication and intertextual complexity. Two moments of the speech especially respond to Ovid's poetry and show how Seneca aims to cap his tales. Laius' speech opens with invective against the house of Cadmus, in particular the incestuous relationship of Oedipus and Jocasta (626–30):

> O Cadmi effera,
> cruore semper laeta cognato domus,
> vibrate thyrsos, enthea gnatos manu
> lacerate potius—**maximum** Thebis **scelus**
> maternus **amor** est. patria, non ira deum,
> sed scelere raperis.

> O savage house
> Of Cadmus, always rejoicing in familial blood,
> Brandish your bacchic wands; it is better to rip up your
> Children with inspired hand—the greatest crime in Thebes
> Is maternal love. Fatherland, you are being plundered by a crime,
> Not the anger of the gods.

While the mythological antecedents evoke Euripides' *Bacchae*, Seneca also has in mind the incestuous relationship of Myrrha and her father in Ovid's *Metamorphoses*.[115] Ovid describes Myrrha's plight as she falls in love with her father, Cinyras, and eventually finds a way to consummate the relationship. In introducing the story, Ovid remarks, "It is a crime to hate your father, / but this love is a greater crime than hatred" (*scelus est odisse parentem, hic amor est odio maius scelus*, 10.314–5). Between the two options of love and hatred, Ovid claims that incestuous love is worse. In looking back to this passage,

---

[114] Laius' squalor (*paedore foedo squalidam obtentus comam*, 625) evokes Tiresias' garb (*squalente cultu*, 554), and both speak *rabido ore* (561–2, 626). Schiesaro (2003) 11 remarks on this inset tale: "As is fitting in a *mise en abyme*, the inset scene is a microcosm of the larger framework, and this makes reflection perceptible."

[115] Cf. Jakobi (1988) 110 and Boyle (2011) ad loc.

Seneca claims that the incestuous relationship between Oedipus and Jocasta (among other Theban crimes involving mothers and sons) is the greatest (*maximus*), capping the comparative found in Ovid (*maius*). Seneca revisits an earlier recollection of the Ovidian passage, when Oedipus spoke of the oracle's prophecy that he would kill his father and sleep with his mother (*nobis **maius** indicunt **scelus**,* 17). Seneca reconfigures the severity of the incest in the necromancy scene to show that even Laius (who, after all, died by Oedipus' hand) believes the worst crime is Oedipus' incestuous relationship with Jocasta.[116] Laius' pronouncement influences Oedipus' contemplation of the proper penalty for his crimes: "What will you give to your sorrowful fatherland, which pays the price for your crime with complete ruin?" (*quae tuum magna luit / **scelus** ruina, flebili **patriae** dabis?,* 940–1).[117] According to Laius (and Oedipus' "reading" of Laius' words), it is incest that truly causes the fatherland to suffer.

Seneca continues to look back to Ovid's tale and debates within his play the proper interpretation of Ovid's incest narrative. Ovid's Myrrha will justify her deed, in part, by finding examples in the animal world (10.324–9), but Laius claims that this impious deed is "scarcely customary among beasts" (*vix mos est feris,* 639). While Myrrha's nurse believed the anger of the gods could be appeased—"If it is the anger of gods, that anger can be appeased by sacrifice" (***ira deum** sive est, sacris placabilis ira,* 10.399)—and that she could help Myrrha to solve her dilemma, Laius stresses that it is this crime, and not the anger of the gods, that is destroying Thebes (*patria, non **ira deum**, sed scelere raperis,* 630–1). Seneca wishes to show that Oedipus' incestuous *scelus* is even worse than Myrrha's and is part of a long line of Theban familial crimes, and the intertext cleverly indicates how Seneca surpasses Ovid's account, even as it points out the root cause of the plague, previously adumbrated by the oracle at Delphi, who closed its prophecy, saying, "You foully returned again to your maternal birthplace" (*turpis **maternos** iterum revolutus in ortus,* 238). In spite of Laius' insistence, the choral song following this scene emphatically claims that Oedipus is blameless and that "the ancient wrath of the gods pursues us" (*veteres **deum** / **irae** secuntur,* 711–2). In doing so, the chorus finds that Thebes itself is problematic from its origin (supported by tales from Ovid's Theban history) and that the plague is a direct result of the gods and not Oedipus.[118] Seneca provides differing internal interpretations in order to question issues such as the role of the gods, personal

---

[116] Oedipus will come to figure his search for knowledge in similar terms; he responds to Jocasta's advice that "truth often has exposed those searching for it to evil" with "Can there be any evil greater than this to be feared?" (***malum** timeri **maius** his aliquod potest?,* 828). He will later tell himself, "Now dare something worthy of your crimes" (*nunc aliquid aude **sceleribus** dignum tuis,* 879).

[117] After his self-blinding, he calls upon the gods, "Come, I beseech you to spare my fatherland!" (*parcite en **patriae**, precor,* 975).

[118] Cf. Jakobi (1988) 121–5 and Hinds (2011) 10–4 for the Ovidian intertexts of this ode.

choice, and fate. While the chorus at this point still supports Oedipus (not realizing that he is Theban) and claims, "No fates of yours stalk the Labdacids" (*non haec Labdacidas petunt / fata*, 710–1), later revelations will force them to reconcile themselves with Oedipus' guilt and fate.[119] Oedipus himself, however, believes at the play's conclusion that he has even surpassed his fates because of Jocasta's suicide: "She was destroyed by my crime. O lying Phoebus; I have surpassed my impious fate" (***scelere*** *confecta est, meo. / O Phoebe mendax, fata superavi impia*, 1045–6).[120]

The second Ovidian intertext comes from the final words of Laius' speech and once again proves that Seneca fashions his characters to act as interpreters of Ovid's poetry. After pronouncing that fecundity and vigor will return to Thebes with the expulsion of Oedipus, he concludes by threatening Oedipus (656–8):

>reptet incertus viae,
>**baculo** senili triste **praetemptans iter**:
>eripite terras, auferam caelum pater.

>He will crawl, uncertain of the way,
>Testing the sad road ahead with an old man's staff:
>You take away the land; I, his father, will remove the sky.

Laius foretells Oedipus' self-blinding and orders the Thebans to exile him from their land. Boyle notes how Seneca's language also has specific Roman connotations: "The standard punishment [for parricide] was to be sewn in a sack with a dog, cock, viper, and monkey and thrown into the local river or into the sea, in order that the parricide may be deprived of the *caelum* while still alive and the *terra* when dead."[121] In addition, Laius' words echo a passage from Ovid's long invective poem *Ibis*.[122] Among the many mythological torments Ovid wishes upon his addressee, Ovid says (259–64):

>Id quod Amyntorides videas, trepidumque ministro
>**praetemptes baculo** luminis orbus **iter**.

---

[119] Note that the chorus concentrates on the question of "fate" (*fata*) from this point forward. It is the first word of each of the subsequent choral odes (883, 980).

[120] Cf. Boyle (2011) ad loc. for the ways in which this concluding address to Apollo recalls the prologue as well as "perhaps also the suggestion of him [Apollo] as the 'speaker of what has been said', i.e. voice of the dramatic tradition, speaking what has been said countless times in other plays, most especially those of the Attic triad."

[121] Boyle (2011) ad loc. with further references to this form of punishment.

[122] See Hinds (2011) 49–55 on Seneca's use of the *Ibis* in his tragedies, including a discussion of this passage.

> nec plus aspicias quam quem sua filia rexit,
>   expertus scelus est cuius **uterque parens**:
> qualis erat, postquam est iudex de lite iocosa
>   sumptus, Apollinea clarus in arte senex.

> May you see what Amyntor's son perceived, and may you
>   Blinded, test the fearful road ahead with a staff as your guide.
> May you see no more than the man whom his own daughter led,
>   Whose crime each of his parents suffered:
> Be such as the old man, famous for Apollo's prophecy,
>   After he was judge of the playful quarrel.

The section of the *Ibis* concerns Phoenix, who was blinded by his father, Amyntor. If Laius takes on the role of Amyntor (with Oedipus as Phoenix), his statement reveals an even more sinister bent, because it implies that he will take Oedipus' eyes himself: "I, his father, will remove the sky."[123] The Ovidian passage goes on immediately to wish a similar fate upon "Ibis" as both Oedipus and Tiresias suffered, thus adding further connections to Seneca's *Oedipus*. In this case, the blindness that Laius predicts may be confirmed, or at least further emphasized by the intertextual connection to the *Ibis* and the mention of Oedipus there. This climactic speech indicates, once again, how Senecan intertextuality often looks at the larger context of the model in order to further articulate Seneca's argument or themes. The necromancy concludes with the words not only of Laius but also of Ovid, menacing Oedipus, and the reader leaves with the ominous impression that Oedipus will soon suffer the blindness intimated here.

This Ovidian passage, however, also acts as a backdrop to Oedipus' response to the story. Oedipus believes that he is the child of Polybus and Merope, and although he admits, "I am accused of having done what I feared to do" (*quidquid timebam facere fecisse arguor*, 660), neither has suffered at his hand. Therefore, "each parent argues against murder and incest" (***uterque** defendit **parens** / caedem stuprumque*, 663–4), a line that responds to the very description of Oedipus in Ovid's *Ibis*.[124] Seneca's Oedipus argues for his innocence in language that recalls Ovid, showing how Ovid's words can be given different interpretations according to the character's own viewpoint (in this case, whether they are used for the prosecution or the defense). Seneca presents his characters as readers of the literary tradition in order to show how these texts can take on a variety of meanings.

---

[123] Cf. Apollod. *Biblio*. 3.13.8 for more on Amyntor and Phoenix.

[124] The phrase is rare outside of Ovid's poetry. In Ovid, it is found at *Am*. 1.3.10, *Her*. 6.62, *Met*. 4.387, and *Fast*. 5.181. Ovid figures Oedipus' crime as a *scelus*, whereas Seneca spells out the charges, including *stuprum*, "the only occurrence in *Oedipus* of this technical legal term for a wide range of sexually prohibited activity, including 'incest'" (Boyle (2011) ad loc.).

While Ovid will claim that Tiresias is a "famous old man" (*clarus...senex*), for Seneca's Oedipus, Tiresias appears to be a "lying elder" (*falsus...senior*, 677) and perpetrator of a trick as pernicious as the Sphinx's riddle.[125] Oedipus will go on to assert that although the gods of the upper and lower worlds condemn him for the death of Laius, his "innocent soul, known to itself better than to the gods, denies it" (*animus contra innocens / sibique melius quam deis notus negat*, 766–7). His view is necessarily limited, based on his incorrect knowledge of his upbringing, and the play goes on to shatter the limits of his intelligence and his way of understanding the world.

This necromancy scene provides a panorama of Seneca's intertextual technique; he blends material that is appropriate and expected, such as Vergil's *katabasis* of *Aeneid* 6, with surprising additions like Ovid's *Ibis*, or the pastoral shade of the *Eclogues*. Such material, marshaled by a *vates* figure such as Tiresias and reported by Creon, provides further evidence of Oedipus' polluting presence in Thebes and the long (tragic) history of Theban figures. In addition, intratextual elements continually remind the reader that Thebes in its plague-ridden state is no different from the Underworld itself and that the *scelus* of Oedipus transcends previous crimes. A reader of this material understands how Seneca's intertextual technique highlights the similarity of this passage to Vergil's *katabasis*, but also the differences. No kind Anchises awaits Oedipus to extol the great future leaders of Rome, but rather a threatening figure who points to Oedipus as the latest in a long line of nefarious Thebans. Intertextual parallels hint at Oedipus' past crime and future suffering and produce dramatic irony in the reader, who recognizes Oedipus' inability to solve the current riddle—namely, that he is the one wreaking havoc on Thebes.

Oedipus himself, however, does not believe this message is true and finds evidence for his innocence in the continued well-being of Polybus and his avoidance of Merope's bed (661–3). Internal "readings" of Ovid's *Ibis* allow us to see how Augustan texts can be interpreted according to the characters' own interests. As Cassandra's message is misconstrued, so the various divinatory scenes of the *Oedipus* are lost on Oedipus, although Creon and Tiresias know that the signs point to Oedipus as the source of pollution.[126] In the play, Oedipus believes that he understands what signs mean, because of his earlier encounter with the Sphinx, whom Seneca similarly imbues with metapoetic traits (her riddle is a

---

[125] Elsewhere in the play, Tiresias is described as *senex* (554, 595). Oedipus claims that he holds the "comrades in a devious plot" (*callidi socios doli*, 668), mirroring his view of the Sphinx (*dolos*, 101; *callidi monstri*, 106).

[126] Tiresias has an inkling that something worse is in store for Oedipus as early as 387. Laius is very clear in pronouncing Oedipus, the "blood-stained king" (*rex cruentus*, 634), the source of the contagion.

carmen at 98, 102; she is a *vates* at 93).[127] Oedipus' confidence springs from this victory, but the play proceeds to reveal his failings in the face of this new evil, which ultimately boils down to an inability to understand himself and his own origins. In fact, as the Sphinx tormented Thebes, so Laius pronounces Oedipus "an entangled evil, and a more mystifying monster than his own Sphinx" (*implicitum malum / magisque monstrum Sphinge perplexum sua*, 640–1). This description hints that Oedipus is the cause of Thebes' present difficulties and that he must depart for peace and tranquility to return to Thebes, a position seconded by the ghost of Laius (647–53).

These divinatory scenes are a departure from the Sophoclean original and are often faulted for being repetitive and stalling the action of the play. Seneca includes them, in part, because they are relevant to their Roman audience. As Ahl states, "Seneca has to adjust the Sophoclean *Oedipus* in many details to make his tragedy work for Romans. Not least, he has to find some way of presenting prophecy to his Roman audience, since, from Cicero's time onward, the Delphic oracle was essentially defunct."[128] While Seneca does feature an account of the Delphic priestess's words, he concentrates on the scenes of *extispicium* and necromancy because these forms of divination were current in the Roman world and would be familiar to the Roman audience. Seneca composes highly literary and allusive accounts of these divinatory practices that speak to their underlying function (namely, to foretell future events) and points out the ambiguity involved in their interpretation. He interweaves the language and imagery of these events with the play as a whole as well as the Latin literary tradition and, in doing so, points to the similar difficulties of interpreting a divinatory event and a work of literature. He means to parallel the reactions of the internal characters to the external reader and point out the difficulty of making sense of the world, especially when under duress. While the external reader may understand the suggestions of the future enmity of Polynices and Eteocles as well as the intertextual references to Latin literature, in the disordered world of the play (**natura versa est!**, 371) Oedipus is blind to the signs and *monstra* around him.[129] Only after cross-examining Jocasta about Laius' murder (782) and receiving the information from Phorbas that Jocasta is his mother (867) does Oedipus realize the truth, that Nature overturned all its laws in the case of Oedipus (*leges*…**Natura in uno vertit** *Oedipoda*, 942–3) and that he has been responsible for the terrible

---

[127] See discussion above, pp. 140–4.
[128] Ahl (2008) 120–1.
[129] Cf. Ahl (2008) 122: "What Manto and Teiresias observe has little to say about any criminality in Oedipus' past actions, since *haruspicina* does not generally reveal the unknown past. And this may well be Seneca's most important point: that the obsession with self and personal past history can blind people, as it blinds Oedipus, to a larger future problem."

suffering of Thebes.[130] Oedipus may be a fallible reader, but it would appear that he has been placed in an environment, namely, Thebes, where a correct reading of the evidence is inherently problematic.

Conclusion

These examples of Senecan intertextuality indicate the pervasive way that metapoetics influences his writing. By creating characters who stand in for the poet himself, Seneca reveals his conception of tragic poetry. Such poetry draws frequently on the works of past writers, but always with an eye to the present scenario and, usually, with an altered focus from the original. Seneca revitalizes the language of the Augustan poets in his tragedies by allowing the various genres and authors to speak both to one another and to the audience. Each context matters for the analysis of Seneca's intertextual poetics, and figures such as Cassandra and scenes such as the *Oedipus'* necromancy allow the reader to understand more fully the ramifications of Seneca's appropriation of the Augustan poets. These words are not passive but rather active components of Seneca's tragic language that have a surfeit of associations—whether it be to a particular moment of the *Aeneid* or *Metamorphoses* or to thematic ties between tales or even their manner of telling. Whereas Cassandra's multiple narratives about the same topic (Agamemnon's death) reach back to the *Aeneid* and Horace's *Ars Poetica* in an attempt to render the subject matter evocatively (and accurately), her tragedy hinges on the inability of those around her to understand her words. Oedipus doubles for the external reader as he attempts to scrutinize the signs around him, including the narrative of Creon, for clues as to the plague's origin and his own guilt. The fear that impelled him to claim, "I've made the sky guilty" (*fecimus caelum* **nocens**, 36) later is verified (*teneo* **nocentem**, 782), only to be surpassed when confronted with the death of Jocasta: "Twice a parricide and more guilty than I feared, I killed my mother" (*bis parricida plusque quam timui* **nocens** / *matrem peremi*, 1044–5). While Jocasta can claim, "Nobody is guilt because of fate" (*nemo fit fato* **nocens**, 1019), the play has proved her wrong.[131] The challenges of Oedipus' "fate" appealed to Seneca, and his play confronts and comments on the philosophical and metaliterary problems of *fata*.[132] From the verb *fari*, this word can indicate "what is said," namely, what has been said previously

---

[130] Seneca revisits this sentiment in his *Phoenissae* (*ipsa se in leges novas / natura vertet*, 84–5).

[131] Cf. Davis (1991) 161, who bridges the perceived divide between fate, intent, and human responsibility: "The play itself presents Oedipus' acts as the result of both fate and crime."

[132] Cf. Boyle (2011) lxxv on the choral odes: "They dwell upon the issue of 'fate', exploiting to the full the semiotic ambiguities of *fatum*, 'what is said', 'death', and 'destiny.'" Cf. Bettini (2008) for more on *fari*.

about a topic, in this case the narratives impacting his Oedipus story. In this play, his "fate" consists, in part, in his previous literary representations and the intertexts that Seneca associates with the Oedipus story. This creates a net from which Oedipus cannot escape and connects his feelings of guilt to the Ovidian and Vergilian texts that help to construct the world of the tragedy. My reading places Oedipus in a decidedly post-Ovidian, post-Vergilian Thebes in which the land itself "always produces new monsters" (*nova monstra semper / protulit tellus*, 724–5), and Oedipus is one in a long line of Theban royals who has undergone transformation and been subject to tragedy beyond their ultimate control. Seneca explores the severity of human "transformation" produced by Oedipus' incestuous and murderous actions from husband to son, from father to brother, from loving son to parricide, from king to scapegoat.

Epilogue

> The almost-but-not-quite-shameful truth was that I could paint only when I thought I was someone else. I'd imitated a style; I'd imitated (though without ever using that word) an artist with his own unique vision and way of painting. And not without profit, for if I had somehow become someone else, I too now had "my" own style and identity. I would take a faint pride in this version. This was my first intimation of the thing that would nag at me in later years, the self-contradiction—a Westerner would call it the paradox—that we only acquire our own identity by imitating others.
>
> —Orhan Pamuk

In this book, I have examined the manner in which Seneca responds to and recasts the language of the Augustan poets in his tragedies in an attempt not only to enrich his dramatic material but also to create his own intertextual poetics. His tragedies consist of a mosaic of texts from a variety of genres, and the confluence of these texts creates tension and polyvalence in Seneca's language. Seneca is a careful reader and rewriter of the poetic tradition and often manipulates his model texts in his new tragic environment to illustrate the limitations of previous depictions (such as Medea in the *Heroides*) or to emphasize his position as the inheritor of a long poetic tradition (such as the topos of the plague or the descent to the Underworld). Seneca consistently and creatively frames his tragedies with a view to his Augustan predecessors and defines his tragic action in relation to Augustan genres. His characters express themselves in a rhetorically heightened manner that demands careful explication in order to decipher how their personae operate in the tragedy. In doing so, they reflect the importance of rhetoric in Seneca's time and the ease by which educated speakers could shift and play with personae. As Boyle states, "Rhetorical training in declamation, most especially mastery of the 'persuasion-speech' *suasoria*, which required diverse and sustained role-playing, gave to contemporary Romans not only the ability to enter into the psychic structure of another...but the improvisational skills required to create a *persona* at will."¹

The various roles that characters play in Seneca's tragedies are indicative of Seneca's view of the self as expressed in the *Epistulae Morales*. Seneca recognizes that individuals play a variety of roles in their interactions with others and that such personae are mutable.² He claims that despite the quest for stability "we continually change our mask [*personam*] and put on one the very opposite of the one discarded."³ Throughout the *Epistulae*, Seneca stresses that he himself is no Stoic *sapiens* but suffers from the same doubts and fluctuations as everyone else.⁴ In his creation of personae, Seneca relies on literary accounts as one of the building blocks of his characters' psychological make-up. The personae that appear throughout the Senecan corpus reveal their constructed nature because their language calls attention to previous manifestations in earlier texts. An intertextual reading of Seneca's tragedies recognizes that the source material influences background information to the characters and reveals the motivation behind both their words and deeds. In some sense, Seneca's characters embody the motto "You are what you read," and Seneca endorses the intertextual component of such reading by anchoring his intertexts within the dramatic context.

Clearly Seneca wrote his tragedies for a highly educated readership that could appreciate the verbal flourishes and intertextual complexity of his poetic language. Quintilian mentions the propensity for *emphasis* ("hidden meaning") in the rhetoric of his time, and the intertextual examples that I have pointed out show how such *emphases* can impact the plot of the tragedies.⁵ To imbue language with such pregnant meaning was common in Seneca's time, as writers and orators attempted to create novel turns of phrase, complex intertextual echoes, and sententiae in order to impress their audience.⁶ While Quintilian (as well as some modern readers) finds such allusiveness troublesome, such a close reading of Seneca's language uncovers hidden connections to Augustan literature and

---

¹ Boyle (2006) 182.

² Seneca on role-playing: *Ep.* 74.7, 76.31, 115.14; *Ad Marc.* 10.1; see Rosenmeyer (1989) 47–56 on the Stoic ramifications of such role-playing.

³ *Ep.* 120.22. Both C. Edwards (2002) and Boyle (2006) 181–2 point out theatrical metaphors in Seneca's Stoic thought. Inwood (2005) 322–52 and Star (2012) discuss self-assertion in Seneca.

⁴ As Pratt (1983) 65 states: "The relationship between the philosopher and his audience is changed, becoming less that of teacher to learner and more that of the still struggling counselor to fellow strugglers."

⁵ *Inst.* 9.2.64: "*Emphasis* is one of these figures by which some hidden meaning is rooted out from another phrase" (*est* **emphasis** *etiam inter figuras, cum ex aliquo dicto latens aliquid eruitur*). Boyle (2006) 229–30 and Fantham (1982) 28–9 both mention how *emphasis* affects Seneca's language. Bartsch (1994) and Rudich (1993) show how such "hidden meaning" can have political implications, as Quintilian recognizes (*Inst.* 9.2.67–75).

⁶ Cf. *Inst.* 9.2.66.

individuates his view of tragedy as a genre.[7] Seneca's tragedies encourage such careful reading and metaliterary language helps to distinguish Seneca's project as an active reenvisioning of his predecessors' works within the tragic genre. This medley of influences does not merely emphasize the "literariness" of his texts but also reinforces the themes and motifs of his plays, for Seneca often stresses the very language from the intertexts by repeating it throughout the play. By creating these internal connections between the intertexts and the tragedy itself, Seneca shows his artistry as a poet and suggests his own particular tragic reception of the Augustan poets (he also encourages his reader to understand the source material in such a manner).

An intertextual reader must determine which references are meaningful, and must interpret the material from his own perspective. My readings are, necessarily, products of my own culture and literary knowledge, and I understand that not every reader of my work will find all of my conclusions persuasive. As Barthes explains:

> A text is made of multiple writings, drawn from any cultures and entering into mutual relations of dialogue, parody, contestation, but there is one place where this multiplicity is focused and that place is the reader, not, as was hitherto said, the author. The reader is the space on which all the quotations that make up a writing are inscribed without any of them being lost; a text's unity lies not in its origin but in its destination.[8]

Each reader creates his own connections from the text, as Seneca himself created his tragedies from the texts and myths of his time. Much of this study has been to unearth Seneca's own predilections as a reader. One can see how self-aware, clever, competitive, and questioning he is through his reception of the Augustan poets. When Seneca reworks the language of his intertexts into the larger fabric of his plays, he encourages the reader to see the importance of the intertext running through the play as a whole or trace the development of this language as focalized by different characters.[9] Often such language has metapoetic implica-

---

[7] Fantham (1982) 29: "In general, however, we find in Senecan tragedy this very overworking of irony and allusion that strains and can even induce resistance in the listener, while the repetitiousness and excessive reliance on aphorism of Quintilian's contemporaries had been an affliction, not only of Seneca's generation (in Quintilian's youth), but of the late Augustans before him."

[8] Barthes (1977) 148. This quote springs from a discussion of Greek tragedy in which Barthes notices the reader-like position of the characters: "Its texts being woven from words with double meanings that each character understands unilaterally (this perpetual misunderstanding is exactly the 'tragic')."

[9] Cf. Mastronarde (2010) 23 on the way that tragedy dispenses with one simple poetic voice for a multiplicity of viewpoints: "Such voices may have different degrees of authority for the audience and may suffer from some partiality in their interpretation.... The shifting process of interpretation

tions that foster the interpretation that part of his purpose in writing these tragedies was to place his works in dialogue with the Augustan poets and highlight that this *aemulatio* is an integral part of his poetics. By tracing Seneca's intertextual connections, one can glimpse his own reading of the Greek and Latin literary canon and see not only how that tradition shaped his writing but also how he continued to shape that tradition for his own literary ends.

---

on the part of the audience, involving an expanded awareness of complexity and conflict, is probably more significant as 'instruction' of the audience than any particular gnomic observation."

BIBLIOGRAPHY

Adams, J. N. (1982) *The Latin Sexual Vocabulary*. London.
Ahern, Charles F. Jr. (1990) "Ovid as *vates* in the Proem to the *Ars Amatoria*." *CP* 85: 44-8.
Ahl, Frederick (1985) *Metaformations: Soundplay and Wordplay in Ovid and Other Classical Authors*. Ithaca.
——— (2000) "Seneca and Chaucer." In G. W. M. Harrison (2000): 151–72.
——— (2008) *Two Faces of Oedipus: Sophocles' Oedipus Tyrannus and Seneca's Oedipus*. Ithaca.
Amoroso, Filippo (1981) "Annunzi e scene d'annunzio nel teatro di L. Anneo Seneca." *Dioniso* 52: 307–38.
Anderson, William S. (1978) *Ovid's Metamorphoses Books 6–10*. Norman.
——— (1996) *Ovid's Metamorphoses Books 1–5*. Norman.
Arcellaschi, André (1996) "La Violence Dans La Médée de Sénèque." *Pallas* 45: 183–90.
Armisen-Marchetti, Mireille (1992) "Pour une lecture plurielle des tragedies de Sénèque: L'exemple de Phèdre, v. 130–135." *Pallas* 38: 379–90.
——— (2008) "Imagination and Meditation in Seneca: The Example of *Praemeditatio*." In Fitch (2008): 102–13.
Armstrong, Rebecca (2006) *Cretan Women*. Oxford.
Austin, R. G. (1955) *P. Vergili Maronis Aeneidos: Liber Quartus*. Oxford.
——— (1964) *P. Vergili Maronis Aeneidos: Liber Secundus*. Oxford.
——— (1971) *P. Vergili Maronis Aeneidos: Liber Primus*. Oxford.
——— (1977) *P. Vergili Maronis Aeneidos: Liber Sextus*. Oxford.
Auvray, C. (1987) "La Citation virgilienne dans les Lettres à Lucilius de Sénèque: Des praecepta aux decreta du Stoïcisme." *BFLM* 15: 29–34.
Aygon, J.-P. (2004) *Pictor in fabula: L'ecphrasis-descriptio dans les tragedies de Sénèque*. Brussels.
Baca, Albert R. (1971) "The Themes of *Querela* and *Lacrimae* in Ovid's *Heroides*." *Emerita* 39: 195–201.
Baertschi, Annette M. (2010) "Drama and Epic Narrative: The Test Case of Messenger Speech in Seneca's *Agamemnon*." In Gildenhard and Revermann (2010): 249–68.
Bakhtin, M. M. (1981) *The Dialogic Imagination*. Trans. Caryl Emerson and Michael Holquist. Austin.
Barchiesi, Alessandro (1993) "Future Reflexive: Two Modes of Allusion and Ovid's *Heroides*." *HSCP* 95: 333–65.
——— (2001) *Speaking Volumes*. London.
——— (2002) "Narrative Technique and Narratology in the *Metamorphoses*." In Hardie (2002): 180–99.
Barrett, James (2002) *Staged Narrative: Poetics and the Messenger in Greek Tragedy*. Berkeley.
Barrett, W. S. (1964) *Euripides: Hippolytus*. Oxford.

Barthes, Roland (1977) *Image, Music, Text*. Trans. Stephen Heath. New York.
Bartsch, Shadi (1994) *Actors in the Audience: Theatricality and Doublespeak from Nero to Hadrian*. Cambridge.
——— (2006) *The Mirror of the Self: Sexuality, Self-Knowledge, and the Gaze in the Early Roman Empire*. Chicago.
——— (2007) "'Wait a Moment, Phantasia': Ekphrastic Interference in Seneca and Epictetus." *CP* 102: 83–95.
Bartsch, Shadi, and David Wray, eds. (2009) *Seneca and the Self*. Cambridge.
Batinski, Emily E. (1991) "Horace's Rehabilitation of Bacchus." *CW* 84: 361–78.
——— (1993) "Seneca's Response to Stoic Hermeneutics." *Mnemosyne* 46: 69–77.
Batstone, William W. (2002) "Catullus and Bakhtin." In Branham (2002): 99–136.
Beacham, Richard C. (1998) *Spectacle Entertainments of Early Imperial Rome*. New Haven.
Beard, Mary, John North, and Simon Price. (1998) *Religions of Rome, Vol. 1*. Cambridge.
Beare, William B. (1951) *The Roman Stage*. Cambridge.
——— (1959) "Contaminatio." *CR* 9: 7–11.
Benton, Cindy (2002) "Split Vision: The Politics of the Gaze in Seneca's *Troades*." In Fredrick (2002): 31–56.
——— (2003) "Bringing the Other to Center Stage: Seneca's *Medea* and the Anxieties of Imperialism." *Arethusa* 36: 271–86.
Berti, Emanuele (2007) *Scholasticorum Studia: Seneca il Vecchio e la cultura retorica e letteraria della prima età imperiale*. Pisa.
Bettini, Maurizio (1983) "L'arcobaleno, l'incesto e l'enigma: A proposition dell'Oedipus di Seneca." *Dioniso* 54: 137–53.
——— (2008) "Weighty Words, Suspect Speech: *Fari* in Roman Culture." *Arethusa* 41: 313–75.
Betts, J. H., J. T. Hooker, and J. R. Oren, eds. (1986) *Studies in Honour of T. B. L. Webster*. Bristol.
Billerbeck, M., and E. Schmidt (1994) *Sénèque Le Tragique*. Genève.
Bishop, J. D. (1972) "Seneca's *Troades*: Dissolution of a Way of Life." *RhM* 115: 329–37.
——— (1985) *Seneca's Daggered Stylus: Political Code in the Tragedies*. Meisenheim am Glan.
Blevins, Jacob, ed. (2008) *Dialogism and Lyric Self-Fashioning: Bakhtin and the Voices of a Genre*. Selinsgrove.
Boal, Augusto (1979) *Theatre of the Oppressed*. New York.
Boldrini, Sandro and Francesco della Corte, eds. (1987) *Filologia e forme letterarie: Studi offerti a F. delle Corte*. Urbino.
Bonner, S. F. (1949) *Roman Declamation*. Liverpool.
Boyle, A. J., ed. (1983) *Seneca Tragicus*. Maryborough.
——— (1985) "In Nature's Bonds: A Study of Seneca's 'Phaedra.'" *Aufstieg und Niedergang der römischen Welt* 2.32.2: 1284–347.
——— (1987) *Seneca's Phaedra*. Leeds.
———, ed. (1988) *The Imperial Muse: Ramus Essays on Roman Literature of the Empire*. Victoria.
——— (1994) *Seneca's Troades*. Leeds.
——— (1997) *Tragic Seneca: An Essay in the Theatrical Tradition*. London.
——— (2006) *An Introduction to Roman Tragedy*. London.
——— (2008) *Octavia: Attributed to Seneca*. Oxford.
——— (2011) *Seneca: Oedipus*. Oxford.
Branham, R. Bracht, ed. (2002) *Bakhtin and the Classics*. Evanston.
Braund, S. M. (2002) *Latin Literature*. London and New York.
——— (2009) *Seneca, De Clementia*. Oxford.
Braund, S. M., and C. Gill, eds. (1997) *The Passions in Roman Thought and Literature*. Cambridge.
Bremmer, Jan N. (1997) "Why Did Medea Kill Her Brother Apsyrtus?" In Clauss and Johnston (1997): 83–102.
Briggs, W. W., Jr. (1980) *Narrative and Simile from the Georgics in the Aeneid*. Leiden.
Brink, C. O. (1963) *Horace on Poetry: Prolegomena to the Literary Epistles*. Cambridge.
——— (1971) *Horace on Poetry: The "Ars Poetica."* Cambridge.

Brissenden, R. F., and J. C. Eade, eds. (1976) *Studies in the Eighteenth Century 3*. Canberra.
Brunschwig J., and Martha Nussbaum, eds. (1993) *Passions and Perceptions: Proceedings of the 5th Symposium Hellenisticum*. Cambridge.
Burden, Michael, ed. (1998) *A Woman Scorn'd: Responses to the Dido Myth*. London.
Burian, Peter (1997) "Myth into *Mythos*: The Shaping of Tragic Plot." In Easterling (1997): 178–208.
Busch, Austin (2007) *"Versane Natura Est?* Natural and Linguistic Instability in the *Extispicium* and Self-Blinding of Seneca's *Oedipus*." *CJ* 102: 225–67.
——— (2009) "Dissolution of the Self in the Senecan Corpus." In Bartsch and Wray (2009): 255–82.
Cairns, F., ed. (1990) *Papers of the Leeds International Latin Seminar, Vol. 6*. Leeds.
Calder, William M. (1970) "Originality in Seneca's *Troades*." *CP* 65: 75–82.
Calvino, Italo (1982) *The Uses of Literature*. San Diego.
Cancik, H. (1967) *Untersuchungen zu Senecas* Epistulae Morales. Hildesheim.
Canter, Howard V. (1925) *Rhetorical Elements in the Tragedies of Seneca*. Urbana.
Casali, S. (1995) "Strategies of Tension (Ovid, *Heroides* 4)." *PCPS* 41: 1–15.
Casamento, Alfredo (2002) *Finitimus oratori poeta: Declamazioni retoriche e tragedie senecane*. Palermo.
——— (2011) *Seneca: Fedra*. Rome.
Clausen, Wendell (1994) *A Commentary on Virgil*, Eclogues. Oxford.
Clauss, James J., and Sarah Iles Johnston, eds. (1997) *Medea: Essays on Medea in Myth, Literature, Philosophy, and Art*. Princeton.
Cleasby, H. L. (1907) "The Medea of Seneca." *HSCP* 18: 39–71.
Coffey, M. and Roland Mayer, eds. (1990) *Seneca: Phaedra*. Cambridge.
Colakis, Marianthe (1985) "Life after Death in Seneca's *Troades*." *CW* 78: 149–55.
Commager, Steele (1962) *The Odes of Horace: A Critical Study*. New Haven.
Connor, P. J. (1971) "Enthusiasm, Poetry, and Politics: A Consideration of Horace, Odes, III, 25." *AJP* 92: 266–74.
Conte, G. B. (1986) *The Rhetoric of Imitation*. Trans. C. Segal. Ithaca.
——— (1994a) *Genres and Readers*. Trans. G. W. Most. Baltimore.
——— (1994b) *Latin Literature*. Trans. J. B. Solodow. Baltimore.
——— (2007) *The Poetry of Pathos*. Oxford.
Copley, F. (1947) "*Servitium amoris* in the Roman Elegists." *TAPA* 78: 285–300.
Costa, C. D. N. (1973) *Seneca: Medea*. Oxford.
Csapo, Eric, and William J. Slater, eds. (1994) *The Context of Ancient Drama*. Ann Arbor.
Curley, Dan (2013) *Tragedy in Ovid: Theater, Metatheater, and the Transformation of a Genre*. Cambridge.
Curley, T. F. (1986) *The Nature of Senecan Drama*. Rome.
Curran, Leo C. (1969) "Catullus 64 and the Heroic Age." *YCS* 21: 169–92.
Dahlmann, Hellfried (1977) "Nochmals 'Ducunt Volentem Fata, Nolentem Trahunt.'" *Hermes* 105: 342–51.
Damon, Cynthia (2010) "Too Close? Historian and Poet in the *Apocolocyntosis*." In Miller and Woodman (2010): 49–70.
Davis, P. J. (1983) "*Vindicat Omnes Natura Sibi:* A Reading of Seneca's *Phaedra*." In Boyle (1983): 114–27.
——— (1991) "Fate and Human Responsibility in Seneca's *Oedipus*." *Latomus* 50: 150–63.
——— (1993) *Shifting Song: The Chorus in Seneca's Tragedies*. Hildesheim.
DeBrohun, Jeri B. (1999) "Ariadne and the Whirlwind of Fate: Figures of Confusion in Catullus 64.149–57." *CP* 94: 419–30.
Degl'Innocenti Pierini, Rita (1990) *Tra Ovidio e Seneca*. Bologna.
DeJong, Irene J. F. (1991) *Narrative in Drama: The Art of the Euripidean Messenger-Speech*. Leiden.
DeLacy, Phillip (1948) "Stoic Views of Poetry." *AJP* 69: 241–71.
De Meo, C. (1978) *Il prologo della "Phaedra" di Seneca*. Bologna.

Depew, Mary, and Dirk Obbink, eds. (2000) *Matrices of Genre*. Cambridge.
DeVito, Ann F. (1994) "The Essential Seriousness of *Heroides* 4." *RhM* 137: 312–30.
De Vivo, Arturo, and Elio Lo Cascio, eds. (2003) *Seneca Uomo Politico e l'età di Claudio e di Nerone*. Bari.
Dickison, Sheila K., and Judith P. Hallett, eds. (2000) *Rome and Her Monuments: Essays on the City and Literature of Rome in Honor of Katherine A. Geffcken*. Wauconda.
Dominik, William J., ed. (1997) *Roman Eloquence: Rhetoric in Society and Literature*. London.
Dominik, William J., and Jon Hall, eds. (2007) *A Companion to Roman Rhetoric*. Chichester.
Dörrie, H. (1971) *P. Ovidii Nasonis Epistulae Heroidum*. Berlin.
Dressler, Alex (2012) "You Must Change Your Life: Theory and Practice, Metaphor and *Exemplum*, in Seneca's Prose." *Helios* 39: 145–91.
Easterling, P. E., ed. (1997) *The Cambridge Companion to Greek Tragedy*. Cambridge.
Easterling, P. E., and E. Hall, eds. (2002) *Greek and Roman Actors*. Oxford.
Eden, P. T. (1984) *Seneca: Apocolocyntosis*. Cambridge.
Edmunds, Lowell (2001) *Intertextuality and the Reading of Roman Poetry*. Baltimore.
Edwards, Catherine (1997) "Self-Scrutiny and Self-Transformation in Seneca's Letters." *G&R* 44: 23–38.
——— (2002) "Acting and Self-Actualisation in Imperial Rome: Some Death Scenes." In Easterling and Hall (2002): 377–94.
Edwards, Mark (1987) *Homer: Poet of the* Iliad. Baltimore.
Eliot, T. S. (1941) *Points of View*. London.
——— (1950) *Selected Essays: New Edition*. New York.
Elsner, J., and J. Masters, eds. (1994) *Reflections of Nero: Culture, History, and Representation*. Chapel Hill.
Erasmo, Mario (2004) *Roman Tragedy: Theatre to Theatricality*. Austin.
Evans, Elizabeth C. (1950) "A Stoic Aspect of Senecan Drama: Portraiture." *TAPA* 31: 169–84.
Fantham, Elaine (1975) "Virgil's Dido and Seneca's Heroines." *G&R* 22: 1–10.
——— (1978) "Imitation and Decline: Rhetorical Theory and Practice in the First Century after Christ." *CP* 73: 102–16.
——— (1981) "Seneca's *Troades* and *Agamemnon*: Continuity and Sequence." *CJ* 77: 118–29.
——— (1982) *Seneca's Troades*. Princeton.
——— (1996) *Roman Literary Culture: From Cicero to Apuleius*. Baltimore.
Fantuzzi, Marco, and Theodore Papanghelis, eds. (2006) *Brill's Companion to Greek and Latin Pastoral*. Leiden.
Farrell, Joseph (1991) *Vergil's* Georgics *and the Traditions of Ancient Epic: The Art of Allusion in Literary History*. Oxford.
——— (1992) "Dialogue of Genres in Ovid's 'Lovesong of Polyphemus' (*Metamorphoses* 13. 719–897)." *AJP* 113: 235–68.
——— (1998) "Reading and Writing the *Heroides*." *HSCP* 98: 307–38.
Feeney, D. C. (1991) *The Gods in Epic: Poets and Critics of the Classical Tradition*. Oxford.
——— (1998) *Literature and Religion at Rome: Cultures, Contexts, and Beliefs*. Cambridge.
Feldherr, Andrew (2010) *Playing Gods: Ovid's* Metamorphoses *and the Politics of Fiction*. Princeton.
Ferri, Rolando (2003) *Octavia: A Play Attributed to Seneca*. Cambridge.
Fitch, John G. (1981) "Sense-Pauses and Relative Dating in Seneca, Sophocles and Shakespeare." *AJP* 102: 289–307.
——— (1987a) *Seneca's Hercules Furens*. Cornell.
——— (1987b) *Seneca's Anapests: Meter, Colometry, Text and Artistry in the Anapests of Seneca's Tragedies*. Atlanta.
——— (2002) *Seneca: Tragedies 1*. Cambridge.
——— (2004a) *Seneca: Tragedies 2*. Cambridge.
——— (2004b) *Annaeana Tragica: Notes on the Text of Seneca's Tragedies*. Leiden.
———, ed. (2008) *Oxford Readings in Classical Studies: Seneca*. Oxford.

Fitch, John G., and Siobhan McElduff (2002) "Construction of the Self in Senecan Drama." *Mnemosyne* 55: 18–40.
Fitzgerald, William (1995) *Catullan Provocations: Lyric Poetry and the Drama of Position*. Berkeley.
Fitzgerald, William and Emily Gowers, eds. (2007) *Ennius Perennis: The Annals and Beyond*. Cambridge.
Foucault, Michel (1986) *The Care of The Self: The History of Sexuality*, vol. 3. Trans. Robert Hurley. New York.
——— (2005) *The Hermeneutics of the Subject: Lectures at the Collège de France 1981–2*. Trans. Graham Burchell. New York.
Fowler, Don (1997) "Virgilian Narrative: Story-Telling." In Martindale (1997): 259–70.
——— (2000) *Roman Constructions*. Oxford.
Fraenkel, Eduard (1957) *Horace*. Oxford.
Frank, Marcia (1995a) "The Rhetorical Use of Family Terms in Seneca's *Oedipus* and *Phoenissae*." *Phoenix* 49: 121–29.
——— (1995b) *Seneca's* Phoenissae: *Introduction and Commentary*. Leiden.
Fredrick, David, ed. (2002) *The Roman Gaze: Vision, Power, and the Body*. Baltimore.
Freudenburg, Kirk (1993) *The Walking Muse: Horace on the Theory of Satire*. Princeton.
Fugmann, Joachim, Markus Janka, Ulrich Schmitzer, and Helmut Seng, eds. (2004) *Theater, Theaterpraxis, Theaterkritik im kaiserzeitlichen Rom*. Munich.
Fulkerson, Laurel (2005) *The Ovidian Heroine as Author*. Cambridge.
Fyfe, Helen (1983) "An Analysis of Seneca's *Medea*." In Boyle (1983): 77–93.
Gadamer, H. G. (1975) *Truth and Method*. Trans. G. Barden and J. Cumming. London.
Gahen, John T. (1988) "Imitation in Seneca, 'Phaedra' 1000–1115." *Hermes* 116: 122–24.
Gaisser, Julia Haig (1995) "Threads in the Labyrinth: Competing Views and Voices in Catullus 64." *AJP* 116: 579–616.
Gale, Monica R. (2000) *Virgil on the Nature of Things: The Georgics, Lucretius and the Didactic Tradition*. Cambridge.
Galinsky, G. K. (1988) "The Anger of Aeneas." *AJP* 109: 321–48.
Garelli-François, M-H. (1998) "Tradition littéraire et creation dramatique dans les tragedies de Sénèque: L'exemple des récits de messagers." *Latomus* 57: 15–32.
Garrison, Daniel H. (1991) *Horace: Epodes and Odes*. Norman.
Garton, Charles (1972) *Personal Aspects of the Roman Theatre*. Toronto.
Gildenhard, I. (2007) "Virgil vs. Ennius, Or: The Undoing of the Annalist." In Fitzgerald and Gowers (2007): 73–102.
Gildenhard, I., and M. Revermann, eds. (2010) *Beyond the Fifth Century: Interactions with Greek Tragedy from the Fourth Century BCE to the Middle Ages*. Berlin.
Gildenhard, I., and A. Zissos (2000) "Ovid's Narcissus (*Met.* 3.339–510): Echoes of Oedipus." *AJP* 121: 129–47.
Gill, Christopher (1987) "Two Monologues of Self-Division: Euripides, *Medea* 1021–80 and Seneca, *Medea* 893–977." In Whitby and Hardie (1987): 25–37.
——— (1997) "Passion as Madness in Roman Poetry." In Braund and Gill (1997): 213–41.
Goldberg, Sander M. (1996) "The Fall and Rise of Roman Tragedy." *TAPA* 126: 265–86.
——— (1997) "Melpomene's Declamation (Rhetoric and Tragedy)." In Dominik (1997): 166–81.
——— (2005) *Constructing Literature in the Roman Republic: Poetry and Its Reception*. Cambridge.
Goldhill, Simon (1986) *Reading Greek Tragedy*. Cambridge.
——— (1997) "The Language of Tragedy: Rhetoric and Communication." In Easterling (1997): 127–50.
Goward, Barbara (1999) *Telling Tragedy: Narrative Technique in Aeschylus, Sophocles and Euripides*. London.
Gowing, Alain (2005) *Empire and Memory: The Representation of the Roman Republic in Imperial Culture*. Cambridge.
Graf (1997) "Medea, the Enchantress from Afar." In Clauss and Johnston (1997): 21–43.

——— (2002) "Myth in Ovid." In Hardie (2002): 108–21.
Gransden, K. W. (1976) *Virgil: Aeneid Book 8*. Cambridge.
Green, Steven J. (2004) *Ovid, Fasti 1: A Commentary*. Leiden.
Greene, Thomas M. (1982) *The Light in Troy: Imitation and Discovery in Renaissance Poetry*. New Haven.
Gregory, Justina, ed. (2005) *A Companion to Greek Tragedy*. Oxford.
Griffin, Miriam (1976) *Seneca: A Philosopher in Politics*. Oxford.
——— (1984) *Nero: The End of a Dynasty*. New Haven.
——— (2003) "Seneca as a Sociologist: *De Beneficiis*." In De Vivo and Lo Cascio (2003): 89–122.
——— (2013) *Seneca on Society: A Guide to* De Beneficiis. Oxford.
Grimal, P. (1963) "L'originalité de Sénèque dans la Tragédie de Phèdre." *REL* 41: 297–314.
———, ed. (1991) *Sénèque et la prose latine*. Vandoeuvres-Geneva.
Guastella, Gianni (2001) "*Virgo, Coniunx, Mater:* The Wrath of Seneca's Medea." *CA* 20: 197–220.
Günther, Hans-Christian, ed. (2013) *Brill's Companion to Horace*. Leiden.
Ter Haar Romeny, H. M. B. (1887) *De auctore tragoediarum, quae sub Senecae nomine feruntur, Vergilii imitatore*. Leiden.
Hachmann, E. (1996) "Die Spruchepiloge in Senecas *Epistulae morales*." *Gymnasium* 103: 385–410.
Hadas, Moses (1939) "The Roman Stamp of Seneca's Tragedies." *AJP* 60: 220–31.
Hall, Edith, ed. (2000) *Medea in Performance: 1500–2000*. Oxford.
Hardie, Philip (1986) *Virgil's* Aeneid: *Cosmos and Imperium*. Oxford.
——— (1993) *The Epic Successors of Virgil*. Cambridge.
———, ed. (2002) *The Cambridge Companion to Ovid*. Cambridge.
Hardie, P., A. Barchiesi, and Stephen Hinds, eds. (1999) *Ovidian Transformations: Essays on Ovid's* Metamorphoses *and Its Reception*. Cambridge.
Harrison, George W. M., ed. (2000) *Seneca in Performance*. London.
Harrison, Stephen J., ed. (2001) *Texts, Ideas and the Classics*. Oxford.
——— (2002) "Ovid and Genre: Evolutions of an Elegist." In Hardie (2002): 79–94.
———, ed. (2005) *A Companion to Latin Literature*. Oxford.
———, ed. (2007a) *The Cambridge Companion to Horace*. Cambridge.
——— (2007b) *Generic Enrichment in Vergil and Horace*. Cambridge.
Heinze, T. (1997) *P. Ovidius Naso. Der 12. Heroidenbrief: Medea an Jason*. Leiden.
Henderson, John (1983) "Poetic Technique and Rhetorical Amplification: Seneca *Medea* 579–669." In Boyle (1983): 94–113.
——— (2004) *Morals and Villas in Seneca's Letters: Places to Dwell*. Cambridge.
Henry, Denis, and B. Walker (1966) "Phantasmagoria and Idyll: An Element of Seneca's 'Phaedra.'" *G&R* 13: 223–39.
——— (1985) *The Mask of Power: Seneca's Tragedies and Imperial Rome*. Warminster.
Herter, H. (1971) "Phaidra in griechischer und römischer Gestalt." *RhM* 14: 44–77.
Hexter, Ralph, and Daniel Seldon, eds. (1992) *Innovations of Antiquity*. New York.
Hijmans, B. L., Jr. (1966) "Drama in Seneca's Stoicism." *TAPA* 97: 237–51.
Hill, D. E. (2000) "Seneca's Choruses." *Mnemosyne* 53: 561–87.
Hill, Timothy D. (2004) *Ambitiosa Mors: Suicide and Self in Roman Thought and Literature*. New York.
Hinds, Stephen (1987) *The Metamorphosis of Persephone*. Cambridge.
——— (1992) "*Arma* in Ovid's *Fasti*: Part 1: Genre and Mannerism." *Arethusa* 81–112.
——— (1993) "Medea in Ovid: Scenes from the Life of an Intertextual Heroine." *MD* 30: 9–47.
——— (1998) *Allusion and Intertext*. Cambridge.
——— (2011) "Seneca's Ovidian *Loci*." *SIFC* 9: 5–63.
Hine, H. M. (1987) Review of *Seneca's Troades, et al. JRS* 77: 256–58.
——— (1989) "Medea versus the Chorus: Seneca *Medea* 1–115." *Mnemosyne* 42: 413–19.
——— (1994) "*Interpretatio Stoica* of Senecan Tragedy." In Billerbeck and Schmidt (1994): 173–220.
——— (2000) *Seneca: Medea*. Warminster.

——— (2005) "Poetic Influence on Prose: The Case of the Younger Seneca." *Proceedings of the British Academy* 129: 211–37.
——— (2009) "Seneca's *Naturales Quaestiones* 1960–2005 (Part 1)." *Lustrum* 51: 253–329.
Hollander, J. (1981) *The Figure of Echo: A Mode of Allusion in Milton and After*. Berkeley.
Holquist, Michael (1990) *Dialogism: Bakhtin and his World*. London.
Hook, Brian S. (2000) "Nothing Within Which Passeth Show: Character and *Color* in Senecan Tragedy." In G. W. M. Harrison (2000): 53–71.
Hooley, D.M. (1997) *The Knotted Thong: Structures of Mimesis in Persius*. Ann Arbor.
Howe, Irving (1992) "The Self in Literature." In Levine (1992): 249–67.
Hutchinson, G. O. (1993) *Latin Literature from Seneca to Juvenal*. Oxford.
Inwood, Brad (2005) *Reading Seneca*. Oxford.
——— (2007) "The Importance of Form in Seneca." In Morello and Morrison (2007): 133–48.
Irvine, William B. (2009) *A Guide to the Good Life: The Ancient Art of Stoic Joy*. Oxford.
Irwin, William (2004) "Against Intertextuality." *Philosophy and Literature* 28: 227–42.
Jacobson, H. (1974) *Ovid's Heroides*. Princeton.
Jakobi, Rainer (1988) *Der Einfluß Ovids auf den Tragiker Seneca*. Berlin.
James, Sharon (2003) "Her Time to Cry: The Politics of Weeping in Roman Love Elegy." *TAPA* 133: 99–122.
Janan, Micaela (1991) "'The Labyrinth and the Mirror': Incest and Influence in *Metamorphoses* 9." *Arethusa* 24: 239–56.
Janka, Markus (2004) "Senecas *Phaedra*: Des Dramas Kern und sein episch-elegischer Rahmen." In Fugmann et al. (2004): 25–57.
Jenkins, Thomas E. (2000) "The Writing in (and of) Ovid's Byblis Episode." *HSCP* 100: 439–51.
Jocelyn, H. D. (1969) *The Tragedies of Ennius*. Cambridge.
Jory, E. J. (1986) "Continuity and Change in the Roman Theatre." In Betts, Hooker, and Oren (1986): 143–52.
Kallendorf, Craig (2006) "Virgil, Milton, and the Modern Reader." In Martindale and Thomas (2006): 67–79.
Kaster, Robert A. (2005) *Emotion, Restraint, and Community in Ancient Rome*. Oxford.
Kelly, Henry A. (1993) *Ideas and Forms of Tragedy from Aristotle to the Middle Ages*. Cambridge.
Kennedy, Duncan F. (1984) "The Epistolary Mode and the First of Ovid's *Heroides*." *CQ* 34: 413–22.
——— (1989) Review of Knox (1986) and Hinds (1987). *JRS* 79: 209–10.
——— (1993) *The Arts of Love*. Cambridge.
——— (2002) "Epistolarity: The *Heroides*." In Hardie (2002): 217–32.
Kennedy, George (1972) *The Art of Rhetoric in the Roman World*. Princeton.
Ker, James (2006) "Seneca, Man of Many Genres." In Volk and Williams (2006): 19–41.
——— (2009) *The Deaths of Seneca*. Oxford.
Kerrigan, John (1996) *Revenge Tragedy: Aeschylus to Armageddon*. Oxford.
Keulen, Atze J. (2001) *L. Annaeus Seneca: Troades*. Leiden.
Kirk, G. S. (1990) *The Iliad: A Commentary. Vol. 2: Books 5–8*. Cambridge.
Knox, Peter E. (1986) *Ovid's Metamorphoses and the Traditions of Augustan Poetry*. Cambridge.
——— (1995) *Ovid Heroides: Select Epistles*. Cambridge.
Kohn, Thomas D. (2013) *The Dramaturgy of Senecan Tragedy*. Ann Arbor.
Laird, Andrew (1999) *Powers of Expression, Expressions of Power*. Oxford.
———, ed. (2006) *Ancient Literary Criticism*. Oxford.
——— (2007) "The *Ars Poetica*." In S. J. Harrison (2007): 132–43.
Larmour, David H. J. (1990) "Tragic 'Contaminatio' in Ovid's 'Metamorphoses': Procne and Medea; Philomela and Iphigeneia (6.424–674); Scylla and Phaedra (8.19–151)." *ICS* 15: 131–41.
Larson, Victoria Tietze (1994) *The Role of Description in Senecan Tragedy*. Frankfurt am Main.
Lawall, Gilbert (1982) "Death and Perspective in Seneca's *Troades*." *CJ* 77: 244–52.
——— (1983) "*Virtus* and *pietas* in Seneca's *Hercules Furens*." In Boyle (1983): 6–26.

Leach, Eleanor W. (1989) "The Implied Reader and the Political Argument in Seneca's *Apocolocyntosis* and *De Clementia*." *Arethusa* 22: 197–230.
Lentricchia, Frank, and Thomas McLaughlin, eds. (1990) *Critical Terms for Literary Study*. 2nd ed. Chicago and London.
Leo, F. (1878) *De Senecae tragoediis observationes criticae*. Berlin.
Lethem, Jonathan (2011) *The Ecstasy of Influence*. New York.
Levine, George, ed. (1992) *Constructions of the Self*. New Brunswick.
Lindheim, Sara H. (2003) *Mail and Female: Epistolary Narrative and Desire in Ovid's Heroides*. Madison.
Littlewood, C. A. J. (2004) *Self-Representation and Illusion in Senecan Tragedy*. Oxford.
Liveley, Genevieve (2011) *Ovid's "Metamorphoses."* London.
Lloyd-Jones, Hugh (1996) *Sophocles: Fragments*. Cambridge.
Long, A. A. (1996) *Stoic Studies*. Cambridge.
Lyne, R. O. A. M. (1979) "*Servitium amoris*." *CQ* 29: 117–30.
MacIntosh, Fiona (2000) "Introduction: The Performer in Performance." In Hall (2000): 1–31.
Mader, Gottfried (1997) "*Duplex nefas, ferus spectator*: Spectacle and Spectator in Act 5 of Seneca's *Troades*." *Latomus* 8: 319–51.
——— (1998) "*Quod Nolunt Velint*: Deference and Doublespeak at Seneca, *Thyestes* 334–335." *CJ* 94: 31–47.
Maguinness, W. S. (1956) "Seneca and the Poets." *Hermathena* 88: 81–98.
Manning, C.E. (1976) "Seneca's 98th Letter and the 'Praemeditatio futuri mali.'" *Mnemosyne* 29: 301–4.
Manuwald, Gesine (2011) *Roman Republican Theatre*. Cambridge.
Marti, B. M. (1945) "Seneca's Tragedies: A New Interpretation." *TAPA* 76: 216–45.
Martina, Antonio (1992) "Alcune considerazioni sul concetto di imitazione in Orazio e in Seneca." *QCTC* 10: 113–32.
Martindale, Charles (1993) *Redeeming the Text: Latin Poetry and the Hermeneutics of Reception*. Cambridge.
——— ed. (1997) *Cambridge Companion to Virgil*. Cambridge.
Martindale, Charles, and Richard F. Thomas, eds. (2006) *Classics and the Uses of Reception*. Oxford.
Mastronarde, Donald J. (1970) "Seneca's *Oedipus*: The Drama in the Word." *TAPA* 101: 291–315.
——— (2010) *The Art of Euripides: Dramatic Technique and Social Context*. Cambridge.
Maurach, G. (1970) *Der Bau von Senecas epistulae morales*. Heidelberg.
Mayer, Roland (1982) "Neronian Classicism." *AJP* 103: 305–18.
——— (1991) "Roman Historical *Exempla* in Seneca." In Grimal (1991): 141–76.
——— (1994) "Personata Stoa: Neostoicism and Senecan Tragedy." *JWCI* 57: 151–74.
——— (2005) "The Early Empire: AD 14–68." In S. J. Harrison (2005): 58–68.
——— (2011) "Latin Pastoral after Virgil." In Fantuzzi and Papanghelis (2011): 451–66.
Mazzoli, G. (1970) *Seneca e la Poesia*. Milan.
McAuley, Mairéad (2012) "Specters of Medea: The Rhetoric of Stepmotherhood and Motherhood in Seneca's *Phaedra*." *Helios* 39: 37–72.
McGill, Scott (2005) "Seneca the Elder on Plagiarizing Cicero's *Verrines*." *Rhetorica* 23: 337–46.
——— (2013) *Plagiarism in Latin Literature*. Cambridge.
McKeown, J. C. (1989) *Ovid: Amores, A Commentary on Book One*. Leeds.
——— (1998) *Ovid: Amores, A Commentary on Book Two*. Leeds.
Merchant, Frank I. (1905) "Seneca and His Theory of Style." *AJP* 26: 44–59.
Merzlak, R. F. (1983) "*Furor* in Seneca's *Phaedra*." *Latomus* 180: 193–210.
Miles, Gary B. (1980) *Virgil's Georgics: A New Interpretation*. Berkeley.
Miller, J. Hillis (1990) "Narrative." In Lentricchia and McLaughlin (1990): 66–79.
Miller, John F. (1993) "Ovidian Allusion and the Vocabulary of Memory." *MD* 30: 153–64.
Miller, John F., and A. J. Woodman, eds. (2010) *Latin Historiography and Poetry in the Early Empire: Generic Interactions*. Leiden.
Morello, Ruth, and A. D. Morrison, eds. (2007) *Ancient Letters: Classical and Late Antique Epistolography*. Oxford.

Morgon, Llewelyn (2003) "Child's Play: Ovid and His Critics." *JRS* 93: 66–91.
Most, Glenn W. (1992) "Disiecti Membra Poetae: The Rhetoric of Dismemberment in Neronian Poetry." In Hexter and Seldon (1992): 391–419.
——— (2000) "Generating Genres: The Idea of the Tragic." In Depew and Obbink (2000): 15–35.
Motto, A. L., and J. R. Clark (1972) "Senecan Tragedy: Patterns of Irony and Art." *CB* 48: 69–76.
Mowbray, Carrie (2012) "Captive Audience? The Aesthetics of *Nefas* in Senecan Drama." In Sluiter and Rosen (2012): 393–420.
Murgatroyd, P. (1981) "*Servitium amoris* and the Roman Elegists." *Latomus* 40: 589–600.
Mynors, R. A. B. (1990) *Virgil: Georgics*. Oxford.
Newlands, Carole E. (1997) "The Metamorphosis of Ovid's Medea." In Clauss and Johnston (1997): 178–208.
Newman, J.K. (1967) *The Concept of vates in Augustan Poetry*. Brussels.
Nightingale, Andrea W. (1995) *Genres in Dialogue: Plato and the Construct of Philosophy*. Cambridge.
Nisbet, R. G. M. (1990) "The Dating of Seneca's Tragedies, with Special Reference to *Thyestes*." In Cairns (1990): 95–114.
Nisbet, R. G. M., and Margaret Hubbard, eds. (1970) *A Commentary on Horace, Odes, Book 1*. Oxford.
———, eds. (1978) *A Commentary on Horace, Odes, Book 2*. Oxford.
Nisbet, R. G. M., and Niall Rudd, eds. (2004) *A Commentary on Horace, Odes, Book 3*. Oxford.
Nussbaum, Martha C. (1993) "Poetry and the Passions: Two Stoic Views." In Brunschwig and Nussbaum (1993): 97–149.
——— (1994) *The Therapy of Desire*. Princeton.
Ogden, Daniel (2001) *Greek and Roman Necromancy*. Princeton.
——— (2009) *Magic, Witchcraft, and Ghosts in the Greek and Roman Worlds*. Oxford.
Owen, William H. (1970) "Time and Event in Seneca's *Troades*." *WS* 83: 118–37.
Palmieri, N. (1989) "'Alia temptanda est via': Allusivita e innovazione drammatica nell'*Edipo* di Seneca." *MD* 23: 175–89.
Panoussi, Lily (2005) "Polis and Empire: Greek Tragedy in Rome." In Gregory (2005): 413–27.
——— (2009) *Greek Tragedy in Vergil's Aeneid: Ritual, Empire, and Intertext*. Cambridge.
Parroni, Piergiorgio (2002) *Seneca: Ricerche Sulla Natura*. Milan.
Paschalis, Michael (1994) "The Bull and the Horse: Animal Theme and Imagery in Seneca's *Phaedra*." *AJP* 115: 105–28.
——— (2010) "Cassandra and the Passionate Lucidity of *Furor* in Seneca's *Agamemnon*." In Tsitsiridis (2010): 209–28.
Pavlock, Barbara (1990) *Eros, Imitation, and the Epic Tradition*. Ithaca.
——— (2009) *The Image of the Poet in Ovid's* Metamorphoses. Madison.
Peirano, Irene (2013) "*Non subripendi causa sed palam mutuandi*: Intertextuality and Literary Deviancy between Law, Rhetoric, and Literature in Roman Imperial Culture." *AJP* 134: 83–100.
Perkell, Christine, ed. (1999) *Reading Vergil's Aeneid: An Interpretive Guide*. Norman.
Pobjoy, Mark (1998) "Dido on the Tragic Stage: An Invitation to the Theatre of Carthage." In Burden (1998): 41–64.
Pratt, Norman T. (1939) *Dramatic Suspense in Seneca and in His Greek Predecessors*. Princeton.
——— (1983) *Seneca's Drama*. Chapel Hill and London.
Prauscello, Lucia (2008) "Juno's Wrath Again: Some Virgilian Echoes in Ovid, *Met*. 3.253–315." *CQ* 58.2: 565–70.
Prince, Meredith (2003) "Medea and the Inefficacy of Love Magic." *CB* 79.2: 205–18.
Pucci, Joseph (1992) "Horace and Virgilian Mimesis: A Re-Reading of 'Odes' 1.3." *CW* 85: 659–73.
Putnam, Michael C. J. (1961) "The Art of Catullus 64." *HSCP* 65: 165–205.
——— (1970) *Virgil's Pastoral Art: Studies in the* Eclogues. Princeton.
——— (1995) *Virgil's* Aeneid: *Interpretation and Influence*. Chapel Hill.

―― (1998) *Virgil's Epic Designs: Ekphrasis in the* Aeneid. New Haven.
―― (2000) *Horace's* Carmen Saeculare. New Haven.
―― (2006) *Poetic Interplay: Catullus and Horace*. Princeton and Oxford.
Raval, Shilpa (2001) "A Lover's Discourse: Byblis in *Metamorphoses* 9." *Arethusa* 34: 285–311.
Rayment, C. S. (1969) "Echoes of the Declamations in the Dialogues of the Younger Seneca." *CB* 45: 51–3, 63.
Regenbogen, Otto (1927–8) "Schmerz und Tod in den Tragödien Senecas." *Vorträge der Bibliothek Warburg* 7: 167–218.
Rehm, Rush (1994) *Marriage to Death: The Conflation of Wedding and Funeral Rituals in Greek Tragedy*. Princeton.
Relihan, Joel C. (1993) *Ancient Menippean Satire*. Baltimore.
Reydams-Schils, Gretchen (2005) *The Roman Stoics: Self, Responsibility, and Affection*. Chicago.
Richardson, L. (1976) *Propertius Elegies 1–4*. Norman.
Ricks, C. (1976) "Allusion: The Poet as Heir." In Brissenden and Eade (1976): 209–40.
Roisman, Hanna M. (2000) "A New Look at Seneca's *Phaedra*." In G. W. M. Harrison (2000): 73–86.
Romm, James S. (1992) *The Edges of the Earth in Ancient Thought*. Princeton.
Rosati, Gianpiero (1999) "Form in Motion: Weaving the Text in the *Metamorphoses*." In Hardie, Barchiesi, and Hinds (1999): 240–53.
Rosenmeyer, T. G. (1989) *Senecan Drama and Stoic Cosmology*. Berkeley.
―― (2000) "Seneca and Nature." *Arethusa* 33: 99–119.
―― (2002) "'Metatheater': An Essay on Overload." *Arion* 10: 87–119.
Ross, David O. (1975) *Backgrounds to Augustan Poetry: Gallus, Elegy and Rome*. Cambridge.
Rudd, Niall (1990) *Horace Epistles Book 2 and Epistle to the Pisones ("Ars Poetica")*. Cambridge.
Rudich, Vasily (1993) *Political Dissidence under Nero*. London.
―― (1997) *Dissidence and Literature under Nero*. London.
Russell, D. A. (2006) "Ars Poetica." In Laird (2006): 325–45.
Schiesaro, Alessandro (1992) "Forms of Senecan Intertextuality." *Vergilius* 38: 56–63.
―― (1994) "Seneca's *Thyestes* and the Morality of Tragic *Furor*." In Elsner and Masters (1994): 196–210.
―― (1997) "Passion, Reason and Knowledge in Seneca's Tragedies." In Braund and Gill (1997): 89–111.
―― (2003) *The Passions in Play*. Cambridge.
―― (2006) "A Dream Shattered? Pastoral Anxieties in Senecan Drama." In Fantuzzi and Papanghelis (2006: 427–50.
Segal, Charles (1982a) "*Nomen Sacrum*: Medea and Other Names in Senecan Tragedy." *Maia* 34: 241–46.
―― (1982b) *Dionysiac Poetics and Euripides'* Bacchae. Princeton.
―― (1983) "Dissonant Sympathy: Song, Orpheus, and the Golden Age in Seneca's Tragedies." In Boyle (1983): 229–51.
―― (1984) "Senecan Baroque: The Death of Hippolytus in Seneca, Ovid, and Euripides." *TAPA* 114: 311–26.
―― (1986) *Language and Desire in Seneca's* Phaedra. Princeton.
―― (1987) "Image and Action in Seneca's *Phaedra*: Five Motifs." In Boldrini and della Corte (1987): 341–57.
Seidensticker, B. (1985) "*Maius solito*: Senecas *Thyestes* und die tragoedia rhetorica." *AA* 31: 116–36.
Setaioli, Aldo (1985) "Seneca e lo stile." *Aufstieg und Niedergang der römischen Welt* 2.32.2: 776–858.
―― (2000) *Facundus Seneca*. Bologna.
Shelton, Jo-Ann (1978) *Seneca's Hercules Furens: Theme, Structure, Style*. Göttingen.
―― (1979) "Seneca's *Medea* as Mannerist Literature." *Poetica* 11: 38–82.
―― (1983) "Revenge or Resignation: Seneca's *Agamemnon*." In Boyle (1983): 159–83.

——— (2000) "The Spectacle of Death in Seneca's *Troades*." In G. W. M. Harrison (2000): 87–118.
Slaney, Helen (2009) "Liminal's Kosky's Hughes's Artaud's Seneca's *Oedipus*." *New Voices in Classical Reception Studies* 4: 52–69.
Sluiter, Ineke, and Ralph M. Rosen, eds. (2012) *Aesthetic Value in Classical Antiquity*. Leiden.
Spika, Josef. (1890) *De imitatione Horatiana in Senecae canticis chori*. Vienna.
Spurr, M. S. (1986) "Agriculture and the *Georgics*." *G&R* 33: 164–87.
Staley, Gregory A. (2000) "'Like Monsters of the Deep' Seneca's Tragic *Monstra*." In Dickison and Hallett (2000): 325–55.
——— (2010) *Seneca and the Idea of Tragedy*. Oxford.
Star, Christopher (2006) "Commanding *Constantia* in Senecan Tragedy." *TAPA* 136: 207–44.
——— (2012) *The Empire of the Self: Self-Command and Political Speech in Seneca and Petronius*. Baltimore.
Sullivan, J. P. (1985) *Literature and Politics in the Age of Nero*. Ithaca.
Sutton, Dana F. (1986) *Seneca on the Stage*. Leiden.
Tarrant, Richard (1976) *Seneca: Agamemnon*. Cambridge.
——— (1978) "Senecan Drama and Its Antecedents." *HSCP* 82: 213–63.
——— (1981) "The Authenticity of the Letter of Sappho to Phaon (*Heroides* XV)." *HSCP* 85: 133–53.
——— (1985) *Seneca's Thyestes*. Atlanta.
——— (1995) "Greek and Roman in Seneca's Tragedies." *HSCP* 97: 215–30.
——— (2002) "Ovid and Ancient Literary History." In Hardie (2002): 13–33.
——— (2006) "Seeing Seneca Whole?" In Volk and Williams (2006): 1–17.
Thomas, Richard F. (1982) "Catullus and the Polemics of Poetic Reference (64.1–18)." *AJP* 103: 144–64.
——— (1983) "Callimachus, the *Victoria Berenices*, and Roman Poetry." *CQ* 33: 92–113.
——— (1986) "Virgil's *Georgics* and the Art of Reference." *HSCP* 90: 171–98.
——— (1987) "Prose into Poetry: Tradition and Meaning in Virgil's *Georgics*." *HSCP* 91: 229–60.
——— (1988a) *Virgil: Georgics. Vol. 1: Books 1–2*. Cambridge.
——— (1988b) *Virgil: Georgics. Vol. 2: Books 3–4*. Cambridge.
——— (2001) *Virgil and the Augustan Reception*. Cambridge.
Töchterle, Karlheinz (1994) *Lucius Annaeus Seneca: Oedipus*. Heidelberg.
Townend, G. B. (1983) "The Unstated Climax of Catullus 64." *G&R* 30: 21–30.
Traina, A. (1999) "Il dolore di Ecuba (Sen. *Troad*. 1062): Alla ricerca di un'esegesi perduta." *Maia* 51: 411–13.
Treggiari, Susan (1991) *Roman Marriage: Iusti Coniuges from the Time of Cicero to the Time of Ulpian*. Oxford.
Trinacty, Christopher V. (2007) "Seneca's *Heroides*: Elegy in Seneca's *Medea*." *CJ* 103: 63–78.
——— (2009) "Like Father, Like Son?: Selected Examples of Intertextuality in Seneca the Younger and Seneca the Elder." *Phoenix* 63: 260–77.
Tsitsiridis, Stavros, ed. (2010) *Parachoregma: Studies on Ancient Theatre in Honour of Professor Gregory M. Sifakis*. Heraklion.
Usher, M. D. (2006) *A Student's Seneca: Ten Letters and Selections from De Providentia and De Vita Beata*. Norman.
Verducci, Florence (1985) *Ovid's Toyshop of the Heart*. Princeton.
Vernant, J. P., and P. Vidal-Naquet (1988) *Myth and Tragedy in Ancient Greece*. New York.
Volk, Katharina (2006) "Cosmic Disruption in Seneca's *Thyestes*: Two Ways of Looking at an Eclipse." In Volk and Williams (2006): 183–200.
Volk, Katharina, and Gareth D. Williams eds. (2006) *Seeing Seneca Whole: Perspectives on Philosophy, Poetry and Politics*. Leiden.
Vottero, Dionigi (1998) *Lucio Anneo Seneca: I frammenti*. Bologna.
Von Albrecht, Michael (2004) *Wort und Wandlung. Senecas Lebenskunst*. Leiden.
Walsh, Lisl (2012) "The Metamorphoses of Seneca's Medea." *Ramus* 41: 71–93.

Warmington, E. H. (1967) *Remains of Old Latin*, 4 vols. Cambridge.
Whitby, M., and P. Hardie, eds. (1987) *Homo Viator: Classical Essays for John Bramble*. Bristol.
Wickkiser, B. (1999) "Famous Last Words: Putting the Sphragis Back into Ovid's *Metamorphoses*." *MD* 42: 113–42.
Wilamowitz-Moellendorff, U. von, ed. (1919) *Griechische Tragödien*, 4 vols. Berlin.
Wilcox, Amanda (2012) *The Gift of Correspondence in Classical Rome: Friendship in Cicero's Ad Familiares and Seneca's Moral Epistles*. Madison.
Wilkinson, L. P. (1955) *Ovid Recalled*. Cambridge.
Williams, Gareth (2003) *Seneca: De Otio, De Brevitate Vitae*. Cambridge.
——— (2012) *The Cosmic Viewpoint: A Study of Seneca's Natural Questions*. Oxford.
Williams, Gordon (1978) *Change and Decline*. Berkeley.
——— (1992) "Poet and Audience in Senecan Tragedy: *Phaedra* 358–430." In Woodman and Powell (1992): 138–49.
Wills, Jeffrey (1996) *Repetition in Latin Poetry: Figures of Allusion*. Oxford.
Wilson, Emily (2004) *Mocked with Death*. Baltimore.
Wilson, Marcus (1983) "The Tragic Mode of Seneca's *Troades*." In Boyle (1983) 27–60.
——— (1988) "Seneca's Epistles to Lucilius: A Revaluation." In Boyle (1988): 102–21.
——— (2001) "Seneca's Epistles Reclassified." In S. J. Harrison (2001): 164–87.
——— (2007) "Rhetoric and the Younger Seneca." In Dominik and Hall (2007): 425–38.
Winkler, John J., and Froma I. Zeitlin, eds. (1990) *Nothing to Do with Dionysus?: Athenian Drama in Its Social Context*. Princeton.
Winterbottom, M. (1974) *Seneca the Elder: Declamations*. Vol. 1. Cambridge.
Wise, V. M. (1982) "Ovid's Medea and the Magic of Language." *Ramus* 11: 16–25.
Wiseman, T. P. (1988) "Satyrs in Rome? The Background to Horace's *Ars Poetica*." *JRS* 78: 1–13.
Woodman, T., and J. Powell, eds. (1992) *Author and Audience in Latin Literature*. Cambridge.
Worton, Michael, and Judith Still, eds. (1990) *Intertextuality: Theories and Practices*. Manchester and New York.
Zeitlin, Froma I. (1990) "Thebes: Theater of Self and Society in Athenian Drama." In Winkler and Zeitlin (1990): 130–67.
Zetzel, J. (1983) "Catullus, Ennius, and the Poetics of Allusion." *ICS* 8: 251–66.
——— (1996) "Poetic Baldness and Its Cure." *MD* 36: 73–100.
Zissos, Andrew (2008) "Shades of Virgil: Seneca's *Troades*." *MD* 61: 191–210.
Zwierlein, O. (1966) *Die Rezitationsdramen Senecas*. Meisenheim am Glan.
——— (1986a) *L. Annaei Senecae Tragoediae*. Oxford.
——— (1986b) *Kritischer Kommentar zu den Tragödien Senecas*. Mainz.
——— (2004) *Lucubrationes Philologae*. Vol. 1: *Seneca*. Berlin.

INDEX OF PASSAGES

Note: Letter *n* designates footnotes. Only specific citations from the text are included. General references to the titles below can be found in the Subject Index.

Apollonius Rhodius
  Argonautica
    3…95n114
    3.1026ff…105n146
Aristophanes
  Ranae
    945–7…129n11
    1005–88…127n2
Aristotle
  Poetics
    1453a18–21…3n8

Catullus
  61…102n137
  62…102n137
  64…173, 174n170
  64.20…173
  64.321…174
  64.326…174
  64.348…173
  64.349–51…173
  64.350…173
  64.351…173
  64.357–60…170, 173
  64.362–4…173
  64.364…173
  64.368…173
  64.368–70…173
Cicero
  Epistulae ad Atticum
    2.19.3…4n13
  Epistulae ad Familiares
    7.1…4n14
  De Inventione
    1.27…153n100
  Pro Sestias
    118–25…4n13
    126…169n153

Ennius
  Annales
    54–5…149n85

Euripides
  Hecuba
    37–41…167n144
    47–50…169n151
  Hippolytus
    380–3…80n62
    856–9…85
  Medea
    1078–80…119n190
    1186–96…117n182
    1342…120n191
  Oedipus
    540…141n57

Fronto
  Aurelium
    2…1, 62n

Greek Anthology
  Anthologia Palatina
    7.487…117n181
    7.710…117n181

Homer
  Iliad
    21…170
    22.396–405…170
  Odyssey
    11.473–540…170n156
Horace
  Ars Poetica
    46…194n30
    47–8…143n66
    81–89…128n4
    86–8…195
    89–118…195n33
    101–3…134n32
    120–2…171n162
    131…12

Horace (continued)
  133–4...12
  139...98n125
  153–204...194n28
  179–183...211
  185...128n6
  190...153n100
  195–6...212
  320...153n100
  339...153n100
  360...194n30
  361...49
  391...155n108
  391–3...155n108
  455...197
  457–9...197
  463...13
  464–6...197
  466–7...197
  467...197
  468–9...197
  471...197
  472...197
  Carmina
    1.1...152
    1.3...158–164
    1.3.9–16...159
    1.3.10–1...159
    1.3.21–4...159
    1.3.25–8...159
    1.3.37–40...159
    1.12...154–158
    1.12.7–12...154
    1.12.15–6...155n109
    1.12.25...158
    1.12.29–32...155n109
    1.19...146n77
    1.19.1–4...146n77
    1.19.6...146
    1.20...154n108
    2.1.17–8...55n89
    2.10...145
    2.10.11–2...145
    2.10.22–4...145
    3.3...146–150
    3.3.1–8...147
    3.3.18–68...149
    3.3.30–31...149
    3.3.40–2...149
    3.3.58...149
    3.3.67–8...149
    3.3.69–72...149n85
    3.3.71–2...150n88
    3.4.49–52...146
    3.23.2...206n68
    3.25...202, 203, 214
    3.25.17–8...204
    3.30...150–154, 152
    3.30.6–9...152
    4.2.2–4...146
    4.6.44...142n62
    4.7...22
    4.7.13–6...22
    4.7.25–6...22
    4.7.25–8...185n207
    4.7.27–8...23
    4.8...152
    4.227–32...15n58
    4.228...15n58
  Epistulae
    2.1.187–8...4n14
    2.1.210–3...186
  Epodes
    5...112n169
  Odes
    1.6...4n14
    3.30...219n100
  Satires
    1.4.62...185n207

Livy
  7.2.7...102n139
Lucretius
  De Rerum Natura
    4.1068–72...70n29
    4.1149–54...70n29
    6.93...143n66
    6.660...76n48
    6.1167...76n48

Ovid
  Amores
    1.1...76
    1.1.2...201n51
    1.1.13–4...76
    1.1.17–8...179n192
    1.1.19...69n26, 100n129
    1.1.24...78n56
    1.3.10...228n124
    1.9...71
    1.9.9–12...71
    1.12.21...119n189
    2.1...74, 76
    2.1.3...77
    2.1.4...74
    2.1.5–6...74
    2.19.36...71
    3.1...78, 112
    3.1.23...113
    3.1.35–6...69n26
    3.1.41–2...100n129
  Ars Amatoria
    1.311–2...69
    1.437–40...88n87
    1.511...67n20
    1.744...67n20
  Ex Ponto
    4.2.30...143n63
  Fasti
    1.523...213n84
    2.418...46n63
    3.261–6...185n207
    4.457–62...120n191
    4.484...191n15
    5.181...228n124
    6.737–62...67n20
  Heroides
    1.69–70...101n134
    3.5–6...101n134
    4...20, 24, 67, 68, 68n22, 78, 83–92 *passim*, 88n92, 89n97
    4.1...86
    4.3–6...88n91
    4.7–10...89
    4.9...88n89
    4.9–10...78, 92
    4.32...91
    4.37–8...88n89, 91
    4.43–6...88n89
    4.51...88n89

Index of Passages 251

4.54–66...88n89
4.63–4...89
4.71–2...90
4.78–83...88n89
4.149...91
4.153...92
4.155...88n89
4.165–6...69n24
4.165–76...88n89
6...94, 94n111, 96, 106n151
6.21...96n119
6.62...228n124
6.83–94...112n169
6.84...114n173
6.124–5...98n123
6.128...124
6.149–51...105
7...20
9...77n51
10...89n97
12...94–109 *passim*, 94n111, 99n126, 112n166, 123
12.1...100
12.16...109
12.33–4...117n183
12.61...108
12.71...109
12.90...124n204
12.90–1...124n203
12.93–108...110n159
12.115...124
12.119–20...96n119
12.137–42...102
12.161–2...104
12.165–6...117n183
12.180...117
12.184...99n126
12.188...98n124
12.189–90...98n123
12.205–6...107
12.208...98
12.209...122
12.214...99
20.230...77n55
Ibis
  259–64...227
Medea
  fr. 2 (Ribbeck)...120, 196
Metamorphoses
  1.1–2...12n51, 93
  1.253–312...10
  1.304...9
  2.103–328...174
  2.161...179n189
  2.202...179n189
  2.202–4...178
  2.205...179n189
  2.315...178
  2.319...179
  2.320...178
  2.333–9...178n184
  2.381–93...178
  2.508–30...131n21
  2.726...75n47
  2.730–1...75
  2.846–75...77n52
  2.850...77n52
  3.334–5...129n13
  4.387...221n104, 228n124
  6.61–8...47
  6.62...47, 49
  6.69...47, 49

6.103–9...77n52
6.636ff...120n191
7...104
7.1–148...105n146
7.1–158...95
7.1–424...94, 95
7.10–1...80
7.12...80
7.17–21...80
7.20–1...119
7.32...120n192
7.40–3...103
7.43–7...103
7.109–10...116
7.137–8...110
7.141–58...110n159
7.149...114n173
7.159–349...95
7.167...114n175
7.175...112n167
7.179–293...112n169
7.192–219...114, 115n178
7.192–293...20
7.199–200...115n177
7.203...96
7.224...114n173
7.232...114n173
7.276...112n167
7.350–1...125n209
7.394...117
7.394–7...95
7.397...125n209
7.405–24...79n61
7.422–3...82n69
7.424...114n175
7.522–613...140n51
7.589–92...139
7.607...140n51
7.611–3...139
7.759–61...142
9.454...84n77
9.454–665...83
9.455...84
9.464–5...85n82
9.466–7...84
9.487...85
9.530...86
9.541...85n82
9.558...86
9.561...85n82
9.586–9...86
9.631–4...86
9.640...85n82
9.734...84n77
10.298–502...82
10.314–5...225
10.324–9...226
10.399...226
10.469–70...82
12.70–145...170
13.339–48...169
13.439–48...167n144
13.442...171
13.443–4...171
13.444...169
13.445–8...171
13.446...171n160
13.448...171, 171n160
13.547ff...120n191
13.565–75...66n16
14.812–6...149n85

Ovid (*continued*)
  15...184, 184n207
  15.120–42...191n16
  15.136–7...191
  15.142...191n16
  15.165...191n16
  15.234–5...219
  15.492–546...174, 175
  15.497–546...67
  15.499...176
  15.503...175n177
  15.508–10...175
  15.511–3...180
  15.524...179n189
  15.525–6...179
  15.527–9...177
  15.528...178n186
  15.529...178
  15.531–2...185n207
  15.538–40...184–185n207
  15.552–3...176n178
  15.871–2...219
  15.879...219
 Remedia Amoris
  63–4...70n30
  64...67n20
  375...122n198
  376...131n18
  379–80...100n129
  743–4...67n20
 Tristia
  2...12
  2.381...69n26, 100
  2.382...123n202
  2.555–6...12
  5.1.59...70n31

Petronius
 Satyricon
  89...180n195
Pseudo-Apollodorus
 Bibliotheca
  3.13.8...228n123
Propertius
 Elegiae
  1.1.7...73n41
  1.3.1...77n53
  1.11.23...104n142
  1.15.31...77n53
  1.18.29–30...101n134
  2.1.1...119n189
  2.16.39–40...77n55
  2.26.29ff...71n34
  2.34.65–6...99n127

Quintilian
 Institutio Oratoria
  2.2.30...45n58
  3.7.3...123n202
  9.2.64...234n5
  9.2.66...234n6
  9.2.67–75...234n5
  10.1.98...4n15
  10.1.125–31...65n11

[Seneca]
 Octavia
  430...59

Seneca the Elder
 Controversiae
  1. *praef.* 6...15n58
  1 *praef.* 10...12n52
  2.2.12...10n47, 65n11
  7.1.27...5n17
  8.4.1...198n41
  9.5.17...10n47, 65n11
 Suasoriae
  3.4–7...5n17
  3.5–7...196
  3.7...13n53, 31n20, 120n191, 125n208
Seneca the Younger
 Ad Marciam
  10.1...234n2
 Agamemnon
  1–8...203
  5...168n148, 213n83
  9...147
  10–2...208
  11...213n83
  19–20...210
  22...210
  25–6...206n70
  34...209
  36...213n83
  48–9...206n70
  57–107...145
  342–7...146
  416–8...167n145
  421–578...148n82
  434–5...200
  444–5...169n154
  466...146n76
  467...213
  474–6...166
  474–84...149
  488–9...209
  495...146n76
  517–26...170n159
  523–4...213
  528...146n76, 149
  535...146n76
  545–52...170n159
  589–636...146
  592...148n82
  593–603...148
  609...147, 150
  610...150
  611...149
  624...149
  625...149
  630...150
  638–9...150
  656–8...150
  659...201
  662–3...200
  664...200
  667...200
  669...149
  670...201n49
  671...201n49
  672...201n49
  676...201n49
  682...201n49
  691–2...201
  708...149
  714–5...209
  718–9...203n60
  720...209, 212
  720–5...201

724...209, 212
724–5...204
726–7...204
728–30...204
730...206
732...206
733...213n84
741–58...206
742...207
747...207
747–8...207
750...208
750–1...200, 214
750–2...208
751...208
752–4...207n71
757...212
758...209, 213
759–64...206n67
769–74...209
791–9...213n82
796...129
808–66...146
867–70...211
868...212
872–5...211
875...213n83
875–80...213n82
880...213n82
883...213n83
885...213
892...212n80
897...214n85
901–3...212n80
908–9...213n83
912...166, 213
996...198n40
1005...213
1006...167
1008...214
1011...200, 214
1012...199, 206n66, 214

Apocolocyntosis
 4.9...58
 4.25–32...59n98
 7.1...7, 9n44

De Amicitia
 F 59.5–6...40

De Beneficiis
 1.3.10...31n22
 1.4.5...143n63
 4.5.1...53
 4.6.4–5...53
 4.7.1...55
 4.9.1...55n85
 5.3...187
 II.14.4...197

De Clementia
 4.1...187

De Ira
 1.1...134n30
 1.5.2...134n30
 1.7.4...134n30
 2.35.5...134n30
 3.1.5...134n30
 3.28.1...134n30

Dialogi
 6.9.1–5...34n29
 7.26.6...45n61
 10.9.2...33n24
 10.16.5...31n22, 45n61

Epistulae
 2.2...15n61
 8.8...26n2
 18...43
 18.2–13...43
 18.5...43
 18.8...44n55
 28.1.6...169n154
 28.4...110n159
 31...44
 31.1...44
 31.8...44n56
 31.11...44
 33.1...12n52
 33.1–4...44n56
 41.3...217n92
 41.9...21
 45.5–13...27n2
 49.8–10...27n2
 58.2...187
 58.26...16n62
 59.5...61
 70.2.3...169n154
 72.1...110n159
 73...51, 56
 73.1...53
 73.10–11...51
 73.14–5...53
 73.15...53
 73.16...53
 74.7...234n2
 76...11
 76.31...153n100, 234n2
 76.33...11
 77.20...153n100
 78...37n36
 78.2...37n36
 79...10, 11, 13, 29n13, 31n21, 197n37
 79.5...10
 79.5–7...10
 79.6...11, 123n202
 79.17...12, 12n52
 79.18...13
 80.1...207n71
 82...52n81
 82.3...52n81
 82.9–10...27n2
 84...10, 13, 13n53, 29n13, 31n21
 84.3...13
 84.5...14
 84.6...15n61
 84.7...15n61
 84.8...15
 84.9...16
 85.5...30n15
 86.15...9, 187
 86.16...9n46
 88...30n15
 88.3...31n22
 88.5...26n1
 88.9...31n22
 88.20...31n22
 88.37–46...30n15
 89.18...30n16
 90.4...21
 90.16...21
 98...34n29
 107...34, 34n28, 35, 35n30, 37
 107.1...35n33
 107.2...35, 35n31
 107.3...34

Seneca the Younger (*continued*)
  107.7...35
  108...29, 30n15, 31, 34n28, 35, 35n30
  108.3...32
  108.8–9...30n17
  108.9...30
  108.10...30, 30n19
  108.11–12...30n17
  108.12...30n17
  108.24...32
  108.26...33n24
  108.27...32, 33n25, 33n26
  108.29...31
  108.30...31
  108.32–4...31
  108.34...31
  108.35...31
  114.13...4n16
  115.14...234n2
  120.22...62, 93, 234n3
  121.22–3...49n69
Hercules Furens
  5...130
  19...131
  22...131n20
  26...132n22
  27–9...130
  29...132
  34...137
  46–7...37n37
  49...132n25
  50–63...132
  63...132
  75...137
  85...132
  99...134
  104–6...133
  105...133
  107–112...134
  108...134n32
  108–14...134n32
  112...135
  116...198n40
  118–23...135
  119...135
  122...135
  181...131n21
  513...198n41
  524–91...145, 152n96
  572–6...157
  588–9...157
  590–1...158
  604–6...37n37
  656–7...136n36
  693–6...36
  696...37
  772–3...157
  957...132n23, 134n32
  974...133, 134n32
  974–5...132n23
  990–1...135n35
  993...135n35
  1025–6...37n35
  1026–7...131n18
  1027...36
  1037–8...134n32
  1052...36
  1092...134n32
  1131–2...140n52
  1167...137n41
  1171–2...135n35
  1192–3...135
  1200...36
  1200–1...37
  1202–18...134n31, 137n40
  1220–1...134n31
  1226...133
  1236...135
  1249...37
  1277...137
  1280...137n43
  1312...133
  1315...137n41
  1316–7...138
  1319...135
  1320...37, 133
Medea
  1...110n160, 126
  15...117
  20...107
  23–4...99, 107
  23–5...118n187
  23–6...98
  25...98
  25–6...122n197
  26...98
  26–8...101
  27...117, 194n30
  32...126
  34...160
  36...160
  43...189n8
  47...189
  48...121
  48–50...98, 100
  49...98, 100, 121n196
  50...98, 112n166, 189
  51...189
  51–55...188
  52...189
  53–4...123
  55...98, 99, 189
  56–74...152n96
  67...117
  108...102
  116...104
  116–20...102
  118...102
  133...156
  135–6...104
  135–58...101
  137–43...106
  140...107n154
  141...107n154
  142...107n154
  155–6...100
  159–60...106n151
  166–7...105n147, 160
  168–71...105
  170...198n40
  171...110, 112n164, 112n165, 118n187
  172...122
  186...109n156
  195...114n175
  201...114n175
  202...114n175
  203...114n175
  205...114n175
  208...114n175
  225–8...196

229...154, 156n111
243...196
266-8...112n165
288-90...112n165
301...159, 159n118
302...158, 159
309-15...158
316-7...158
318...159
319-20...156n111
320...115
326...159n118
331-4...158
335-9...159
346...159
356...154
358...154
360-3...159
361...117n185
361-4...117n185
362-3...111, 112n165
364...163
364-79...161
382...118n186
396...109n156
397-8...108
398...117
399...190n10
405...118n186
406...108n156
407-14...108n155
415-9...108
416...108
419...108
422...108
437-8...108
465...104n141
466...110n159, 116
516-7...111
524...112n164
549-50...109
550...110
556-7...110n159
560...110
560-5...109
564...110
579...156n111
579-82...110n162, 115
582...158n117
584...156n112
584-5...115
604...155
607...159n118
613...157
616-69...115
625-33...155
628-9...112n165
639-42...115n179
644-6...115n179
670-739...165n135, 167n145
670-848...95
673-5...111
675-739...112
680-704...113n171
682...118n186
683-4...112n165
684...154
688...154
690-704...170n159
692-3...113

694...156n112
703...114n173
704...114n173
705-30...113n172
720-1...114n173
722...114n173
730...114n173
731...114n173
734...113
737...106
737-9...113
740-848...114, 165n135
740ff...156n112
752-3...120
752ff...156n112
754...115
755-6...115
757...115
759...115
760...114
761...115
762-70...118n186
763-4...115
765...115
765-6...115
765-7...156
767...114
768-70...115
769...114
775-6...115, 118n186
777-8...115
779...117
779-81...115
793...117n183
800...117
812...159n118
823-4...110
829-30...116
832...197
833...106
834...197
836-9...116n180
837-42...116
841...160n121
842...117
857-62...194
862...196
863...120
863-6...119
866...119
866-9...195
867...119n189
867-70...97n122, 158n117
869...123
880...116n180
894...102, 117
895...123n201
898...100
901...100, 121n196
905-7...100n130
905-8...121
908-9...124
908-10...112n165
910...98n124, 106, 122
911-2...156
914-5...123
924-30...121
925-6...118n187
933-4...112n165
934...112n164

Seneca the Younger (*continued*)
- 943–4...120n195
- 947–8...112n165
- 953...122
- 954–7...122
- 986...117n184
- 986–7...124
- 988–9...124
- 990–2...122
- 992–4...124
- 1001...125
- 1005...118n186
- 1010–1...125
- 1011...159n118
- 1012–3...122n197
- 1015...189
- 1016–7...190
- 1021...104n141, 125
- 1025–7...125
- 1027...126

Naturales Quaestiones
- 1.3.4...48
- 2.32.4...190n12
- 3.27.13–3.28.2...27n6
- 3.27.14...10n47
- 3.27.15...10
- 6.2.2...33n24

Oedipus
- 3...39
- 4...144n68, 222n107
- 14...138
- 17...226
- 29...143n67
- 36...138, 231
- 39–40...217
- 52–6...138
- 55...144n68
- 56...140
- 62–3...38
- 70...39n41
- 84–5...231n130
- 92–102...141, 142
- 93...144n68, 230
- 98...230
- 101...229n125
- 102...230
- 106...229n125
- 106–8...143
- 108–9...33n24
- 130...140n51
- 132–3...217n93
- 152...144n68
- 159...222n107
- 164...222n107
- 171–5...140n53
- 187...218n96
- 214–5...216n89
- 215–5...141
- 216...51
- 221–38...215
- 228...143
- 230...143
- 235...51n78
- 238...226
- 244...143n67
- 246...143n67
- 295...51n79
- 314–20...49
- 315...50
- 319...51
- 331...51n78
- 333...216n89
- 334...218
- 341–50...190
- 352...51, 51n78
- 359–60...190
- 366...191
- 371...139, 230
- 372...140, 191n16
- 372–80...190
- 373...140
- 384...191, 216n89
- 387...192n17, 229n126
- 390...221
- 390–2...191
- 392...192
- 394...215
- 403–508...145n72
- 411...222n107
- 509...51n78
- 522...216
- 530–6...216
- 530–658...187
- 536...219
- 536–7...219
- 542...218
- 546–7...219n101
- 550–1...220
- 551–2...220
- 552...215
- 553...220
- 554...220, 225n114, 229n125
- 555...220
- 556–8...220
- 559–63...220
- 561–2...225n114
- 567–8...220
- 568...220, 221
- 569...221n103
- 571...215
- 571–3...221
- 573...221
- 577...193
- 579...193, 221
- 584...218
- 589...222, 222n107
- 590–4...216n91
- 591–2...221
- 592...221
- 592–4...37
- 593...221
- 594...221
- 595...222
- 600...223
- 600–7...222
- 607...223, 224
- 620...219
- 625...225n114
- 626...225n114
- 626–30...225
- 630...224
- 630–1...226
- 632...39n42
- 634...142, 229n126
- 634–5...139n49
- 638–40...139n49
- 639...226
- 640–1...143, 230
- 642...142
- 647–53...230

Index of Passages

656–8...227
660...228
661–3...229
663–4...228
668...143n66, 229n125
677...229
710–1...227
711–2...226
724...144
724–5...232
764–77...51n78
766–7...229
770–1...38, 139
782...230, 231
828...226n116
849...50
857–9...144n67
859...144n67
867...230
879...226n116
883...227n119
896–8...146
919–20...142
926–34...170n159
937...142n59
940–1...226
942...142n59
942–3...230
943...139
947...142n59
949–51...51, 193n23
965...140, 191n16, 222n107
968...142
974...192n18
975...226n117
977...139n48
980...227n119
987–94...145
999...51
1007...50n75
1010...50n75
1019...231
1031–2...193n23
1044–5...231
1045–6...227
1052...39n41
1059...39

Phaedra
7–8...71
9–10...71
30...178
60...72n37
64...181
80–90...33n24
83–4...129n13
89–92...70
96...80n62
99...72
101...70n31
102...72
103–4...85n82
103–9...88n88
110–2...88n89
112–4...68
113...70n31
115...70n31
124–5...78
124–8...88n89
127–8...69
128...73

132–5...69
138...86
143...73
152–3...86
153...73
153–4...91
171–2...82
173–77...78
177–9...80, 119n190
178...72, 72n37
184...72
184–5...80
186–94...81
188–94...85n82
195–6...45, 46, 68
195–217...81n63
203...46
218...71
233–5...71
235...72n37
239...72n37
240...69
241...71n35, 72n37, 73n42
250–66...73
254...72n37, 73n42
268...80n62
270...81n64
271...73
272...73
273...73
274...183
274–8...146n77
274–357...67, 73–78
276...73, 74
277...73
279...80n62
280...178
290–5...73, 74
291–2...77
296–8...85n79
296–316...73
299...77, 92n105
301–2...77
303–8...77
304...181
307...183
309...74
317–24...77
317–29...74
330...74, 76n48
330–4...75
335–51...73
336–7...184
337...74
341–2...77
343...176
351–3...184
352–7...77
354...92
355...74
356–7...81
363...73n44, 80n62, 86n83
371–2...46
372–3...73n44
376...90n98
377...178
387ff...73n44
394–404...88n89
396...72n37
450–1...33n24

Seneca the Younger (*continued*)
466–8...21
481...21, 72n37
483–539...72n36
483–564...72n40
491...72n37, 72n38
496...46, 68n23
558...81
559–64...72n38
563–4...81
566–8...21n83
578–9...89n93
592–9...89n94
596...72n37
607...176n178
609...76
609–12...84
612...85
618...72n37
621...87
623...85n82, 88n89
634...85, 89
636...85n82, 88n89
637...89
639–40...87
641–4...85n82
651–2...90
665...89
665–8...90
671...85, 85n82, 88n89
689...81
693...87
697...81, 91
698–9...71n34, 91
699–702...88n89
700...72n37
700–1...72
703...91
704...22n85
704–9...91n101
707...22n85
719...176n178
727...75
728...22n85
735...22n85
743...89
748...154n106
761...75n47, 178n188
761–3...89
773...75n47
797...146
820–4...184n207
840...87n84
847–8...185n207
849...72n37
858...86n83
899–900...82n69
915...46
947–8...83n72
959–88...145
972...154n106
980...81
987...72n37
991–5...167n145
991–1122...174
997...175n175
998...175n175
1000–1114...120n193
1007...183n203
1012...183n203
1013...183n203
1015...183n203
1018...183n203
1019...183n203
1019–20...83n73, 87
1025–7...176
1030...183n203
1032–3...183n204
1033...183n203
1034...72n37
1036...180, 184
1036–7...181
1036–49...180
1037...180
1039...183
1040...183
1041...184
1043...180
1044...183
1046–8...181
1047...184
1051...72n37
1059–61...182
1064...175n175
1068...176
1077...72n37, 92
1083–4...178
1085...90, 178, 181n198
1087...181n198
1089...178
1090–6...177
1096...178
1097...183n203
1098–1102...179
1100...179n190
1104...181n198
1105–10...178n184
1114–6...76
1118–22...175n175
1141...87n84
1141–8...145
1159...183n206
1160...183n206
1170–3...182n201
1171...176
1172...176
1173...178n185
1180...72, 72n37, 87
1183–4...71
1185–6...83
1186–7...78n57
1190...87
1191–2...81
1192...81
1194...46, 68n23
1196...22
1199–200...201n52
1200...82
1210...72n37
1213–43...178
1240...72n37
1249...177n182
1256...185n207
1256–79...178n184
1258...181n198
1260...177n182
1265...46, 68n23
1265–6...90
1266...178
1267...178n186
1270...178n185
1278...181n198

Index of Passages 259

Phoenissae
  35...198n40
  84–5...231
  98–102...197
  100...197
  122...143n67
  151–3...198n42
  193–6...198
  223...198
  261...198n40
  353...198
Thyestes
  57...81n65
  66...125n206
  122–35...57n92
  122–75...152n96
  249–250...55n90
  267...99n127
  358–62...148n81
  360–2...150n90
  395...57
  396...57
  397...58
  407...57n92
  546–662...55
  559...55
  560–6...55
  561–2...56
  573–6...55n89
  634–40...167n145
  684...57
  689...58
  693...57
  742...57n93
  876...58n95
  877–80...57
  888...57
  1005–6...125n207
Troades
  17...163n129
  67–163...144
  83–129...173
  84...173n169
  93–4...173n103
  98–9...173n169
  106...173n169
  114...173n169
  120–1...173n169
  140...43n53
  156–60...151
  164...168n147
  164–202...129
  166...168n147
  168...167
  168–202...152
  169–70...167
  174...168
  175...168
  180...168
  181–9...169
  181–202...151
  182...170, 170n158
  183...170
  184...173
  189...170
  190...171n161
  191...172
  191–6...170
  196...168
  199–202...172
  202...173

  236–7...173n167
  245–9...170n158
  248...171
  286–91...170n158
  298–9...170n158
  360–1...174n171
  361...170n158, 171
  371...151
  371–408...151
  376–80...151
  381...151
  400...152
  401...153n99
  402...153n99
  406...153
  407–8...151
  428...42n51
  438–60...151n92
  441...194n30
  443–60...152
  453...33n24
  464...43
  577...153
  614–5...64
  621...153
  623–4...168n148
  625...153n98
  681...189
  683–5...151n92
  834–5...171
  869...152
  943...171
  994–5...172n165
  1002...171
  1063...171
  1078–87...124n206
  1087...168n149
  1110...168n149
  1112–3...43
  1117...42, 43
  1118–64...124n206
  1121...168n149
  1128...154n103
  1131...154n103
  1159...172
  1164...168n149, 169
  1165...172
  1167...172
  1167–8...42n51
  1168...172
  1956–9...167n145
Sophocles
  Polyxena
    frag. 523 (Lloyd-Jones)...167n144
Statius
  Silvae
    4.5...145n73
    4.7...145n73
  Thebais
    12.816–7...207n71

Tacitus
  Dialogus
    35.4...123n202
Theocritus
  18...102n137
Tibullus
  1.4.41ff...71n34
  1.6.30...77n55
  2.3.11–30...85n79

Vergil
 Aeneid
  1.24...131n17
  1.25–6...130
  1.26–8...131n17
  1.36...130
  1.47...131
  1.84–5...166
  1.203...136n36
  1.283–5...163
  1.432–3...14
  1.474–8...207
  1.483...170
  1.668...136n38
  2...169n154, 180n195, 208
  2.206...181
  2.207–8...181
  2.215...181n198
  2.217...181n198
  2.220...181n198
  2.238–40...150
  2.242–3...150
  2.270–97...42n51
  2.272–6...206n69
  2.354...33n24
  2.499...150
  3...169n151
  3.22...168
  3.26...168
  3.29–30...168
  3.63...168
  3.65...169
  3.67...169
  3.72...169n154
  3.183–7...210n76
  3.490...41n46
  3.588ff...102n138
  4.23...69n24
  4.301...204n63
  4.384–7...206n65
  4.461...204
  4.464...210n77
  4.465...204
  4.469–70...205
  4.471–3...205
  4.532...104n144
  4.569...189
  4.612–29...206
  5.636...210n76
  5.865...142n58
  6...208, 220, 229
  6.8...220
  6.102...220
  6.103–5...11
  6.126–9...132n25
  6.237–8...216n91
  6.257–8...221n103
  6.274...221
  6.274–81...216n91
  6.275...34, 36, 221
  6.276...221
  6.299...220
  6.300...220
  6.301...220
  6.304...220
  6.306...223n111
  6.309–12...223
  6.427–8...140n52
  6.428–9...140
  6.438–9...219n101
  6.494–534...206n69
  6.706–9...224
  7...131n20, 132n24, 133, 134, 135n34, 209n74
  7.41...142n62
  7.44...136
  7.311...136
  7.312...132n24
  7.327–8...134n31
  7.338...133
  7.761–82...185n207
  8...137n43
  8.228...136n39
  8.230...136n39
  8.291–2...136
  8.352–3...216n92
  8.364–5...40, 45
  8.634...46n63
  9.13...189
  9.176–204...131n21
  10.68...210n76
  10.264–6...223n110
  12.71...183
  12.101–2...183
  12.101–6...182
  12.808–28...149n85
  12.946–7...136
 Eclogues
  1...56, 57n93
  1.4...163n127
  1.6...57n94
  1.6–8...56
  1.24–5...218
  1.27–9...129n13
  1.59–62...162
  2...54
  2.4...54
  4.1...99n127
  4.3...58n95
  4.4–5...57
  4.9...58
  6.56...69n24
  8...112n169
 Georgics
  1.29–31...163
  2.108...223
  3...181n196, 187, 191–193, 218n94
  3.3–12...190
  3.9–10...192
  3.13–6...192
  3.40–3...189
  3.46...189
  3.46–7...192
  3.66–8...32
  3.209...182n200
  3.209–11...182n200, 183
  3.219ff...77n54
  3.232–4...182
  3.237...183n203
  3.238...183n203
  3.260–1...31n21
  3.282...77n54
  3.284...32
  3.330–4...217
  3.465...217n93
  3.478–566...140n51
  3.566...76n48, 218n96
  4.162–9...14
  4.473–4...222
  4.475–7...223n111
  4.478–80...219n101

SUBJECT INDEX

Note: Letter *n* designates footnotes. Headings which appear periodically throughout the page range are designated with *passim*.

Achilles
  Agamemnon and, 207
  ghost of *Troades* and, 151–154, 154n102, 167–174
    passim
  ira and, 171, 171n161
  Vergil and, 167–169
aemulatio
  Augustan poets and, 16, 212
  Ovid and, 49, 89, 114, 185
  Seneca on, 13, 31
  Seneca the Elder on, 15
  Vergil and, 185
Aeneas
  Agamemnon and, 147, 204, 208, 210n76
  Carmina and, 22
  De Amicitia and, 41
  Epistulae and, 11, 35, 45
  Hercules Furens and, 131, 131n17, 136, 136n38, 137
  Oedipus and, 193, 221, 223
  Troades and, 41, 42n51, 168–169, 169n151
Aetna
  Ars Poetica and, 13
  Epistulae and, 10
  Hercules Furens and, 133
Agamemnon (Seneca)
  Achilles and, 207
  Aeneas and, 147, 204, 208, 210n76
  Apollo and, 204n61
  Cassandra and, 25, 129n13, 167, 187, 198–214, 204n63, 206n66–213n84 *passim*, 231
  chorus/choral ode and, 146–150, 146n77, 148n83, 200–203, 203n60, 211
  color and, 208
  Dido and, 204–206, 206n65, 210n77, 212, 214
  Euripides and, 204
  furor in, 199–214 *passim*, 206n65–66, 214n85
  Hercules in, 211
  imagery in, 208
  nature and, 209
  Vergil and, 147–150 *passim*
Ahl, F., 230
ambiguity of language, 6n23
  Hercules Furens and, 133

messenger speech and, 165, 180
  Oedipus and, 50n76, 141, 216, 230, 231n132
  Phaedra and, 85, 87, 88
  Troades and, 153
Andromache
  De Amicitia and, 41
  Troades and, 41–43, 42n51, 151–153, 151n92
Annales (Ennius), 149, 149n85
Apocolocyntosis (Seneca), 6–7, 6n28, 55n86, 59, 145n74
Apollo
  Agamemnon and, 204n61
  Hercules Furens and, 136n37
  Oedipus and, 220, 227n120, 228
  Phaedra and, 85n79
Apollonius, 93n107–108
Ariadne, as exemplum, 89
Astyanax
  De Amicitia and, 41
  Troades and, 42–43, 42n51, 151, 151n92, 153, 154n103, 168n149, 172
Atreus, 1, 55–59, 63–64, 167n143
Augustan poets. *See also specific poets*
  aemulatio and, 16, 212
  character and, 2
  genre and, 95n115
  imagery and, 25, 61
  imitatio and, 16n63
  reception of (*see* reception of Augustan poets)
Augustus/Octavian
  Hercules and, 136n37, 148
  Horace and, 147–148, 154, 154n107, 155n110, 158, 158n116, 202, 202n57
  as tragedian, 4n13
  Vergil and, 28, 53, 53n82–83, 56, 56n91, 162–164, 188, 192

Bacchae (Euripides), 204, 225
Bacchus
  Horace and, 147, 202–204, 204n61–62
  Oedipus and, 145n72
Bakhtin, M. M., 19, 23
Barchiesi, A., 17, 99

261

Barrett, J., 165
Barthes, R., 235, 235n8
Boyle, A. J., 1, 42, 78, 111, 124, 125, 199, 200, 227, 233
Burian, P., 3
Byblis
   Cupid/Venus and, 84, 84n77
   Phaedra and, 67–68, 68n22, 79, 83–93 *passim*, 83n74–85n82 *passim*

Caligula, 1, 7n30
Cassandra
   Agamemnon and, 25, 129n13, 167, 187, 198–214, 204n63, 206n66–213n84 *passim*, 231
   Horace and, 199–204, 210–219
   Juno and, 210n76
   Vergil and, 203–208
character
   Augustan poets and, 2
   depth of, elegy and, 104
   as exemplum, 63
   genre and, 19–21
   interpretation and, 16–18
   intertextuality and, 21–23, 62–126 *passim*
   messenger speech and, 165–185 *passim*
   metapoetry and, 199–215 *passim*
   prologue speech and, 129–144 *passim*
   as reader, 227–231
   restricted nature of, 3–8
   Stoic ideas of, 1n2
chorus/choral ode, 144–164. *See also* lyric
   Agamemnon and, 146–150, 146n77, 148n83, 200–203, 203n60, 211
   Epistulae and, 15
   genre and, 18, 20
   Greek and Roman tradition and, 128
   Hercules Furens and, 152n96, 157–158
   Horace and, 24, 145–164 *passim*
   imagery in, 145–146, 149
   interpretation and, 6n28
   Medea and, 94, 101–102, 101n135, 110n162, 111, 115–119, 123, 152n96, 155–165, 158n117, 194–197
   messenger speech and, 165
   Oedipus and, 140n51, 140n53, 142n61, 222n107, 226–227, 227n119, 231n132
   Phaedra and, 72n39, 73–81 *passim*, 76n49, 77n54, 84n78, 85n79, 92n105, 176, 178, 178n188, 181n196, 183–184
   Thyestes and, 55–58, 150n90, 152n96
   Troades and, 150–154, 168n147, 171–173
   Vergil and, 158–167 *passim*
Claudius, 6, 7, 164, 164n131
Clytemnestra, 146, 199, 205–206, 206n66, 210, 214, 214n85
Coffey, M., 69, 89, 180, 188
color
   Agamemnon and, 208
   Carmina and, 149
   intertextuality and, 61, 63, 128
   Medea and, 194–196
   Metamorphoses and, 46–51
   Naturales Quaestiones and, 46–49, 49n70
   Oedipus and, 49–51, 50n74, 224
   Ovid and, 46–51
   Phaedra and, 23, 194
contaminatio, 14, 14n56, 74, 92n105, 168, 176, 181, 185, 224
Conte, G. B., 18, 60, 71, 100
Creon
   Medea and, 100, 105–115 *passim*, 196

messenger speech of, 187, 199
Oedipus and, 37, 140, 141n55, 143n67, 187–221 *passim*
Cupid/Venus
   Byblis and, 84, 84n77
   Hercules Furens and, 131
   Medea and, 80, 81n63, 100n129, 119
   Phaedra and, 46, 68, 74–76, 76n49, 78, 84, 88, 88n89, 146n77, 182n200, 183

De Amicitia (Seneca)
   Aeneas and, 41
   Andromache and, 41
   Astyanax and, 41
   Vergil and, 39–41
De Beneficiis (Seneca), Vergil and, 53–55
De Ira (Seneca), 94n109, 134, 143n30
Dido
   Agamemnon and, 204–206, 206n65, 210n77, 212, 214
   imagery and, 204n63
   Medea and, 104n144
   Phaedra and, 20
   Troades and, 41
drama, 2–25 *passim*
   epic and, 164n133, 205
   Greek foundations of, 3
   Horace on subject matter of, 12
   intertextuality and, 16–25 *passim*
   language of, 5
   Roman foundations of, 3–4, 4n12
   in Seneca's plays, 2n7, 8–9, 8n41, 16, 63
   tragic praxis and, 3

ecphrasis, 38, 174n173, 216
   epic and, 207–208n72
elegy, 73n41
   depth of character and, 104
   furor in, 73n41
   gender and, 83, 84n79
   genre of, 101
   language of, 77n53, 85n80, 100n129
   meter of, 70n31
   perspective of, 66, 66n15, 92
   in Seneca's plays, 6
   tragedy and, 69, 69n26, 72, 87–112 *passim*
Eliot, T. S., 29
Ennius, 4, 128, 149, 149n85, 192
   genre and, 62, 62n1
epic
   drama and, 164n133, 205
   ecphrasis and, 207–208n72
   intertextuality and, 127–131, 129n10, 185–186
   language of, 149, 212n80, 222–223
   messenger speech and, 165–184 *passim*, 169n154, 171n161, 175n175, 180n195, 193, 200
   meter of, 115
   time and, 205
   tone of, 221
   tragedy and, 18, 20, 24, 93, 127–131, 129n10, 162n125
epinician poetry, imagery and, 190
Epistulae (Seneca)
   Aeneas and, 11, 35, 45
   Aetna and, 10
   choral nature of, 15
   katabasis in, 35
   nature and, 35, 187
   stoicism and, 43, 53
   Vergil and, 30–35, 43–45, 51–53

Subject Index

Erasmo, M., 1
Euripides, 16, 88n90, 128n8
  Agamemnon and, 204
  Medea and, 93–95, 125
  Oedipus and, 225
  Phaedra and, 181n197
  Polydorus' ghost and, 168, 168n150, 169n151
  prologue speech and, 129
exemplum
  Ariadne as, 89
  character as, 63
  of greatness, 62
  Hippolytus as, 22
  intertextuality and, 93
  language of, 15n59
  literary vs. historical, 45
  Medea as, 79
  Phaedra as, 69, 79
extispicium, 49, 50n76, 51, 144, 187, 190–193, 192n17, 215–216, 230

Fantham, E., 42, 171
Fitch, J. G., 7, 67, 85, 133, 157, 198
Frank, M., 198
furor, 20
  in *Agamemnon* (Seneca), 199–214 *passim*, 206n65–66, 214n85
  in elegy, 73n41
  in *Hercules Furens*, 129–137 *passim*, 133n28, 134n31, 137n40
  in *Medea*, 80, 108–109n156, 121, 124, 188
  in *Oedipus*, 198
  in *Phaedra*, 20, 21n83, 72, 73n44, 80, 82n62, 86n83, 88, 88n89

gender, elegy and, 83, 84n79
genre-generic escalation/enrichment
  ascent of, 99–101, 99n128
  Augustan poets and, 95n115
  character and, 19–21
  chorus/choral ode and, 18, 20
  diction and, 195
  of elegy, 101
  Ennius and, 62, 62n1
  imagery and, 183
  impact of, on use, 26–27
  intertextuality and, 18–21, 18n72, 26–27, 53, 58, 64, 127–129, 128n4, 128n8, 131n20, 185–187
  language and, 95, 183
  lyric as, 3, 6, 164m133
  in *Medea*, 94, 101, 122n199
  messenger speech and, 165
  meter of, 114–115
  misreading of, 83
  Ovid and, 65–68, 126
  in *Phaedra*, 72
  Seneca on, 9–10, 16–17n64, 24
  Seneca's choice of, 1–8
  tone and, 196
  tragedy as, 69n26
  Vergil and, 53, 58, 164
Goldberg, S. M., 5, 195
Goldhill, S., 63–64

Hadas, M., 63
Harrison, S. J., 149n86

Hecuba
  Euripides and, 168, 168n150, 169n151
  suffering and, 63
  Troades and, 42n51, 66n16, 151, 153, 163n129, 172, 172n165, 173, 174
Hecuba (Euripides), 168, 168n150, 169n151
Hercules, 37n37–39
  in *Agamemnon*, 211
  in *Apocolocyntosis*, 7, 9n44
  Augustus/Octavian and, 136n37, 148
  divinity of, 147–148
  Horace and, 147
  Juno and, 129–140 *passim*, 131n21–140n52 *passim*
  katabasis and, 136
  literary tradition and, 63
  in *Medea* and, 115, 115n179, 118, 118n186, 160, 160n121
  Orpheus and, 154–158
  in *Phaedra*, 77, 77n51
  Vergil and, 36–37
Hercules Furens (Seneca)
  Aeneas and, 131, 131n17, 136, 136n38, 137
  Aetna and, 133
  ambiguity of language and, 133
  Apollo and, 136n37
  chorus/choral ode and, 152n96, 157–158
  Cupid/Venus and, 131
  furor in, 129–137 *passim*, 133n28, 134n31, 137n40
Hercules Oetaeus, 7
Hinds, S., 100
Hippolytus
  as exemplum, 22
  Horace and, 22–23
  nature and, 21–22, 21n83
  in *Phaedra*, 21–24, 21n83–23n86, 33n24, 45–46, 46n63, 67–92 *passim*, 67n19–90n98 *passim*, 129, 146, 167, 174–185, 175n175–185n207 *passim*
  stoicism and, 21n83
Hippolytus (Euripides), 181n197
Horace
  Augustus/Octavian and, 147–148, 154, 154n107, 155n110, 158, 158n116, 202, 202n57
  Bacchus and, 147, 202–204, 204n61–62
  Cassandra and, 199–204, 210–219
  chorus/choral ode and, 24, 145–164 *passim*
  dramatic subject matter and, 12
  Hercules and, 147
  Hippolytus, 22–23
  Medea and, 194–197
  Oedipus and, 197–198
  Pollux and, 147
  reception of, 12–25 *passim*
  rhetoric and, 195–198

imagery
  in *Agamemnon*, 208
  Augustan poets and, 25, 61
  in chorus/choral ode, 145–146, 149
  Dido and, 204n63
  Epinican, 190
  genre and, 183
  intertextuality and, 24–25, 33, 33n26, 35–36, 185, 230
  in *Medea*, 95n113, 97, 100–101, 110, 116–118, 126
  messenger speech and, 175–176, 176n179
  in *Oedipus*, 50, 138–139, 144, 219, 221
  Ovid and, 61, 66–67
  in *Phaedra*, 24, 68–88 *passim*, 69n27, 70n30, 83n73, 95, 175–176, 180, 182–183, 182n201
  prologue speech and, 129
imago, 15, 40–45, 154, 154n108, 211

Subject Index

imitatio
  Augustan poets and, 16n63
  language of, 207n71
  reading and, 29
  Seneca on, 31
  Seneca the Elder on, 5n17, 15, 15n58, 31n20
intertextuality
  character and, 21–23, 62–126 *passim*
  color and, 61, 63, 128
  drama and, 16–25 *passim*
  epic and, 127–131, 129n10, 185–186
  exemplum and, 93
  genre and, 18–21, 18n72, 26–27, 53, 58, 64, 185–187
  imagery and, 24–25, 33, 33n26, 35–36, 185, 230
  metapoetry and, 199–215
  plot and, 127–185 *passim*
ira
  Achilles and, 171, 171n161
  Juno and, 131
  in *Medea*, 104n145, 197
  Ovid and, 122n198, 131n18
  in *Phaedra*, 182
  tragedy and, 122n198, 131n18

Jason, 79–80, 94–125 *passim*, 188–190, 196–197
Jocasta, 50, 50n75, 140, 190, 193n23, 224, 225–227, 226n116, 230–231
Julius Caesar, 4n13, 164, 164n131
Juno, 37n37
  Cassandra and, 210n76
  as deity, 66n16
  fall of Troy and, 149–150
  Hercules and, 129–140 *passim*, 131n21–140n52 *passim*
  ira and, 131
  Medea and, 132n22
  Ovid and, 130–131
  in *Phaedra*, 185
  prologue speech of, 130–138
  Vergil and, 130–138

Kallendorf, C., 2
katabasis
  in *Epistulae*, 35
  Hercules and, 136
  Seneca's description of Hades and, 39
  Vergil and, 35, 192–193, 220–221, 229
Ker, J., 41

Laius, ghost of, 38–39, 39n42, 139n49, 142–143, 192n18, 193, 199, 215, 218, 220n102, 221n104, 224–230, 225n114, 229n126
language
  of drama, 5
  of elegy, 77n53, 85n80, 100n129
  of epic, 149, 212n80, 222–223
  of exemplum, 15n59
  genre and, 95, 183
  of *imitatio*, 207n71
Littlewood, C. A. J., 1, 7–8, 43, 113, 200
lyric. *See also* chorus/choral ode
  dialogism and, 19n76
  as genre, 3, 6, 164n133
  meter of, 102n137, 146, 201n52
  tragedy and, 24, 145

Maguinness, W. S., 55
Manto, 49–50, 50n74, 140, 190, 230n129

Martindale, C., 18, 25
Mastronarde, D. J., 61, 142
Mayer, R., 69, 89, 180, 188
McElduff, S., 67, 85
Medea, 93–126, 158–164 *passim*, 194–197, 212
  Apollonius and, 93n107–108
  Creon and, 100, 105–115 *passim*, 196
  as exemplum, 79
  Horace and, 194–197
  Jason and, 79–80, 94–125 *passim*, 188–190, 196–197
  Juno and, 132n22
  messenger speech and, 165, 165n134–135
  nature and, 113, 156n113
  Orpheus and, 154–158
  Ovid and, 19–24, 65–68, 79–82, 93–126 *passim*
  persona of, 97, 104, 111, 118–125 *passim*, 196
  stoicism and, 8, 8n38
  Vergil and, 188–190
Medea (Euripides), 95
Medea (Ovid), 4
Medea (Seneca)
  chorus/choral ode and, 94, 101–102, 101n135, 110n162, 111, 115–119, 123, 152n96, 155–165, 158n117, 194–197
  color and, 194–196
  Cupid/Venus and, 80, 81n63, 100n129, 119
  Dido and, 104n144
  Euripides and, 93–95, 125
  furor in, 80, 108–109n156, 121, 124, 188
  genre in, 94, 101, 122n199
  Hercules in, 115, 115n179, 118, 118n186, 160, 160n121
  imagery in, 95n113, 97, 100–101, 110, 116–118, 126
  ira in, 104n145, 197
messenger speech
  ambiguity of language and, 165, 180
  character and, 165–185 *passim*
  chorus/choral ode and, 165
  of Creon, 187, 199
  epic and, 165–184 *passim*, 169n154, 171n161, 175n175, 180n195, 193, 200
  genre and, 165
  imagery and, 175–176, 176n179
  Medea and, 165, 165n134–135
  Ovid and, 166–184 *passim*
  Vergil and, 166–184 *passim*
metapoetry, 21–25 *passim*, 47, 94–112 *passim*, 122, 126, 136, 164, 181, 185, 193–195, 231, 235
  Cassandra and, 200
  intertextuality and, 199–215
  Sphinx and, 229
metatheater, 1, 8, 45, 125, 200
meter
  of elegy, 70n31
  of epic, 115
  of genre, 114–115
  of lyric, 102n137, 146, 201n52
Myrrha
  Oedipus and, 225–226
  Phaedra and, 67, 79, 82–83, 82n70, 93

Nature/nature, 9, 46–49, 49n70, 53, 55
  Agamemnon and, 209
  color and, 46–49, 49n70
  Epistulae and, 35, 187
  Hippolytus and, 21–22, 21n83
  Medea and, 113, 156n113
  Oedipus and, 139, 143, 190n12, 191, 230
  Orpheus and, 154
  Phaedra and, 76–78, 76n50, 83n73
Nero, 1, 5, 7, 7n 33, 28, 53–59 *passim*, 59n98

Subject Index

Octavia, 1n1, 7
Octavian. *see* Augustus/Octavian
Oedipus, 38–39
  blinding of, 50–51, 50n76
  Creon and, 37, 140, 141n55, 143n67, 187–221 *passim*
  Horace and, 197–198
  impiety of, 198
  madness of, 198
  messenger speech to, 187, 199
  necromancy and, 37–39, 143n66, 144, 187, 192–193, 199, 215–216, 226–231
  Ovid and, 138–144 *passim*, 214–232 *passim*
  prologue speech of, 129–130, 138–144
  as reader, 214–215
  Sphinx and, 140–144
  suicide and, 197
  Vergil and, 138–144, 190–193, 215–224
Oedipus (Seneca)
  Aeneas and, 193, 221, 223
  ambiguity of language and, 50n76, 141, 216, 230, 231n132
  Apollo and, 220, 227n120, 228
  Bacchus and, 145n72
  chorus/choral ode and, 140n51, 140n53, 142n61, 222n107, 226–227, 227n119, 231n132
  color and, 49–51, 50n74, 224
  Euripides and, 225
  extispicium in, 49, 50n76, 51, 144, 187, 190–193, 192n17, 215–216, 230
  furor in, 198
  imagery in, 50, 138–139, 144, 219, 221
  Jocasta in, 50, 50n75, 140, 190, 193n23, 224, 225–227, 226n116, 230–231
  Laius, ghost of, in, 38–39, 39n42
  Manto in, 49–50, 50n74, 140, 190, 230n129
  Myrrha and, 225–226
  nature and, 139, 143, 190n12, 191, 230
Orpheus, 118, 118n186
  Hercules and, 154–158
  Medea and, 154–158
  nature and, 154
otium, 51–59 *passim*
Ovid, 4
  aemulatio and, 49, 89, 114, 185
  Byblis and, 67–68, 68n22, 79, 83–93 *passim*, 83n74–85 n82 *passim*
  color and, 46–51
  genre of, 65–68, 126
  imagery and, 61, 66–67
  ira and, 122n198, 131n18
  Juno and, 130–131
  Medea and, 19–24, 65–68, 79–82, 93–126 *passim*
  messenger speech and, 166–184 *passim*
  Oedipus and, 138–144 *passim*, 214–232 *passim*
  Phaedra and, 24, 65–93 *passim*
  reception of, 9–13, 16–24 *passim*
  rhetoric and, 65, 96
  Sphinx and, 140–144 *passim*

Pasiphae, 68–70, 70n30, 80, 83n73, 87, 182
persona, 64, 234
  of Medea, 97, 104, 111, 118–125 *passim*, 196
  of Phaedra, 24, 45, 64, 66n15, 67, 69, 79, 83, 85, 92
Phaedra
  as *exemplum*, 69, 79
  Neptune and, 183n206
  Ovid and, 24, 65–93 *passim*
  persona of, 24, 45, 64, 66n15, 67, 69, 79, 83, 85, 92
  Vergil and, 45–46, 180–185

Phaedra (Seneca)
  ambiguity of language and, 85, 87, 88
  Apollo and, 85n79
  Byblis and, 67–68, 68n22, 79, 83–93 *passim*, 83n74–85 n82 *passim*
  chorus/choral ode and, 72n39, 73–81 *passim*, 76n49, 77n54, 84n78, 85n79, 92n105, 176, 178, 178n188, 181n196, 183–184
  color and, 23, 194
  Cupid/Venus and, 46, 68, 74–76, 76n49, 78, 84, 88, 88n89, 146n77, 182n200, 183, 184
  Dido and, 20
  Euripides and, 181n197
  furor in, 20, 21n83, 72, 73n44, 80, 82n62, 86n83, 88, 88n89
  genre in, 72
  Hercules in, 77, 77n51
  Hippolytus in, 21–24, 21n83–23n86, 33n24, 45–46, 46n63, 67–92 *passim*, 67n19–90 n98 *passim*, 129, 146, 167, 174–185, 175n175–185n207 *passim*
  imagery in, 24, 68–88 *passim*, 69n27, 70n30, 83n73, 95, 175–176, 180, 182–183, 182n201
  ira in, 182
  Juno in, 185
  Myrrha and, 67, 79, 82–83, 82n70, 93
  nature and, 76–78, 76n50, 83n73
  Pasiphae in, 68–70, 70n30, 80, 83n73, 87, 182
Phaethon, 126n211, 174, 177–179
Phoenissae (Seneca), 7, 7n30, 39
Pollux, 147
Polydorus, ghost of, 168, 168n150, 169n151
prologue speech, 129–144
  character and, 129–144 *passim*
  Euripides and, 129
  imagery and, 129
  of Juno, 130–138
  of Oedipus, 129–130, 138–144
  Vergil and, 130–144 *passim*
Putnam, M. C. J., 18, 131

rainbow, 46–51, 141n57, 191
Raval, S., 85
reader
  character as, 227–231
  imitatio and, 29
  Oedipus as, 214–215
  Seneca as, 26–61
reception of Augustan poets, 2, 12, 18, 25–83 *passim*, 137, 158–197 *passim*, 235
  Horace and, 12–25 *passim*
  Ovid and, 9–13, 16–24 *passim*
  Vergil and, 9–24 *passim*
rhetoric, 214, 225, 233–234
  Horace and, 195–198
  Ovid and, 65, 96
  tragedy and, 2–22 *passim*, 61
Rosenmeyer, T. G., 7n32, 164n133

Schiesaro, A., 1, 38, 134, 192, 200
Segal, C., 1, 112
Seneca the Elder
  on *aemulatio*, 15
  on *imitatio*, 5n17, 15, 15n58, 31n20
"Senecan Drama and Its Antecedents" (Tarrant), 3
sententia, 5, 10, 30, 59, 198, 234
Setaioli, A., 55
Sphinx, 140–144
Staley, G. A., 28, 55

Still, J., 27, 29
Stoicism, 1, 6–8, 7n32, 7n34, 8n39, 9n44, 11, 21, 26–34 *passim*, 55, 65, 150, 197, 234
    Epistulae and, 43, 53
    Hippolytus and, 21n83
    ideas of character and, 1n2
    Medea and, 8, 8n38
surrogate poet, 25, 47n64, 118, 186–187

Tantalus, 124n206, 133n28, 207–210, 210n75
Tarrant, R., 3, 56, 66
Theseus, 22, 22n84, 36, 36n34, 37n39, 46, 46n63, 67, 76–92 *passim*, 137, 174–185 *passim*, 201n52
Thomas, R. F., 217, 218n94
Thyestes, 55–59
    Atreus and, 1, 55–59, 63–64, 167n143
    ghost of, 129, 199, 206, 208–209, 212
Thyestes (Seneca)
    chorus/choral ode and, 55–58, 150n90, 152n96
    Vergil and, 55–59
Thyestes (Varius), 4
Tiberius, 7n30
Tiresias, 37, 49, 51, 190–193, 199, 215, 220–229 *passim*
tragedy
    drama and, 3
    elegy and, 69, 69n26, 72, 87–112 *passim*
    epic and, 18, 20, 24, 93, 127–131, 129n10, 162n125
    as genre, 69n26
    ira and, 122n198, 131n18
    lyric and, 24, 145
    rhetoric and, 2–22 *passim*, 61
Troades (Euripides), 168
Troades (Seneca)
    Aeneas and, 41, 42n51, 168–169, 169n151
    ambiguity of language and, 153
    Andromache and, 41–43, 42n51, 151–153, 151n92
    Astyanax and, 42–43, 42n51, 151, 151n92, 153, 154n103, 168n149, 172
    chorus/choral ode and, 150–154, 168n147, 171–173
    Dido and, 41
    ghost of Achilles and, 151–154, 154n102, 167–174 *passim*
    Hecuba and, 42n51, 66n16, 151, 153, 163n129, 172, 172n165, 173, 174
    Vergil and, 41–43, 167–169

Ulysses, 63–64, 153, 171, 172n165
Underworld, 32–39, 61, 72, 87, 114, 132–140 *passim*, 153–154, 157, 168, 185–233 *passim*

Varius, 4, 4n14
vates, 38, 142, 199–215 *passim*, 220, 229–230
Venus. *See* Cupid/Venus
Vergil
    Achilles and, 167–169
    aemulatio and, 185
    Agamemnon and, 147–150 *passim*
    Augustus/Octavian and, 28, 53, 53n82–83, 56, 56n91, 162–164, 188, 192
    Cassandra and, 203–208
    chorus/choral ode and, 158–167 *passim*
    De Amicitia and, 39–41
    De Beneficiis and, 53–55
    Epistulae and, 30–35, 43–45, 51–53
    genre of, 53, 58, 164
    Hercules and, 36–37
    Juno and, 130–138
    katabasis and, 35, 192–193, 220–221, 229
    Medea and, 188–190
    messenger speech and, 166–184 *passim*
    Oedipus and, 138–144, 190–193, 215–224
    Phaedra, 45–46, 180–185
    prologue speech and, 130–144 *passim*
    reception of, 9–24 *passim*
    Thyestes and, 55–59
    Troades and, 41–43, 167–169
    Underworld, and, 32–39, 35–39, 61, 132–140 *passim*, 168, 185–233 *passim*
Vernant, J. P., 20, 87
Vidal-Naquet, P., 20, 87

Wilson, M., 153
Worton, M., 27, 29